Fundamentals of Contract Law

THIRD EDITION

Laurence M. Olivo
Jean Fitzgerald

emond

Toronto, Canada
2013

Emond Montgomery Publications Limited
60 Shaftesbury Avenue
Toronto ON M4T 1A3
http://www.emond.ca/highered

Printed in Canada.
Reprinted November 2015.

We acknowledge the financial support of the Government of Canada.
Nous reconnaissons l'appui financier du gouvernement du Canada.   Canada

The events and characters depicted in this book are fictitious. Any similarity to actual persons, living or dead, is purely coincidental.

Publishers, college division: Bernard Sandler and Sarah Gleadow
Developmental editor: Sarah Gleadow
Supervising editor: Jim Lyons
Production editor: Andrew Gordon
Copy editor: Anita Levin
Proofreader: David Handelsman
Cover and text designer and typesetter: Tara Wells
Indexer: Paula Pike
Cover image: © Blue Jean Images/Corbis

Library and Archives Canada Cataloguing in Publication

Olivo, Laurence M., 1946-
    Fundamentals of contract law / Laurence M. Olivo, Jean Fitzgerald. — 3rd ed.

Order of authors reversed on previous eds.
Includes bibliographical references and index.
ISBN 978-1-55239-385-7

    1. Contracts—Ontario—Textbooks.   2. Contracts—Canada—Textbooks.
I. Fitzgerald, Jean   II. Fitzgerald, Jean. Fundamentals of contract law.   III. Title.

KEO299.O45 2012   346.71302   C2012-907776-3
KF801.O45 2012

In memory of Josef Stavroff (1942–2005),
my friend and colleague and a gifted teacher,
too soon gone from us. — L.M.O.

Contents

Preface   vii
Acknowledgments   ix

CHAPTER 1
Introduction to the Law of Contracts . . .   1
Introduction   2
Features of Legally Enforceable Contracts   2
How Contract Law Developed   5
Chapter Summary   8
Key Terms   8
Review Questions   8

CHAPTER 2
Formation of a Contract   11
Introduction   12
Intention to Create a Legal Relationship   12
Offer and Acceptance   15
Consideration   23
Introduction to Legality   30
Form and Writing Requirements   36
Chapter Summary   46
Key Terms   46
Review Questions   46

CHAPTER 3
Protecting Weaker Parties   51
Introduction   52
Legal Capacity to Contract   52
Minors   53
Capacity of Drunkards and Persons Under
    Mental Disability to Contract   62
Chapter Summary   67
Key Terms   67
Review Questions   67

CHAPTER 4
Contractual Defects   71
Introduction   72
Misrepresentation   72
Duress   83
Undue Influence   85
Unconscionability   87
Mistake   90
Chapter Summary   108
Key Terms   108
Review Questions   108

CHAPTER 5
Contractual Rights   113
Introduction   114
Privity of Contract   114
Assignment of a Contract   121
Chapter Summary   125
Key Terms   125
Review Questions   125

CHAPTER 6
Contract Interpretation   129
Introduction   130
Contract Provisions: Representations, Terms,
    Conditions, and Warranties   131
The Search for Certainty: The Parol Evidence
    Rule, Its Exceptions, and Rectification   134
Exclusion and Penalty Clauses   139
Frustration   148
Chapter Summary   156
Key Terms   156
Review Questions   156

CHAPTER 7

Discharge of Contract 159
Introduction 160
Discharge by Performance 160
Discharge by Agreement 163
Discharge as of Right 167
Discharge by Operation of Law 168
Chapter Summary 169
Key Terms 169
Review Questions 169

CHAPTER 8

Breach of Contract and Remedies 173
Introduction 174
Method of Breach 174
Nature of Breach 176
Remedies 177
Choice of Remedies 191
Chapter Summary 194
Key Terms 194
Review Questions 194

CHAPTER 9

**Electronic Contracts and
    E-Commerce** 199
Introduction 200
The Legislative Framework for E-Commerce 201
E-Commerce Issues: Problems and Solutions ... 207
Chapter Summary 220
Key Terms 220
Review Questions 220
Appendix: Electronic Commerce Act, 2000 223

CHAPTER 10

Contract Preparation and Drafting 231
Introduction 232
Preparing to Draft a Contract 232
Drafting a Contract 234
Structure of a Contract 247
Contract Administration 254
Chapter Summary 258
Key Terms 258
Review Questions 258
Recommended Texts on Interpretation
    and Drafting 261
Appendix: Sample Contracts 262

Glossary of Terms 281
Index 289

Preface

Since the second edition, both the authors and publisher have given considerable thought as to how we can present material about contract law that is accurate and comprehensive and also accessible and practical. The third edition is the result of all this thinking. To begin with we have updated the law, noting, for example, that fundamental breach is no longer good law in Canada. We have also recognized the rapid expansion of e-commerce since the last edition, and responded with a new chapter that examines how contract law is evolving to deal with e-commerce issues.

We also recognize that our readers are involved in law-related programs and activities where they may not only have to know basic contract law concepts, but also be able to apply those concepts in practical ways to use, interpret, and apply contract law, or to administer contracts in a variety of circumstances. To meet this need we have redesigned the text. The format is more user-friendly and easier on the eyes, and to help students master the subject matter, there is greater reliance on summary boxes, real life case law examples, practical tips, samples and models of different types of contracts, materials on how to draft contracts and how to avoid common drafting problems, and an expanded Review Questions section that includes True or False?, Multiple Choice, Short Answer, and Apply Your Knowledge questions. It is our expectation and hope that students will find the new approach helpful and more enjoyable.

Jean Fitzgerald
Laurence Olivo
November 2012

Acknowledgments

No text writes itself. We would like to thank various individuals, including our students and colleagues, for sharing their ideas about how this text could be improved. In this third edition, Jean Fitzgerald was unable, for a variety of reasons, to participate fully. Her humour, common sense, and practical approach to teaching contract law are evident in the new edition, nevertheless, and we hope to have her fully involved in the next and subsequent editions.

In preparing this edition, we acknowledge the valuable feedback of professors Francine Roach (Algonquin College) and Hilary Findlay (Brock University). In preparing the second edition, Professors Mary Ann Kelly, Jo Ann Kurtz, and Liz Thoms (Seneca College) provided detailed feedback and suggestions about how the contents should be organized, and, trusting to their extensive experience in teaching contracts courses, we adopted almost all their suggestions. In particular, Liz Thoms was extraordinarily helpful in providing us with some of her teaching materials, including fact situations, questions, and examples. Her material on the law of mistake, always an area to trap the unwary, was a model of clarity and lucidity. We incorporated this into the text with enthusiasm and thanks.

This edition also would not have been born without the able assistance of the editors at Emond Montgomery.

Laurence Olivo

Introduction to the Law of Contracts

1

Introduction 2

Features of Legally Enforceable Contracts 2

How Contract Law Developed 5

Chapter Summary 8

Key Terms 8

Review Questions 8

After completing this chapter, you should be able to:

- Define the term "contract."
- Identify the features of legally enforceable contracts.
- Understand how contract law developed.

Introduction

Contracts are agreements made between two or more persons that the law recognizes and will enforce.

Contracts are not simply long documents written in legalese and covered in ribbons and seals. They are part of everyday life in our society, where economic exchange is an essential part of getting things done. For example, buying a bus token, paying a parking fee, buying a cup of coffee, using a credit card to buy a jacket, leasing an apartment, and buying this textbook all involve agreements between you and someone else where you agree to do something (pay money) in exchange for the other person doing something (giving you a parking space for your car, a cup of coffee, or a book). These common, everyday contracts can be in writing, or they can be oral; they can be explicit, like an apartment lease that spells out in writing the details of what was agreed to, or they can be implicit, like buying a cup of coffee where you serve yourself and hand over money, and no one exchanges a word.

Features of Legally Enforceable Contracts

Not all agreements are recognized by the law as contracts. For example, if you invite me to dinner and I agree to come but then fail to show up, I have breached the rules of good manners, but not the law. The law would define our agreement as a social agreement rather than as an enforceable contract primarily because certain things that make an agreement a contract appear to be missing. For example, an intention to create legally binding relations is missing, as is a promise from me to do something for you of legally recognizable value in exchange for the invitation, other than just showing up and eating your food.[1]

> ### Some Basic Terms
>
> - The terms **contract** and **agreement** are used interchangeably to refer to the same thing: a binding contract.
>
> - A party to a contract or agreement who undertakes to do something is sometimes referred to as a **promisor**. The party who receives the benefit of the promise made by the promisor is sometimes referred to as the **promisee**.
>
> - In the bargaining process that precedes making the contract or agreement, the promisor may be referred to as the **offeror** and the person to whom the offer is made may be referred to as the **offeree**.

---

1   Where parties promise to exchange something of recognizable value, there is said to be *valuable consideration*. Because of the commercial origins of contract law, the courts look for an exchange of promises involving things of monetary cost or value, although consideration need not be money or even be reduced to a specific dollars and cents amount. Consideration is discussed in more detail in Chapter 2, Formation of a Contract.

contract/agreement
an agreement made between two or more persons that the law recognizes and will enforce; a binding contract

promisor
the party to a contract who undertakes to do something

promisee
the party to a contract who receives the benefit of a promise made by another party to the contract

offeror
a person who, during the bargaining process that precedes making a contract, agrees to do something for the other party; once the offer is accepted, the bargain is concluded and the parties have made an agreement

offeree
a person to whom an offer is made during the bargaining process

Agreements that the law recognizes as contracts have certain features in common, described below.

Offer and Acceptance of the Offer

For a contract to be created, one party must offer to do something, and the other party must promise to accept that offer. This exchange of promises in contract law is referred to as **offer** and **acceptance**. To constitute an agreement, the mutual exchange of promises that includes an offer and an acceptance must relate to acts that are performed at the time the agreement is made, or acts to be performed in the future. However, an offer may be followed by a counteroffer rather than acceptance. This exchange, or bargaining behaviour, may go on for some time until the parties reach an agreement. When the parties have reached an agreement there is said to be, in the words of older cases, *consensus ad idem* (a "meeting of the minds"), and the parties may be referred to as being *ad idem*. The concepts of offer and acceptance and agreement are discussed in more detail in Chapter 2, Formation of a Contract.

Intention to Create Legally Binding Relations

The parties to an agreement must intend that the promises each makes to the other will be legally binding. This means that if one party breaks a promise, the other may ask the courts to enforce the contract by providing a remedy for the breach. Generally, the courts have held that social agreements (such as a dinner invitation), agreements between family members, and moral vows (such as a vow to join a religious order or to give to charity) are not legally enforceable because an intention to create legally binding relations is missing. But in other types of agreements, uncertainty about parties' intentions can arise, as the Case in Point feature below illustrates.

In deciding whether an agreement is legally binding, the courts have taken two different approaches. In some cases, the courts have taken a subjective approach, examining the evidence of what the parties actually thought they were doing or said they were doing to determine whether they intended to create legally binding rules to govern their behaviour. In other cases, the courts have taken an objective approach, determining the intention of the parties not by what they thought they said they intended, but by what a "reasonable person" would think they intended, considering the surrounding social context. Much of the case law on this issue uses the objective method, which has resulted in an approach where a fictional "reasonable person" relying on an understanding of social norms and values in our society would simply "know" that a dinner invitation was a social agreement and outside the law of contract.

Exchange of Valuable Consideration

Although there are some exceptions, both parties must promise something of value to the other. Usually this takes the form of payment or giving something of value in exchange for some goods or services of value. For example, when you park your car in a parking lot, the lot owner is promising a parking space for your car as valuable consideration, and you accept the offer by promising to pay an agreed price for the

offer
a promise to do something or give something of value to another person; if the other accepts the offer, a binding contract exists

acceptance
when there has been acceptance of an offer made by one party in the bargaining process, the parties are assumed to have reached an agreement on contract terms, and a binding contract exists from that time

consensus ad idem
when there has been acceptance by the offeree of an offer, the parties have reached an agreement on terms, and they have an intention to be bound by those terms; they are said to have reached a *consensus ad idem* (a "meeting of the minds"); sometimes a shorter form is used, and the parties are said to be *ad idem*

ad idem
see *consensus ad idem*

Determining Whether the Parties Intended to Form Contractual Relations

Skibinski v. Community Living British Columbia, 2010 BCSC 1500 (CanLII)

Facts

The plaintiff sued Community Living British Columbia in contract and unjust enrichment for provision of care services to Ms. Savone. The plaintiff had a long career and a good reputation in caring for people with mental disabilities. Savone was 48 years old and had serious medical problems and mental disabilities. She clearly could not look after herself. The plaintiff, acting on her own, assumed responsibility for Savone's care and took her home, where she was being paid by the defendant for the care of two other clients. The defendant did not provide a care contract because the plaintiff did not have a licence for having a third resident in her care. The parties continued to negotiate, but they never reached a formal contract. The plaintiff alleged that the defendant had agreed that it would retain her services with an implied term that they would negotiate for fair compensation. Alternatively, she sought compensation based on unjust enrichment in that she provided services for which the defendant was responsible. The defendant denied that it was liable in contract because there was no contract and argued that the plaintiff's actions were as a volunteer acting gratuitously.

Decision

The court granted judgment to the plaintiff on the ground of unjust enrichment, despite the absence of a formal contractual agreement between the parties, based on a finding that the plaintiff did work and incurred expenses for which the defendant was responsible. The court outlined criteria that the plaintiff satisfied: (1) that she provided necessary services and incurred expenses of a kind the defendant was obligated to pay for, (2) that the defendant likely would have had to pay someone for those expenses and services, and (3) that it was reasonable that she would expect that she would receive something for her services despite the absence of a formal agreement. Savone's needs were great, the plaintiff was ready, willing, and able to care for her, and suitable alternatives were not readily available at that time. It was fair and just for the defendant to pay the plaintiff for the benefit it had received.

Practical Tip

If you are acting gratuitously (without compensation) in an emergency, generally, you will have some difficulty later claiming compensation. For that reason, those who make a living dealing with emergencies, such as tow truck operators, should either get paid up front or insist on a simple written contract. Be careful, however, not to create detailed contracts with lots of fine print—they may cover all of the terms to your advantage, but where the other party is under pressure, courts may well find that the party was under duress and disallow parts or all of such contracts. These issues are discussed in Chapter 4, Contractual Defects.

space. What constitutes valuable consideration is discussed in more detail in Chapter 2, Formation of a Contract.

Legal Capacity to Contract

Not everyone is eligible to enter into a contract. Generally, for a contract to be enforceable, the parties are assumed to be roughly equivalent in bargaining power and must meet minimum standards of intelligence, rationality, and maturity. More important, they must meet these standards to have the contract enforced against them if they fail to keep the promises they made. For this reason, minors and persons under certain types of mental disability may not have to honour their contractual obligations in whole or in part. This is discussed in more detail in Chapter 3, Protecting Weaker Parties.

Compliance with Legal Formality Requirements

Not every agreement where the parties have the capacity to enter into a contract, where there is an agreement to enter into legal relations, and where valuable consideration has been given will result in a legally binding contract. An agreement may meet all of these requirements and still be held to be unenforceable because it fails to meet formality requirements. While many contracts may be based on an exchange of oral promises, some contracts—such as contracts for the sale of land—must be in writing. Others must be in writing *and* be witnessed, have seals attached, or meet other formal requirements to be enforceable. Formality requirements are discussed in more detail in Chapter 2, Formation of a Contract.

How Contract Law Developed

You may wonder why some agreements are recognized as binding contracts while others are not, why some people are eligible to enter into contracts but others are not, or why there must be valuable consideration for an agreement to be a valid contract. An understanding of how contract law developed can help to answer some of these questions.

Canadian contract law outside Quebec is based on English common law. While there are some minor differences in contract law in England and Canada, the main elements are derived from English law. Before the 16th century, there was no law of contracts as we now know it in England and Canada. However, from the late Middle Ages on, there did exist the tort of owing a debt and failing to repay it.[2] Here the law focused on the wrongful act of failing to repay money owed on a debt. If the agreement involved an exchange of services or goods, it was not enforceable under this rule of law. The lack of a modern law of contract was not important as long as commercial transactions were primarily simple and local. But in the early modern period, trade and commerce expanded and became more complex, and a national economy began to develop. As commercial transactions became more complex, the law evolved to permit merchants and others to enter into complex legal arrangements to govern their activities, and to provide remedies when parties found themselves in a commercial dispute. In *Slade's Case*[3] in 1602, the law finally broke away from enforcing only monetary debts to enforcing other kinds of commercial promises. From this point, the common law began to enforce all kinds of commercial bargains where there was valuable consideration, and began to evolve on a case-by-case basis to the kind of contract law we have now.

After *Slade's Case*, the law recognized virtually any kind of contractual breach, not just breach by failure to pay a contract price. Contract law as we know it was born.

---

2   For a more detailed discussion on the tort origin of contract law, see G.H.L. Fridman, *The Law of Contract in Canada*, 5th ed. (Toronto: Carswell, 2006), c. 1.

3   *Slade's Case* (1602), 4 Co. Rep. 91 (KB).

Slade's Case: The Beginnings of Modern Contract Law

Slade's Case (1602), 4 Co. Rep. 92b, 76 ER 1074 (Ct. Exch. Chamb.)

Facts

John Slade contracted to sell grain he was growing to Humphrey Morley for £16. The day for payment came but Morley reneged on the deal and refused to pay. Slade could sue in *assumpsit* for the tort of failing to pay a debt, though this was still a novel and controversial approach, but his lawsuit also involved an action on the case. This was a special form of pleading that allowed Slade to recover not only the contract price, based on *assumpsit*, but also compensation for other additional damages suffered by Slade as a result of Morley's failure to honour his obligation. Morley was represented by Francis Bacon, a prominent lawyer and Renaissance scholar and writer. Slade was represented by Sir Edward Coke, a famous lawyer and later chief justice of England, whose commentaries on the common law were a staple of legal training for two centuries.

Decision

The courts were initially divided over whether the action could succeed, but the higher court found that a person harmed by another's breach of a contract was not limited to suing only for non-payment of the debt, but could seek compensation for all of the damages sustained that resulted from the contract breach.

Case Law and Statute Law

Contract law arose from attempts by judges to solve individual commercial disputes brought before them on a case-by-case basis. Over several centuries, the principles of contract law were derived from the reasons for judges' decisions in cases. Very little contract law came from statute law.

When legislatures have passed statutes that create new rules or principles of contract law, they have usually focused on several areas:

- *Consumer protection* provides consumers, who have weaker bargaining power, with some protection from sophisticated and powerful sellers.

- *Prevention of fraud* provides for formality requirements and the protection of persons who lack full capacity to enter into contracts.

- *Rationalization of the common law* creates uniform rules in areas where the common law has become confused or chaotic, as, for example, with respect to legislation in the 19th century governing the sale of goods.

precedent
an essential doctrine of common law that requires judges to follow the rule in a previously decided case when that case deals with similar facts or issues to the case currently being decided

Developing contract law on a case-by-case basis had certain advantages: real rather than theoretical commercial problems could be resolved in a practical way, and legal principle derived from one case could evolve and change in subsequent cases to meet changing commercial realities. But there were some disadvantages, too. Because judges were resolving specific, narrow problems, they did not always focus on establishing clear principles to guide changes in the law so that the law could develop in a rational and coherent way. In some cases, judges following **precedents** where the rationale for a decision is not clear have applied the law rigidly and mechanically, relying strongly on the similarity of facts in the cases rather than on the legal principles that may lie below the surface. For example, the law of contract determining what happens when parties are mistaken about the terms of the contract often seems to focus on classifying the type of mistake made by a party rather than on whether it was reasonable to make the mistake in question. The result, in the view of some observers, has been that the law on the issue of mistake has become confused, although courts in England and Canada have recently taken steps to sort out some of the confusion.

Positivism Versus Judicial Interventionism

Another factor that contributes to difficulties in interpreting case law on contract issues is the tension in the courts between two points of view about how the law should be interpreted. Under the **positivist** approach, judges take the position that it is not up to them to impose their own interpretation of a contract on the parties. Judges who take this view try to give a dictionary or literal meaning to the words used in a contract, regardless of the outcome. These judges assume that parties to the contract have equal bargaining power and are free to bargain as they wish without the court meddling in the process. The judges will often say that it is not their job to remake a bad bargain or rewrite a badly written contract. Underlying this view is the idea that governments in general, and courts in particular, should not interfere in private persons' economic affairs.

Under the **judicial interventionist** approach, judges may look at the economic forces surrounding the making of a contract, at notions of fundamental fairness, and at other contextual facts as a background to interpreting the language of a contract. This approach is more likely to be used when there is an inequality of bargaining power between the parties—for example, in consumer contracts. However, some judges take this interpretive approach where the parties are equal in bargaining power but in the judge's view the likely outcome is socially or economically undesirable.

The positivist approach has been the principal, and older, approach to interpreting contract law in England, Canada, and the rest of the common-law world up to the mid-20th century. As judicial interventionism or judicial activism has become more commonly used in Canadian courts in general, it has also had an increasing impact on modern contract law. To some extent, this approach is the source of some of the differences in contract law between Canada and England today, since Canadian courts tend to be more interventionist than English courts. However, the differences should not be overstressed. The basic law of contract is very similar in both jurisdictions, and Canadian judges have tended to be sparing in their use of an interventionist approach to contract law.

positivism
an approach to the interpretation of law that states that the meaning to be given to the words in legal rules should be the ordinary, dictionary meaning without resorting to social, economic, or political values to aid in interpretation

judicial interventionism
an approach to the interpretation of law that draws on social, economic, and political values in interpreting the meaning and application of legal rules and principles

CHAPTER SUMMARY

Contracts are agreements between two or more persons that the law will recognize and enforce. Not all contracts are enforceable, however. There must be an intention to create an enforceable legal relationship that the law will recognize. The law will usually enforce a contract if there is a clear agreement, valuable consideration has been exchanged, the parties have the capacity to contract, and legal formality requirements have been complied with.

Contract law developed from tort law and evolved into modern contract law in the 17th century. It developed from case law as judges tried to adapt contract law to modern business practices. Very little contract law is based on statutes. Statutory contract law usually "corrects" problems arising in case law—preventing fraud, protecting consumers and other weaker contract parties, and rationalizing the case law in an area when it becomes confusing.

KEY TERMS

acceptance, 3
ad idem, 3
consensus ad idem, 3
contract/agreement, 2
judicial interventionism, 7
offer, 3
offeree, 2
offeror, 2
positivism, 7
precedent, 6
promisee, 2
promisor, 2

REVIEW QUESTIONS

True or False?

_____ 1. Some statutes governing contracts have been passed in order to protect weaker parties or to rationalize the common law when it becomes confusing.

_____ 2. A valid contract requires the exchange of something of value by each of the parties.

_____ 3. All oral contracts are enforceable.

_____ 4. A contract is legally binding, but an agreement is not.

_____ 5. The offeree is the person who makes the offer.

Multiple Choice

1. The following person may not be capable of entering into a valid contract:

   a. an adult who is physically incapacitated

   b. an unmarried 22-year-old woman

   c. a person suffering from advanced Alzheimer's disease

   d. none of the above

2. *Slade's Case* was important because

   a. it made it possible for a party to sue to recover a debt

   b. it made it possible to sue for any kind of breach of contract

   c. it established that farmers could sue grain merchants

   d. the decision was firmly based on statute law

3. An advantage of developing common law on a case-by-case basis is that

   a. legal principles derived from cases can be adapted over time to meet evolving commercial realities

   b. focusing on narrow, practical problems is a good way to establish clear legal principles

   c. the use of case precedents ensures that the law will be applied flexibly and sensibly

   d. none of the above

4. Which of the following is *not* an example of a contract:

   a. I offer to rent you a room in my house and you accept the offer.

   b. I bring a cup of coffee to the cash desk in your store and hand you some money, which you accept.

   c. I park my car in a parking lot and pay the parking lot attendant.

   d. I invite you to attend my choir concert and you accept my invitation.

5. In order for a contract to be enforceable,

   a. it must be of considerable financial value

   b. it must be in writing

   c. it must be entered into at a place of business

   d. there must be valuable consideration exchanged

Short Answer

1. What is a contract?

2. What is the difference between a contract and an agreement?

3. What main features must a contract have to be binding?

4. What does it mean for the parties to an agreement to be *ad idem*?

5. What is the difference between a subjective and an objective approach to legal interpretation?

6. Explain what is meant by the term "valuable consideration."

7. Why do we limit the contractual rights of minors and persons who have certain types of mental disabilities?

8. Provide an example of a formality requirement in contract law, and explain its purpose.

9. How important is case law to the development of the law of contracts? How important is statute law to the development of the law of contracts?

10. What is the doctrine of precedent?

11. What are some of the advantages of having a law of contracts that is based on case law? What are some of the disadvantages?

Apply Your Knowledge

1. Explain whether, in the following fact situations, you could sue for breach of contract:

   a. You invite me to dinner, and I agree to come. You spend a lot of time and money preparing the meal, but I fail to show up.

   b. Your sister promises to lend you some money because you are in debt, but she later changes her mind and refuses to do so.

   c. You invite me to dinner and agree to pay me an amount of money if I praise an invention of yours to another dinner guest who is interested in investing in your invention. I agree to attend, but I fail to show up, and the other guest decides not to invest in your invention.

2. Read *Skibinski v. Community Living British Columbia* (Case in Point on page 4). Was this case decided on the basis of a "reasonable person" objective standard, or on a subjective reading of the evidence about what the parties thought they were doing? Explain your answer.

Formation of a Contract

2

LEARNING OUTCOMES

Introduction 12

Intention to Create a Legal
Relationship 12

Offer and Acceptance 15

Consideration 23

Introduction to Legality 30

Form and Writing Requirements . . . 36

Chapter Summary 46

Key Terms 46

Review Questions 46

After completing this chapter, you should be able to:

- Explain the "reasonable person" test for determining whether a party intended to be legally bound by his or her promise.

- Describe the features of a valid offer, counteroffer, and acceptance and explain how the effective timing of an offer and acceptance is determined.

- Understand how an offer can effectively be revoked and how an offer can lapse.

- Define "consideration" and describe the qualities of valid consideration.

- Identify which contracts have to be in writing to be enforceable.

- Define "estoppel" and explain how the doctrine of estoppel is relevant to contract law.

- Explain the difference between void and illegal contracts.

Introduction

As discussed in Chapter 1, for an agreement to be a valid, binding, and enforceable contract, certain elements must be present. If any of these elements are missing or defective, the courts will not enforce the rights and duties created by that agreement. An unenforceable or defective contract is also known as a **void contract**. A void contract is no contract at all, since it has no legal force or binding effect. The parties to a void contract may have gone through some form of making a contract, but because one or more of the necessary elements were missing, no contract came into being. Hence, a void contract is one that may be "avoided" by one or both parties.

void contract
a contract that does not exist at law because one or more essential elements of the contract are lacking; an unenforceable contract

The essential elements of a contract are:

- the intention to create a legal relationship;
- offer and acceptance of the offer;
- an exchange of something of value, usually referred to as consideration; and
- legality.

Intention to Create a Legal Relationship

The parties to a contract must have intended from the beginning of their negotiations that legal obligations would result from their agreement. This is based on the premise that the contract will be the result of a meeting of the parties' minds, or *consensus ad idem*, on the terms and conditions that will form the contract.

The first requirement of a contract is the intention of the promisor to be bound by the promise he or she made. All agreements contain some kind of a promise, either to do something or to refrain from doing something. But while all contracts contain promises, not all promises become contracts. Some promises carry with them a moral obligation, but only a valid contract carries with it a legal obligation. The question to be determined, then, is whether the person making the promise (the promisor) intended to be bound by his or her promise. Some people make promises intending to be bound by them. Some people make promises with no intention of becoming legally obligated to fulfill them. Without the intention to be bound, a promise cannot form the basis of an enforceable contract.

presumption of law
an inference in favour of a particular fact; a rule of law whereby a finding of a basic fact gives rise to the existence of a presumed fact or state of affairs unless the presumption can be rebutted, or proved false, by the party seeking to deny the presumed fact

Since examining intention requires finding out what was in the promisor's mind at the time the promise was made, proving intention can be difficult. As a result, the courts rely on a **presumption of law** that promisors intend to be bound by the promises they make. Once this presumption has been made, the **onus**, or burden of proof, shifts to the promisor to prove that the intention did not exist. The courts look to evidence such as the conduct of the parties at the time the promise was made, the circumstances surrounding the making of the promise, the statements made by the parties, and the relationship between the parties. The test to be applied is: "Would a reasonable person hearing the promise assume that the promisor intended to be bound?"

onus
the burden of responsibility or proof

The relationship between the parties is an important factor to be considered. If the promise occurs in an **arm's-length transaction** where the parties are "strangers" to each other or unrelated, or in commercial or business dealings, the courts assume that the promise is binding unless one or both parties can convince the court that there was no intention.

> **arm's-length transaction** a transaction negotiated by unrelated parties, each acting in his or her own independent self-interest; "unrelated" in this context usually means not related as family members by birth or marriage, and not related by business interests

EXAMPLE

"Reasonable Person" Test

In the US case of *Higgins v. Lessig*,[1] a farmer who had a $15 harness stolen from him angrily exclaimed in front of several people, "I will give $100 to any man who will find out who the thief is!" Immediately, one of the people present named the thief and claimed the reward. The farmer refused to pay and the informer sued for the $100. The court held that the statement was "the extravagant exclamation of an angry man" and that a reasonable person would not assume that the farmer intended to be bound.

However, the courts also recognize that promises made between people who are not at arm's length may not be intended to be binding. Promises made between family members and in social situations are usually not assumed to be binding. In addition, the courts assume that promises to donate money to charity or to join a religious order are generally not intended to create a binding contract.

EXAMPLE

Non-Arm's-Length Transaction

Your sister promises to come to your daughter's ballet recital. You buy her a ticket but she does not show up, nor does she pay you for the ticket. It is unlikely that the courts would presume that your sister intended to be legally bound by her promise.

EXAMPLE

Arm's-Length Transaction

You are selling tickets to your daughter's ballet recital to help raise funds for a new dance studio. A company promises to buy a block of tickets from you but never pays for them. The courts would be more likely to presume that the company intended to be legally bound by its promise, because it is at arm's length.

---

1 *Higgins v. Lessig*, 49 Ill. App. 459 (1893).

Did Mom and Daughter Have a Deal?

Jones v. Padavatton, [1969] 2 All ER 616 (CA)

Facts

A mother and daughter agreed that the mother would pay an allowance to her daughter if the daughter would leave her current employment and study for the bar in England. Relying on this arrangement, the daughter quit her job and started her legal studies. Mom paid the allowance as agreed. Because the daughter couldn't find suitable housing, they altered the agreement with the mother providing a house for the daughter to live in. Mother and daughter then had a dispute and the mother began proceedings to evict the daughter. The daughter argued that a deal is a deal, and that this was a contractual arrangement that the mother was required to honour.

Decision

All the judges agreed that there was some kind of contractual arrangement, with some elements of flexibility due to unforeseeable circumstances. The subsequent arrangement to provide a house for the daughter was an adaptation to circumstances, and was an amendment to the original agreement. But was it a contract? Lord Justice Salmon stated that the daughter was not a youngster, had a good job, and was well established. By accepting the mother's offer, she was setting aside her career and prospects, uprooting herself and her child, and moving to England for the possibility of becoming a barrister, something that would please the mother. The daughter was induced by the mother's promise of financial assistance, later confirmed by the mother's solicitor. Applying an objective test of what a reasonable person would think, Salmon LJ held that there was sufficient evidence to support a serious intention on the part of both parties so that the arrangement was in fact a contract and enforceable by the daughter, even though some of its terms were uncertain. But he held that she had no right to stay in the house, on the grounds that the time for completing legal studies had elapsed, and with it the right to remain in the house, so that the contract, while enforceable, was discharged by the passage of time.

Practical Tip

Agreements with family members are often made orally and informally so it may be difficult for a court to determine whether the family members intended to create an enforceable contract. If the parties intend the agreement to be enforceable, it would be wise to have such arrangements reduced to writing.

Advertisers also often make statements that they do not intend to be legally binding. The courts allow advertisers some latitude in their advertisements as long as they do not mislead the public. The courts sometimes accept exaggeration as an indication that the advertiser did not intend to be bound (for example, "Come to Joe's Diner for the best Wiener schnitzel in the world!"). As a general rule, the courts view advertisements as "invitations to do business" (sometimes referred to as "invitations to treat" in older cases) rather than promises to the public at large. So if you sued Joe's Diner because its Wiener schnitzel was not the best in the world, a court would be unlikely to find that Joe's Diner intended to be held to its promise.

However, while advertisers are not generally subject to the presumption that they intend to be bound by their promises, the courts will enforce those promises if the party seeking to rely on the promise can convince the court that the advertiser intended to be bound. To find this intent, the courts examine the advertisement carefully, applying the "reasonable person" test.

Offer and Acceptance

Nature of an Offer

A valid contract does not come into existence until one party, the offeror, has made an offer and the other party, the offeree, has accepted it. An offer is normally conditional—that is, the offeree must do something or give some promise in exchange. The initial offer is tentative. Once an offeree accepts and agrees to fulfill the conditions contained in the offer, the contract is formed and the promise becomes binding. To be valid, an offer must contain all of the terms of the contract, either expressly or impliedly.

An invitation to do business by displaying goods for sale or by advertising these goods does not constitute an offer. For example, a business that uses a newspaper advertisement to sell goods for a certain price is not making an offer because the business does not intend to sell its goods to every person who reads the advertisement. The supply of those goods is likely to be limited. If the advertisement was an offer, the business would be bound to sell the goods to every person who saw it and accepted the offer by agreeing to pay the price. The purpose of the advertisement is to attract potential customers. Those customers might make an offer to purchase the goods, which the merchant can accept, or the merchant can make an offer to customers once the customers express an interest in the goods, which the customers can accept. The advertisement is simply a way to start the negotiation process.

CASE IN POINT

"Mere Puffery" or an Intention to Be Bound?

Carlill v. Carbolic Smoke Ball Co., [1893] 1 QB 256 (CA)

Facts

This English case is an example of the factors the courts examine in determining intention to be bound by a promise made in the form of an advertisement. In this case, the Carbolic Smoke Ball Co. manufactured and advertised a product that it claimed would cure or prevent influenza. In fact, it went so far as to advertise that it would pay £100 to anyone who used its product and contracted influenza. The advertisement also stated that the company intended to be bound by its promise and, as a sign of good faith, it had deposited £100 with a bank to be used for this purpose. Mrs. Carlill purchased the product, used it according to the company's instructions, and contracted influenza. The company refused to pay her the £100, claiming that it never intended to be bound by its promise and that the advertisement was a "mere puff."

Decision

The court found that the words of the advertisement clearly expressed the intention to be bound and ordered the company to pay the £100 to Mrs. Carlill.

Practical Tip

Product manufacturers may be legally bound by the advertising claims they make. As a business person, make sure that your products or services do what you say they can do, and do not exaggerate their qualities or characteristics.

Offer

I offer to sell you my car for $5,000. My offer is conditional on your agreeing to fulfill the condition in my offer—paying me $5,000. Once you accept my offer by agreeing to fulfill the condition, our mutual promises become binding. I must sell you my car, and you must pay me $5,000.

However, some advertisements have been found to be offers. For example, an advertisement stating that a store will sell a television set at a greatly reduced price to the first ten people who arrive at the store on a certain date (a "gate-crasher special") can be interpreted as an offer. The offer of a reward for information or for the return of a lost item made to the public at large can be interpreted as an offer. However, these types of advertisements are the exception to the rule that advertisements are not offers but merely invitations to do business.

Communication of an Offer

There is no particular format in which the offer must be made, as long as it is understood by the offeree to be an offer. Offers can be made verbally, in writing, or through gestures (for example, raising your hand to make a bid at an auction). A general rule is that the offer must be communicated by the offeror to the offeree before it is capable of being accepted.

Is It an Offer or an Invitation to Treat?

Fisher v. Bell, [1960] 3 All ER 731 (QB)

Facts

This English case is an example of what constitutes an "invitation to treat" as opposed to the making of an offer. In 1959, Parliament made it an offence to sell a spring blade knife commonly known as a "flick knife" or "switch blade." A police constable noticed that Bell had such a knife in his shop window, with a price tag. Bell was prosecuted for offering flick knives for sale, contrary to statute.

Decision

Both at trial and on appeal, the court held that displaying the knife with a price tag was an invitation for a potential customer to make an offer, and was not in itself an offer to sell capable of being accepted. Chief Justice Parker of the Court of Queen's Bench said:

I think that most lay people would be inclined to the view ... that if a knife were displayed in a window like that with a price attached to it, it was nonsense to say that that was not offering it for sale. ... [B]ut any statute must be looked at in the light of the general law of the country, for Parliament must be taken to know the general law. ... [A]ccording to the ordinary law of contract, the display of an article with a price on it in a shop window is merely an invitation to treat.

Practical Tip

As a seller you do not make an offer to sell merely by displaying goods with a price marked. This gives you flexibility in changing the price, or refusing to sell the goods at all if circumstances warrant.

This may seem self-evident, but it becomes important when offers are not made face to face. For example, if an offer was made by letter, telegram, fax, email, or other method, it is vital to know when the offeree became aware of the offer, because the offer is not valid until it is received by the offeree, and the offeror is not bound by the offer until it has been accepted. No person can accept an offer of which he or she was unaware.

Another general rule is that only the person to whom an offer is made may accept the offer, even if others are aware of it. This prevents people from being forced to enter into contracts with persons not of their own choosing. However, if an offer is made to the public at large, it is assumed that the offeror is implying that the identity of the offeree is unimportant to the contract, and anyone may accept the offer.

EXAMPLE

Lack of Communication of an Offer

- A person posts a notice on his office bulletin board offering a reward of $100 for the return of his lost briefcase. A co-worker finds his briefcase and, unaware of the reward, returns it to him. If she later sees the notice, she cannot go back and demand the reward. Because she was not aware of the offer when she returned the briefcase, she cannot later accept the offer. No contract was created.

- You leave a note for your neighbour in his mailbox that you will pay him $200 if he will cut down a tree on your property. Before he sees the note, another neighbour takes it and cuts down the tree in your absence. Upon your return, the other neighbour demands payment of the $200. You are not obligated to pay him the $200, even though you benefited from his labour. The offer was not made to him, and therefore was not capable of being accepted by him. No contract was formed.

Acceptance of an Offer

Acceptance of an offer may be made verbally or in writing, or it may be inferred from the conduct of the parties. However, certain rules must be complied with before acceptance of an offer is valid.

First, acceptance must be communicated by the offeree to the offeror in the manner requested by or implied in the offer. Second, the acceptance must be clear, unequivocal, and unconditional.

Communication of the Acceptance

Communication of the acceptance is simple if the offer states the method of acceptance. An offer might state that the offer may be accepted only in writing or in person. In that case, the acceptance must be communicated in the stated manner.

However, the offer may not contain such a precise stipulation. The courts look at a number of variables to determine what may constitute a valid form of communication of an acceptance. For example, they look at the form in which the offer was made, the usual and ordinary way of doing business in a particular industry, and the history of dealings between the parties to determine whether the method of communication was valid.

While the form of acceptance must generally be positive in nature, even silence can be a valid form of acceptance if the parties have agreed in advance that silence is sufficient, or where the parties have habitually used this method in previous transactions.

EXAMPLE

Silence as Acceptance

You belong to a music club. Each month the club mails you a notice advising that it will send you that month's selection of CDs unless you mail back the notice stating that you do not want them. The agreement you have with the club states that failure to send back the notice constitutes acceptance of the CDs. In this case, then, silence constitutes acceptance.

If a person's conduct, though silent, leads the offeror to believe that the offeree has accepted the offer, especially where the person receives some benefit from the offeror, and knows that the offeror expects to be compensated for the services or goods supplied, the courts may find that a contract has been formed.

There is consumer legislation to deal with the situation that arises when sellers send unsolicited goods to members of the public. For example, the Ontario *Consumer Protection Act, 2002*,[2] s. 21, provides a "cooling-off" period for a consumer who accepts unsolicited goods or services. In this case, the supplier shall refund a payment received from a consumer in respect of unsolicited goods or services within 15 days after the day the consumer demands the refund.

In some cases, performance of the terms of the offer may constitute acceptance. In those cases, acceptance is complete when the offeree performs all of the terms contained in the offer. In such a case, notifying the offeror of the acceptance is unnecessary.

EXAMPLE

Acceptance by Performance

You send a letter or email to a company requesting that the company send you an item that it carries. You do not hear back from the company, but then receive the item in the mail accompanied by an invoice requesting payment. In this case, performance of the terms of the offer (sending you the items) can constitute acceptance.

---

2 *Consumer Protection Act, 2002*, SO 2002, c. 30, sched. A.

Silence Can Constitute Acceptance of an Offer

Saint John Tug Boat Co. Ltd. v. Irving Refining Ltd., [1964] SCR 614

Facts

The plaintiff made its tugboat available for use by the defendant. The terms of the rental of the tug were never agreed upon in writing, but a verbal agreement was made and extended twice. No formal authorization was made for a further extension, but the defendant continued to make use of the tug. The defendant then tried to deny liability for all charges arising from the continued use of the tug.

Decision

Ritchie J, writing for the Court, stated:

1. Liabilities are not to be forced upon people behind their backs any more than you can confer a benefit upon a man against his will.

2. But if a person knows that the consideration is being rendered for his benefit with an expectation that he will pay for it, then if he acquiesces in its being done, taking the benefit of it when done, he will be taken impliedly to have requested its being done: and that will import a promise to pay for it.

Practical Tip

It is always a good idea to reduce verbal agreements to writing, confirming the verbal terms by letter or email, not just to make the contract enforceable but also to make the terms clear and explicit.

The issue of communication of an acceptance was raised in the case of *Carlill v. Carbolic Smoke Ball Co.*, discussed above. The company raised the argument that Mrs. Carlill had not communicated her acceptance of its offer before using its product, so no contract was formed. The court did not accept this argument, holding that the offer implied that notification of acceptance was not necessary. The company had asked that its customers buy and use the product, and performance of these terms was sufficient acceptance of the offer, without communication to the company.

Rules for Determining Communication of Acceptance

The moment of acceptance can be important, and rules have been established to determine when communication of an acceptance takes place.

If acceptance is to be made verbally, acceptance takes place when the words are spoken, either by telephone or in person.

If acceptance may be made in writing, the "postal acceptance rule" applies. Using the mail to make and accept offers has been so common that the courts have established a rule that states that when acceptance of an offer may be validly made by mail, acceptance takes place when the properly addressed and stamped letter of acceptance is placed in the mailbox. The contract is formed at the time of mailing, even though the offeror may not be aware of the acceptance until several days later. Even if the letter is then lost or is delivered late, the contract is valid. The reasoning is that offerees who use the mail to accept an offer have done everything they must do at that point. While it can be argued that it may be harsh to expect offerors to be bound by contracts if they have no knowledge of the acceptance, an offeror who invited acceptance by mail must be prepared to accept the risk that the acceptance may be delivered

TIP

If you make an offer, you can stipulate an action or activity that will constitute acceptance, rather than a verbal or written communication. For example, you can make an offer to someone to sell your guitar for a certain price, and if you are going to be absent from your home, you can ask them to drop the money through the mail slot if they agree to purchase it. Such an action, though not direct communication, will be considered an acceptance.

late or go astray. However, an offeror may stipulate in the offer that acceptance by mail is acceptable but will only be binding when the letter is actually received by the offeror. Such a specific term in the offer overrides the postal acceptance rule.

While the general fallback rule is that an offer is accepted when it is received, the development in the late 20th century of email, fax, voice messaging, and interactive websites has complicated the determination of when an offer or acceptance has been communicated. These issues are discussed in Chapter 9, Electronic Contracts and E-Commerce.

Counteroffers and Inquiries

If the acceptance of an offer is not clear, unequivocal, and unconditional, it is not an acceptance but may be a counteroffer or an inquiry. If a person, upon receiving an offer, states that he or she "thinks it is a great deal but would like to think about it," this is not an acceptance because it is not clear and unequivocal. If he or she agrees to some of the terms but not others, or wants to add or vary terms, this is not an acceptance because it is conditional. Until an offer is accepted without qualification, no contract is formed.

Offers, counteroffers, and inquiries are common in most negotiations. However, it can sometimes be difficult to determine what was an offer, what was a counteroffer, and what was an inquiry, in the midst of negotiations.

A **counteroffer** is a response by the offeree that does not unconditionally accept the terms of the offer but proposes to add to or modify the terms of the offer. By making a counteroffer, the offeree rejects the original offer and puts a new offer on the table. Note that by rejecting the original offer by making a counteroffer, the offeree cannot then go back and accept the original offer unless the offeror makes the original offer again.

An **inquiry** by the offeree as to whether the offeror will consider other terms or is willing to modify the terms of the offer does not constitute a counteroffer and will not result in rejection of the original offer. In this case, the offeree can still accept the original offer.

counteroffer
a response to an offer by an offeree that does not unconditionally accept the terms of the offer but proposes to add to or modify the terms

inquiry
questioning by the offeree as to whether the offeror will consider other terms or is willing to modify the terms of the offer; an inquiry does not constitute a counteroffer and is not a rejection of the original offer

EXAMPLE

Counteroffer and Inquiry

Michelle:	I will sell you my motorcycle for $4,500. *(offer)*
Sanjay:	I can pay you $3,500 for it. *(rejection and counteroffer)*
Michelle:	I could lower the price to $4,200, just for you. *(rejection and counteroffer)*
Sanjay:	Would you consider $3,800? *(inquiry)*
Michelle:	Not a chance. *(answer to inquiry)*
Sanjay:	I will accept your offer to sell for $4,200, but I'll need three months to pay you. *(rejection and counteroffer)*
Michelle:	I need the money now. Forget it. I can sell it to someone else. *(rejection)*
Sanjay:	Don't be so hasty. I'll pay you the $4,200 now. *(fresh offer)*

In this case, no contract has been formed. Even though Sanjay's last counteroffer only added a term to Michelle's last offer (payment over time), it constituted a rejection of Michelle's offer. Once Sanjay rejected Michelle's offer, he was unable to go back and accept it. Even though he is willing to accept the terms of Michelle's last offer, his intervening counteroffer took it "off the table" and Michelle is under no obligation to accept Sanjay's fresh offer.

Lapse and Revocation of an Offer

An offer may **lapse** or it may be **revoked**, rendering the offer a **nullity** and not capable of being accepted.

An offer may lapse under any of four conditions:

- Either of the parties dies, declares bankruptcy, or is declared insane prior to acceptance of the offer.
- The offeree rejects the offer or makes a counteroffer.
- The offeree fails to accept the offer within the time period specified in the terms of the offer.
- No time period is specified in the terms of the offer, and the offeree fails to accept the offer within a reasonable time period.

Once an offer has lapsed, it cannot be accepted even if the offeree was unaware of the lapse.

What constitutes a "reasonable time period" where no time period has been specified in the terms of the offer depends on the circumstances in each case and the nature of the anticipated contract. An offer to sell a crop of tomatoes will have a much shorter reasonable time period for acceptance than an offer to sell concrete blocks.

lapse
the termination or failure of an offer through the neglect to accept it within some time limit or through failure of some contingency

revoke
to annul or make void by recalling or taking back; to cancel or rescind

nullity
nothing; something that has no legal force or effect

CASE IN POINT

What Is a Reasonable Time for Acceptance?

Barrick v. Clark, [1951] SCR 177, [1950] 4 DLR 529 (SCC)

Facts

In this Supreme Court of Canada case, Barrick wrote to Clark on November 15, offering to sell his farm to Clark for $150,000. The letter stated that the deal could close immediately and title would be transferred on January 1. In the letter, Barrick stated, "trusting to hear from you as soon as possible." Clark was away when the letter arrived, and did not accept the offer until December 10. But in the meantime, Barrick had sold the farm to a third party. Both the third party and Clark claimed they had a valid contract with Barrick.

Decision

The Supreme Court of Canada ruled that Clark's acceptance was valid; as the offer did not set out a specific time period, it was reasonable to determine how long the offer should

remain open from the surrounding circumstances. In particular, Estey J stated:

Farm lands ... are not subject to frequent or sudden changes or fluctuations in price and, therefore ... a reasonable time for the acceptance of an offer would be longer than that with respect to such commodities as shares of stock upon an established trading market. It would also be longer than in respect to goods of a perishable character.

Practical Tip

To avoid "reasonable time" problems, consider providing how acceptance is to be communicated and how long the offer is open for before it lapses. To avoid having a contract lapse due to bankruptcy, death, or insanity of a party, consider providing that the contract will survive those changes in status.

The offeror may revoke the offer at any time prior to acceptance. The revocation must be communicated to the offeree before the offeree accepts the offer. Generally, the offeror must communicate the revocation directly to the offeree. For direct communication, the revocation is effective when it is received by the offeree. However, the offer can also be revoked indirectly. If the offeree has actual knowledge (from a reliable source) of the revocation of the offer or of circumstances in which it would be unreasonable for the offeree to expect the offeror to stand by the offer, this knowledge may prevent the offeree from accepting the offer. The onus of proving that the offeree had this knowledge rests on the offeror.

breach of contract
failure, without legal excuse, to perform any promise that forms part of a contract

Such circumstances might be the sale of the offered goods to another party, or the loss or destruction of the goods. However, an offeror who sells goods without revoking an outstanding offer runs the risk of the first offeree accepting the offer and thus becomes liable for **breach of contract** with the first offeree.

EXAMPLE

Revocation

Dawn offers to sell her horse to Maria. Maria says she needs time to think about it, and Dawn says she will keep the offer open until the end of the week. The next day, Dawn sells the horse to Miguel without revoking her offer to Maria first. The following day, Maria communicates her acceptance of Dawn's offer.

If Maria is unaware of the sale to Miguel, she is still entitled to accept Dawn's offer and a contract is formed. Dawn, of course, will be unable to fulfill the terms of the contract (delivering the horse to Maria) and will be in breach of contract.

If Maria hears from a reliable source that Dawn sold the horse to Miguel, Dawn may be able to argue that this was a form of indirect communication of the revocation of the offer and that Maria was no longer able to accept the offer once she had this information.

The box below summarizes the basic rules for acceptance. The table below it summarizes offer, acceptance, counteroffer, lapse, and revocation as they relate to the steps in the formation of a contract.

Basic Rules for Acceptance

1. Acceptance must be clear, unequivocal, and unconditional.
2. Acceptance must be communicated by the offeree to the offeror in the manner requested by or implied in the offer.
3. Acceptance must be within the time stipulated in the offer or, if time is not stipulated, within a reasonable time.
4. Silence can be a valid form of acceptance if the parties have agreed in advance that silence is sufficient, or where the parties have habitually used this method in previous transactions.
5. In some cases, performance of the terms of the offer may constitute acceptance.
6. Once an offer is accepted, there is a contract, and neither the offer nor the acceptance can be revoked.
7. The general rule is that acceptance is effective when it is communicated to the offeror.

Steps in the Formation of a Contract

Scenario	Contract formed?	Reason
A makes an offer. B accepts.	Yes	Both offer and acceptance have occurred.
A makes an offer. B rejects the offer. B later accepts the offer.	No	Offer is no longer open after B rejects it.
A makes an offer stating deadline for acceptance. B accepts after this date.	No	Offer has lapsed. B's acceptance is a new offer.
A makes an offer. B makes a counteroffer. A rejects the counteroffer. B accepts the original offer.	No	Offer is no longer open as a result of B's counteroffer.
A makes an offer stating the offer remains open until a certain date. A revokes the offer prior to this date. B accepts the offer after revocation but before the original deadline.	No	Offers can be revoked prior to acceptance, even if they include a promise to stay open.
A makes the same offer separately to B and C. B accepts, then C accepts shortly thereafter.	Yes—two are formed.	Acceptance of offer by one party does not revoke the offer made to another party.

Consideration

The law makes a distinction between a **gratuitous promise** and a contract. In a gratuitous promise, one party agrees to do something for free or without reward. In contrast, a contract is essentially a bargain in which each party gets something in return for his or her promise to perform the obligations in the contract. The price paid in return for the promise is called consideration. Without **consideration** there is no contract.

Consideration can take many forms. Most commonly, of course, consideration is the payment of money. However, consideration can also be the exchange of goods or services, an agreement to refrain from doing something, or the relinquishment of a right. Where a party has made a statement or a promise relinquishing a right, or refraining from doing something, the party may be **estopped** (stopped or prevented) from later repudiating the statement or promise, if the other party relied on it in good faith. Factual and promissory estoppel are discussed later in this section.

The consideration in a contract must also be legal. If the consideration is illegal (for example, paying a sum of money to a person to murder someone else), the consideration fails and the contract is unenforceable. The legality of contracts will be discussed in detail later in this chapter.

gratuitous promise
a promise made by someone who does not receive consideration for it

consideration
the price, which must be something of value, paid in return for a promise

estopped
stopped or prevented

Gratuitous Promises

In most circumstances, the courts will not enforce gratuitous promises. Because they lack consideration, gratuitous promises are not contracts. However, there are some exceptions to this rule.

The promise of a donation to a charity is a gratuitous promise. The promisor who pledges to donate a sum of money to a charity receives nothing in return apart from the thanks of the charity and the knowledge of a good deed done (and possibly a tax receipt). Most people do honour their pledges to charities, and most charities would not consider legal action to try to enforce a subscriber's pledge. However, there are cases in which the courts have upheld the promise of a donation to a charity on the basis that the subscribers pledged to donate funds for a specific undertaking.

Note that if the pledge constitutes only a small part of the total funds needed for the undertaking, the courts are unlikely to enforce the promise. The pledge must constitute a substantial portion of the funds needed. In addition, if the moneys are pledged not for a specific project or undertaking but for the day-to-day expenses of the charity, the courts will not enforce the promise.

under seal
bearing an impression made in wax or directly on paper, or affixed with a gummed paper wafer, to guarantee authenticity

A gratuitous promise that is made **under seal** will be enforced even without consideration. Originally, a seal was used on a document to prove its authenticity and to substitute for a signature at a time when few people were literate. The seal was usually wax, and a signet ring was impressed into the wax. Over time, gummed wafers were substituted, or impressions were made directly onto the paper. Even the word "seal" or "LS" (short for *locus sigilli*, or "the place of the seal") can constitute a seal. To properly execute a document under seal, the promisor must sign the document and affix the seal at the time of signature. A document under seal is called a **deed**.

deed
a written contract, made under seal by the promisor(s); also called a formal contract

A promise made under seal does not require consideration to make it binding. The courts have traditionally viewed the seal on a document as an indication that the promisor understands the significance of his or her act and intends to be bound by the promise contained in the document.

CASE IN POINT

Are Gratuitous Promises Enforceable?

Sargent v. Nicholson (1915), 9 WWR 883 (Man. CA)
YMCA v. Rankin (1916), 10 WWR 482 (BCCA)

Facts

In the cases of *Sargent v. Nicholson* and *YMCA v. Rankin*, the charity (the YMCA in both cases), relying on the pledges received from its subscribers, committed itself to constructing new buildings. The subscribers then refused to honour their pledges.

Decision

The court held that there was an implied request from the subscribers that the charity undertake the project as the "price" for the pledge. The court held that this was sufficient consideration.

Practical Tip

Do not make a pledge to a charity that specifies the project to be undertaken with the funds unless you are certain you will donate the money.

Estoppel Based on Fact

When one person asserts as true a certain statement of fact and another relies on that statement to his or her detriment, the maker of the statement will be estopped from denying the truth of his or her original statement in a court of law, even if it turns out to have been untrue.

> **EXAMPLE**
>
> **Estoppel Based on Fact**
>
> Alberto leased a retail shop from Ewalina. Alberto wanted to get rid of furniture at the back of the shop but believed that it belonged to Ewalina. She told Alberto it had belonged to the previous tenant but it came with the lease and Alberto could do what he wanted with it. Alberto sold the furniture for a profit. Subsequently, Ewalina realized that her husband had inherited the furniture from his mother. Ewalina sued Alberto for the value of the furniture, but was unsuccessful. Ewalina was estopped from denying the truth of her statement to Alberto when they negotiated the lease, that he could do as he liked with the furniture, even though the statement was untrue. Because Alberto relied on her statement, he should not have to suffer detrimental consequences because he acted in good faith on what Ewalina had told him.

Promissory Estoppel

Another exception to the rule that most gratuitous promises cannot be enforced occurs in cases involving **promissory estoppel** (also known as equitable estoppel). Once a party makes a promise or representation to the other party, and the other party relies on this statement of fact to his or her detriment, the statement or promise cannot later be denied. The party is estopped from denying the promise previously made. In other words, the party who relied on the promise can "raise estoppel" against the party who made the statement to ensure that he or she fulfills the promise.

Five elements must be present to constitute promissory estoppel:

promissory estoppel
a rule whereby a person is prevented from denying the truth of a statement of fact made by him or her where another person has relied on that statement and acted accordingly

1. There must be an existing legal relationship between the parties at the time the statement on which the estoppel is founded was made.
2. There must be a clear promise or representation made by the party against whom the estoppel is raised, establishing his or her intent to be bound by what he or she has said.
3. There must have been reliance, by the party raising the estoppel, on the statement or conduct of the party against whom the estoppel is raised.
4. The party to whom the representation was made must have acted on it to his or her detriment.
5. The promisee must have acted equitably.[3]

---

3 G.H.L. Fridman, *The Law of Contract in Canada*, 3d ed. (Scarborough, ON: Carswell, 1994), 129-35.

When Is a Gratuitous Statement Enforceable?

Central London Property Trust, Ltd. v. High Trees House, Ltd., [1947] KB 130

Facts

In this English case, a landlord gratuitously promised to reduce the rent on a long-term lease because of the difficulties the tenant was experiencing due to the war. After the war, the landlord's representative sued the tenant for the full amount of the rent owing. Clearly, no consideration passed from the tenant to the landlord in exchange for the promise to reduce the rent. However, the tenant relied on the promise to his detriment.

Decision

The court stated:

[A] promise was made which was intended to create legal relations and which, to the knowledge of the person making the promise, was going to be acted on by the person to whom it was made, and which in fact was so acted on. In such cases the courts have said that the promise must be honoured.

Practical Tip

Promissory estoppel is hard to prove, because you need reliable evidence. If the promises relied on are oral it is a good idea to send a letter or an email, confirming what was promised. Documentary evidence made at the time of the event is much more credible evidence than oral "he said, she said" recollections long after the event.

Promissory estoppel usually involves an assurance by one party that it will not enforce its legal rights with the intention that the assurance be relied on and acted on by the other party.

Adequacy of Consideration

The courts insist that the consideration exchanged have some value to the parties, but will not examine the adequacy of the consideration to determine whether the promise and the consideration are of equal value. The adequacy of the consideration is a matter of personal judgment. As long as consideration is present, the requirement is satisfied. The consideration may be as little as one dollar or less, or may take the form of an item that has value or significance to no one apart from the parties to the contract, such as a book or a photograph.

If a party agrees to a contract in which he or she receives grossly inadequate consideration for his or her promise, the courts will nevertheless enforce the contract. However, this lack of interference occurs only where both parties are equally capable of looking after their own interests and there is no evidence of **fraud**, undue influence, or duress. If one party can prove that the consideration in the contract was grossly inadequate *and* can prove the existence of some form of fraud, undue influence, or duress, the court may hold that the contract is unenforceable. This is dealt with in more detail in Chapter 4, Contractual Defects.

fraud
false or misleading allegations for the purpose of inducing another to part with something valuable or to give up some legal right

Past Consideration

Consideration must be something that is to be received at the instant the promise is made (*present consideration*) or at a later date (*future consideration*). It cannot be something that the person has received before the promise was made (**past consideration**). Even if a person promises to reward another who has previously done an act gratuitously, the promise is not binding because past consideration is no consideration at all. To be a valid and enforceable contract, the promise and the consideration must be exchanged for each other. This is not the case when the act is done first and the promise is made later.

past consideration
an act done or something given before a contract is made, which by itself is not consideration for the contract

---

EXAMPLE

Present, Future, and Past Consideration

- Fazil purchases a book from Margaret. Margaret gives him the book and Fazil pays the money immediately. The act (Margaret giving Fazil the book) and the promise (Fazil promising to pay for the book) occur at the same time. This is *present consideration*.

- Fazil purchases a book from Margaret on credit and agrees to pay her for it in a month. The act (Margaret giving Fazil the book) occurs in the present and the promise (Fazil promising to pay for the book) is made at the same time as the act, although the payment will occur at a later date. This is *future consideration*.

- Margaret gives Fazil a book as a gift (a gratuitous act). A few months later, Fazil finds out that it is a valuable first edition and offers to pay Margaret for it but later changes his mind and refuses to pay. The act (Margaret giving Fazil the book) occurred before the promise was made (Fazil promising to pay for the book). This is *past consideration*, and Fazil's promise to pay Margaret cannot be enforced.

Existing Legal Obligation

The promise to do something that a party is already obligated to do under another contract or under a statute cannot be consideration. If an existing contract obligates one party to perform a certain act for another party, that same act cannot form the consideration for another contract. There must be *fresh consideration* for a new promise. Otherwise, the promise is gratuitous.

Similarly, if a party has an obligation under a statute to perform certain duties, agreeing to perform those duties cannot be consideration for another contract. This applies to persons who have obligations to perform public duties, such as police officers.

More recently, starting in England, courts have begun to reconsider the idea that the modification of an existing contract always requires fresh consideration. In *Williams v. Roffey Bros. and Nicholls (Contractors) Ltd.*,[4] the English Court of Appeal held that the requirement of fresh consideration could be relaxed to make enforceable a gratuitous promise (one made without fresh consideration) to pay more, so long as:

- the promisor obtains some benefit or advantage from the new arrangement, and

- the promise was not made under duress—for example, a refusal to carry out essential parts of an existing contract unless further payment is made.

---

4   *Williams v. Roffey Bros. and Nicholls (Contractors) Ltd.*, [1990] 1 All ER 512, [1991] 1 QB 1.

Existing Legal Obligation

Bruce and Patrice enter into a contract whereby Bruce agrees to build a backyard deck for Patrice. Patrice needs to have the deck completed by a certain date, and Bruce agrees to this term. However, Bruce later finds that he cannot complete the deck on time without hiring extra workers. He tells Patrice that he will need an additional $5,000 if she wants the deck completed by the date specified. Patrice agrees to pay the extra $5,000, and Bruce then completes the deck on time. However, Patrice refuses to pay Bruce the additional $5,000.

Bruce cannot enforce Patrice's promise to pay the additional $5,000 because Patrice received no consideration for her promise to pay. The only thing Bruce offered her in exchange for the additional $5,000 was the completion of the deck by a certain date, something he was already obligated to do in the original contract. Patrice received no fresh consideration for her promise. However, if Bruce had offered her fresh consideration (such as offering to stain the deck as well), Patrice's promise to pay would have been enforceable because it would have been supported by consideration. Bruce could also have had the agreement to pay the additional $5,000 executed under seal, which would have made fresh consideration for the promise to pay the additional $5,000 unnecessary.

Debtor–Creditor Relationships

While the requirement for fresh consideration for a promise makes good sense in most instances, it can lead to unfair results in others, particularly in debtor–creditor relationships. In a debtor–creditor relationship, the debtor is obligated to pay to the creditor a certain sum of money. The debtor's obligations are discharged when the full amount of the debt is paid in accordance with the terms of the contract (loan, credit card, financing agreement, and so on). However, it is common practice, especially where a debtor has defaulted in payment, for debtors and creditors to enter into an agreement to allow the debtor to pay a lesser amount than the total owed.

For example, Marcel, a debtor, owes $10,000 and offers to pay $9,000. The creditor, Su Mei, agrees to accept the sum of $9,000 in full and final settlement of the $10,000 debt. For many reasons, Su Mei may find that it is to her benefit to accept the lesser amount rather than to pursue Marcel through the courts for the full amount. In addition, Marcel ought to be able to rely on Su Mei's promise that she will take the lesser amount in full satisfaction for the debt. However, the requirement of fresh consideration makes the agreement to accept the lesser amount unenforceable. Because Marcel was already obligated to pay that sum of money (and more), Su Mei received no fresh consideration for the promise to pay the lesser amount. Su Mei would then be free to sue Marcel for the outstanding sum of $1,000.

To address this problem and to allow debtors and creditors to enter into such arrangements with the knowledge that they are enforceable, many provinces in Canada have passed legislation that states that a creditor who accepts a lesser sum in satisfaction of a debt will not later be allowed to claim the balance. In Ontario,

When Is the Modification of an Existing Contract Enforceable?

NAV Canada v. Greater Fredericton Airport Authority Inc., 2008 NBCA 28 (CanLII)

Facts

Nav Canada was responsible, under a contract, for providing aviation services and equipment to the airport. The airport decided to extend one of its runways and asked Nav Canada to relocate the instrument landing system. Nav Canada concluded that part of that system should be replaced and upgraded at a cost of $223,000. Nav Canada, however, refused to make provision in its budget for the new equipment unless the airport agreed to pay the cost. The airport stated that it was not contractually required to do this, but would pay under protest. Nav Canada relied on this statement and ordered the equipment. The airport then refused to pay for it.

The dispute went to arbitration. The arbitrator ruled that Nav Canada had the exclusive right to decide whether to replace equipment, but that there was nothing in the existing contract that permitted Nav Canada to make the airport pay for it. However, the arbitrator ruled that the subsequent exchange of correspondence about who was to pay constituted a new and separate contract that was supported by consideration (the airport got new equipment that would make the use of its new runway more effective). The use of the term "under protest" was not in itself enough to negate the airport's obligation to pay Nav Canada.

Decision

The Court of Appeal examined the consideration doctrine at some length, and while the fresh consideration doctrine was not abandoned by the court, the court was, in this case, of the view that it was unsatisfactory. The court recognized that the doctrine of consideration that developed in the 19th century might not be entirely relevant in every modern situation. Consequently, on a case-by-case basis, the court should be prepared to accept as valid and binding post-contractual modifications unsupported by additional consideration, provided there is no coercion. This case, the court held, was such a case.

Practical Tip

It is best for oral collateral communications outside a contract to be reduced to writing in the form of letters, emails, or memoranda. For emails, preserve the meta data (information about when something was sent, who sent it, and to whom it was sent), as timing of these communications may be important.

---

such a provision is found in the *Mercantile Law Amendment Act.*[5] However, where the creditor agrees to accept a lesser amount, he or she can change his or her mind at any point before receiving the lesser sum.

Quantum Meruit

It is not unusual for one party to request goods or services from another and for that person to deliver such goods or services without a price being discussed. This is not a situation of a gratuitous promise. Even though the consideration is not specifically mentioned in the request, an agreement of this type will not fail for lack of consideration. The law will imply a promise to pay in a request for goods or services.

Quantum meruit is a concept that is relied on by someone whose occupation is to provide services or goods in a situation where payment is understood and expected.

quantum meruit
an equitable doctrine that states that no one should unjustly benefit from the labour and materials of another; under those circumstances, the law implies a promise to pay a reasonable amount, even in the absence of a contractual term for price; loosely translated as "as much as is deserved"

---

5   *Merchantile Law Amendment Act*, RSO 1990, c. M.10, s. 16.

Where there is no mention of price, the implied promise is for payment of what the services are reasonably worth, or payment for *quantum meruit*. Parties who have negotiated a contract that contains a term as to the price to be paid for the goods or services cannot later rely on the doctrine of *quantum meruit* to get a better price. *Quantum meruit* can be relied on only when the contract is silent as to the amount (or quantum) of the consideration, in circumstances where payment is clearly required.

In determining what goods or services are reasonably worth, the courts look to the prices charged by similar suppliers and fix the contract price accordingly. *Quantum meruit* also applies to situations where there has been substantial performance, although performance is not complete. To prevent one party from getting some benefit for the work done without having to pay would be unfair. Where there has been substantial performance, the court therefore will try to determine the value of the work that has been done and award compensation for that work. *Quantum meruit* in connection with substantial performance is discussed in more detail in Chapter 8, Breach of Contract and Remedies.

Introduction to Legality

In order to be binding and enforceable on the parties, a contract must have a legal purpose. To have a legal purpose, a contract cannot violate any statute, and it cannot violate public policy. If, for either reason, the contract is found to have an unlawful purpose, the courts will not enforce it and will declare it to be void, or illegal, or both.

The distinction between a contract that is merely void for having an unlawful purpose and a contract that has an unlawful purpose and is illegal as well is important. If the contract is merely void for being unlawful, the court may grant some remedies to parties who entered into the contract by attempting to restore them to their original positions. For example, if money and goods have changed hands but the contract is unlawful, the court may order the goods and the money returned.

However, if the contract is not only unlawful but also illegal, the court will not grant any remedies to any party who knowingly entered into the illegal contract. In the case of *Archbolds (Freightage), Ltd. v. Spanglett, Ltd.*,[6] the court stated:

> The effect of illegality upon a contract may be threefold. If at the time of making the contract there is an intent to perform it in an unlawful way, the contract, although it remains alive, is unenforceable at the suit of the party having that intent; if the intent is held in common, it is not enforceable at all. Another effect of illegality is to prevent a plaintiff from recovering under a contract if in order to prove his rights under it he has to rely upon his own illegal act. … The third effect of illegality is to avoid the contract ab initio [void from the time it is made] and that arises if the making of the contract is expressly or impliedly prohibited by statute or is otherwise contrary to public policy.

Remedies are discussed in more detail in Chapter 8, Breach of Contract and Remedies.

---

6   *Archbolds (Freightage), Ltd. v. Spanglett, Ltd.*, [1961] 1 QB 374 (CA).

Contracts That Violate Statute Law

It is important to look closely at the wording of the statute in question to determine whether a contract that violates the statute is void, or void and illegal.

- Some statutes impose certain requirements on certain activities. A contract that provides for activities that do not comply with those requirements has an unlawful purpose by implication.
- Some statutes expressly prohibit certain activities and may describe contracts that provide for such activities and the activities themselves as "unlawful" and "illegal" and may impose criminal penalties, such as a fine or imprisonment. Such contracts have an unlawful purpose and may be illegal as well.
- Some statutes prohibit certain kinds of agreements; only a few will be discussed here.

A contract to commit any act prohibited by the *Criminal Code*[7] is both void and illegal. This includes, for example, any agreement to commit murder, rob, assault, or kidnap. The courts will not enforce such a contract and will not provide any remedies to parties who enter into the contract. Because it is a criminal offence to conspire to commit a crime, entering into a contract to commit a crime is a form of conspiracy and a crime in itself. Even if the crime is not carried out, the parties to the illegal contract can be charged with conspiracy.

The *Competition Act*[8] prohibits business practices that are contrary to the public interest and unduly restrict business, such as an agreement to fix prices, eliminate competition, allocate markets, or create monopolies. Such business practices represent forms of **restraint of trade**. The Act renders illegal any contract entered into whose purpose is to engage in the prohibited practices. It is possible to obtain governmental approval to enter into contracts to engage in such practices (such as for mergers) to avoid violating the Act. However, without approval, such contracts are void and illegal.

The *Workplace Safety and Insurance Act, 1997*[9] prohibits any agreement between employers and employees that attempts to deprive employees of the protection of the Act. For example, a contract in which an employee agrees not to make any workplace injury claims if he or she is injured on the job is void, although it is not illegal. Contracts to sell land that violate the provisions of the *Planning Act*,[10] and in which the parties do not obtain approval from the government, are void but not illegal. The *Customs Act*[11] prohibits contracts to smuggle, and such contracts are both void and illegal. The *Bankruptcy and Insolvency Act*[12] renders void, but not illegal,

restraint of trade practices that are designed to artificially maintain prices, eliminate competition, create a monopoly, or otherwise obstruct the course of trade and commerce

---

7   *Criminal Code*, RSC 1985, c. C-46, as amended.

8   *Competition Act*, RSC 1985, c. C-34.

9   *Workplace Safety and Insurance Act, 1997*, SO 1997, c. 16, sched. A.

10   *Planning Act*, RSO 1990, c. P.13.

11   *Customs Act*, RSC 1985, c. 1 (2nd Supp.).

12   *Bankruptcy and Insolvency Act*, RSC 1985, c. B-3.

any contract a person enters into in which that person transfers property either as a gift or for inadequate compensation within one year before declaring bankruptcy.

Various statutes and bylaws require tradespeople and professionals to be licensed before they can offer services to the public. If an unlicensed tradesperson or professional enters into a contract for services that he or she is not licensed to provide, such a contract is void but not illegal. However, this generally applies only to the services provided, not to any goods provided. An unlicensed plumber, then, could not enforce that part of the contract for payment for the work he or she did, but could enforce that part of the contract that provided for the supply of goods, such as pipes and fittings. However, this issue cannot be raised as a defence by the unlicensed tradesperson to the enforcement of the contract by the other party. If the unlicensed plumber did shoddy work and caused damage, the plumber could be sued for breach of contract by the customer. The plumber could not then claim that he or she incurred no liability under the contract because of being unlicensed. This is an application of the general principle that a party may not rely on his or her own wrongdoing to gain an advantage in court.

Contracts That Violate Public Policy

Contracts that violate public policy are void and may be illegal as well. These contracts are contrary to the public good.

Such contracts include those designed to interfere with the administration of justice (for example, paying a witness to give a certain kind of evidence in court), injure the public service (for example, giving "kickbacks" to a public official), promote unnecessary litigation (for example, paying someone to start a lawsuit to generate publicity), or suppress evidence of a crime (for example, entering into an agreement not to report a theft if the wrongdoer pays back the money). Note that while most contracts that violate public policy are merely void, statute law may be in place that makes them illegal as well (for example, bribing a public official).

Other contracts may be void because they involve an agreement to commit a dishonest or immoral act. For instance, contracts for loans that charge an unconscionably high rate of interest are void. Contracts for loans that charge an interest rate higher than 60 percent are also illegal. Contracts that involve prostitution are void. Some contracts that involve gambling are void. However, societal mores change, and some acts that may once have been considered immoral by the courts are no longer illegal. For example, in the 1965 case of *Prokop v. Kohut*,[13] the court stated that it would not enforce an agreement made between a man and a woman that granted the woman a half interest in the man's estate based on the couple's commitment to live together as a married couple although they were not married. Despite the fact that the couple lived together for 16 years, the court dismissed the woman's claim, stating that any such contract would be "void as having been made for an illegal consideration and the plaintiff can recover nothing." However, the

---

13 *Prokop v. Kohut* (1965), 54 DLR (2d) 717 (BCSC).

more recent case of *Chrispen v. Topham*[14] dismissed the traditional approach, with the judge stating, "In my opinion, it cannot be argued that the [cohabitation agreement] between the plaintiff and the defendant was made for an immoral purpose, and therefore, [is] illegal and unenforceable. Present day social acceptance of common-law living counters that argument."

Business contracts can be challenged as void for containing **restrictive covenants** that constitute a restraint of trade. While these contracts may not violate the *Competition Act*, discussed above, they nonetheless may be void for violating public policy. There is a presumption at law that all restrictive covenants that constitute a restraint of trade are void. However, this presumption can be rebutted by the party wishing to enforce the contract showing that the restrictive covenant did not generally restrain trade.

restrictive covenant
a provision in a contract that prohibits certain activities or uses of property

EXAMPLE

Restrictive Covenant

Newco Ltd. buys a dry-cleaning business in Toronto from Oldco Ltd. In the sale agreement, Newco states that it does not want Oldco opening a dry-cleaning business anywhere in the province of Ontario for a period of 25 years. The courts would likely find that such a restrictive covenant is contrary to public policy and therefore void. However, if the covenant stated that the restricted area was within a 10-kilometre radius from the business site and for a period of four years, the courts would likely uphold the restrictive covenant.

When a business is sold, the purchasers usually want to ensure that the vendors do not engage in a business that would compete with them. The parties often include a restrictive covenant in the sale agreement that the vendors will not open a competing business for a certain period of time within a certain geographical area. If the time period and the geographical area of restriction are reasonable, the courts will uphold the contract. However, if they are unreasonable, the courts will find that the restrictive covenant is a restraint of trade and will not enforce it. What is reasonable depends on the circumstances of each case and the standards of the industry or business in question.

Contracts between employers and employees that unreasonably restrict the employee's right to compete with the employer or to work for a competitor after the employment agreement terminates can also be void for restraint of trade. However, if the time period and geographical area are reasonable, the courts may enforce the contract. It is harder to enforce a contract of this nature than a contract for the sale of a business, since the courts are reluctant to restrict an individual from earning a living. However, if the restraint is reasonable and necessary, it will not offend the public interest and will be enforced.

---

14 *Chrispen v. Topham* (1986), 28 DLR (4th) 754 (Sask. QB).

Restitution: A More Modern Approach to Legality Issues

Modern commentators have been highly critical of the courts' refusal to soften the impact resulting from a contract found to be void because it is illegal. There is a tendency in some recent court decisions to look beyond an automatic and rigid response to a finding that a contract is illegal, and to mitigate the impact of such a finding in circumstances where the illegality is a technicality or where one of the parties was innocent of illegal intent. In such cases, courts have severed illegal parts of a contract, or introduced a concept of notional severance, in effect rewriting parts of a contract that had made it illegal.[15] A more recent trend has been to develop the law of restitution to put a party back in the position he or she would have been in had the contract not been illegal. The cases so far, as the Case in Point that follows illustrates, may permit restitution in cases where

- a contract is illegal and it is clearly not contrary to public policy to grant relief; and
- a party had acted in good faith, or in justifiable ignorance of whether or not the contract was legal.

Summary: Legality of Contracts

	Void	Void and Illegal
Contracts Against Statute	• **Some contracts made against specific provisions of a statute are considered void.**	• **Some contracts made against specific provisions of a statute are considered void *and* illegal.**
	Examples: • *Workplace Safety and Insurance Act* violations (restricting injury claims) • *Planning Act* violations (failing to obtain severance approvals) • *Bankruptcy and Insolvency Act* violations (transfers of property within one year before declaring bankruptcy) • Contracts with unlicensed tradespersons or professionals: contracts void but claim available for goods reimbursement to the supplier and damages claim by the customer	*Examples:* • *Criminal Code* violations (e.g., agreement to commit murder, robbery, assault, or kidnap) • *Competition Act* violations (e.g., agreement to fix prices, eliminate competition, allocate markets, or create monopolies (restraint of trade)) • *Customs Act* violations (contracts to smuggle)
	Restitution: • Restitution may be ordered if money and goods have changed hands if not contrary to public policy and party has acted in good faith	*Restitution:* • No restitution, generally
	Sanctions: • No criminal sanctions	*Sanctions:* • May include criminal sanctions

---

15   *Transport North American Express Inc. v. New Solutions Financial Corp.*, [2004] 1 SCR 249; *William E. Thomson Associates Inc. v. Carpenter*, 1989 CanLII 185 (ON CA).

	Void	Void and Illegal
Contracts Against Public Policy	• **Contracts that are contrary to the public good are void.**	• **Contracts that are against public policy (void) can *also* violate statutes and thus be rendered illegal.**
	Examples: • Promoting unnecessary litigation (e.g., paying someone to start a lawsuit to generate publicity) • Dishonest or immoral acts (e.g., contracts for loans with unconscionably high interest rates) • Restrictive covenants that constitute a restraint of trade (onerous employee restrictions after employment ends)	*Examples:* • Suppressing evidence of a crime (e.g., agreeing not to report a theft if the thief repays the money) • Injuring the public service (e.g., bribing a public official) • Interfering with the administration of justice (e.g., bribing a witness)

CASE IN POINT

Can a Party Obtain Relief When a Contract Is Held to Be Illegal?

Still v. MNR, [1998] 1 FC 549

Facts

Still had married a Canadian citizen and immigrated to Canada to join her husband. Having applied for permanent resident status, she was provided with a document that stated she would be granted permanent resident status and that declared her eligible to apply for employment and/or student status. Still assumed this meant that she could work, and she did from May to October 1993, when she was laid off. She then applied for employment insurance. She had received her permanent resident status in September. Her claim was denied on the ground that her employment contract was void because she was not technically a permanent resident until September. Although her employment contract from September to October was valid, this period of time was not long enough to support a claim for employment insurance. Still appealed to the Tax Court, and then to the Federal Court of Appeal.

Decision

The Federal Court of Appeal noted that the classic model of the contract being strictly unenforceable was no longer persuasive, as it was far too rigid and ill-suited for solving the problem at hand. The court favoured the following principle, to be applied on a case-by-case basis: "where a contract is expressly or impliedly prohibited by statute, a court may refuse to grant relief to a party when, in all of the circumstances of the case, including regard to the objects and purposes of the statutory prohibition, it would be contrary to public policy, reflected in the relief claimed, to do so." Consequently, the court should "identify those policy considerations which outweigh the applicant's *prima facie* right to" employment insurance benefits. The court found that Still had acted in good faith and that the denial of employment insurance benefits was disproportionate to the breach of statute, and ordered restitution in the form of payment of the benefits.

Practical Tip

Where the subject matter involves a regulated activity, such as a consumer transaction, an extension of credit, or an activity requiring licensing, it is wise to obtain legal advice about legal limits on the activity prior to entering into a contract. While the court may forgive an unwitting, innocent person straying into an area of illegality, it will still impose a reasonable person test, and a reasonable person might well be expected to obtain legal advice, particularly in commercial transactions subject to regulation.

Form and Writing Requirements

Formal and Simple Contracts

Contracts can be classed in terms of form or appearance as either **formal contracts** or **simple contracts**. Formal contracts, also called deeds, are in writing and sealed by the promisor. Deeds were the first type of contract to be recognized as valid, enforceable contracts. The early common law did not recognize most promises, whatever the form, for the purpose of enforcement. However, if a contract was written and sealed by the promisor, the formal act of applying a seal to the document was seen as evidence of a serious intention to make and keep a promise. If the promise was broken, it raised a serious issue of moral wrongdoing, which might bring the promise breaker before the church courts or local manorial courts to enforce the promise. By the late Middle Ages, the king's common-law courts began to assume jurisdiction and enforce some contracts if they were in writing and made under seal, on the basis that the seal was evidence of a serious intention. At first, only contracts under seal were enforced; the courts would not recognize oral or unsealed written contracts as worthy of enforcement.

Contracts that are not formal contracts are called simple contracts. "Simple" does not refer to the complexity of the contract. A simple contract can be very complicated and may go on for pages. It may be oral or in writing. In the medieval period, the common-law courts would not recognize simple contracts as worthy of enforcement, although church and manorial courts might enforce them in some limited circumstances, as they did for formal contracts, provided there was some evidence of serious intention—for example, a deal confirmed by a handshake made in public. However, while the king's courts began to enforce formal contracts on evidence of a breach of the promise made by a party, they did not enforce simple contracts on the basis of a breach of the promise made. Instead, if one party performed his or her obligations but performed them badly, the other party could sue in **tort** for damages resulting from the other party having performed the promise poorly. Here, liability rested on a legally recognized civil wrong, or tort, rather than on the contractual basis of the breach of a promise. However, if the promisor did nothing at all to fulfill his or her obligation, he or she was not liable in tort to the promisee for the omission. This problem was solved not by recognizing contractual rights but by creating the tort of deceit, which made those who did nothing to fulfill a promise liable for damages. However, by the beginning of the 17th century, as modern contract law began to develop, the common law began to enforce simple contracts as contracts rather than as parts of tort law. In fact, by the end of the 17th century, the law was well on its way to enforcing all simple contracts and abandoning prescribed formality requirements altogether. Today, simple contracts do not depend on any particular ceremony or prescribed form to be enforceable. However, there are some areas of contract law where enforceability depends on some formality requirements having been met.

As you will see in this chapter, contracts of certain types that cover certain subject matter must be in writing and signed by the party or parties to be bound to be valid and enforceable. As well, when a contractual promise is made by one party to another without any valuable consideration, a seal is required. In the absence of consideration, the seal is still seen as evidence of a serious intention to create legal relations.

The Statute of Frauds

The *Statute of Frauds* was enacted in England in 1677[16] and was adopted during the colonial period in Canada and the United States. It is still part of the law in most Canadian provinces, except for British Columbia, Quebec, and Manitoba, and in some American states. It requires that certain types of contracts be in writing and be signed by the parties who are to be bound by their promises. Such contracts do not necessarily have to be made under seal unless there is an absence of consideration. The Statute was originally passed in the wake of the English civil war and other upheavals that began in 1640 and was designed to introduce order and stability to the law, particularly with respect to fraudulent claims concerning long-term leases and other land rights (which had required deeds or formal contracts). It also covered situations that are now dealt with by simple contracts, although because of the Statute, these contracts must be in writing.

The Statute has long been regarded as an anachronism and has been repealed in England. Sections 1–4 are relevant to the law of contract today in most parts of Canada. The Statute was amended in Ontario,[17] and the Ontario Statute is the basis for discussion in this chapter. Some parts of the original Ontario *Statute of Frauds* have found their way into other statutes. The content of s. 17 is now found as part of sale of goods legislation in most provinces. It requires contracts for the sale of goods in excess of a stated price to be in writing unless the existence of the contract is established in other ways: by part payment or by acceptance of some of the goods. Similarly, the requirement that marriage contracts be in writing, formerly part of s. 4, is now found in s. 55 of the Ontario *Family Law Act*[18] and in the family law legislation of other provinces.

Contracts That Must Be in Writing and Signed

Under the *Statute of Frauds*, certain types of contracts must be in writing and signed by the person to be bound:

- contracts by an executor of an estate to pay debts of the estate from personal funds (s. 4),
- contracts by a person to guarantee the debts of another or be responsible for the *tort* obligations of another (s. 4),
- contracts for the sale of land or affecting any interest in land except for leases of less than three years (ss. 3 and 4), and
- contracts made after attaining the age of majority to ratify debt obligations incurred as a minor (s. 7).

CONTRACTS BY A TRUSTEE OF AN ESTATE TO PAY ESTATE DEBTS

If the trustees of an estate decide to pay the debts of the estate out of their own personal funds, their promise to do so must be put in writing if they are to claim from the

---

16 *Statute of Frauds (An Act for the Prevention of Frauds and Perjuries)* (1677), 29 Car. II, c. 3.

17 *Statute of Frauds*, RSO 1990, c. S.19.

18 *Family Law Act*, RSO 1990, c. F.3.

estate what they paid out to third parties. This might happen if an estate debt is pressing and a penalty may be imposed or interest is accumulating on the debt. The estate trustee might pay the debt out of personal funds to prevent the estate from losing money. Then, when estate funds later become available, he or she may claim from the estate the amount paid.

EXAMPLE

Payment of Estate Debts from Personal Funds

Sandra is the trustee of her mother's estate. Her mother had a personal loan at the time of her death and owned some bonds. There is interest running against the personal loan, which is now a debt of the estate. Sandra would like to pay off the loan as soon as possible to avoid further interest charges against the estate. The bonds are assets of the estate and could be used to pay off the loan, but the estate would lose money if the bonds are cashed in now. Sandra pays off the personal loan out of her own money. She sets out in a document the fact that she is acting as the estate trustee and paying off the personal loan, setting out the amount and the recipient, and that she is entitled to be reimbursed from the estate. She signs and dates the document, and has a friend witness her signature. She also obtains an acknowledgment and receipt from the creditor to show that the payment has been received. Both of these documents will be necessary to prove that Sandra is entitled to be reimbursed from the estate assets when they become available if she is challenged by other beneficiaries of the estate.

CONTRACTS TO ASSUME THE LIABILITIES OF ANOTHER

Contracts where a third party promises to perform the obligation of another person must, under the Statute, be in writing and be signed by the third party. If the promise is not in writing, it cannot be enforced against the third party. The Statute describes two contractual situations where third parties agree to assume another's liability: guarantees and assumed liability for torts.

◇ Guaranteeing Debt

guarantee
a promise by a third party to pay the debt of another person if that person fails to pay the debt when it is due

guarantor
a third party who gives a guarantee to the creditor of another person

A **guarantee** arises where the **guarantor** promises to pay the debt of another person if that other person fails to pay the debt when it is due. In this situation there are two levels of liability. The original debtor is primarily liable to pay the debt. Only after the original debtor fails to pay the debt does the liability of the guarantor arise. The guarantor's liability in this situation depends on the principal debtor's failure to pay the debt when it is due and extends only to the terms of the original guarantee. If the primary debtor and the creditor agree to change the terms, the guarantor is released from his or her obligation to pay the debt unless the guarantor also agrees in writing to the new terms.

It is important for a third party to examine a loan agreement carefully to see if the terms indicate that he or she will be a guarantor of payment by the principal debtors or primarily liable along with other debtors to pay the debt. A person who co-signs a loan or accepts joint liability with another to pay a debt is primarily liable along with that other debtor. A guarantor, on the other hand, is liable only when the principal debtor defaults on payment when the debt is due. If a guarantor pays a debt for the primary debtor, the guarantor has a right to demand payment of the amount of the debt from the primary debtor. Guarantees are sometimes confused with indemnity agreements. An indemnifier is assuming or sharing primary liability on the debt, whether the other debtor fails to pay or not. An indemnity agreement need not be in writing.

Creditors who are lending to someone who is a poor credit risk often ask the debtor to find someone who has a good credit rating to guarantee repayment. In this situation, if the creditor wishes to enforce the guarantee, it must be in writing and signed by the guarantor. In some jurisdictions, the guarantor may also be required to sign a document indicating that the responsibilities of a guarantor have been explained to him or her, and that the guarantor understands those responsibilities. The amount of consideration, however, does not have to be in writing.[19]

EXAMPLE

Guarantee of a Debt

Johann wants to borrow money from the Caring Bank. The bank manager knows that Johann doesn't have a full-time job, has few assets, and is a poor credit risk. The bank manager says the bank will lend Johann the money if Johann can find someone to guarantee the loan. Johann asks his friend Antonio to act as guarantor. Antonio goes to the bank and gives his guarantee in writing, signing the guarantee. A few weeks later, Johann misses a payment installment. On default, the manager calls Antonio and tells him that the bank is looking to him to repay the loan and will be relying on the signed guarantee to enforce Antonio's obligation.

◇ Assuming Responsibility for Tort

If a third party promises to pay the damages that may be found to be owing by another person to a tort victim, the third party must give this promise in writing and sign the document if he or she is to be held liable for the torts of another. If there is no signed, written document, a mere oral promise is unenforceable.

EXAMPLE

Guaranteeing Damages for Another's Tort

Jocasta's son Oedipus drove his car into Tiresias's parked van. Jocasta, who owns the insurance policy on her son's car, does not want to have to pay a higher insurance premium as a result of the accident. She promises Tiresias that she will pay for the damage to his van out of her own pocket if he agrees not to notify the insurance company. Tiresias, having read this text, insists that she set out her promise in writing and place her signature on it so that he can enforce the agreement if she tries to back out of it.

---

19 *Statute of Frauds*, supra footnote 17, s. 6.

CONTRACTS FOR THE SALE OF LAND OR AFFECTING ANY INTEREST IN LAND

Contracts in which one person gives an interest in land to another must be in writing under the terms of the Statute. In addition, in various jurisdictions in Canada, transfers of interests in land must meet other formality requirements, including the use of a prescribed form, seals, and other mandatory information. "Interest in land" includes not only the sale of the freehold interest but also the transfer of interests that are less than freehold: leases for more than three years, **life estates**, and **easements**, but probably not most **licences**, which the courts usually see as a right to a particular use of land without any interest in it being transferred. For example, your right to occupy a space in a parking lot is usually seen as an occupational licence rather than the transfer of an interest in the space itself. Deciding whether you are dealing with an interest in land is important, since oral agreements to convey an interest in land are not enforceable, subject to some exceptions discussed later in this section.

The rules requiring written agreements for transfers of interests in land have given rise to two problems. First, the courts have had great difficulty in determining what kinds of agreements are concerned primarily with land and not something else. Second, where an agreement is unenforceable because it is not in writing, the courts have had to decide what remedies can be provided where one person performed his or her part of the bargain, relying on the agreement, and the other was using the technical requirements of the Statute to unfairly get out of the deal by getting the benefit of the other's part performance without having to do anything in return.

◇ Determining What Constitutes a Contract Regarding Any Interest in Land

The vagueness of the Statute regarding a definition of "any interest … concerning [land]"[20] has caused great confusion in the case law. The courts have had to develop some principles by which they can sort claims into two categories: contracts that are concerned primarily with the sale of land or the transfer of some interest in land, and contracts that may have involved a transfer of an interest in land but are also concerned with other things. The Statute requires contracts that are concerned primarily with land transfers to be in writing to be enforceable; contracts that are about land but also about something else may not have to be in writing.

> **EXAMPLE**
>
> **Contract Concerned with a Transfer of an Interest in Land**
>
> Cain promises to sell Canaan to Abel for $10. For Abel to enforce this agreement, it must be in writing and signed by Cain because it is primarily concerned with the transfer of an interest in land.

One of the reasons why so much attention has been focused on deciding whether a contract is primarily a land transaction is that the courts have wanted to limit the application of the Statute requiring land contracts to be in writing. Situations arise where it would be unfair to not enforce the conveyance of an interest in land where the conveyance is not in writing. For example, Abelard promises Eloise that he will

life estate
a transfer of interest in land for a term of years measured by the life of the transferee or by the life of another person; when the person dies, the life estate ends, and the property goes back to the transferor or other persons designated to receive the interest in land

easement
an interest in land that permits certain uses without interruption or interference by the person who has legal title to the land

licence
a grant of a right; in real property law, a grant of a right to some use of land that does not amount to a grant of an interest in the land

---

20 Ibid., s. 4.

convey his house to her on his death if she accepts only room and board and looks after him as a housekeeper until his death. If Eloise performs her part of the bargain, it seems unfair to allow Abelard or his heirs to avoid conveying the land to Eloise solely because the agreement is not in writing. The courts have met this problem by sometimes classifying the contract as having to do with something other than land, thus taking it outside the Statute so that an oral agreement can be enforced. The court can also accept that the contract falls within the Statute but use the equitable doctrine of part performance to achieve a fair result. Part performance is discussed below.

EXAMPLE

Contract Concerned with a Transfer of an Interest in Land and Something Else

Vivaldi wishes to hire Offenbach to play in his orchestra. Vivaldi offers Offenbach a large salary and promises that if Offenbach stays with the orchestra, Vivaldi will also transfer a parcel of land to him. The contract may not need to be in writing to be enforceable by Offenbach because it is primarily about something other than the transfer of a parcel of land.

◇ **The Doctrine of Part Performance**

A contract that involves the transfer of an interest in land may be enforceable through the equitable doctrine of part performance, even if the contract is not in writing, if the promisee performs some acts in reliance on the promisor's oral offer to convey land. However, the doctrine of part performance in Canada has received a narrow interpretation. A person arguing against the requirement that the contract be in writing must come within all of the following four requirements:

1. *Performance must be directly related to land.* The party claiming part performance must show that the acts performed are done only with respect to the promise to convey a specific parcel of land. If part performance is related to something other than the conveyance of land, or if the acts are not in respect of the specific land itself, the doctrine cannot be successfully invoked.

EXAMPLE

Clare promises to sell Swamp Acre to Chloe for $10. The offer is oral, and Chloe accepts it. She moves onto the land and begins to build a house. Clare then says that she is backing out, and since the agreement is not in writing, there is no contract. Here there is a promise to convey by Clare and part performance by Chloe, who has begun to build the house. Part performance is exclusively based on the agreement to convey land. Without the promise to convey, Chloe would never have begun building the house. Further, the acts done are with respect to the land itself, so that Chloe can rely on part performance.[21]

---

21 If Chloe had sent a letter or email confirming the oral arrangements with Clare, she would have had an easier time proving her case. And it would have been easier yet, if she could have gotten Clare to sign the letter or email back that she accepts and acknowledges the terms.

2. *Enforcement of the statutory requirement would defraud the party and cause hardship.* The party claiming part performance must show that enforcing the statutory requirement of a written contract would defraud the party relying on the promise and cause hardship.

> **EXAMPLE**
>
> If the contract between Clare and Chloe could not be enforced, then Chloe, who relied on the promise, would be defrauded of the cost of building a house and of the house itself. She would also have suffered hardship from losing a substantial sum of money.

3. *There must be a valid and enforceable oral agreement.* The party claiming part performance must show that, aside from the requirement of writing, there is a valid and enforceable oral agreement. There must be cogent and persuasive oral evidence to support the existence of the agreement.[22]

> **EXAMPLE**
>
> Chloe and Clare have a valid contract: an offer, an acceptance, and valuable consideration that would support the existence of a valid oral agreement. Cogent evidence of the agreement might include a receipt for $10 or a cancelled cheque, oral evidence of witnesses present when the agreement was reached, the building of the house without interference by Clare, or any other rational explanation for undertaking such work.

4. *The agreement must be primarily about an interest in land.* The party claiming part performance must show that the agreement primarily involves an interest in land. Something less than a legally defined interest does not suffice.

> **EXAMPLE**
>
> The promise made by Clare was clearly a conveyance of the freehold to Chloe, which is an interest in land.

A more flexible approach that expanded the application of the doctrine of part performance was followed in England by the House of Lords in *Steadman v. Steadman*.[23] In this case, a husband and wife had separated. The husband was in arrears in his support payments. The husband and wife orally agreed that she would release her half-interest in the house if he paid £1500 and £100 in arrears of maintenance.

---

22   J.A. Willes, *Contemporary Canadian Business Law*, 4th ed. (Toronto: McGraw-Hill Ryerson, 1994), 196-97.

23   *Steadman v. Steadman*, [1976] AC 536 (HL).

Was Part Performance Enough Performance?

Deglman v. Guaranty Trust Co. of Canada and Constantineau, [1954] SCR 725

Facts

Deglman lived with his aunt in her house while he attended a course. She also owned the property next door (property X). During this time, the aunt said that if Deglman was good to her and would do such services for her as she might request during her lifetime, she would make adequate provision for him in her will and, in particular, she would leave him property X. While he lived with her, Deglman did chores around her house and odd jobs on both buildings, ran other errands for her, and took her on trips and drives. She died six months after he moved in, and the will left no provision for him at all. Deglman sued her estate, claiming enforcement of the oral agreement for the transfer of land.

Decision

The Court, in reviewing the evidence, held that none of the numerous acts done for the aunt were "by their own nature, unequivocally referable to" property X, so the doctrine of part performance could not be invoked. The court did go on to hold, on other grounds, that there was some kind of contractual relationship that justified some payment to Deglman.

Practical Tip

If you care for an ill or elderly relative with the promise of receiving the person's house in appreciation, make sure you obtain this promise in writing signed by both parties, or if signed by the owner only, then under seal.

He paid the arrears, but the wife refused to transfer her interest, arguing that the promise to convey was not in writing and there was no part performance because the payment of the arrears was not specifically referable to the land itself. The House of Lords took the view that if the husband paid the arrears, this could be used to prove the existence of the agreement to convey the property and his reliance on it. If so, looking at all the circumstances, to require the husband's acts to be with respect to the property itself was too narrow an approach. Acts to improve the property, for example, certainly provided evidence of his reliance on the agreement, the existence of the agreement, and the expectation of the property being transferred to him, but they were not the only evidence that could prove the existence of the agreement. If there was other cogent evidence of the existence of the agreement to transfer the property, and his reliance on it, then that should be sufficient. In this case, his payment of the arrears constituted acceptable evidence of the existence of the agreement and his reliance on it. This approach is broader than the Canadian approach, but it is consistent with the idea that the *Statute of Frauds* should be used to prevent fraud, not to escape one's obligations on a technicality.

CONTRACTS MADE AFTER ATTAINING THE AGE OF MAJORITY TO RATIFY DEBT OBLIGATIONS INCURRED AS A MINOR

If a minor incurs a debt before reaching the age of majority, and the debt is not related to necessities, the contract cannot be enforced against the minor once he or she has reached the age of majority unless the individual ratifies the contract in writing. The effect of minority status on contract enforcement is discussed in Chapter 3, Protecting Weaker Parties.

TECHNICAL REQUIREMENTS FOR WRITTEN CONTRACTS

The Statute requires that an agreement be in writing. Whether required by the Statute or generally, the following considerations apply. A formal document drafted by lawyers is not necessarily required. The contract can consist of written notes on the back of a menu or on a restaurant tablecloth, or an exchange of letters, faxes, or emails. Whatever the form, a written agreement, whether it is one document or several letters between the parties, should

- identify the parties to the contract by name or by description;
- identify the terms of the contract, including the offer that has been accepted and the consideration to be given;
- be signed by the party whose promise is being enforced; it is not necessary to have other parties' signatures if the agreement is not being enforced against them; and
- include a printed or stamped signature, which may suffice in place of an actual signature. But an actual signature is preferable if there is an issue about whether a party actually "signed" an agreement.

Formal contracts (deeds) must be in writing and under seal. This means that the document should be signed by the persons being bound, with a gummed paper seal or a wax impression attached next to the signature. Drawing a circle next to the signature and labelling it "LS" (*locus sigilli* or "the place of the seal") is sufficient evidence that the document is meant to be under seal. It is also usual for the document to be signed by a person who witnessed the promisor signing and affixing the seal to the document.

Signatures are not legally required in theory, but are invariably present because seals are usually gummed and do not by themselves identify the person to be bound. When contract law was developing, seals were usually made by impressing a signet ring with a person's identifying sign or coat of arms into hot wax applied to the document. This is obviously no longer done, since most people don't have coats of arms, signet rings, or seals, or carry around hot wax.

The existence of the seal indicates that the party signing the document intends to be bound by the agreement even when he or she receives no consideration from other parties, as in cases where the promisor is promising a gift to someone. This can be important if, as in tax cases, it matters that a conveyance of something is to be seen to be a gift and not something else.

Must the seal be affixed for the contract to be enforceable? The fact that a person has gone to the trouble of affixing a seal is, in theory, evidence of serious intent, so that validity and enforceability arise from the solemn form of the agreement itself. In most cases, if there is evidence that the document was intended to be sealed, that will suffice to make it a deed and have it enforced as if it were a deed. However, there are still cases where some evidence that seals were affixed (even if they later fell off) is required.[24]

---

24 See *Township of South-West Oxford v. Bailak* (1990), 75 OR (2d) 360, 73 DLR (4th) 411 (Gen. Div.), per Meisner J.

If a corporation or other legal "person" who is not an individual, such as a government department, is a signatory to a contract, it usually will execute an agreement using a corporate seal that identifies the corporation by name. Some statutes require that a signing officer of the corporation sign his or her name next to the seal. Often, the seal alone or the signature of a corporate officer is sufficient. Legislation governing business corporations in many jurisdictions no longer requires a corporation to have and use a seal.

Generally, most contracts need not be witnessed unless there is some statutory requirement. But it is a good idea to have the signatures witnessed so that if proof of a signature on a contract is required it can be more readily obtained. For some deeds, witnesses are required, and an **affidavit of execution** by the witness may also be required in which the witness swears that he or she was present and saw the party sign the document. In this situation, the affidavit of execution itself becomes evidence that a party to the contract signed it.

affidavit of execution
a sworn statement in writing, signed by the witness to a contract, stating that the witness was present and saw the person signing the contract actually sign it; the affidavit can be used to prove that a party to a contract actually signed it

CHAPTER SUMMARY

A contract is an agreement that is enforceable at law. A contract that is not enforceable is a void contract. For a contract to be enforceable, the essential elements of a contract must be present. The parties must have the intent to create an agreement that is legally binding. An offer, or a promise, must be made by the offeror and communicated to the offeree. The offer must not lapse or be revoked. The offeree must communicate his or her unequivocal acceptance to the offeror. The contract must include consideration, or an exchange of something of value between the parties. An agreement without consideration is a gratuitous contract and will not be enforced unless it is under seal. The purpose of the contract must be legal, and any agreement that violates statute law or public policy is void and may be illegal as well.

In considering formality requirements, contracts are either formal or simple contracts. Formal contracts, also called deeds, are in writing and under seal. Simple contracts may be oral or in writing but are not formal contracts, usually because they are not under seal. While many oral contracts are enforceable, some contracts must be in writing and in some cases must be under seal as well.

The *Statute of Frauds* requires that certain contracts involving estate debts, guarantees for third parties, and the transfer of interests in land must be in writing. To prevent rigid and unfair application of this rule requiring written contracts, the courts have developed some exceptions where there has been part performance by one party.

KEY TERMS

affidavit of execution, 45
arm's-length transaction, 13
breach of contract, 22
consideration, 23
counteroffer, 20
deed, 24
easement, 40
estopped, 23
formal contract, 36
fraud, 26

gratuitous promise, 23
guarantee, 38
guarantor, 38
inquiry, 20
lapse, 21
licence, 40
life estate, 40
nullity, 21
onus, 12
past consideration, 27

presumption of law, 12
promissory estoppel, 25
quantum meruit, 29
restraint of trade, 31
restrictive covenant, 33
revoke, 21
simple contract, 36
tort, 36
under seal, 24
void contract, 12

REVIEW QUESTIONS

True or False?

_____ **1.** An offer cannot be revoked after acceptance.

_____ **2.** Contracts made between family members are arm's-length transactions.

_____ **3.** An advertisement is considered an offer to do business.

_____ **4.** An offer lapses when the offeree rejects the offer or makes a counteroffer.

_____ **5.** A gratuitous promise is legally binding.

_____ **6.** There is no difference between an illegal and an unlawful contract.

_____ **7.** A one-year lease for an apartment must be in writing for the tenant to be held to the full term of the lease.

_____ **8.** An oral agreement need not have been witnessed in order for it to be binding.

Multiple Choice

1. Henry invites Sarah to dinner. Sarah accepts his invitation. In preparation, Henry goes to a gourmet food store and spends several hundred dollars on food and spends hours in the kitchen. Sarah fails to show up.

   a. Sarah is contractually liable for half of the money Henry spent on groceries.

   b. Sarah is contractually liable to compensate Henry for his time spent preparing the dinner.

   c. Sarah is not contractually liable because the contract was oral.

   d. Sarah is not contractually liable because this was merely a social arrangement.

2. If I make you an offer and require that you signify acceptance in writing and by mail,

   a. you can phone me up and tell me you accept, at which point I am bound by your acceptance.

   b. if you hand deliver the written acceptance I am bound by your acceptance.

   c. once you mail the written acceptance, I am bound by your acceptance.

   d. if you mail me your acceptance, I am not bound if I never receive the letter in the mail.

3. Consider the following exchange between Suki and Harinder, and identify what each statement would be considered.

   Suki: I hear you have a pet aardvark you wish to sell.

   a. This statement is an offer.

   b. This statement is an acceptance.

   c. This statement is a counteroffer.

   d. This statement is an inquiry.

   Harinder: I have an aardvark and am prepared to part with it for $250.

   a. This statement is an offer.

   b. This statement is a rejection and counteroffer.

   c. This statement is an acceptance.

   d. This statement is an inquiry.

   Suki: I can pay you $200 for it and take delivery today.

   a. This statement is an offer.

   b. This statement is an acceptance.

   c. This statement is a rejection and counteroffer.

   d. This statement is an inquiry.

   Harinder: I could lower the price to $225 for you.

   a. This statement is an offer.

   b. This statement is an acceptance.

   c. This statement is a rejection and counteroffer.

   d. This statement is an inquiry.

   Suki: OK, but I need three days to pay.

   a. This statement is an offer.

   b. This statement is an acceptance.

   c. This statement is a rejection and counteroffer.

   d. This statement is an inquiry.

   Harinder: OK.

   a. This statement is an offer.

   b. This statement is an acceptance.

   c. This statement is a rejection and counteroffer.

   d. This statement is an inquiry.

4. In the preceding question, suppose Suki doesn't come up with the money at the end of three days; in this case,

   a. the offer has lapsed.

   b. Suki has breached the contract.

   c. Harinder can resell to someone else.

   d. b and c

5. The Hangnail Society, a registered charity, sent Felicity a letter asking for a donation. She completed the form indicating that she would donate $200, but never sent the money.

   a. This is a gratuitous promise and is probably unenforceable.

   b. Because she completed the form, the promise is enforceable.

   c. If she made the pledge, or promise, under seal, it would be enforceable.

   d. a and c

6. George had a contract to supply fuel to Eberhardt for Eberhardt's fleet of tugboats at the fluctuating market price. Due to supply problems, fuel prices doubled in a week. Eberhardt, realizing he couldn't pay the cost of running his fleet, tied his tugs up at the wharf. George, facing no sales of fuel at all to Eberhardt, promised to reduce what he charged to Eberhardt to a lower price. Eberhardt agreed to put his fleet back on the water and resume purchasing fuel at the new price offered by George. After a few weeks, George tried to collect the cost of fuel at the old price, reneging on his offer to reduce the price.

   a. There was no new consideration, and so the old contract stands.

   b. Eberhardt is entitled to rely on the new price.

   c. This is an example where the doctrine of promissory estoppel applies.

   d. b and c

7. In the question above, if George had contracted with Eberhardt to supply fuel at a fixed price for a specific period, and then said he could not supply the fuel unless he had a 20 percent increase because his costs had risen by that much,

   a. Eberhardt would be obliged to pay the new price, as he cannot expect George to absorb all of the rising costs of fuel.

   b. George can stop supplying fuel if he is going to run up losses in honouring the agreement.

   c. Eberhardt is under no obligation to pay the surcharge, as George has to honour the terms of the existing contract.

   d. George can always rely on an increase in the market price to raise the price under the existing contract since the contract involves goods subject to fluctuating market prices.

8. Which of the following is an example of an enforceable contract?

   a. Two competitors agree on the price they will charge to the public for goods they both sell.

   b. Avram agrees not to report a theft by Bertil if Bertil repays what he has stolen.

   c. A plumber who is unlicensed sues for the price of goods supplied where he is supplying both goods and services.

   d. Morris agrees to lend Miguel money at 120 percent interest per annum.

9. Contracts involving the transfer of an interest in land

   a. may be enforced whether they are oral or in writing

   b. may be enforced if they are oral, provided that the promisee relied on the oral offer to make improvements to the land

   c. may be enforced if they are oral, provided that the promisee does something or gives something of value to the promisor

   d. none of the above

10. April and May entered into an agreement under seal. Both signed the agreement and there were circles where little gummed red seals were to be affixed, and the agreement states that it is under seal. There is no evidence that the seals were actually applied to the paper, or if they were, they have fallen off.

   a. If the contract is one that does not have to be under seal, the absence of the seals are of no relevance.

   b. If the contract had to be under seal, if there is evidence of some intent to attach a seal, the contract will likely be enforceable, even if the seals have fallen off.

   c. If the contract had to be under seal, and there are no seals affixed to the contract, it is unenforceable, whatever the intention of the parties was with respect to affixing seals.

   d. a and b

Short Answer

1. Explain why an offer must be communicated before it can be accepted.

2. When does an offer lapse?

3. How may an acceptance be communicated? When does silence constitute acceptance?

4. What is the "postal acceptance rule"?

5. How may an offer be revoked, and when is such revocation effective?

6. What distinguishes a counteroffer from an inquiry?

7. What is promissory estoppel?

8. Explain the differences among past, present, and future consideration.

9. Where a contract is modified, are there circumstances in which it will be held to be valid and enforceable

despite the absence of fresh consideration? Explain your answer.

10. In what circumstances might a court grant relief where a contract is found to be illegal?

11. What kinds of contracts does the Ontario *Statute of Frauds* require to be in writing and signed by the parties to be enforceable?

12. What is an "interest in land" that would bring a contract within the *Statute of Frauds*?

Apply Your Knowledge

1. Willie the electrician receives a telephone call late at night from Colin. Colin explains that he has just come home and his house has no power. Colin insists that Willie come over immediately because it is the middle of winter and he is without heat. Willie explains that he charges extra for emergency calls, but no actual price is ever discussed over the phone. Willie arrives at Colin's house. He finds that the house has no power because Colin tripped the main circuit breaker by plugging in too many appliances. Willie simply turns the main circuit breaker back on and leaves. He sends a bill to Colin for $400. Is Colin obliged to pay this amount? Explain.

2. Sharri places an advertisement in the paper offering to sell her piano for $4,000. Aaron writes to Sharri in response to the advertisement and offers to buy her piano for $3,000. Sharri receives Aaron's offer on January 3 and telephones him to ask if he will consider increasing his offer. Aaron tells her he will think about it. Mary writes to Sharri, offering to buy her piano for $3,200. Sharri receives the letter on January 5. She writes to Mary the same day and tells her she will sell the piano for $3,500. Mary receives the letter on January 7 and writes back the same day advising Sharri that she accepts the offer to buy the piano for $3,500. Unfortunately, the letter is lost in the mail, and Sharri never receives it. Aaron writes to Sharri on January 5 stating that he will pay her $4,000 for her piano by paying her $3,000 now and $1,000 in one month. Sharri receives Aaron's letter on January 8 and telephones Aaron the same day to confirm that the payment terms are acceptable. Sharri then receives a telephone call from Mary on January 9 in which she learns of Mary's acceptance by letter dated January 7. Sharri then tells Mary she now wants $4,000 for the piano. Is Sharri bound to sell her piano to either Mary or Aaron? Why or why not?

3. Upon his death, Phillippe left his entire fortune in trust to his daughter, Danielle. Because she was a child when he died, Elizabeth was appointed Danielle's guardian. When Danielle turns 21, she is entitled to her inheritance. However, under the terms of the trust, Danielle cannot access the trust moneys until then. Elizabeth spends a great deal of money on Danielle's education, sending her to expensive private schools and to university. Elizabeth incurs personal debt as a result of Danielle's educational costs. When Danielle turns 21, she gets her inheritance and promises to repay Elizabeth for the money Elizabeth spent on her education. Danielle fails to repay Elizabeth. Can Elizabeth enforce Danielle's promise? Why or why not?

4. Diego owns an automobile repair business. He also owns the land on which the business operates. Dorion has worked for Diego as a mechanic. Diego is interested in retiring and suggests that Dorion buy the business as an ongoing operation. Diego offers to sell for $100,000. Dorion says he doesn't have that kind of money and doesn't have the kind of credit that would allow him to get a loan. Diego says that is no problem. If Dorion can raise $25,000, Diego will give him a mortgage on the garage property for $75,000 at a very low rate of interest. Dorion agrees to this proposal provided, he says, that he can raise the $25,000 downpayment. Diego says that's fine. The agreement is entirely oral. Dorion raises the $25,000 and pays it to Diego. Before he can make the first mortgage payment, Diego dies. Diego's executors find out about these arrangements but refuse to honour them, claiming there was no enforceable contract. Assess the likelihood that the executors will be able to resist Dorion's claim.

5. The Parliament of Canada, after many years of staying out of the bedrooms of the nation, passed a statute "prohibiting anyone from selling post-coital contraceptive medication, otherwise known as the 'morning after pill.'" Cheapo Pharmacy put a poster up by the prescription drop-off, advertising the Cheapo Morning-After Pill for only $10. Cheapo is charged with violating the statute. Would Cheapo be likely to be convicted? If not, what would Parliament have to do to ensure a conviction in this case? Explain your answer.

Protecting Weaker Parties

3

Introduction 52

Legal Capacity to Contract 52

Minors 53

Capacity of Drunkards and Persons Under Mental Disability to Contract 62

Chapter Summary 67

Key Terms 67

Review Questions 67

LEARNING OUTCOMES

After completing this chapter, you should be able to:

- Explain what the term "legal capacity" means.

- Explain the difference between an unlawful and an illegal contract, and describe the impact on the remedy available to the parties in the event of a breach.

- Describe the difference between a simple contract and a formal contract.

- Distinguish between the treatment of contracts for necessaries and contracts for non-necessaries.

- Identify when employment contracts with minors are enforceable.

- Explain the effect of drunkenness on the validity of a contract.

- Explain the effect of mental disability on the validity of a contract.

Introduction

From the 17th century on, the development of modern contract law was driven by the needs of an expanding trading, manufacturing, and banking economy. These needs included a legal system that would enforce commercial agreements without interfering with the bargaining process that led to them. The common law met these needs by interpreting commercial agreements and then enforcing them. The courts rarely inquired into the process that led to forming a contract; they assumed that in commercial agreements, business people were roughly equal in bargaining power and could look after themselves. If a party made a bad bargain because he or she was not as sharp or clever as the other party, that was his or her misfortune.

While this "hands-off" approach is the one usually taken in contract law, the courts do sometimes intervene where parties are clearly unable to protect themselves in the bargaining process. Sometimes this is because one party lacks the intellectual capacity to protect herself or himself, the other party acts dishonestly during the bargaining process or takes advantage of a position of trust, or the other party has expert knowledge of the subject matter of the contract that the weaker party cannot have and takes unfair advantage of that knowledge. This chapter explores some of the circumstances in which the courts protect weaker parties where the capacity of a party to enter into a contract is at issue.

Legal Capacity to Contract

Not everyone is legally entitled to enter into contracts. Some persons, by their status, are presumed not to have the ability to enter into contracts or have limited rights to contract. The purpose here is to protect the weaker party from the stronger and more able party. This class of persons who lack or have limited capacity to contract includes **minors** and **persons under mental disability**.

minor
at common law, an individual under the age of 21; minority status has also been defined by statute law, lowering the age of majority to 18 or 19 in most provinces

persons under mental disability
a general term that includes persons who are delusional and insane so as to be a danger to themselves and others, and those who, while not insane and dangerous, lack the ability to manage their own affairs

There are other situations where the capacity of a party to contract is based on the nature of the contracting entity or on public interest or public policy issues, and not on the strength or weakness of the parties' bargaining power. Enemy aliens, for policy reasons, do not have the capacity to contract, and their contracts in Canada are void and unenforceable by them unless they hold a licence from the Crown. Corporations, as artificial entities, may enter into contracts but do not have the capacity to enter into ones that deal with subject matter that is entirely outside the corporate purposes and objects set out in the company's articles of incorporation or corporate charter, or, where the corporation has been created by statute, outside the powers granted by the statute. Trade unions, which can act like corporations for some purposes and are certified under labour legislation, cannot usually sue or be sued as legal entities absent enabling legislation. Bankrupts may not enter into any contract except for necessaries until they are discharged from bankruptcy. The discharge from bankruptcy relieves the bankrupt of personal liability under contracts entered into before the bankruptcy occurred, except where the bankrupt engaged in fraud or breach of trust.

Minors

The general rule is that contracts with minors are not enforceable against the minor. At common law, a minor is an individual who is under 21 years of age. The common-law definition of age has been replaced by statutory definitions in most provinces, where, as in Ontario, the age of majority is now 18 for the purposes of entering into contracts.[1] The reason for this rule is that minors are presumed to be naive, inexperienced, and easily taken advantage of, so some protection is required.

Contract Rights and Obligations Generally

While the general rule is that contracts with minors are not enforceable against minors, contracts for necessaries of life made by a minor are enforceable, but other contracts are not *if* the minor repudiates them. The reason for enforcing contracts for necessaries is that some minors may have to meet some of their basic needs themselves; if a seller could not enforce a contract against a minor in these circumstances, the seller might choose not to sell at all rather than risk not being able to collect the debt. Because this might leave a minor in a position of not being able to purchase food or shelter, these contracts are enforceable and minors may not repudiate them.

Contracts with minors for non-necessaries are another matter. Here, the law recognizes two types of contracts:

- contracts that are **void *ab initio***
- contracts that are **voidable** at the option of the minor

Because minors may be taken advantage of, the law creates various opportunities for them to treat contracts for non-necessaries that provide some benefit as voidable by allowing minors to repudiate them, in some cases even after the age of majority has been reached. However, if the contract is prejudicial or of no benefit, it may be treated by the courts as void *ab initio*. This means the court will treat the contract as invalid from the beginning and of no force or effect. No rights can ever arise under such a contract, and the minor gets no choice as to whether it is enforceable against him or her or not.

If the contract is voidable, the minor may enforce it if he or she chooses, or repudiate it and recover money paid under it, or the minor may use it as a defence to enforcement by the other party. However, until the minor does what is required to treat the contract as voidable, unless the contract is void *ab initio*, it is presumed to be valid and enforceable.

void *ab initio*
invalid from the beginning; no rights can arise under a contract that is void *ab initio*

voidable contract
a contract that may be avoided or declared void at the option of one party to the contract; once it is declared invalid no further rights can be obtained under it, but benefits obtained before the declaration are not forfeit

---

1 In some provinces the age of majority is 19. There are also other statutes that grant rights on the basis of age. For example, an individual in Ontario can enter into contracts as someone of full age and capacity at 18 but cannot buy alcoholic beverages until the age of 19. See *Age of Majority and Accountability Act*, RSO 1990, c. A.7.

Enforceable Contracts: Purchases of Necessaries

executory contract
a contract between a buyer and seller in which full payment is not made at the time of the contract; a contract to buy on credit

As in most provinces, the Ontario *Sale of Goods Act*[2] provides that a minor is liable to pay a reasonable price for goods that are necessaries that have been sold and delivered to the minor. It follows from this that a minor may be able to repudiate a contract for the sale of goods if it is an **executory contract**. An executory contract is one where the obligations are performed after the contract is made. Thus a minor may repudiate a contract for the sale of necessary goods between the time the minor agreed to purchase the goods but before they are delivered. If the contract is partly performed—for example, goods are delivered but not yet paid for—the minor is bound. If the minor borrows money to purchase necessaries and the money is used for that purpose, then the debt is enforceable against the minor. The Act also describes necessaries as goods "suitable to the conditions in life of the minor" and as goods actually required when ordered. This means that if the goods are necessaries and they are ordered and delivered when the minor is amply supplied with such goods, then the minor may be able to repudiate the contract on the ground that they were not actually required when ordered.

As to what goods are actually necessaries "suitable to the conditions in life of the minor," the case law indicates that the context determines what is suitable given the minor's "conditions in life" or social and economic class. The necessaries for a minor from a wealthy family may be luxuries for a minor from a less wealthy family. How goods are used may also determine whether they are necessaries. If a minor buys clothes so that he or she will be "cool," they may be seen as non-necessaries, but if the minor buys clothes, even expensive ones, to be properly dressed at work, they may be classed as necessaries because they are used in connection with earning a living. Even where a contract is binding because it is for necessaries, the law will not

---

> ### EXAMPLE
>
> #### Contracts for Necessaries
>
> - Tamar, age 17, moves into a dormitory at school because she is far from home. She signs a rental contract. She also decides to rent a TV. Both of these are executory contracts. A month later, Tamar decides to move back home and tries to repudiate both contracts. She may be held to the dorm rental contract, since this was for necessary services. The TV is arguably not a necessary; she may be able to avoid this contract by pleading her minority status and get her money back, and be relieved of future rental charges. She will also have to return the TV.
>
> - Stanislaus, age 16, orders a new winter coat, although he already has three others. Before the coat is delivered, he changes his mind and repudiates the contract. The coat is a necessary item, but it has not been delivered at the time of repudiation, so he can repudiate the agreement. Stanislaus could also argue that the coat is not a necessary because he has three others and is amply supplied with winter coats.

---

2 *Sale of Goods Act*, RSO 1990, c. S.1.

CASE IN POINT

Necessaries or Extravagance?

Nash v. Inman, [1908] 2 KB 1 (CA)

Facts

An action was brought by a tailor for clothes supplied to the defendant while the latter was an undergraduate at Cambridge University. The defendant was a minor at the time of the sale and delivery of the goods. He was the son of well-to-do parents. The clothing supplied included, among other things, 11 expensive waistcoats. The only evidence for the plaintiff was that of its travelling salesperson, who said that he visited Cambridge to solicit business, and had heard that the defendant was a big spender. The plaintiff rested his claim on the ground that the defendant was a minor and that the goods were necessaries. The defendant argued that there was no evidence to go to a jury that the goods were necessaries, in which case the contract could not be enforced against him. The trial judge agreed and dismissed the case. The plaintiff appealed.

Decision

The Court of Appeal held that the defendant had proved both his minority status and that the purchases were extravagant in the circumstances, so that the contract could hardly be described as one for the purchase of necessaries.

Practical Tip

Merchants who take orders for necessaries from minors must be cautious. If payment is not received at the time the order is placed, then the minor may be able to repudiate the contract if the goods turn out not to be necessaries.

make the minor pay more than a reasonable price. Thus, a merchant suing a minor on a contract for necessaries may find recovery of the purchase price limited to what the court thinks is a reasonable price.

It is also clear that contracts for necessary services are binding on a minor. Medical and dental services and, in some cases, contracts for training for employment have been classed as necessaries.[3] An executory contract for necessary services, unlike the situation for the sale of goods, is probably not voidable by the minor.[4]

Enforceable Contracts: Employment

Generally, minors who enter into employment contracts, formal or informal, are bound by their terms unless the terms are not beneficial to the minor. Presumably, minors accept employment to meet their needs, so an employment contract could be viewed as a contract for necessaries. However, just as an article of clothing can be a luxury or a necessity, depending on what it is for, so can a job be classed that way. A minor who works because his or her needs would not be met otherwise is in a different position from a minor who works to acquire spending money for luxuries.

---

3   G.H.L. Fridman, *The Law of Contract in Canada*, 3d ed. (Scarborough, ON: Carswell, 1994), 144. The scheme for analyzing the enforceability of contracts on minors is taken from Fridman because it is a rational and sensible analytic scheme.

4   Ibid.

Minors' Employment Contracts

Arturo, age 16, is hired to work in a factory. He is paid less than the minimum wage and has to sign a form that he will not make a workers' compensation claim if he is injured on the job. He quits without notice and repudiates the contract. The employer will have difficulty enforcing the contract since these conditions appear to be detrimental to Arturo, and a prudent and informed parent would not likely permit a child to work under these conditions.

However, the case law does not focus on whether work is a necessity; rather, it accepts a service contract as enforceable by both parties unless the contract does not benefit the minor. "Benefit" has been held by the courts to include an appropriate salary, but also may include consideration of whether there was a general advantage for the minor in acquiring skills and satisfying aims or desires, and whether the minor was taken advantage of. It has also been suggested that the test of "benefit" may be whether a "prudent and informed parent" would have approved this contract for his or her minor child.

CASE IN POINT

Employment Contract Must Be for the Minor's Benefit

Toronto Marlboro Major Junior "A" Hockey Club et al. v. Tonelli et al. (1979), 23 OR (2d) 193 (CA)

Facts

John Tonelli was a young hockey player of exceptional ability. When he was 17 years old, he entered into a contract with the Toronto Marlboro Junior "A" Hockey Club (the Marlies), an amateur club from which professional hockey players were normally recruited. Tonelli agreed to play hockey only for the Marlies for a period of three or, at the plaintiff's option, four years for minimal salary and to pay to the plaintiff 20 percent of his earnings during his first three years as a professional hockey player. The contract contained other terms highly unfavourable to Tonelli. On attaining the age of 18, Tonelli repudiated the agreement and entered into an agreement with a professional hockey club in Houston, Texas, at a professional's salary. An action for damages against Tonelli and his agent for breach of contract was dismissed on the ground that the contract, not being on the whole beneficial to Tonelli, was voidable at his option. The Marlies appealed to the Ontario Court of Appeal.

Decision

The court held, Zuber, JA, dissenting, that the appeal should be dismissed.

Justices Arnup and Blair said that a contract of service is only enforceable against a minor if it was for his benefit when made, the onus being on the adult party to establish the benefit. In the circumstances, considering Tonelli's exceptional ability and the terms of the contract, it could not be said that the contract was beneficial to him and, in fact, it could be considered very onerous and one-sided. Consequently, Tonelli could not be liable.

Mr. Justice Zuber, dissenting, said that the test should be whether a prudent and informed parent would approve the minor's contract. In this case, a parent would have done so since the alternative was exclusion from the junior league, which would not have been in Tonelli's best long-term professional interest.

Practical Tip

When contracting for employment services with a minor, make sure the terms are fair and reasonable for the minor. Ask yourself whether his or her parent would approve it as being in the minor's best interest.

Contracts for Non-Necessaries

Where a minor has entered into a contract for non-necessaries, the contract is always enforceable by the minor, but the minor may be able to avoid enforcement of the contract against him or her in some circumstances.

If the contract is not fully executed, the minor may avoid the contract (as is the case for contracts for necessaries). If the minor as a buyer repudiates the contract, he or she must return the goods, whatever state they are in. He or she will not be liable for the wear and tear to the goods but may be liable for damage to them that goes beyond reasonable wear and tear. If the minor is the seller, he or she must be able to return the money if the minor wishes to repudiate and have the goods returned to him or her.

If the contract for non-necessaries has been fully executed so that goods and money have changed hands, the contract cannot be set aside. However, the court may order a refund to the minor of the difference between the price actually paid and a court-determined price, as would be the case for necessaries.

If the contract is ongoing, as, for example, if the minor has joined a monthly CD or book club, he or she can repudiate any future liability, but cannot recover money spent for benefits already received.

If the creditor has loaned money for non-necessaries to a minor, the creditor cannot recover the debt if the minor chooses not to pay.

Effect of Reaching the Age of Majority on Minors' Contracts

Where a contract is for necessaries, the liability continues. However, if the contract is for non-necessaries and has not been repudiated by the minor during his or her minority, the contract has to be classified as to type. For this purpose there are two types.

1. *Contracts for non-necessaries that are valid unless the minor repudiates them.* These are contracts that confer ongoing or continuous benefits that are made while an individual is a minor, and which carry on after the age of majority has been reached. The contract will continue to bind the individual unless he or she, before or shortly after reaching the age of majority, does something that constitutes repudiation of the agreement.

2. *Contracts for non-necessaries that are invalid unless ratified by the minor.* These are contracts that confer a one-time benefit, for example, where goods are ordered while the individual is a minor but are not to be delivered to complete contract performance until the minor has reached the age of majority. These contracts must be ratified in writing by the minor during his or her minority or shortly thereafter. If the minor does not ratify the contract, the seller must return the deposit. These two types of contracts are discussed below.

Voidable Ongoing Benefit Contracts for Non-Necessaries: Valid Unless Repudiated

Where a minor acquires by contract permanent property that carries some obligations for the minor, the contract is presumed to be valid and enforceable unless the minor repudiates it during his or her minority or shortly after reaching the age of majority. "Shortly after" appears to be measured in weeks or months rather than years.[5] The classes of contracts affected are contracts that transfer shares to a minor, partnership agreements, and marriage contracts. If the minor, after reaching the age of majority, acts to accept the contract, he or she cannot repudiate it.[6] If he or she does repudiate it, no special form of repudiation is required.[7] It can be written, oral, or inferred from an act. Repudiation is an all-or-nothing affair: the minor cannot repudiate the non-beneficial parts of the contract and hold the other party to the rest of the agreement.[8]

EXAMPLE

Contract That Is Valid Until Repudiated

Luc bought 80 shares in a private company when he was a minor. He paid $8,000, and a further $2,000 is due when he is 22 years old. Two days after reaching the age of majority, Luc considers repudiating the contract. Luc would be able to repudiate this contract because it is in a contract category—share transfers—that permits repudiation while he is a minor or shortly thereafter; two days is certainly "shortly thereafter." However, suppose that a dividend cheque arrives that same day and he cashes it. Because Luc has engaged in an act that affirms his acceptance of the contract by cashing the dividend cheque, he may now be barred from repudiating the contract.

Consequences of Repudiation

- Contracts are enforceable and effective until they are repudiated.
- The minor, on repudiating the contract, is relieved of future obligations and accrued but undischarged obligations.[9]
- Money paid by the minor before repudiation may not be recoverable if the adult party performed his or her obligations under the contract before repudiation by the minor.[10]
- The minor may also recover property such as goods after repudiation if the goods have not been consumed and can be restored to the minor.

---

5 *Foley v. Canada Permanent Loan and Savings Society* (1883), 4 OR 38; *Whalls v. Learn* (1888), 15 OR 481 (CA).

6 *In the Matter of Prudential Life Insurance Co.: Re Paterson*, [1918] 1 WWR 105 (Man. SC).

7 *Butterfield v. Sibbit and Nipissing Elec. Supply Co.* (1950), 4 DLR 302 (Ont. HC).

8 *Henderson v. Minneapolis Steel & Machinery Co.*, [1931] 1 DLR 570 (Alta. SC).

9 *Re Central Bank and Hogg* (1890), 19 OR 7 (Ch.).

10 *Steinberg v. Scala (Leeds) Ltd.*, [1923] 2 Ch. D. 452 (CA).

Voidable One-Time Benefit Contracts for Non-Necessaries: Void Unless Ratified

All other contracts for non-necessaries made by a minor must be ratified when the minor reaches the age of majority or they cease to be valid and enforceable against the minor who has now reached the age of majority. Such contracts, being for non-necessaries, also could have been repudiated by the minor before reaching the age of majority, but were presumed valid unless challenged. In Canada, the ratification must be in writing and signed by the minor.

EXAMPLE

Contract That Must Be Ratified to Be Valid

Michelle, age 17, decides to buy a sailboat. She pays $10,000 as a first installment and will pay the balance in June of next year. She will be 18 in April of next year. Michelle decides she doesn't want the sailboat and refuses to ratify the contract when she turns 18. Because she must ratify the contract and the sailboat is not a necessary, the contract ceases to be enforceable by the seller and is now void. Michelle is entitled to get her money back because the seller can be restored to his or her previous position.

Consequences of Invalidation from Failure to Ratify

- Prior to validation, the minor can enforce the contract against the adult, but not vice versa.
- A third party cannot rely on the invalidity of a contract to escape liability. For example, an adult who agrees to indemnify another for a minor's debt is still bound even if the minor fails to validate the contract by ratifying it.[11]
- If the minor does not ratify, he or she is not liable for future accrued liabilities under the contract.
- If the minor does not ratify, money can be recovered provided the minor can restore the adult to his or her pre-contract position. If the minor has paid in part and then refuses to ratify, he or she must return the goods and may lose the deposit, although he or she may recover other moneys paid.[12]

Void Contracts

In Canada, some minors' contracts have been held to be void *ab initio*. Some cases have held that a contract that is not beneficial is void without the minor having to do anything. But the better view is that to fall into the void *ab initio* category, a

---

11 *McBride v. Appleton*, [1946] OR 17 (CA). An adult who gives a guarantee, however, is not bound, since the guarantee can apply only to a valid contract. Once the contract has been voided it is gone, and there is nothing to guarantee.

12 Fridman, supra footnote 3, at 153.

contract would have to be more than "not beneficial"—it would have to be clearly prejudicial or harmful, which is a more stringent requirement for holding a contract to be void.[13]

EXAMPLE

Contract Void Ab Initio

Henry is a wealthy minor. He is prevailed upon by his cousin Anna to lend her a large sum of money at a very low rate of interest. Anna has been bankrupt three times and is clearly a poor credit risk. Because the interest is unreasonably low and the risk of loss of the money is very high, the contract would be prejudicial to Henry, and it is arguably void *ab initio*.

Consequence for Void Contracts

The minor is entitled, not being bound, to have all of his or her money or property returned, and the adult need not be restored to his or her pre-contract position.

Alternative Remedies for Void or Void Ab Initio Contracts

If a minor is immune from liability in contract because the contract is void, the adult cannot make an end run around contractual immunity by suing the minor in tort. This is certainly true for the tort of negligence, but wilful destruction of the subject matter of the contract by the minor may give rise to an action for an intentional tort such as trespass to goods.[14]

If the minor misrepresents his or her age, claiming to have reached the age of majority, at common law an action for the tort of fraudulent misrepresentation will not be permitted.[15] However, the adult may invoke equitable remedies under which the minor must restore goods purchased in a contract where the minor fraudulently misrepresented his or her age.

TIP

It would be best for an adult who contracts with a minor to find another adult to be jointly liable with the minor for the contractual liability. It is not a good idea to have an adult guarantee the obligation as a secondary debtor, because if the minor's contract is made void, the liability on the guarantee is also void, although an agreement by an adult to indemnify a person who contracts with the minor may survive if the minor contract is found to be void.[16]

---

13   *Beam v. Beatty* (1902), 3 OLR 345 (HC).

14   *Burnard v. Haggis* (1863), 143 ER 360.

15   *Stocks v. Wilson*, [1913] 2 KB 235.

16   Fridman, supra footnote 3, at 155-57.

Beware of Contracting with Minors

R v. Rash (1923), 41 CCC 215 (CA)

Facts

The defendant, a minor, was tried under what was then s. 417 of the *Criminal Code* with defrauding his creditors by concealing, removing, or disposing of property. The defendant, while a minor, had purchased groceries at wholesale with the intent of selling them at retail. The argument of the defendant was that he was a minor when he committed the offence, so he could not be found guilty, even though he had disposed of his wholesale stocks without paying his creditors. The magistrate convicted him.

Decision

The Court of Appeal held that the conviction should be set aside. The defendant, as a minor, was under no legal obligation to pay his creditors. During his minority they had no enforceable claim against him, and upon attaining his majority he had the legal right to repudiate liability, which he did by refusing to pay. Therefore, those who sold him the groceries were not his "creditors" within the meaning of s. 417. The conviction was quashed.

Practical Tip

Merchants who sell non-necessaries on credit to young people should make sure they find out whether their customer is a minor. A minor in these circumstances can repudiate the contract by refusing to pay.

Law Affecting Minors in British Columbia

The law affecting minors in British Columbia is somewhat different from the law in other common-law provinces and Quebec. It is summarized as follows.

A minor's contract is unenforceable against the minor unless one of these conditions is met:

- the contract is enforceable under some statute,
- the minor validates the contract on attaining the age of majority,
- the minor wholly or partly performs the contract shortly after attaining the age of majority, or
- the contract is not repudiated by the minor within a year of having attained the age of majority.

Where a contract is invalid, the court has broad discretion to provide remedies and may discharge parties from contractual obligations, or order restitution or compensation.[17]

---

17   Ibid., at 157-58.

Summary: Liability Under Contracts by Minors

Contracts for Necessaries	Contracts for Non-Necessaries

• as a general rule, these contracts are enforceable against the minor
 	
• if the contract is executory, the minor can repudiate it
 	
• if the minor borrows money to purchase necessaries and the money is used for that purpose, the debt is enforceable
 	
• because necessaries are goods "suitable to the conditions in life of the minor" and goods actually required when ordered, if the goods fail to satisfy either condition, they may be deemed non-necessaries and the minor may be able to repudiate the contract
 	
• contracts for necessary services are binding on a minor
 	
• generally, employment contract terms are binding on a minor unless the terms are not beneficial to the minor
	• as a general rule, these contracts are not enforceable against the minor if the minor repudiates them
	
	• the contract is always enforceable by the minor
	
	• there are two types:
	  – void *ab initio*: these contracts are prejudicial or harmful to the minor and are never enforceable
	  – voidable: these contracts are presumed to be valid; the minor may enforce them or repudiate them
	
	• if the contract is not fully executed, the minor may repudiate it, but must return the goods or money
	
	• if the contract is fully executed
	  – it cannot be set aside by the minor, but a court may order a refund of part of the purchase price to the minor if the purchase price is "unfair"
	  – it cannot be set aside by the other party and that party cannot sue for debt
	
	• when the minor reaches the age of majority:
	  – if the contract is a voidable ongoing benefit contract, the contract continues to be valid unless the minor repudiates it
	  – if the contract is a voidable one-time benefit contract, the contract ceases to be valid unless the minor ratifies it

Capacity of Drunkards and Persons Under Mental Disability to Contract

Drunkenness

The law will intervene in some circumstances where someone who is intoxicated enters into an agreement. Intoxication alone is not sufficient, but it can be a defence to enforcement by the sober party, and the intoxicated party may void the contract on the basis of his or her own intoxication in the following circumstances:

- the intoxicated party, because of the intoxication, did not know what he or she was doing;
- the sober party was aware of the intoxicated state of the other party; and
- upon becoming sober, the intoxicated party moved promptly to repudiate the contract.[18]

---

18   *Gore v. Gibson* (1845), 153 ER 260.

Repudiation for Intoxication—If It Is Clear That the Person Is Intoxicated

Bennet v. Latitude 49 Developments Ltd., 1999 CanLII 6513 (BCSC)

Facts

Jack Bangay and his wife were joint shareholders of a company. The company ran a pub that the plaintiffs wished to purchase. The sale documents were for the sale of assets—the pub, its stock in trade, and so on. Bangay maintained that his instructions were to sell the shares, not the assets. When the sale of assets was completed, Bangay attempted to repudiate the sale on the basis of his own intoxication. The court found that Bangay was indeed an alcoholic with a serious drinking problem. There was evidence, including from his wife, that when he was drinking, he was very good at concealing its effects so that a stranger might not know that he was intoxicated. The court also noted that the documents for the sale were very clearly for the sale of the pub as an asset, and not for the sale of shares. The plaintiff's evidence was that the contract was regular on its face as to its terms, and that there was no evidence that Bangay was intoxicated when the deal was finally completed. Further, there was ample time beforehand to examine the sale documents.

Decision

In the circumstances, the court determined that even if Bangay was intoxicated, the other party could not reasonably have been aware that he was. The court determined that the contract was valid and enforceable.

Practical Tip

Where you think there might be an issue of intoxication by one of the parties, it is a good idea to meet with the party, observe his or her demeanour, go over the terms and provisions, and then attend to formally signing the contract. Avoid using email or other electronic means to sign the contract. You (or another person) should take notes of your observations of the other party to rebut claims of intoxication as a ground for repudiation. If the party does appear to be intoxicated, it is wise not to proceed with signing the contract at that time.

The basis for this approach is not that one party is drunk but that the other party might defraud the drunkard. Thus, even where the sober party is not aware of the intoxicated state of the other party, if there is evidence of intoxication so that it may be presumed, the unfairness or one-sidedness of a contract might result in its being voided.[19] This view moves the law toward a position that an unconscionable or markedly unfair agreement permits the court to presume that the sober party had knowledge of the intoxication of the other party once there is evidence of intoxication.

How intoxicated does a party have to be to avoid a contract? Merely being in an excited state with one's judgment somewhat impaired may not be sufficient to allow a contract to be voided. If the intoxicated party knew what the basics of the contract were and what he or she was being asked to do, that may not be enough to allow for repudiation.[20] The cases do not indicate that intoxication from substances other than alcohol would give rise to a right to repudiate a contract. Perhaps because intoxication from sources other than alcohol are often illegal, litigants on this issue have been reluctant to come forward.

---

19   *Black v. Wilcox* (1977), 70 DLR (3d) 192 (Ont. CA).

20   *Watmough v. Cap's Const. Ltd.*, [1977] 1 WWR 398 (Alta. Dist. Ct.).

> **EXAMPLE**
>
> **Repudiation for Drunkenness**
>
> Melissa has had so much to drink that she cannot stand, her words are slurred, and her conversation makes little sense. Semareh has an old sofa she would like to get rid of. She persuades Melissa to buy the sofa for a price that is almost the price of a new sofa. Melissa sobers up the next morning, realizes what she has done, and calls Semareh to tell her the deal is off. Melissa was clearly very drunk; it would have been hard for Semareh to be unaware of that. It is doubtful that Melissa was coherent enough to know what she was doing when she bought the sofa. Melissa repudiates at the first reasonable opportunity once she sobers up. She will probably succeed in repudiating the contract.

Mental Disability

Some types of mental disability may be sufficient to allow a person to repudiate a contract in certain circumstances. Generally, the law is concerned with the lack of capacity arising from mental disability. For example, people who have schizophrenia may have delusions, but if they can manage their own daily and business affairs and look after their personal finances, they may have the capacity to enter into some contracts. The mentally disabled persons that the law protects are those who are unable to manage their own affairs or are unable to appreciate the nature and consequences of their actions.

The law deals in the following ways with those who are unable to manage their affairs:

- Provincial legislation provides that a person can be declared to be unable to manage his or her affairs. If there has been such a judicial finding, contracts made after the judicial finding are void on the ground that there is a lack of capacity to consent to the provisions of a contract.[21] Contracts made prior to the finding may be voidable, as noted below.

- If a person lacks capacity because he or she is unable to handle his or her affairs, but there has been no judicial finding, the contracts made are voidable at the option of the person who is mentally disabled. If the contracts are not repudiated, they are presumed to be enforceable.[22]

As is the case with drunkenness, for repudiation to succeed where no judicial finding of incapacity has been made, the other party must know of the mental disability. There need not be actual knowledge if there is wilful disregard of the surrounding circumstances from which the mental state could be presumed. Thus, if the non-disabled party suspects from the other's conduct that the other might lack capacity due to mental disability, that may be sufficient knowledge.[23]

---

21 *Rourke v. Halford* (1916), 37 OLR 92 (CA).

22 *Fykes v. Chisholm* (1911), 3 OWN 21 (HC).

23 *Grant v. Imperial Trust Co.* (1934), 3 DLR 660 (SCC).

Mental Disability as a Ground for Avoiding a Contract

◼ François has been diagnosed with Alzheimer's disease and has been found by a court to be incompetent to handle his own business affairs. After this finding, François contracts to have aluminum siding installed on his house. His brother finds out and tells the contractor. The contractor has no right to proceed, because a contract made by a person found by a court to be incompetent is void *ab initio*.

◼ François's brother also discovers that François had contracted to have aluminum siding installed by another contractor two weeks before being found incompetent by the court. François has memory problems that are obvious to a casual observer, but the terms of the contract are reasonable. Because the contractor has not taken advantage of François, this contract may be difficult to repudiate. However, if there is already new or adequate aluminum siding on the house, François (through his brother) may be able to argue that the contract is unfair because it is unnecessary, and that, on the whole, the contract is inequitable.

Be Cautious When Dealing with Persons Suspected of Having a Mental Disability

Elliott v. Parksville (City of), 1990 CanLII 806 (BCCA)

Facts

This was an appeal to the Supreme Court of British Columbia from a decision dismissing an action for wrongful dismissal. Ms. Elliott had been the municipal clerk, having risen through the ranks of municipal employees. She sent two letters to the municipal council, one resigning her position, and a second asking to go on sick leave. The letters were contradictory, there was a known history of mental illness, and there was evidence that she was mentally ill when she sent both letters. The council accepted her resignation and offered her three months' sick leave. Her work record to this point had been less than satisfactory: she had been late, had failed to perform duties as assigned, had been insubordinate, had had a negative impact on other staff, and had given herself an unauthorized salary increase. She had been notified of these deficiencies and the council considered them when accepting her letter of resignation.

Decision

At trial, the judge had found that the letter of resignation was of no force and effect as the appellant lacked capacity, but that she had been properly dismissed for cause. The trial judge's decision was upheld by the appellate court.

Practical Tip

As with intoxicated parties during the contract formation process, it is wise to deal in person with anyone who you suspect might be mentally incapacitated. If you discover this to be the case, you should inquire to see if there is someone who holds power of attorney with authority to enter into a contract with the grantor (the incapacitated person) or if there is a court order appointing a guardian. If so, you can deal with the guardian or person granted power of attorney (referred to usually as "the attorney," although this does not mean the person is or has to be a lawyer).

The fairness of the contract is also important because there must be evidence that the contract is fair to the mentally disabled party. Some cases go on to require that, to be voidable, the contract must be unconscionable, although that view has been rejected in Canada and England.[24] It follows that if the contract is fair, or the other party is unaware of a mental disability that affects capacity, then the contract is enforceable and not voidable by the person who is mentally disabled.

As with minors, persons under a mental disability are liable to pay a reasonable price for necessaries, and contracts for necessaries cannot be repudiated.

---

24 *Archer v. Cutler*, [1980] 1 NZLR 386.

CHAPTER SUMMARY

While the courts normally do not interfere with the rights of parties to contract, they will in some circumstances intervene to protect a weaker party from a stronger one where it is likely that one side will extract an unfair advantage from the other.

Some parties to a contract are protected on the basis of their status. Protective rules apply to minors, drunkards, and persons under a mental disability. Minors can be held to contracts for necessaries and to beneficial employment contracts. But if the contract is for non-necessaries, these may not be enforced against minors in most instances. If the minor accepts the contract and does not repudiate during his or her minority, the minor may be able to repudiate the contract on reaching the age of majority. In some cases, the contract must be positively ratified or affirmed by the minor on reaching the age of majority. A minor's contract that is prejudicial or harmful may be void *ab initio*.

In the case of drunkards, if intoxication results in the drunkard not knowing what he or she was doing, but the other party knew it, and on becoming sober, the intoxicated party moves to repudiate the contract, a court may well set the contract aside because of diminished capacity.

In the case of those under a mental disability, a person found by a court to lack mental capacity is unable to enter into valid contracts except for necessaries; contracts for non-necessaries are void. When the person suffers from a mental disability but has not been so declared by a court, and if the other party to the contract knew or ought to have known of the disability, the mentally disabled party may be able to avoid the contract.

KEY TERMS

executory contract, 54
minor, 52
persons under mental disability, 52
void *ab initio*, 53
voidable contract, 53

REVIEW QUESTIONS

True or False?

_____ **1.** In the case of a minor, an expensive business suit may be considered a necessity under certain circumstances.

_____ **2.** An executory contract is one where both parties have completed their obligations at the time the contract is made.

_____ **3.** If a contract for non-necessaries made by a minor is not repudiated at or about the time the age of majority is reached, the contract continues in force and is valid.

_____ **4.** Ali, age 15, bought an expensive snowboard, paid for it, and had it delivered. As a minor he can repudiate this contract.

_____ **5.** Employment contracts entered into by minors are unenforceable if they are not in the best interests of the minor.

_____ **6.** In the case of a minor entering into a contract, the contract will be considered void *ab initio* if it is prejudicial or harmful to the minor.

_____ **7.** Just as people are accountable for the crimes they commit when they are drunk, so are they liable for the contracts they enter into when they are drunk.

_____ **8.** Persons suffering from a medically recognized mental illness are never liable under any contracts they sign.

Multiple Choice

1. Morris, a minor who is a paraplegic and who cannot swim, bought a sailboard (a surf board with a sail on it). Shortly thereafter, he attained the age of majority.

   a. He can repudiate because this is a non-necessary.

   b. He is no longer a minor, and is therefore bound.

   c. The contract is void *ab initio* because it could not be of benefit to him.

   d. He can repudiate, provided he does so around the time of attaining the age of majority.

2. Avril, age 16, has just moved from the tropics to a cold climate. She doesn't have a winter coat, so she goes looking for one. She finds what she refers to as "an old lady coat" for $150, and another winter coat for $160 that she thinks is "way cool." She buys the cool coat, but wants to return it the next day because her girlfriends don't like it.

   a. She can repudiate the contract because she is a minor and a "way cool" coat is not a necessary.

   b. She cannot repudiate the contract because a winter coat is a necessary and the price difference between the two coats is small. This is not an unreasonable price to pay for a winter coat for Canadian winters.

   c. She cannot repudiate the contract because she has paid for the coat, and once a minor pays for goods, he or she cannot repudiate the contract.

   d. None of the above.

3. Supposing in the previous example, the seller saw how much Avril wanted the coat and told her it would cost $300, though he normally sold it for $160.

   a. Avril would be liable for the price agreed to.

   b. Because it is a necessary, Avril has to pay for it, but is liable only for what would be a reasonable price.

   c. It is not a necessary, and Avril can repudiate at any time.

   d. Because of the cost, the contract is void *ab initio*.

4. Ivo, age 17, signs a contract to work as a baker's apprentice. He is paid almost nothing, and though he has room and board, his room is freezing and the food is very low quality. His parents, glad to have Ivo off their hands, tell him to stick with it. In determining whether Ivo can repudiate the contract, you should consider

   a. whether there is a benefit to Ivo

   b. whether the contract is too one-sided in favour of the employer

   c. whether Ivo's parents think the contract will benefit him

   d. all of the above

5. Melish, age 15, joined an Internet movie service where he can pay to download movies, and is charged $10 a month whether he uses the service or not. He decides that it is not worth the membership fee, so he repudiates the contract.

   a. He can recover the amounts previously paid to download movies.

   b. He is locked into the deal and cannot get out.

   c. He can give notice that he is repudiating the contract, and is not obliged to pay the future monthly fees.

   d. a and c

6. Soshona bought a Zipmobile, which is not a necessary; it had not been delivered at the time she reached the age of majority.

   a. Once it is delivered she is obliged to pay the contract price.

   b. The price must be reasonable or the contract is void.

   c. She must ratify the contract, or the seller is obliged to return the price paid.

   d. None of the above.

7. Orrin bought shares in a company for $10,000 when he was a minor; he paid $8,000 at the time of the purchase and the balance is due when he is 21.

   a. He must ratify the contract at or around the time he reaches the age of majority.

   b. He can repudiate before or shortly after reaching the age of majority.

   c. If he receives a dividend cheque on the shares and cashes it after reaching the age of majority, he may be barred from repudiating the contract.

   d. b and c

8. Henry has had a few drinks and is in a good mood. He goes out to buy a new car. The salesman can smell alcohol on his breath, and sees that Henry is quite animated as a result of his alcohol intake. Henry knew he was buying a car, and negotiated a good price, but decides later to repudiate the deal, based on the fact that he was intoxicated.

    a. Henry cannot rely on his intoxication to repudiate the contract.

    b. The contract can be repudiated as the salesperson knew Henry had consumed alcohol and that his judgment was affected by it.

    c. Even if he got a good deal, Henry can still repudiate based on intoxication.

    d. All of the above.

Short Answer

1. Why do courts usually take a "hands-off" approach when it comes to examining the bargaining process?

2. What does the phrase "inequality of bargaining power" mean?

3. In what circumstances must minors honour their contractual obligations? In what circumstances can they escape their contractual obligations?

4. If a contract is detrimental to a minor, is the contract void *ab initio* or voidable? What is the difference between a contract that is void *ab initio* and one that is voidable?

5. Suppose the contract made by a minor is binding. Must the minor pay the price set by the seller? Why or why not?

6. If a minor orders goods that are necessaries, can he or she back out of the deal if the goods have been delivered? Does it matter if the minor already has three of what was ordered? Explain.

7. In what circumstances can a minor's contract be repudiated if it is not for necessaries and not an employment contract?

8. What are the consequences if a minor misrepresents his or her age when entering into a contract and presents himself or herself as having reached the age of majority?

9. How can adults who wish to contract with minors protect themselves from repudiation of a contract by a minor? What will work? What will not work?

10. In what circumstances can a drunkard avoid a contract?

11. Describe the way the law treats contracts of persons under a mental disability.

Apply Your Knowledge

1. Greta is 17 and lives with her mother, who does not earn much money. Greta needs to work part time to contribute to the family income while going to school. She gets a job in an office as a receptionist. Because she has few clothes suitable for business purposes, she buys several suits to wear to work. She gets a good price and buys them on sale. After bringing them home, Greta decides she wants to return some of them. The seller says they were sold on sale with no right of return. Can Greta argue her minority status and repudiate this agreement?

2. Read the Court of Appeal decision in *Toronto Marlboro Major Junior "A" Hockey Club et al. v. Tonelli et al.* You will find the citation in the Case in Point on page 56. Compare the approach of the majority with that of the dissent by Mr. Justice Zuber. What are the standards adopted by the majority and the minority to "test" a minor's employment contract? Are the differences, if any, significant? Which do you prefer and why?

3. Edgar, age 15, would like to buy a really expensive snowboard. To earn the money to buy the board, he takes a job at The Grill as a busboy. He is paid $4.00 per hour on the grounds that he has to learn the job and is apprenticing. This is well below the statutory minimum wage. There are no deductions for employment insurance, income tax, or Canada Pension Plan, which is fine with Edgar, as it means more take-home pay for him. After a few days he walks off the job without notice, demanding his pay to date. The boss refuses to pay him because he left without notice. Explain whether Edgar is entitled to his unpaid wages.

Contractual Defects

4

Introduction	72
Misrepresentation	72
Duress	83
Undue Influence	85
Unconscionability	87
Mistake	90
Chapter Summary	108
Key Terms	108
Review Questions	108

LEARNING OUTCOMES

After completing this chapter, you should be able to:

- Define "contractual defect" and list five types.

- Distinguish between innocent, negligent, and fraudulent misrepresentations.

- Distinguish between duress and undue influence.

- Explain what is meant by "unconscionability" in the context of the validity of a contract.

- Explain the consequences of the various kinds of mistakes on the part of contracting parties.

Introduction

A contractual defect is a defect in one of the elements of a valid contract. In some cases, the contractual defect will render the contract void *ab initio* (that is, it is void from the beginning because it fails to meet the requirements of a valid contract) and in other cases, it will render the contract voidable (made void by the action of either party to it). In yet other cases, the contract may continue to be valid but the injured party may be able to sue for what amounts to a breach of contract. This chapter discusses several types of contractual defects:

- misrepresentation
- duress
- undue influence
- unconscionability
- mistake

All of these types of defects are factors that can affect the parties' intention to create a legal contract.

Misrepresentation

Overview

A **misrepresentation** is a false statement that induces someone to enter into a contract. It generally arises as part of the bargaining process. For example, if you are considering ordering a carload of tomatoes and while you examine them you ask the seller, "Are these grade A tomatoes?" and the seller replies "Yes," then the "Yes" may be a statement made to induce you to enter into the contract. If you enter into the contract because of the answer, then the inducement is a **material representation**. If the statement is false and the seller is not aware that it is false, it is an **innocent misrepresentation**. If the statement is false and the seller knows it is false, it is a **fraudulent misrepresentation**. If you are aware that the statement is a misrepresentation and enter into the contract anyway, or you are not influenced by the statement to enter into the agreement but enter into it for other reasons, then you may not **rescind** the contract because of the false statement because you were not induced by it to enter into the contract.

What happens if a statement is not material? If the misrepresentation induces you to enter into the agreement but it is not related to a material fact that induces you to enter into the contract, then you may not rely on it to rescind the contract.

Does a material representation always require a statement? Usually, failing to say anything does not give rise to rescission. If you ask the seller, "Are these grade A tomatoes?" and the seller says nothing and the tomatoes turn out not to be grade A, there is no misrepresentation, particularly if you could look at the tomatoes and decide for yourself. However, if the seller has special information that you could not reasonably know, his or her omission may amount to a misrepresentation. Some statutes,

Margin glossary

misrepresentation
a false statement that induces someone to enter into a contract

material representation
a statement made before a contract is made that induces, or influences, a party to enter into the contract

innocent misrepresentation
a false statement made to induce a party to enter into a contract that the maker of the statement does not know is false

fraudulent misrepresentation
a false statement made to induce a party to enter into a contract that the maker knows is false

rescission
the cancellation, nullification, or revocation of a contract; the "unmaking" of a contract

EXAMPLE

Non-Material Misrepresentation

If the seller says, "Tomatoes are necessary for good health," this general statement about tomatoes may be a misrepresentation (you can enjoy good health and never eat a tomato), but it is not the kind of statement that has anything directly to do with material concerns that affect the decision to buy a carload of tomatoes.

in particular those protecting consumers from sophisticated sellers, also permit rescission for an omission by a seller that amounts to a material misrepresentation.

A statement that is a misrepresentation must be a statement of fact and not an opinion. The words themselves do not always make it easy to decide whether a statement is a fact or an opinion. In our example, the seller's answer "Yes" to a question could be seen as a statement. However, if the seller had instead said, "I *think* these are grade A tomatoes," this would be his or her opinion and no more than that. The cases indicate that an opinion is usually not seen as sufficient to induce you to enter into a contract, because it lacks the certainty and emphasis of a statement of fact. This may be an impractical and illogical distinction, because the opinion of a knowledgeable seller might very well induce you to enter into a contract.

TIP

If you wish to prove reliance on an opinion so that it will be treated as a statement of fact, it is a good idea to make it clear in writing to the other party that you do not have expert knowledge, that you acknowledge that he or she does, and that you are relying on his or her professional or expert opinion.

EXAMPLE

Statement of Opinion

A car salesman says, "I think this car will meet your fuel efficiency requirements." This is a statement of opinion and is not a fact on which the buyer can rely if it turns out that the car is not particularly fuel efficient.

However, if the car manufacturer's engineers, with knowledge of the buyer's requirements where the buyer does not have expert knowledge, make this statement, a court may treat the statement made in this context as a material statement to be relied on, rather than mere opinion.

Does a material misrepresentation automatically void a contract? A material misrepresentation does not make a contract void *ab initio*. It will make the contract voidable by the party who was misled by the misrepresentation (or material omission). But it is the misled party's choice; though misled, a party may, for a variety of reasons, choose not to void the contract and continue with it. But once the misrepresentation is discovered, if the misled party intends to treat the contract as void, the misled party should act as soon as possible to rescind the contract. In doing so, he or she must accept no further benefits under the contract, or he or she may be deemed to have affirmed the contract notwithstanding the misrepresentation and, by doing so, waived the right of rescission.

A misrepresentation may not only induce you to enter into a contract, it may also become a term of the contract. When a misrepresentation is found by a court to have become a contract term, the contract is not subject to rescission for misrepresentation, but is subject to an action for breach of contract.

Statements That Are Not Misrepresentations

- statements of belief or opinion that turn out to be false
- statements of future conduct or intention that turn out to be false
- honest misstatements as to what the law is (although there is conflicting case law)
- silence or non-disclosure (generally)

Exceptions:

- statements that do not present the whole truth, or half-truths, may be regarded as misrepresentations.
- statements that are true when made but become false by the time they are acted upon may constitute a misrepresentation if the maker does not advise the other party of the change.

TIP

If you discover that you were misled by a material misrepresentation, you should give the other side notice in writing that you consider statements made by the other party to be a material misrepresentation and that you consider the contract to be void. Or, you might indicate that you are *considering* treating the contract as void, as you may decide to continue the contract, but plan to use the misrepresentation as the basis for renegotiating the contract on more favourable terms, rather than treating it as void. For business reasons, using a material misrepresentation as a springboard for altering the terms of a contract in your favour may be an attractive alternative approach.

EXAMPLE

Misrepresentation Becoming a Term of a Contract

The seller may not only make a misrepresentation that the tomatoes are grade A, he or she may also make it a term of the contract by describing the tomatoes as being grade A. It might then be seen as a term of the contract, and if the tomatoes are not grade A, you could sue the seller for breach of contract.

Innocent Misrepresentation

Innocent misrepresentation is the misrepresentation of a material fact that the person making it believes to be true, but which is discovered to be false after the contract has been made. If the innocent party can show that he or she was induced by the statement to enter into the contract and that the statement was material, he or she may ask for the equitable remedy of rescission. At common law, the party who has suffered loss cannot obtain a remedy unless the untrue statement can be construed as a term of the contract or the untrue statement was made negligently. If it is a term of the contract, then the victim can sue for breach of what is a perfectly valid contract and obtain damages for whatever losses he or she sustained. If the false statement was negligently made, though the maker thought it was true, then although there is no contractual remedy at common law, the innocent party could sue the other party for negligent misrepresentation in tort,[1] in which case the maker of the statement would be liable for all the foreseeable damage actually sustained.

The common law, then, leaves the victim of a "pure" innocent misrepresentation without a remedy. However, the doctrine of equity—a special branch of our law designed to promote fairness by creating exceptions to the unfair application of the strict rules of common law—provides relief in this situation. The victim of a pure misrepresentation may request the equitable remedy of rescission. Rescission does not include an award of damages for the victim's losses; it does, however, revoke a voidable contract at the instance of the injured party and, as far as possible, restores the parties to their pre-contract positions. Doing this may mean that the party who suffered the loss may receive his or her money back, but other consequential damages (for example, in a contract for manufacturing supplies, the loss of an opportunity to fill an important order), even in equity, cannot be recovered. This means that of the three types of innocent misrepresentation, the pure type may lead to something less than full recovery of all of the losses causally connected to the contract. Consequently, it is important to classify the innocent misrepresentation further because of the different remedies available.

- An innocent misrepresentation that can be classified as a term of the contract can give rise to an action for breach of the term of the contract.
- An innocent misrepresentation that is made negligently can give rise to an action in tort for negligent misrepresentation.
- An innocent misrepresentation that is classified as "pure" will give rise to revocation of the contract and some indemnification to restore the injured party as much as possible to his or her pre-contract position. This remedy is referred to as **restitution**. But if the contract has been partly performed, and restitution is not possible, rescission may not be available to the plaintiff. However, unlike the English courts, Canadian courts have been relatively flexible in allowing rescission where there has been part performance.[2]

restitution
a remedy by which one seeks to rescind a contract; if granted, restitution restores the party, as far as possible, to the pre-contract position

There has been some question as to whether the victim can obtain more damages by suing in tort for negligent misrepresentation than by suing for breach of a term of the contract. In practical terms, there is probably little difference. It is clear that while a contract matter may give rise to a lawsuit, it does not have to be a contract suit if an action in tort is made out. If a misrepresentation is material, whether it is innocent, innocent and negligent, a minor representation, or a term, a party may be able to sue in tort or contract in the alternative, and leave it to the trial judge to decide the basis of liability and the damages that flow from that finding.

---

1 *Hedley Byrne and Co. Ltd. v. Heller and Partners Ltd.*, [1964] AC 465 (HL).

2 S.M. Waddams, et al., *Cases and Materials on Contracts*, 4th ed. (Toronto: Emond Montgomery, 2010), 450.

Innocent Misrepresentation Can Lead to Rescission

Kosior v. Motz, 2006 SKPC 35

Facts

The plaintiff Kosior purchased an 18-foot boat, equipped with a 175-horsepower inboard motor, from the defendant Motz. Kosior paid $8,900 to Motz. The boat and trailer were sold "as is subject to water tryout." It is clear on the evidence that the defendant believed the motor to be in good operating condition and indicated that it was to the plaintiff. There was no real opportunity to test the engine until the plaintiff got it home and into the water. When he did try it out, the plaintiff discovered that the engine had been frost damaged and would require expensive repairs. The plaintiff asked for his money back, and the defendant said the sale was on an "as is" basis and refused to refund the purchase price or take back the boat. The plaintiff therefore sued for rescission: the defendant would return the purchase price, and the plaintiff would return the boat to the defendant.

Decision

The plaintiff was entitled to rescind the contract, return the boat to the defendant, and get his money back. The defendant made an innocent misrepresentation that the motor would work. The fact that it did not deprived the plaintiff of virtually the whole of what he had bargained for as the boat was useless without a properly working motor. Further, the plaintiff clearly had to rely on this misrepresentation as there was no real opportunity to test or inspect the motor, so that the defendant could not fall back on the argument that the purchase was on an "as is" basis where the plaintiff could not assess whether he was getting what he bargained for. As the innocent misrepresentation was about an essential matter, relied on by both parties, the plaintiff was entitled to rescind the contract and get his money back.

Practical Tip

When negotiating a contract where you are relying on representations made by the other party, insist on those representations being included in the text of the contract to make it easier to rescind if an innocent representation turns out to be a misrepresentation.

It is possible to get around narrow interpretations of representations about land in rescission cases. Carefully drafting the contract to state clearly, for example, that the exact acreage or amount of the land that is the subject of the contract is material to the buyer may make it possible for a court to rule in your favour if the land turns out to be less than you bargained for.

For an innocent misrepresentation to be material, it must result in a substantial difference between what the party bargained for and what the party obtained from the contract.[3] This requirement has been narrowly interpreted. For example, if the victim bargained for land, and a misrepresentation was made that it was 5 hectares when it turned out to be 3 hectares, the victim may ask for rescission on the ground that he or she was induced to enter into the agreement by the representation as to size. However, in one case, the court held that the victim bargained for land and he got land in the contract; the size was immaterial.[4] Rights of rescission have been further narrowed in Canada and England by cases that have had the effect of making it almost impossible to obtain rescission for innocent misrepresentation if the subject matter of the contract was real property, the transfer had been completed, and the contract had been fully executed. The reasons for protecting contracts

---

3   *Alberta North West Lumber Co. v. Lewis*, [1917] 3 WWR 1007; *Kennedy v. Royal Mail Co. of Panama* (1867), LR 2 QB 580.

4   *Komarniski v. Marien*, [1979] 4 WWR 267 (Sask. QB).

EXAMPLES

Innocent Misrepresentation

▪ Eduardo wants to buy a vacant lot on which to build a warehouse. He asks Marlene, the seller, if the lot is zoned for a warehouse. Marlene asks the municipality and is told the land is zoned for a warehouse. She tells Eduardo this. Eduardo agrees to purchase the vacant land at an agreed price. After the contract is made but before the property is transferred to Eduardo, Marlene discovers that since she inquired, the city has changed the zoning to residential use only. She tells Eduardo, who states that he is rescinding the contract. In this case, Eduardo wanted to buy vacant land but the statement about the zoning was a material inducement considering what he wanted to do with the land. The statement probably is not a term of the contract, since the sale was for land, not for land zoned commercial. However, as he probably would not have bought the land if the zoning did not meet his needs, it is arguable that Marlene's statement is a "pure" misrepresentation (it is not a term and it was not made negligently, because she made inquiries). Because the contract is not fully executed (the land has not yet been transferred), the facts of the case come within the case law that allows rescission on land transfers if the contract is not fully executed.

▪ Suppose instead that when Eduardo asks Marlene whether the lot is zoned for a warehouse, she replies, "Sure." She honestly thinks it is, but she does not check with the municipality to see if she is correct. Because Marlene may be negligent in not checking the zoning before answering the question, she may be held to have made a negligent misrepresentation on which Eduardo relied to his detriment.

▪ In an unrelated transaction, Eduardo says to Marlene, "I am looking to purchase a truck with a 10-ton capacity. I am prepared to buy your truck if it can carry 10 tons, but not otherwise." Here it could be argued that Eduardo is not just bargaining for a truck but for a truck with specific qualities, which could be seen to be a term of the agreement. Marlene says the truck can carry 10 tons, without actually determining whether this is so. It turns out that the truck cannot carry this load. Marlene's misrepresentation, because it leads to a breach of the term of the contract, gives rise to an action for breach of contract with damages as the remedy, rather than an action for rescission.

for real property more than contracts for goods are not convincing, particularly since restitution is probably no more difficult with real property than with some goods or **intangible property**. A better approach would be to follow the English statutory solution and permit rescission on an executed contract where there has been an innocent misrepresentation unless restitution at or near the loss sustained is impossible, third parties acquired legitimate rights and would be harmed by rescission, or damages are available for negligent misrepresentation or for breach of a term of the contract.[5]

intangible property
personal property where the interest in it or its value rests in rights it confers rather than in its physical properties

---

5   G.H.L. Fridman, *The Law of Contract in Canada*, 3d ed. (Scarborough, ON: Carswell, 1994), 305-8.

Fraudulent Misrepresentation

A fraudulent misrepresentation is one in which an apparent statement of fact is made without any belief by the maker that it is true and with the intent that the person to whom it is made will act on it and be induced to enter into the contract.[6] The fact stated must be a positive misstatement of a past or present fact, although in some cases a representation of a future event may be seen as a fact about what is certain to happen rather than an opinion about what might happen. For example, you invest in a business because you are told that it will expand to all major Canadian cities within two years. The statement is known by the maker to be false, but because it is unqualified and certain in tone, it may be classed as a fraudulent misrepresentation of a fact rather than an opinion. Otherwise it could be seen as an opinion as to what is expected to happen in the future, which as mere opinion could not be held to be an actionable misrepresentation. If a statement about the future is made and qualified by words such as "likely to happen," "fully expect," or "strongly anticipate," then it is likely, because of the qualifications, to be seen as a statement of opinion, not fact.[7]

> **TIP**
>
> In contract negotiations where statements are made about future expectations, ask the maker of such statements to set out the factual information on which he or she relies in making such statements. Not only will this allow you to assess the statements for accuracy and reliability, it may also result in the maker of the statement crossing the line from a statement of mere opinion to something that is much more like a statement of fact, which can be classed as a material misrepresentation. So, if you have to sue the maker of the statements in these circumstances, you may be on firmer legal ground.

If the statement of fact is one that the intended victim could check, the law normally expects the victim to look after his or her interests, and affords no remedy if he or she fails to do so. However, even where the victim could find out, if the statement is made fraudulently the law will step in, because eliminating fraud is more important than teaching contracting parties to be careful and alert.[8]

A fraudulent statement about the state of the law, as opposed to a statement of fact, however, cannot amount to a misrepresentation because everyone is presumed to know the law. In practical terms, this makes little sense, particularly where the maker of the statement is presumed to have some expert knowledge or experience so that a listener might reasonably rely on the statement.

The speaker must make the fraudulent statement with no belief in the truth. This means that the speaker knew the statement was untrue, or the speaker made the statement with reckless disregard as to whether it was true or not, but the speaker believed it to be untrue. If the speaker is reckless in making the statement but believed it to be true, it would not amount to a fraudulent statement.[9] But if the speaker was reckless in making a statement he or she believed to be true, the victim could of course sue for negligent misrepresentation, for which damages are available.

---

6 Ibid., at 295.

7 *Allen v. Allen* (1976), 15 Nfld. & PEIR 362 (Nfld. Dist. Ct.).

8 *Sager v. Manitoba Windmill Co.* (1914), 23 DLR 556 (SCC).

9 *Derry v. Peak* (1889), 14 App. Cas. 337 (HL).

CHAPTER 4   Contractual Defects   79

For an action to succeed, the representation must be fraudulent, but it must also be made with the intent of having the intended victim act on it. Thus the statement must be material and must be made to induce the other party to enter into the contract. It must also be made or at least directed at, among others, the person who acts on it. If a knowingly false statement is made to X, who enters the contract, and X later sells to Y, who knew nothing of the statement, Y cannot sue for fraudulent misrepresentation because the statement was not directed at Y or intended by the speaker to be made to Y, and the statement did not induce Y to enter into the agreement.

Not only must the statement be directed to the victim, it must also influence the victim to enter into the contract. The statement cannot be material if the intended victim is not induced by it to enter into the contract. Reliance on the statement by the victim is something that must be shown. The statement does not have to be the only reason the victim enters the contract, but it does have to be an important reason.

If the victim is successful in showing that he or she was induced to enter into the agreement by a fraudulent misrepresentation, the following remedies may be available:

- Fraudulent misrepresentation is equivalent to the tort of deceit and thus gives rise to a claim in tort for damages.
- Fraudulent misrepresentation results in a contract induced by fraud that is voidable at the option of the victim. It is not, however, void *ab initio*. If rescission is granted, the court will attempt to restore the victim to his or her position before the contract was made. If this cannot be done, then the court will award damages. Damages for other losses not covered by rescission may also be available. If damages are awarded, they should put the victim back into the position he or she would have been in had the fraud not occurred. If the injured party wishes to rescind, he or she must not delay in making the claim and must not affirm the contract by accepting any benefits from it once he or she discovers the fraud.

EXAMPLE

Fraudulent Misrepresentation

Rory has founded a software company and is trying to sell shares to raise capital. His prospectus states that he has secured government support. He knows that in fact he has not done so, and has no idea whether he will be successful in getting it. Sonia, smelling a winner (she thinks), buys some shares. Later the government refuses to give Rory's company a cent. Sonia moves to rescind for fraudulent misrepresentation on the ground that she would not have invested if she had known the government would not support the company, and that Rory made a statement that was untrue at the time, so that he fraudulently misrepresented the situation. This gives Sonia a right to rescind the contract so that she can be restored to her pre-contract position as far as possible. In the alternative, she may sue him for the tort of deceit and claim damages for the fraudulent misrepresentation.

Misrepresentation by Omission

While silence usually cannot be interpreted as misrepresentation, in some circumstances a failure to disclose may amount to misrepresentation. If the failure to disclose has the effect of making previous statements or disclosures untrue and fraudulent, then it can give rise to an action for fraudulent misrepresentation. If the failure to disclose results in previous statements being true but misleading, this does not result in a fraudulent misrepresentation unless there is a clear duty to inform.

EXAMPLE

Misrepresentation by Omission

Sara is the trustee for her disabled sister Rachel and invests in property for the trust to earn income for Rachel. Sara decides to borrow money from Rachel's trust to invest in her own highly risky company. Sara fails to disclose this to Rachel. Later, Rachel finds out and rescinds the loan contract on the ground that Sara has, as trustee, a duty of the utmost good faith that requires Sara to disclose to Rachel that she is investing for her own benefit. Sara's omission, where the information is material and where Rachel relies generally on Sara to behave toward her with the utmost good faith, amounts to a misrepresentation that allows Rachel to rescind the contract.

CASE IN POINT

No Remedy for Mere Statement of Opinion

Robert & Webster v. Hebert, 2011 BCPC 275 (CanLII)

Facts

The plaintiffs purchased a building structure from the defendant for $25,000, thinking that the structure could be moved to their property in a different town and converted into a home. After paying, the plaintiffs discovered that the structure could not be moved without first making significant structural changes. The plaintiffs alleged that it was the responsibility of the defendant to know the building code requirements and that he fraudulently misrepresented that the building was fit for living and that all the plaintiffs needed to do was move it and place it on a new foundation. The defendant denied making any such representations and claimed that he was not fraudulent or negligent in any representation he made.

Decision

The defendant in no way fraudulently or negligently misrepresented anything. He made no statement recklessly or with knowledge that it was false. The defendant was not in the business of moving buildings and there was no reason to assume he knew anything about the building code, nor did he hold himself out as knowledgeable about building code requirements. Nor did he make any fraudulent statements other than give his opinion that it was possible to move the building. As both parties knew that a building inspector would need to authorize a permit before the structure could be moved, potential problems were or should have been obvious.

Practical Tip

If a seller has made representations, they should be incorporated into the terms of the contract. Having it in writing eliminates the problem of deciding who is telling the truth about the content of oral representations when both sides give contradictory oral evidence.

The duty to inform is restricted to a range of contracts where "utmost good faith" is required between the parties (sometimes referred to by the Latin term as **_uberrimae fidei_ contracts**). These contracts are characterized by a marked power imbalance between the parties, where one party is in the position of having to trust and rely on the other and has placed confidence and trust in the other. Many family agreements fall into this category, as do trust agreements where a trustee has ownership and control over property that he or she exercises for a beneficiary of that property. Other types of trust agreements include the lawyer–client relationship, doctor–patient relationship, partnership contracts, and corporation–corporate director contracts. Lastly, insurance contracts require full disclosure. An insurance company is absolutely dependent on the insured party disclosing all risks before the insurance rate is fixed. The insurance company has no way of knowing some of the risks unless the party who has the knowledge cooperates by providing information about these risks. For all of these "good faith" contracts there is a positive duty to disclose and not to remain silent. A knowing silence may amount to a fraudulent misrepresentation.

> *uberrimae fidei* **contracts**
> a class of contracts where full disclosure is required because one party must rely on the power and authority of another, who must behave with utmost good faith and not take advantage of the weaker party

Summary of Remedies for Misrepresentation[10]

Misrepresentation	Description	Remedy
Non-Material	A misrepresentation that is unrelated to a material fact that is essential to you in entering into a contract.	• no remedy
Material	A statement made before a contract is made that induces, or influences, a party to enter into a contract.	• does not make the contact void *ab initio* • makes the contract voidable by the party who was misled by the misrepresentation: the party may request rescission or, if not possible, damages • the misled party may at his or her option continue the contract and treat it as valid
	Innocent Misrepresentation The misrepresentation of a material fact that the maker believes to be true but which is discovered to be false after formation of the contract.	• if it forms a term of the contract, damages for breach of contract • if negligently made, then liability for all foreseeable damages • if it does not form a term of the contract, rescission and restitution

(The table is concluded on the next page.)

---

10   Note that an opinion is not a misrepresentation; therefore, no remedy is available. However, a court may treat the opinion of an expert as a material statement to be relied on, making a remedy possible.

Misrepresentation	Description	Remedy
Material (cont.)	*Negligent Misrepresentation* A representation made without the exercise of due care as to whether the representation is true or not.	• liability for foreseeable damages in tort
	Fraudulent Misrepresentation An apparent statement of fact made without any belief by the maker that it is true and with the intent that the person to whom it is made will act on it and enter the contract.	• voidable at the option of the victim • if rescission is granted, then restoration of the victim to his or her former position • if rescission is not possible, then damages
	Misrepresentation by Omission 1. A failure to disclose that has the effect of making previous statements or disclosures untrue and fraudulent; or 2. A failure to disclose that results in previous statements being true but misleading where there is a clear duty to inform. Results in fraudulent misrepresentation.	• voidable at the option of the victim • if rescission is granted, then restoration of the victim to his or her former position • if rescission is not possible, then damages

CASE IN POINT

Misrepresentation by Omission in Insurance Contracts

Landmeyer v. Economical Mutual Insurance Co., et al. (1985), 66 NSR (2d) 139 (SC)

Facts

Landmeyer claimed on his fire insurance policy for fire damage to his duplex. He also claimed against his agent. The defendant insurance company refused to honour the claim on the ground that the plaintiff had breached statutory conditions in the policy by failing to make full disclosure of all facts affecting risk. The duplex was located in the commercial and industrial core of the city. The plaintiff rented one half to his father and lived in the other half. But he also rented out upstairs rooms to two or three roomers. The plaintiff was 55 years old and had not been employed in the past 20 years. He lived off his rental income. His tenants, like himself, were alcoholics. At the time of applying for insurance, the agent asked the plaintiff who lived in the house and the plaintiff replied that he lived in one half and that his father lived in the other half. He did not disclose that he rented rooms.

Decision

Landmeyer's lawsuit was dismissed. The plaintiff's response to the agent's questions contained a non-disclosure of material facts in breach of the *Insurance Act*. The failure to disclose also amounted to a misrepresentation by omission in breach of the Act. While a misrepresentation by omission is not actionable in circumstances where the other party has an opportunity to research, insurance companies have to rely on the insured to act in the utmost good faith in disclosing information about all known risks.

Practical Tip

When taking out insurance of any kind, be sure to do your homework and disclose all known risks to avoid having an insurance company refuse to honour a claim for failure to make full disclosure.

Duress

At common law, a party to a contract can ask that it be declared void or can defend against its enforcement on the ground that the party was induced to enter into the contract by actual or threatened physical force or unlawful confinement directed against the party or his or her spouse, children, or near relatives.[11] Because **duress** can rest on threats made to immediate family, the contracting party need not be threatened directly, but the threat must be the reason that he or she enters into the contract. Because the effect of threats is to negate real consent to enter into the agreement, one can argue that if there is no consent there can be no contract so that the contract is void *ab initio*. However, the law in Canada and England treats duress like fraud by making the contract voidable.[12]

For duress to succeed, it is not always necessary for the person making the threat to be a party to the contract. If a third party threatens one of the contracting parties and the other contracting party knows of the threat and takes advantage of it, that is sufficient for a defence of duress to succeed.[13] However, since the contract is voidable, if there are grounds for a defence based on duress and the threatened party delays taking steps to void the contract or takes steps to affirm and accept the contract, the threatened party loses the right to rescind the agreement.

This doctrine of duress is very narrow and is based on tort and criminal law concepts that are older than the modern law of contract and have simply been carried over to contract law. However, the common law does expand and evolve, and courts have recognized that this narrow concept of duress may be inadequate for contract law situations. Consequently, the concept of duress has been expanded to include physical threats to property as well as to people, and also to include economic duress.[14] For example, in *North Ocean Shipping Co. v. Hyundai Construction Ltd.*, there was a contract to build a ship at a stated price. Due to currency devaluation, the price became worth less than it had been when the contract was made. The shipbuilder knew that the customer needed the ship to fulfill its own shipping contracts. The shipbuilder refused to complete the ship unless the customer paid more money to cover the losses from currency devaluation. In this situation, the court held that the knowledge of the customer's urgent need of the completed ship was used to pressure the customer into paying more, something it would not otherwise have done. However, no remedy was granted because the customer affirmed the contract by paying the money and accepting the ship when it was completed. The result of this

duress
an unlawful threat or coercion used by one person to induce another to perform some act against his or her will

> **TIP**
>
> In the event you are subject to duress in a contract situation, remember that acquiescence in the demands may prevent, in cases of economic or functional duress, the court granting you any remedy. It is usually a good idea in situations involving duress to keep careful records of communications between the parties, and to act quickly to rescind or seek other remedies. Delay is usually not helpful to the victim of duress.

---

11 Fridman, supra footnote 5, at 314.

12 *Saxon v. Saxon*, [1976] 4 WWR 300 (BCCA); *Barton v. Armstrong*, [1975] 2 All ER 465 (PC).

13 *CIBC v. Beaudreau* (1982), 41 NBR (2d) 596 (QB).

14 Fridman, supra footnote 5, at 317-20; *North Ocean Shipping Co. v. Hyundai Construction Ltd.*, [1978] 3 All ER 1170 (QB); *Pao On v. Lau Yiu*, [1979] 3 All ER 65 (PC).

expansion of the law of duress is that the courts now look not so much at the particular form that duress takes but at whether

- there is commercial pressure that amounts to a coercion of the will, which negates contractual consent,
- there are alternative ways of avoiding the coercion, or
- the pressure exerted was legitimate.

This functional view of duress suggests that a variety of circumstances other than merely physical harm can give rise to the defence of duress. You should also be aware that duress in the form of threats may amount to criminal extortion, which opens up the possibility of criminal remedies as well as civil ones. In this context, however, the threat of civil proceedings to collect a debt is neither extortion nor duress provided there is a bona fide belief that there is a right to sue to collect the debt.

EXAMPLES

Duress

Threat by a Party to the Contract

Spiro has just been made an offer that he cannot refuse; Mariella has told him that if he does not lend her $10,000 at 1/2 percent interest (when current interest rates are 5 percent), he might not live to attend next year's New Year's Eve party. Spiro lends her the money and then moves to rescind the contract on the ground of duress, arguing that threats to his life caused him to enter into this disadvantageous contract.

Threat by a Non-Party to the Contract

Zainab received a letter from Zeke stating that if she did not leave town, she had but a short time to live. Zainab, frightened, decides to sell her house and leave town. Juan heard about the threat made to Zainab and offered to buy her house for far less than it was worth. Zainab accepts in a panic because of the threat by Zeke, but then refuses to complete the sale. She can rescind the contract on the ground of duress, even though the threat was made by a non-party to the contract.

Economic or Functional Duress

Albert had ordered three flatbed trucks from Truckworks for fixed prices. After the parties entered into this contract, Albert was offered a large, long-term shipping contract that he could not fulfill unless he had the three flatbed trucks delivered by a certain date. Truckworks heard about the new contract and, knowing Albert would be desperate, demanded a 10 percent surcharge on the current contract price. Provided Albert didn't cave in and pay the price, he could rescind the contract, or possibly also sue for specific performance, with the court requiring Truckworks to complete the contract on the original terms.

Economic Duress Determined by Objective Test

Sun Life Financial Distributors (Canada) Inc. v. Everett, [2011] OJ No. 1468 (Sm. Cl. Ct.)

Facts

Leanne Everett, looking for a career, was hired by Sun Life to eventually sell life insurance. She started as a trainee, where she was not paid, and when her training was completed, she was told to sign an Advisor's Agreement. Everett testified that her manager told her she had to sign the document, failing which she would be out of a job. She wanted time to review it. The supervisor then said she could have a lawyer look at it if she wanted, but that it didn't matter because if she did not sign it she would not have a job. Everett signed the document. She had reviewed it for perhaps 10 or 20 minutes, but did not understand its effect. She later resigned and denied that the Advisor's Agreement was enforceable against her on the ground of duress.

Decision

The court found that economic duress was established. Economic pressure can amount to duress if two elements are present: (1) pressure amounting to compulsion of the will of the victim and (2) the illegitimacy of the pressure exerted. Duress, if established, renders a contract voidable unless the party later affirms the contract. In this case, Everett had a significant investment in her position as an advisor with Sun Life, a position for which she had worked hard and which she had in fact accomplished, as of some two months before the Advisor's Agreement was put to her. Sun Life, through her supervisor, gave her a clear ultimatum: sign this document or be fired; and there would be no negotiation over terms. On that basis, the court was satisfied that Everett was subjected to pressure amounting to compulsion against her will.

Practical Tip

Where one of the parties to a contract is in a much better bargaining position than the other, care must be taken to give the weaker party opportunity to examine a contract carefully, and to negotiate, in order to avoid repudiation by the weaker party based on duress.

Undue Influence

The common law of duress depended on a finding of physical duress to persons or property, although it has expanded to include economic duress and could well expand further. **Undue influence** developed under the law of equity to provide remedies for more subtle forms of oppressive behaviour. The doctrine can be applied in two types of contract situations:

- actual undue influence, which covers contracts, including gifts, where one party actually engages in conduct that results in applying moral or other undue pressure to obtain a desired contractual result; and
- presumed undue influence, which arises when the relationship between the parties raises a presumption of undue influence at or before the time the contract was made.

In both situations the court is concerned with the same thing—the domination of one party by another so as to prevent the dominated party from making an independent decision. The difference between the two situations is in the onus of proof. In the case of actual undue influence, the party that is claiming undue influence must prove that the other party used undue influence to compel the first party

undue influence
persuasion, pressure, or influence short of actual force that overpowers a weaker party's judgment and free will and imposes the will of the stronger party

to enter into the contract. In the case of presumed undue influence, once the relationship is shown to exist there is a presumption of undue influence. This reverses the evidentiary burden; the person alleged to have resorted to undue influence must prove that the transaction was free of its effects to escape liability.

The kinds of relationships that give rise to a presumption of undue influence include, not surprisingly, many of the relationships that give rise to the requirement of utmost good faith in contractual relations: family, solicitor–client, doctor–patient, guardian–ward, and trustee–beneficiary relationships. The Supreme Court of Canada has made it clear that the presumption is not restricted to existing categories but may extend to any other "special" relationships, such as **fiduciary** relationships, confidential relationships, or advisory relationships.[15] However, the reasoning behind this expansion is not clear. The recent cases have produced concurrent decisions with different reasons being given by different judges in the same case to explain the development of the concept of "special" relationships.[16] Where there is a "special" relationship, it is not necessary to show that the party affected by undue influence is also disadvantageously affected by the contract.

fiduciary
a relationship where one person is in a position of trust to another and has a duty to safeguard the other's interests ahead of his or her own interests

---

EXAMPLES

Undue Influence

- Ian has befriended the elderly Enrique and does various things for Enrique, including running errands, doing chores, and generally being helpful. Enrique has become quite dependent on Ian both for help and for company. One day Ian announces that he needs money to repay a debt and unless Enrique can give him a temporary loan, Ian will have to move away to find other work. Enrique does not want to lose Ian's help and company so, against his better judgment, he lends him the money. Enrique then has misgivings and moves to rescind the loan, arguing that Ian used friendship and the dependent relationship to unduly pressure Enrique into lending him the money. If Enrique can demonstrate this, he may prove undue influence to a degree that is sufficient to void the loan agreement. It is also possible that the court might view the relationship as a "special" relationship given Enrique's age, needs, and dependence on Ian, in which case undue influence would be presumed. Here, Ian would have to rebut the presumption by showing that Enrique had independent legal advice.

- Assume the same fact situation, but suppose Enrique and Ian are father and son. Here, because the nature of the relationship falls into a category where undue influence is presumed, the burden would be on Ian to demonstrate that Enrique had independent advice sufficient to give Enrique a clear and objective view of what he was doing.

---

15   *Geffen v. Goodman Estate* (1991), 81 DLR (4th) 211 (SCC). The English House of Lords has moved in the same direction: *Barclay's Bank plc v. O'Brien*, [1993] 4 All ER 417.

16   Fridman, supra footnote 5, at 323-25.

Undue Influence Determined by Objective "Reasonable Person" Test

Credit Lyonnais Bank Nederland NV v. Burch, [1997] 1 All ER 144 (CA)

Facts

Burch worked for a small company where Pelosi was the primary owner and shareholder. Burch was a loyal employee and had a close relationship with Pelosi, who was, in effect, her employer. Pelosi asked Burch to provide the bank with an unlimited loan guarantee, supported by a mortgage on her home. She gave the guarantee, though she did not have the means to repay it. The business failed, and the bank sued Burch on her guarantee.

Decision

The court found that there was no commercial advantage to Burch in giving the guarantee, which was beyond her ability to repay. It was clear that she gave the guarantee at Pelosi's request and out of friendship for him. The bank was clearly aware of this, as it advised her to get independent legal advice (which she did not do). The loan guarantee was given as a result of undue influence by Pelosi, in circumstances where no reasonable person would otherwise have given the guarantee. That being so, and the bank being aware that this was so, the bank could not then benefit from an improvident agreement due to undue influence, even where it did not exercise undue influence itself. The transaction was therefore set aside.

Practical Tip

It is unwise to be party to contractual arrangements by which you stand to benefit where undue influence has been exercised, even if not by you.

Where the presumption applies, the transaction is set aside unless the party benefiting from the contract can demonstrate that the party allegedly influenced had independent advice of some kind, often independent legal advice, so that the party allegedly influenced could be said to be entering into the contract with his or her eyes open. Independent legal advice, in particular, may be important, and it requires the adviser to do a proper and thorough job and not just go through the motions in giving independent advice.

Unconscionability

The law of equity will relieve a party in some circumstances from the effects of unconscionable conduct by the other contracting party. The focus here is not on conduct that affects consent, as is the case for undue influence or duress. With an unconscionable transaction, the focus is on the reasonableness of the contract itself and the way in which the party whose conduct is in question behaved during the bargaining process. This is very broad, and you should appreciate that not every "unfair" contract will result in a court declaring the transaction to be unconscionable when someone, through stupidity, recklessness, or foolishness, has made a bad bargain.

Finding the balance between unconscionability and stupidity is not always easy, and the case law is not particularly helpful because the cases seem to turn on a judge's subjective view of particular facts. However, where an action based on undue influence or duress may fail because pressure on the victim did not interfere too much with consent by the victim, the contract may still be avoided because its terms are unconscionable or the behaviour of the other party was unconscionable. For example, where one party is illiterate or intellectually disadvantaged and the other party knows this and takes advantage by persuading the disadvantaged party that "this is a good deal" when in fact it is not, if the disadvantaged party is keen to close the deal, there may be no duress or undue influence. In fact, no pressure or coercion may have been necessary. The wrong is in one party knowing that there was a lack of bargaining power or ability by the other and taking advantage of that fact, leaving the victim with a grossly unfair and inequitable bargain.

Another approach to this issue has developed in England. In *Lloyd's Bank v. Bundy*,[17] a father placed a mortgage on his house in order to secure a loan for his son. The son was in financial difficulty, and the father was emotional, upset, and ready to do just about anything to help his son. The majority found that there had been undue influence by the bank regarding the father, its customer, who should have had but did not have independent legal advice before agreeing to what turned out to be a very bad bargain. However, Lord Denning arrived at the same result by a different route: he combined undue influence and other equitable doctrines to develop a ground for rescinding contracts on the basis of "inequality of bargaining power." This approach includes undue influence and possibly duress, where there is a lack of independent consent to the terms of the contract, as well as unconscionability, where the nature of the bargain and the state of mind of the victim in entering into the contract are relevant. Where, in the circumstances, the bargain—because of its contents, the behaviour of the advantaged party, and the state of mind of the disadvantaged party—is grossly one-sided, that may be sufficient evidence of inequality of bargaining power to warrant court interference.

EXAMPLE

Unconscionable Contracts

Derek, who has a hearing disability, thinks it would be cool to have a good stereo. He wears a hearing aid and reads lips. It is obvious to anyone talking to Derek that he is hearing impaired and that the better sound in a high-quality system would be useless to him. Derek walks into Sam's Stereo Shop and tells Sam that he wants a stereo system that is really cool. Sam notices that Derek is hearing impaired and realizes that the quality of a high-priced system would be useless to him, but he tells Derek he has a "good deal" on a cool system for $8,000. This is in fact an extremely high price. Derek eagerly puts his money down but later changes his mind and moves to rescind on the ground that the transaction is unconscionable. Because Sam knew that Derek could not derive any substantial benefit from a high-quality sound system, it may be shown that the bargain is such a poor one for Derek that it is unconscionable. The fact that the price is unduly high may be further evidence of unconscionability, but there is no evidence that Derek's disability affects his bargaining power on price—this may simply be a bad bargain and will not attract court interference. However, if the price was represented as a good price when Sam knew it was not, that may be a fraudulent misrepresentation, which would void the contract apart from the outcome on the unconscionability issue.

---

17 *Lloyd's Bank v. Bundy*, [1974] 3 All ER 757 (QB).

Whether the English "inequality of bargaining power" approach or the Canadian "unconscionability" approach is taken, the result may be the same—overturning immoral and inequitable bargains. What the case law has not developed so far is a methodology for identifying inequitable bargains that would cause the court to interfere with an individual's freedom to contract.

Unconscionability Legislation

Legislatures in common-law jurisdictions have often passed legislation to protect certain classes of persons from unconscionable transactions where duress and undue influence would not necessarily offer protection, and where the application of the unconscionability principle is uncertain. This type of legislation usually tries to define unconscionability and then turns the matter over to the courts for adjudication. There are two types of such legislation in the Canadian provinces, discussed below.

Unconscionable Transactions Acts

All provinces have legislation that permits a court to interfere with the terms of a loan where the contract is harsh and oppressive and the cost of the loan is excessive.[18] The legislation does not add significantly to the common law, except that it clearly brings loans within the reach of unconscionability doctrines. A loan is excessively expensive if it can be obtained elsewhere at a lesser rate, but this is not reliable as a test because the rate can be based on a variety of risk factors that make comparisons difficult or impossible. This is particularly so with high-risk loans, where interest rates are high, the pool of comparable lenders is small, and risk assessment is somewhat subjective. A very high interest rate will attract attention if there is an element of unfairness about the loan; for example, if the borrower is desperate and the lender knows it, a statutory remedy might be provided. By way of remedy, the court can reopen the loan and make the lender accept a fair amount, order the lender to repay any overcharges, or cancel or alter any security given by the borrower to obtain the loan. This is different from the remedies available for duress, undue influence, and unconscionability, for which the usual remedies are rescission and damages.

Unfair Business Practices

Several provinces, including Alberta, British Columbia, Ontario, Newfoundland, and Prince Edward Island, have all passed legislation that goes well beyond the common law in giving individuals remedies where a consumer transaction is unfair.[19] These acts permit consumers who have entered into contracts with business

---

TIP

Be aware of who your contracting party is; if the party is under a disability you should proceed with caution and, where possible, suggest that the other party have legal or other necessary advice before proceeding further, as a safeguard against later rescission by the party.

---

18   See, for example, the *Unconscionable Transactions Relief Act*, RSO 1990, c. U.2.

19   *Consumer Protection Act, 2002*, SO 2002, c. 30, sched. A; *Business Practices and Consumer Protection Act*, SBC 2004, c. 2; *Fair Trading Act*, RSA 2000, c. F-2; *Consumer Protection and Business Practices Act*, SNL 2009, c. C-31.1; and *Business Practices Act*, RSPEI 1988, c. B-7.

Unconscionability Test: Both Subjective and Objective

Loans Till Payday v. Brereton, 2010 ONSC 6610 (CanLII)

Facts

The plaintiff, Loans Till Payday, brought a Small Claims Court action alleging that the defendant Brereton defaulted on a $450 payday loan. The loan was advanced on July 22. The defendant signed a promissory note agreeing to pay $563 one week later. The promissory note set out additional liabilities in the event of default, including $500 if the matter required legal action and a 59 percent interest rate on any amounts owed as of July 29.

In its action, the plaintiff sought to recover $1,114, consisting of the amount the defendant agreed to repay, plus $500 in liquidated damages plus pre-judgment interest at 59 percent. Brereton did not defend, the plaintiff obtained default judgment, and the matter was referred to determine the amount owing on the loan. The judge awarded $450, being the amount of the loan, plus pre-judgment and post-judgment interest of 18 percent from the date of default, plus court costs of $185. The plaintiff submitted that the judge erred in concluding that the claimed interest rate offended the *Criminal Code*, that the $500 claim for liquidated damages was not a genuine pre-estimate of loss and was unreasonable, and that the plaintiff was not entitled to the post-default interest rate set out in the promissory note.

Decision

The appeal was dismissed. The effective interest rate charged under the agreement was clearly in excess of the legal rate of interest. The judge properly found that the claim of $500 for liquidated damages was unreasonable, as the evidence in support of the plaintiff's actual legal costs and damages was insufficient and did not constitute a genuine pre-estimate of damages. No error was made in the determination of pre-judgment and post-judgment interest. It was within the trial judge's discretion to find that the cost of the loan was excessive and that the transaction was harsh and unconscionable at common law and under the *Unconscionable Transactions Relief Act*.

Practical Tip

A wise lender should examine the limits imposed by unconscionability legislation and other legal limits used to protect weaker parties, and should not create an excessively one-sided contract that imposes heavy penalties.

---

sellers on the basis of representations that are false, misleading, or deceptive to rescind those contracts and obtain damages. Most important, these remedies are available on proof of a misrepresentation in situations where the common law would have given no remedy. Punitive damages are also available. Sellers cannot escape the reach of this legislation: neither party can agree in a contract to exclude the operation of the act on the contract. In addition to private lawsuits to set aside contracts, an unfair practice may become subject to administrative proceedings before a regulatory board to ensure compliance by business sellers with the terms of the statute.

Mistake

Overview

Parties may negotiate all the terms of a contract and appear to come to a meeting of minds, yet fail to make an enforceable contract because they discover that they did not mean the same thing with respect to an essential element. When this happens the parties are said to be *mistaken*, so that their true intentions about something fundamental and important are not reflected in the contract. While not every mistake leads to a void or voidable contract, as a result of a mistake,

- a contract may be declared at common law to be void *ab initio*;
- if equitable doctrines are invoked, a contract may be
  - voidable by either party,
  - rescinded in some cases, or
  - rectified in other cases.

Traditionally, the courts have been very reluctant to terminate agreements that appear to be complete contracts on the ground that a bargain once made must be kept. A party to a contract who says, "I made a mistake, please let me out of this contract" is likely to meet with the judicial response, "Having made a bargain, you will have to live with it." On the other hand, for some mistakes the courts have ruled that it would be unjust to enforce an agreement if it does not represent what the parties were really bargaining about. What has been difficult for the courts in Canada and England to decide, whether using common-law rules or equitable ones, is where to draw the line between a mistake that leaves a contract unenforceable and a mistake that does not. If you review mistake cases, you may come away with the impression that decisions turn on the court's subjective view of whether enforcement would be unfair or unconscionable rather than on some universal objective test or set of criteria that could be applied to measure the nature and effect of the mistake.

Principles of the Law of Mistake

While predicting whether a mistake will give rise to relief in a particular case is difficult, the courts appear to have applied some principles in analyzing mistake cases.

- If what was offered was offered in error, it may be impossible for the other side to accept an unintended offer. Here it could be said that there was no meeting of minds and no real offer and acceptance from which to create a valid contract.[20]
- If there is a mistake that is about something fundamental in the contract, such as the existence of the thing contracted about or a term of the contract, the contract may be void, voidable, or subject to rescission or rectification.[21]
- A mistake in the motive or intention for contracting is likely to be seen as irrelevant.[22]
- Unexpected and exceptional contractual consequences that stem from a mistake may well lead to a contract being declared void, voidable, or subject to rescission or rectification.

---

20 Per Estey J in *R v. Ron Engineering and Construction (Eastern) Ltd.* (1981), 119 DLR (3d) 267, at 277 (SCC). For a detailed discussion of judicial principles used to analyze mistake cases, see Fridman, supra footnote 5, at 248-67.

21 *Bell v. Lever Bros.*, [1932] AC 161 (HL).

22 Ibid.

- If one party is mistaken, the other knows it and says nothing, and the mistake is about something fundamental, then the contract may be treated as void, voidable, or subject to rescission or rectification.
- If both parties are mistaken about something fundamental, the contract may be treated as void, voidable, or subject to rescission or rectification.
- If the mistake was due to one party's carelessness or negligence, that party may have to live with the consequences.
- When dealing with a case of mistake, the courts tend toward upholding agreements, and when they do intervene, they are likely to try to save the contract by creating opportunities for rectification before they grant rescission or declare the contract voidable or void.

Remember that just because one or more of these principles could logically be applied to the facts of a case that involves a mistake, it does not follow that the principles will be applied or that, if applied, a court will grant a remedy. Cases about mistake with similar facts are often decided quite differently. For example, the Canadian and English courts have gone in quite different directions with respect to cases that involve fundamental mistake. While various theoretical reasons may be advanced to explain these differences, they may also be explained in terms of the English courts making more creative use of equitable doctrines to take a more flexible position in enforcing contracts where fundamental mistakes have been made.[23]

Treatment of Mistake at Common Law and Equity

The preceding discussion suggests that mistake cases are treated differently under common-law rules from the way they are treated under equitable doctrines. At common law, a contract is valid and exists, or is invalid and does not exist. If it is valid and exists, that is the end of the matter. Equity, which is designed to introduce flexible responses to common-law rigidity, takes a different approach: a contract that is not void *ab initio* may still be subjected to equitable remedies if it is inequitable or unconscionable. In equity, a contract could be treated as voidable or be subject to rescission, rectification, or relief from forfeiture. In England, and to a lesser extent in Canada, there has been a trend away from rigid and formalistic application of common-law rules in mistake situations and toward increasing use of equitable doctrines; the focus is more on fairness in outcome and less on enforcing bargains regardless of fairness.[24]

Mistake cases can be categorized in terms of

- mistakes about particulars of the contract, and
- effects of the mistakes determined by which party is mistaken.

---

23   Fridman, supra footnote 5, at 252-57.

24   Ibid., at 265.

Mistakes of Law and Fact

MISTAKE OF LAW

Generally, because everyone is expected to know the law, if either or both parties are mistaken about the law as it affects their contract, the law affords no remedy for the mistake. Because ignorance of the law is no excuse, to be ignorant is to be at the least negligent, and a negligent party cannot ask that his or her mistake, based on that negligence, be corrected.

Permitting rectification or rescission when a mistake is factual, but not when it is legal, is not a very satisfactory analytic distinction. Courts have often had great difficulty in distinguishing between a mistake of fact and one of law.

EXAMPLE

Mistake of Fact or Law

A sells land to B. A and B assume that A owns the land but both are unaware that C actually owns it. This could be characterized as a mistake of law regarding the legal rights of ownership, or it could be characterized as a mistake of fact where both A and B believe as a fact that A owns the land and are unaware that in fact C owns it. It has also been argued that the rule presuming knowledge of the law is derived from criminal law that affects citizens and the state, which may not be appropriate to law that regulates the rights of citizens among themselves.

Some jurisdictions have taken steps to counter the effect of the rule that all are presumed to know the law by allowing remedies for a mistake in law for contracts that concern the payment of money. The Supreme Court of Canada confronted this issue directly in 1989 in *Air Canada v. British Columbia*,[25] holding that it did not matter whether the mistake was a mistake of fact or of law in determining whether there could be recovery for a mistake. The *Air Canada* case applied to the recovery of money paid under a contract where one party claimed that the payment was made on the basis of a mistaken assumption in law that it was owing. There is no clear indication that this case necessarily applies to other types of contract, but there is no logical reason why it should not.

EXAMPLE

Mistake of Law

Bach and Handel enter into a lease agreement in which Handel rents a house from Bach. At the time, both parties mistakenly believe that a rent control law sets the rent at a lower rate than Bach would otherwise have charged. Bach discovers that the law does not apply and moves to rescind the contract on the ground that both parties were mistaken about the amount of payment required. Depending on how narrowly the *Air Canada* case is applied, Bach may be able to rescind the contract or have it rectified.

---

25 *Air Canada v. British Columbia*, [1989] 1 SCR 1161, 59 DLR (4th) 161.

Liability Avoided with Mistake in Law

Air Canada v. British Columbia, [1989] 1 SCR 1161

Facts

In this complicated case, Air Canada, as one of the parties, challenged the constitutionality and applicability of an act that imposed specific taxes on the airline. The Crown, by way of defence, argued that Air Canada had paid the taxes under a mistaken interpretation of the law, and that a mistake of law could not be the basis for recovery of taxes paid.

Decision

The Court held that the province of British Columbia's taxation statute did not apply to Air Canada, and consequently British Columbia had no authority to collect the taxes, and

Air Canada was entitled to the return of taxes paid on the basis that the legislation did not apply to it. The fact that Air Canada made a mistake of law in interpreting the act and paying the tax did not bar its recovery, as the legislation was unenforceable against it.

Practical Tip

If you make a mistake about the facts on which a contract is based, or on the underlying law, you may have to live with the consequences. Be sure you have researched the background law and investigated the facts before you enter into a contract.

The Supreme Court, in the case above, continued to erode the distinction between a mistake of law and a mistake of fact, increasing the scope for remedies when a party has made a mistake of law, although the extent to which the Supreme Court is prepared to extend remedies for a mistake of law beyond invalid or inapplicable statutes is not yet clear.

MISTAKE OF FACT

◇ Identity of the Subject Matter

The focus here is on the subject matter of the contract: what it is about, the obligations involved, or what a term means. "Subject matter" is defined broadly to include the identity of the goods, land, or service; the price to be paid; and the obligations undertaken, provided that these are major or fundamental terms. If the mistake is about a minor matter or collateral term, it cannot cause a contract to be declared void, although it may result in other remedies such as rectification.

The test for determining whether there is a mistake regarding the identity of the subject matter is whether a reasonable person looking at the contract formation

Mistake as to Identity of the Subject Matter

Simon wanted to buy a road bike. He was induced by an error in the photographs in an online catalogue to buy a commuter bike, though he thought that he was buying a road bike. On discovering his error, he could sue to rescind the contract on the ground that there was a fundamental misunderstanding between the parties of what they were contracting for.

process and the resulting contract can determine whether the parties have identified what is fundamental to the agreement. A reasonable person need not look at the reasons or motives of the parties in deciding what is fundamental. The search is to see that important terms about the identity of the subject matter have been determined so that a reasonable person could say that the parties have reached consensus, in which case the contract is valid.

If there is a mistake, it must be about the identity of the subject matter, not some quality of it, unless the quality is so fundamental that it becomes part of the subject matter. The courts shy away from granting remedies when a mistake about quality is at issue, since this usually affects the value of the contract, which is perceived to raise issues about whether a party has bargained carefully. If a party has not bargained well, the courts are not likely to interfere to remake a bad bargain. Some cases have granted relief for a mistake relating to the quality of the subject matter, but only when the quality is a fundamental part of the identity of the subject matter.[26] Again, the difficulty is deciding where to draw the line between quality of the subject matter and quality assuming characteristics of identity of the subject matter. The quality of the subject matter would become part of the identity of it if a reasonable person would expect the quality to be essential to the contract. For instance, in the Example box below, the type of wheat (winter wheat) would become part of the identity if Karl indicated that he needed wheat for his baking operation instead of indicating just that he needed wheat. When it has been determined that there is a mistake as to the identity of the subject matter of a contract, because it is fundamental, the parties have failed to reach consensus so there is no contract, and what appears to be a contract is void *ab initio*.

TIP

In negotiating the terms of a contract, be explicit and informative in describing what you are contracting for, and consider including in the contract the details about what you require the contract goods for, or why you want them. This may minimize unintended mistakes about identity or existence of the subject matter of the contract.

> **EXAMPLE**
>
> ### Mistake as to Identity/Quality of the Subject Matter
>
> Karl wants to buy a carload of winter wheat that is suitable for making bread. He mistakenly believes that Tara has a carload of winter wheat for sale and offers to buy it. Karl says nothing to Tara about the type of wheat he wants, and Tara is unaware that Karl wants winter wheat. The wheat Tara is selling is not winter wheat. Karl completes the purchase and takes delivery. He realizes his mistake and seeks to rescind the contract on the ground that there is a mistake as to the identity of the subject matter: winter wheat versus another type of wheat.
>
> Is this a mistake going to the identity or the quality of the subject matter? If it is the latter, there is no remedy for Karl. To answer this question, the court uses the objective test of a reasonable person analyzing the bargaining process and the final contract. In doing so, a reasonable person is likely to conclude that the parties contracted for the sale of a carload of wheat and that there was no mistake about this. There was nothing apparent in the contract or the bargaining process to indicate that the type of wheat was at issue. There was no objective evidence to alert Tara to what Karl was thinking; Karl never communicated his thoughts, and nothing

---

26   *Clay v. Powell*, [1932] SCR 210.

he did indicated that he was thinking about winter wheat. Karl could be seen to have ideas, motives, or beliefs about the subject matter and reasons for entering into the contract. But he would have to communicate these so that a reasonable person could see and be aware that the type of wheat was fundamental and therefore that the identity of the subject matter included winter wheat, not just wheat. Note that it does not matter whether Tara knew or did not know what Karl wanted— it is what a reasonable person would conclude that counts.

How mistakes are characterized is a matter of factual interpretation, as shown by the Case in Point features on page 97. The defendants in the first case, *Clay v. Powell*, argued that the second case (*Smith v. Hughes*) supported their claim, and they were successful in the Court of Appeal. However, they were not successful in the Supreme Court, which took a different view of what is a quality and what is subject matter. Predicting the outcome in cases such as these is difficult, as the distinction between a mistake as to subject matter and a mistake as to quality may at times appear subjective.

◇ Existence of the Subject Matter

In this situation, the parties intend to contract about the same subject matter and there is no confusion or disagreement about what that subject matter is. However, they may be mistaken about the existence of the subject matter:

- It may never have existed.
- It may have existed but ceased to exist before the parties entered into an agreement.
- Both may think they can contract about it, but it is not something that can be the subject of a contract for legal or other reasons.
- Both may have contemplated the non-existence of the subject matter but may not have reached consensus on how to deal contractually with its non-existence.

If the parties are mistaken about the existence of the subject matter at the time the contract is made, then the contract is usually void *ab initio* and both parties must be returned to their pre-contract positions. The reasoning here is that the parties cannot be *ad idem* (of the same mind) over something that does not exist, so there can be no agreement.[27] It can also be argued that the existence of the subject matter is a condition precedent to the existence of a valid contract. The application of this approach illustrates a common situation in contract interpretation cases: a fact situation can be analyzed under more than one legal rule or doctrine. How a fact situation is categorized or identified may well determine the outcome of a case.

TIP

It is quite permissible, where only one of several competing rules or doctrines will determine the outcome of the case, for your legal representative to argue them all "in the alternative," leaving the judge to decide whether one of the arguments will resolve the issue.

---

27   *Barrow, Lane and Ballard Ltd. v. Phillips & Co.*, [1929] 1 KB 574.

Mistake as to Very Subject Matter Allows for Rescission

Clay v. Powell, [1932] SCR 210

Facts

Clay had placed surplus funds for investment in the hands of S.P. Powell & Company, Limited. The defendant had to account for the funds and could only use the funds in accordance with Clay's instructions. They were authorized to debit his account of $2,000 for the purchase of the company's treasury stock. Instead, Powell, an owner of the defendant, sold Clay personal stock in the company. Clay argued that the defendant was not properly accounting for the sale: Clay had thought he was buying treasury stock. When he discovered what he had actually bought, he sued to rescind the agreement and get his money back.

Decision

The Supreme Court of Canada reversed the appellate court's decision on this issue. The Court of Appeal characterized the purchase as one of stock and the type of stock (company treasury stock or Powell's personal stock) was a question of quality of the subject matter, allowing rescission only if the quality of the subject matter had been a matter of warranty in the contract. The appeal court relied on the English case of *Smith v. Hughes*, discussed below. The Supreme Court held, in this case, that what was at issue was the subject matter of the contract itself. The purchaser did not get the thing he contracted for. An offer duly accepted to sell treasury shares of a company is not satisfied by the transfer to the purchaser of an individual shareholder's personal stock. This was a mistake as to the very subject matter of the contract and a proper case for Clay to rescind the contract.

Mistake as to Quality of Subject Matter Does Not Allow for Rescission

Smith v. Hughes (1871), LR 6 QB 597

Facts

Smith, a farmer, showed a sample of oats to Hughes, a horse trainer, saying he had "good oats for sale." Hughes agreed to purchase some oats. When the oats were delivered, Hughes complained that the oats were *new* oats, and not what he had bargained for. Smith admitted that the oats were indeed new oats and said he didn't have old oats for sale. Hughes claimed he said he would purchase good old oats. Smith denied there was any mention of old oats, and refused to take the oats back. When Hughes refused to pay, Smith sued for the price of oats, sold and delivered to Hughes.

It was unclear whether the defendant had specified that he was interested in buying old oats. But it was clear there was a sample of oats shown, which Hughes may or may not have looked at, and that Hughes purchased oats after Smith offered them for sale.

Decision

In these circumstances, the court held that there being no representation or warranty by Smith as to the age of the oats—the quality of the oats was not in issue—Hughes bargained for oats and he got oats. That he was mistaken as to the quality was a matter not communicated to Smith, and therefore was not something Hughes could rely on to rescind the sale.

Practical Tip

In both this case and *Clay*, the outcome turned on an assessment of the oral evidence given by the parties. How the subject matter of a contract is characterized may determine the outcome of a claim to rescind based on mistake. It is important that the evidence be clear, so the wise buyer or seller should carefully describe the subject matter of the contract in sufficient detail, and where quality is concerned, make quality standards a matter of contractual warranty.

> ### EXAMPLE
>
> #### Mistake in Existence of the Subject Matter
>
> Albert, a grain merchant, contracts to purchase from Bertha a load of grain currently being shipped to London. Unknown to both of them, the grain had spoiled en route and was sold at a distress price by the captain of the ship. In this case, the subject matter of the contract, the load of grain, had ceased to exist when the parties entered into their agreement. Consequently, they cannot reach consensus, and there is no sale.[28]

Suppose that the parties contemplate the possibility of the non-existence of the subject matter of the contract. They may assign the risk for loss or non-existence of the subject matter to one party or the other. Sale of future goods on an executory contract might give rise to this kind of arrangement. A tomato canner, for example, might enter into an agreement in spring for the purchase of field tomatoes that do not now exist but are expected to exist at the end of August. A prudent party would take care to assign risk for goods that do not yet exist and are perishable and fragile. Even where the parties make no specific arrangements to cover destruction before delivery, the courts have occasionally extended the law of mistake as to existence of the subject matter to cover subject matter that did not exist when the contract was made and never existed in the form that could be delivered under the contract. A better approach might be to avoid twisting the law of mistake beyond recognition and to treat this kind of case as a contract that requires a condition precedent—the existence of the subject matter—before the contract can be valid.[29]

◇ Identity of the Party

The common law has long held that a mistake as to the identity of a party to a contract renders the contract void. The basis for this rule is that only the person to whom an offer is made can accept it; another person has no right to the bargain. The rule has a practical basis as can be seen from the cases, many of which arise when a cheat with whom the victim would not ordinarily contract impersonates someone with whom the victim would be prepared to contract. For example, in *Cundy v. Lindsay*,[30] a person named Blenkarn fraudulently induced the respondents to sell him material. The respondents mistakenly believed that Blenkarn was Blenkiron and Co., a reputable firm with whom they would have contracted. If the respondents had known they were dealing with Blenkarn, they would not have entered into the contract. It was held that the mistake as to identity made by the respondents resulted in there being no contract, because they thought they were contracting with Blenkiron, not Blenkarn. They were not simply mistaken as to Blenkarn's attributes; they were

---

28 See *Couturier v. Hastie* (1856), 5 HL Cas. 673; Atiyah, "*Couturier v. Hastie* and the Sale of Non-Existent Goods" (1957) 73 LQR 34.

29 See Fridman, supra footnote 5, at 279-81.

30 *Cundy v. Lindsay* (1878), 3 App. Cas. 459 (HL).

mistaken as to his identity. They believed him to be someone other than the person he was pretending to be. Because no offer was intended to be made to Blenkarn, he was not in a position to accept.

While a mistake about identity voids a contract, a mistake about the attributes of a party is likely to have no effect on the contract. However, it can be difficult to determine whether a mistake is about a party's identity or his or her attributes. One eminent English judge called it "a distinction without a difference."[31] If Y represents himself as a wealthy man when he is not, and X, who does not know anything about Y other than that he appears to be wealthy, deals with Y in the mistaken belief that Y is wealthy, it could be said that X was mistaken as to the identity of the party because Y was not a wealthy man. Here "wealthy man" is presumed to be the identity. But one could also argue that X thought she was dealing with someone called Y, and she did deal with Y, so there was no mistake about Y's identity, but there was a mistake about one of Y's attributes, his wealth. This is similar to the problem of distinguishing between identity of the subject matter and quality of the subject matter.

EXAMPLE

Mistake as to Identity of the Party

Ivan the Terrible, seeking to kill off all his enemies without making a fuss, wishes to contract with Lucretia Borgia for the purchase of poisons that do not leave a trace. Lucilla Borgia hears about Ivan's desires and, carrying a nice line of poisons herself, contacts Ivan. Thinking he is dealing with Lucretia, he purchases a variety of poisons from Lucilla. Later, in a fit of remorse after he discovers that Lucilla is not the same person as Lucretia, Ivan demands his money back, saying he was mistaken as to the identity of the person he was contracting with. Because Lucilla and Lucretia are two different people, there is a mistake in identity, not in attributes, because Ivan intended to contract with Lucretia, not Lucilla. Contracting with Lucretia may be seen as important to Ivan and fundamental, because she has a reputation for high-quality poisons, and he would not have contracted with Lucilla had he known he had mistaken her for Lucretia. The fact that Lucilla's poisons were the equal of Lucretia's is not important because this does not affect the formation of Ivan's intent to contract.

Nevertheless, the cases do distinguish between intending to contract with someone who appears to have wealth, a business, or commercial influence where there is a mistake about the person being wealthy, having a business, or having commercial influence, and intending to contract with someone in the mistaken belief that the person is someone else. But even here, the key appears to be that the mistake in identity is fundamental. For example, B represents that he has authority to receive bonds from A. In fact, B is a thief and has no authority. A checks on B's identity and, satisfied that B is the person he says he is, delivers the bonds. Here B was who he said he was, and A was contracting with the person she thought she was contracting

---

31   *Lewis v. Averay*, [1971] 3 All ER 907, at 911 (CA), per Lord Denning.

with. If there is a mistake, it is about B's attribute of being a thief. If there is a solution for A, it may lie in the area of fraudulent misrepresentation, not in mistake as to the identity of a party. Mistake as to identity remains limited to situations where offers are accepted by a person for whom the offer was not intended where the identity of the offeree is important or fundamental. This type of mistake can also be treated as a unilateral mistake, where one party is mistaken about something fundamental, and the other party knows it and takes advantage of the mistake. Unilateral mistake is discussed later in this chapter.

◇ Nature of the Contract (Non Est Factum)

A party may plead as a defence to an attempt to enforce a contract that he or she made a mistake about the type of contract. For example, a party may think he or she is guaranteeing a debt when in fact he or she is becoming a principal debtor. This might happen where A is illiterate, blind, or otherwise disabled and is relying on B to prepare the agreement for signature. If B substitutes a document creating primary indebtedness for a guarantee and A signs it, A would say that this was not the type of contract he had agreed to. This defence, called the **non est factum** defence, denies that there was consent to the terms of an agreement. If there is no consent, then there is no enforceable contract.

non est factum
(Latin) "I did not make this"; a defence used by one who appears to be a party to a contract but who did not intend to enter into this type of contract; in effect, the party is denying that he or she consented to this contract

The plea of *non est factum* is available only in certain circumstances:

- The party relying on the plea must be illiterate, unable to understand English, blind, or affected by some other disability that prevents the person from reading and sufficiently understanding the document, at least to the extent of understanding the difference between the document the party signed and the document he or she thought he or she was signing.[32]

- The party must not be careless or negligent in signing the document. Blindness or other disability alone is not enough. The party must make some effort to determine what the document is or to obtain assistance before signing it. The effort does not necessarily have to be successful or effective.

- The party must be entirely mistaken as to the type of transaction or contract that he or she is signing. Ignorance of the terms or confusion about the effects of the contract is not sufficient for a successful plea.

- The party relying on the plea must prove that he or she was mistaken as to the type of contract, was not negligent or careless in signing, and had a disability that prevented him or her from appreciating that the document was entirely different from what he or she thought it was.

- The party relying on the plea need not prove fraud, misrepresentation, or fault by the other party.

---

32 *Saunders v. Anglia Building Society*, [1971] AC 1039 (HL).

CASE IN POINT

Courts Reluctant to Use Non Est Factum Defence in Absence of Duress, Fraud, or Undue Influence

Michiels v. Kinnear, 2011 ONSC 3826 (CanLII)

Facts

Michiels, a widow, sued for damages to compensate her for the loss of her real and personal property, for return of personal property, and for punitive damages. In 1978, the plaintiff and her husband purchased a house as joint tenants. In February 2004, the plaintiff's husband was advised that he had approximately six months to live. The plaintiff accompanied her husband to his lawyer's office and was presented with a transfer/deed to sign and was told that she had to sign it if she wanted to continue to use the property. Upon her husband's death, Michiels would have inherited the whole of the property as the surviving joint tenant. The transfer/deed gave the plaintiff's niece, nephew-in-law, and sister-in-law ownership, subject to a life interest in favour of the plaintiff and her husband for the sum of $2. This would allow the plaintiff to live in the house during her lifetime, after her husband died.

The plaintiff had a grade 4 education and could not read or write. She alleged that the transfer/deed was not explained to her. Soon after her husband's death, the plaintiff moved into an apartment and her niece and nephew-in-law moved into the house. In 2005, the plaintiff's niece and nephew-in-law wished to mortgage the property, but could not do so due to the plaintiff's life estate. The plaintiff attended another lawyer at the request of her sister-in-law and signed documents giving up her life interest.

The plaintiff alleged that she did not understand that she had given up her ownership of the property until 2006, when she went to sell the property. She argued *non est factum*, claiming she did not have the ability to understand what she had been asked to sign in 2004, and that her husband's lawyer did not explain it to her.

Decision

The action was dismissed. The gift transactions were not unconscionable as the plaintiff was able to protect herself, and she was not taken advantage of and was not the victim of any undue influence. Furthermore, she could not argue *non est factum*. Although the plaintiff was not fully literate, she was functionally literate and understood the nature and intent of the documents she signed.

Practical Tip

When dealing with a person whose literacy and capacity may be at issue, be sure the person has separate legal representation.

EXAMPLE

Mistake as to Nature of the Contract

Allen is an illiterate farmer. Larissa negotiates a contract to lease 40 hectares of land from Allen. Allen goes to Larissa's lawyer's office to sign the lease. He tells the lawyer he has come to sign the lease. At Allen's request, the lawyer goes over the terms with him, but by mistake she gives Allen the lease with an option to purchase attached. When Allen discovers what happened, he seeks to negate the contract and pleads *non est factum*. He may be successful, since he has a disability that prevented him from determining the true nature of the document. Allen was not careless—he asked for and received assistance. The mistake was not due to fraud or intentional misrepresentation, but that is not something Allen has to show to succeed with the plea.

The trend in the case law in Canada and England is to narrow this defence, in particular by confining it to situations where the document signed is completely different from the one the party thought he or she was signing. Further, while the courts have been inclusive as to the types of disability that might underlie a plea of *non est factum*, they have required that the mistake go to the nature of the contract itself and that the party show some effort to try to understand the nature of the contract.[33]

The Mistaken Party

So far, we have examined mistakes about particulars of the contract, chiefly mistakes of law and fact. We now turn to an analysis of the doctrine of mistake in the context of who makes a mistake and what the consequences of the mistake are.

In many cases of mistake, it is possible to analyze the fact situation in terms of a mistake of fact or as a mistake by a party or parties. For example, where A and B are contracting over the sale of a boat and, unknown to both of them, the boat has been destroyed by fire, there is no contract. This conclusion could be based on the argument that there is a mistake about the existence of the subject matter—a mistake of fact—or it could be based on the argument that both parties have made a common mistake, since both believed that the subject matter existed when it did not. Whichever route is taken, the conclusion is the same. However, there may be cases where focusing on mistakes of fact or law may lead to different conclusions from an analysis based on which party made the mistake.

Unilateral Mistake

unilateral mistake
one party to a contract
is mistaken about a
fundamental element
of the contract

Unilateral mistake occurs when one party to a contract is mistaken about some fundamental element of the contract. What follows from such a mistake depends on whether the unmistaken party knew or ought to have known about the mistake.

OTHER PARTY IS UNAWARE OF THE MISTAKE

If one party makes a mistake and the other is unaware of it and could not have reasonably been expected to know of it, then the contract is valid and cannot be rescinded or nullified.[34] This result may be explained in terms of the law that requires the mistaken party to bear the cost of his or her own negligence or carelessness. At common law, the test of the unmistaken party's knowledge is objective: what would a reasonable person who is looking at the bargaining process and contract think the unmistaken party knew or ought to have known? The equitable approach is more subjective, since it looks at the intentions of the parties.

---

33   Ibid.; *Marvco Color Research Ltd. v. Harris* (1982), 141 DLR (3d) 577 (SCC).

34   *Commercial Credit Corporation v. Newall Agencies Ltd.* (1981), 126 DLR (3d) 728 (BCSC).

Unilateral Mistake: Other Party Is Unaware

Ravi has leased a car from 4 Wheels Ltd. He wants to buy the car at the end of the lease period. He asks 4 Wheels to quote him a buyout price, and 4 Wheels does so. Ravi agrees to the price, unaware that 4 Wheels has made a mistake and quoted a lower price than it intended. Ravi does not have the knowledge or background to know that a pricing mistake has been made and in fact has no real idea of what the market price is. Consequently, it could not be said that he knows or ought to know that 4 Wheels made a mistake, and the contract is binding on 4 Wheels.

OTHER PARTY SHOULD HAVE BEEN AWARE OF THE MISTAKE

If one party makes a mistake and the other is unaware of it but in all of the circumstances should have been aware of it, then the unmistaken party cannot rely on enforcing the contract. Although the contract may or may not be void *ab initio* at common law, it is voidable and could be rescinded in equity at the option of the party who made the mistake on the ground that it would be unconscionable to permit the unmistaken party from taking advantage of an error in offering or accepting the terms of an agreement.[35]

Unilateral Mistake: Other Party Should Have Been Aware

Marek has seen an invitation to tender on a contract to provide fuel to Elizavetta's business. He submits a tender in which he mistakenly miscalculates the unit price. Elizavetta, seeing that the price is very low, accepts the tender immediately. She suspects that Marek has made an error, but she does not know what it is and does not inquire further. Even if she does not know that there is a mistake, a reasonable person would be expected to know that the price was low and would expect the buyer to be aware of an error.

OTHER PARTY IS AWARE OF THE MISTAKE

If one party makes a mistake and the other is aware of it and snaps up the bargain, the contract is voidable by the mistaken party. There is no requirement to show that the unmistaken party misled or deceived the mistaken party, and the results are the same as they would be for a situation where the unmistaken party did not know of the mistake but should have known about it. Where the unmistaken party knows of the mistake, the test is subjective, and the courts will hear evidence from the mistaken party as to what he or she actually intended to do.

---

35 *BCE Development Corp. v. Cascade Investments Ltd.* (1987), 55 Alta. LR (2d) 22 (QB); aff'd. (1987), 56 Alta. LR (2d) 349 (CA).

> **EXAMPLE**
>
> **Unilateral Mistake: Other Party Is Aware**
>
> In the above example, if Marek's calculation error was easily evident on the face of the tender, then Elizavetta either would have had actual knowledge of the miscalculation, or ought to have known of the miscalculation.

REMEDIES

The law is not entirely clear on what remedies are available in cases of unilateral mistake. In Canada, it appears that the mistaken party has a choice between rectification of the contract and rescission. If rectification is chosen, the contract is rewritten by the court to correct the mistake. If rescission is chosen, the contract is voided and the parties are returned to their pre-contract positions.[36] This solution has been rejected in England, where rectification is the only remedy.[37] With unilateral mistake, the courts are inclined to resort to the law of equity, which allows for flexible remedies that maximize opportunities for keeping the contract alive.

Mutual Mistake

mutual mistake
both parties to a contract are mistaken but each makes a different mistake

A **mutual mistake** arises where both parties are mistaken but they each make a different mistake. The test of whether mistakes have been made is objective. If a reasonable person is of the view that the parties appear to be in agreement on the terms of the contract, then there is apparent assent to the terms of the contract, making the contract valid. As one case put it, "[m]utual assent is not required … only apparent manifestation of assent is required."[38] The subjective, inward secret beliefs of a mistaken party are considered to be irrelevant, which prevents the doctrine from being exploited to undo what, in effect, is a bad bargain by either party.

> **EXAMPLE**
>
> **Mutual Mistake**
>
> Farid is selling a second-hand mountain bike. Marsha indicates that she would like to buy it. She is looking for a new bike and thinks that Farid's, which is clean and shiny, is new. Farid is unaware that Marsha thinks she is buying a new bike—he thinks she wants to buy a second-hand one. The objective view of the reasonable person might be that the condition of the bike might provide reasonable support for the mistake Marsha made, and that there was no evidence to prevent Farid from being mistaken about Marsha's intent. If so, it might be argued that the parties did not reach consensus and there was no contract.

---

36 *Devald v. Zigeuner* (1958), 16 DLR (2d) 285 (Ont. CA).

37 *Riverlate Properties Ltd. v. Paul*, [1975] Ch. D. 133 (CA).

38 *Walton v. Landstock Investments Ltd.* (1976), 13 OR (2d) 693 (CA), quoted in Fridman, supra footnote 5, at 258.

No Mutual Mistake Where Party Fails to Inform Itself

0707448 B.C. Ltd. v. Cascades Recovery Inc., 2011 BCSC 1065 (CanLII)

Facts

The plaintiff landlord sued for breach of lease as a result of the defendant failing to pay rent. The defendant was in the recycling business. It rented a warehouse for the purpose of a "multi-stream recycling and processing facility" and applied for a licence from the city. The defendant expected its licence to be approved and began making various alterations to the building without obtaining a building permit. The city posted a stop-work order at the property. The defendant's business licence application was then rejected on the grounds that its operation was contrary to the zoning bylaws for the property and the alterations were unauthorized.

Rent had been paid for only a few months. The plaintiff's solicitors wrote to the defendant, terminating the lease and giving notice of the plaintiff's intention to claim damages. In response, the defendant claimed, among other things, that there had been a mistake at common law; alternatively, it claimed that there had been a mistake in equity, as both parties were under the mistaken assumption that performance of the lease was, at all times, possible under the zoning bylaws, and more specifically, that the defendant's proposed

use was permissible. Finally, in the alternative, the defendant argued there was a prior oral collateral agreement between the parties that, in the event the defendant was unable to obtain the necessary permission from the city to use the building to carry on its recycling business, the parties would be relieved from their obligations under the lease.

Decision

The doctrine of mutual mistake was not available to the defendants, as the doctrine could not be used to re-allocate risk away from the party that should bear it. The burden of investigating zoning, the risk of making alterations without a building permit, and the risk that the premises were not fit for the lessee's purpose, was on the defendants. If there was a mistake, it was solely that of the defendants. Judgment was granted in favour of the plaintiff for breach of contract.

Practical Tip

When licences or permits are required by one of the parties, make sure you spell out the terms clearly, and insert conditions precedent for performance into the contract.

Common Mistake

A **common mistake** is one where both parties are mistaken and make the same mistake. They have not reached consensus on essential terms, and there is no enforceable contract. Not every common mistake yields these results—there must be a fundamental common mistake about the subject matter or a term of the contract.[39] Fact situations that give rise to analysis using the doctrine of common mistake can also be analyzed in terms of mistake as to identity, quality, and existence of the subject matter. In the end, using any of these analytic approaches, the contract may be avoided if the mistake is about something fundamental and the party appears to have received far less than what he or she had apparently contracted for.

common mistake
both parties to a contract are mistaken and make the same mistake

---

39 *McMaster University v. Wilchar Construction Ltd.*, [1971] 3 OR 801 (HC); aff'd. (1973), 12 OR (2d) 512 (CA).

Common Mistake

Millicent wants to sell her fur coat, which she thinks is mink. Emily agrees to buy it; she too thinks it is mink. Both intend the transaction to be about a mink coat. In fact, both are mistaken—the coat is made of some other kind of fur dyed to look like mink and is worth far less than a mink coat. Assuming that neither Millicent nor Emily is careless in failing to find the true quality on examining the coat, it appears that both have made a common mistake. Because a mink coat is perceived to be different from other kinds of coats, the mistake could be said to be fundamental and to give rise to rescission. Note that on these facts, this could also be seen as a mistake about the identity or quality of the subject matter.

The Consequences of a Serious Common Mistake

Miller Paving Limited v. B. Gottardo Construction Ltd., 2007 ONCA 422 (CanLII)

Facts

The plaintiff, Miller Paving Ltd., sold materials to the defendant for use in a construction project. The parties signed an agreement in which the plaintiff acknowledged that it had been paid in full for all the materials it had supplied. The plaintiff later found it had mistakenly failed to bill the defendant for some of the materials sold, and rendered a further invoice. The defendant refused to pay. The plaintiff brought an action to recover the outstanding amount. The action was dismissed at trial. The trial judge found that the agreement stood as a complete bar to the plaintiff's claim and that the misapprehension as to the facts did not justify setting the agreement aside. The plaintiff appealed, arguing that the trial judge erred in failing to properly apply the doctrine of common mistake to the agreement.

Decision

The plaintiff's appeal was dismissed. The court set out a test to consider the application of the doctrine of common mistake:

- The court should look to the contract itself under both the common law and equitable approaches to common mistake to see whether the parties have provided for who bears the risk of the relevant mistake.

- If they have so provided, that provision will govern.

- If they have not, the court will examine the evidence to see who bears the risk.

In this case, the agreement clearly allocated to the plaintiff the risk that payment in full had not been received, as it acknowledged that it had in the contract itself. Even if the plaintiff could resort to the doctrine of common mistake, it could not succeed in setting aside the agreement. First, if the court applied the common-law approach, the plaintiff had to show that as a result of the common mistake, the subject matter of the contract had become something essentially different from what it was believed to be. The subject matter of the agreement was the release of all further claims. Nothing about the mistaken assumption changed that subject matter.

Second, to engage the equitable doctrine of common mistake, the plaintiff had to show that it was not at fault. The finding of the trial judge was that the mistake was due to the plaintiff's errors and was not in any way the responsibility of the defendant.

Summary of Unilateral, Mutual, and Common Mistake

Unilateral Mistake

- only one party has made a mistake and the mistake is about a fundamental element of the contract
- if the other party is unaware of the mistake and could not have reasonably been expected to know of it, then the contract is valid
- if the other party is aware or should have been aware of the mistake, then the contract is voidable at the option of the mistaken party

Mutual Mistake

- both parties have made a mistake, but they have made different mistakes
- determined by the objective "reasonable person" test: Do the parties appear to be in agreement about the terms of the contract?
- if the parties appear to be in agreement on the terms of the contract, then the contract is valid
- if the parties do not appear to be in agreement on the terms of the contract, then the contract is voidable

Common Mistake

- both parties are mistaken and make the same mistake
- if the mistake is with respect to a fundamental term, then the contract is voidable

CHAPTER SUMMARY

Where one party makes a statement that is a misrepresentation and induces another to enter into a contract on the basis of the misrepresentation, the law will intervene, depending on whether the statement was a term of the contract or an inducement to enter into it, and whether the misrepresentation was innocently made, negligently made, or made with the intent to defraud or deceive. Depending on the nature of the misrepresentation, it can give rise to damages for breach of contract, or to rescission of the contract where the contract is voided.

The courts also will void a contract on the ground that one party was induced by duress or undue influence to enter into a contract that he or she would otherwise not have entered into. In other circumstances, where there is no apparent undue influence or duress, the court may intervene on the ground that the contract in its terms is so unfair that it is unconscionable.

When a party makes a mistake, the courts examine the situation carefully in deciding whether or not a party should be let out of his or her contractual responsibilities. If the mistake is fundamental and concerns the identity or existence of the subject matter, a term of the contract, or the nature of the contract itself, the court will often allow for rescission, rectification, or termination of the contract. The basis for these remedies is that the parties were not really in agreement about essential terms and that a reasonable person would assume that it was reasonable in the circumstances for the party or parties to have made the mistake in question.

The courts also examine mistake from the perspective of who makes the mistake and what the consequences are or should be for the mistaken party. If one party makes a unilateral mistake about a fundamental element of the contract, what happens depends on whether the other party knew or ought to have known of the mistake. One cannot take advantage of a reasonable mistake by the other party. If both parties make a mistake and it is the same one, it is a common mistake. If the mistake is fundamental, then the parties are not *ad idem* and there is no valid contract. If both parties make a mistake, but each party's mistake is different, they have made a mutual mistake. If the result is that they are not *ad idem* about something fundamental, then the contract may be avoided.

KEY TERMS

common mistake, 105
duress, 83
fiduciary, 86
fraudulent misrepresentation, 72
innocent misrepresentation, 72

intangible property, 77
material representation, 72
misrepresentation, 72
mutual mistake, 104
non est factum, 100

rescission, 72
restitution, 75
uberrimae fidei contracts, 81
undue influence, 85
unilateral mistake, 102

REVIEW QUESTIONS

True or False?

_____ 1. In some cases a misrepresentation in a contract may give rise to a tort action as well as an action in contract.

_____ 2. If there is a mistake about a fundamental term of the contract, the contract may be void or voidable.

_____ 3. A *consensus ad idem* is a prerequisite to successful enforcement of a contract.

_____ 4. Where a party has made a mistake, courts, when they do intervene, will try to save the contract through rectification rather than rescind the contract or declare it to be voidable.

_____ 5. The remedy of restitution allows a judge to alter the terms of the contract to reflect what the parties had initially intended.

_____ 6. Silence can never be considered to be a misrepresentation.

_____ 7. The defence of *non est factum* will not likely be successful where independent legal advice was obtained.

_____ 8. Mistakes as to the identity of the subject matter are treated differently than mistakes as to the quality of the subject matter.

_____ 9. A common mistake arises where both parties are mistaken but they each make a different mistake.

Multiple Choice

1. An innocent misrepresentation
   a. automatically will result in rescission if the other party sues for rescission
   b. is a false statement
   c. is when the maker of the statement is unaware that it is false
   d. b and c

2. A material representation that you make that you know is false is called
   a. an intentional misrepresentation
   b. a misleading misrepresentation
   c. a fraudulent misrepresentation
   d. none of the above

3. If you are the victim of a material misrepresentation and seek to rescind the contract and have it declared void,
   a. you must stop carrying out your part of the contract
   b. you should notify the other party of your intentions
   c. you can rescind at any time if you are the victim of a misrepresentation
   d. a and b

4. If I ask you, "Are these good rutabagas?" and you say nothing, this may be a misrepresentation by omission for which I may be able to obtain rescission
   a. if I have the opportunity to inspect the rutabagas that are the subject of the contract
   b. if your failure to say anything has the effect of making a previous statement by you untrue
   c. if I have very little knowledge about rutabagas and I am relying on your knowledge and experience
   d. b and c

5. A threatens B that if he doesn't buy goods from C, he, B, will be "swimming with the fishes at the bottom of Hamilton Harbour." C is aware of the threat against B.
   a. This does not amount to duress because the threat is not made by C, the other contracting party.
   b. B, though not threatened by C, may nevertheless sue C for duress.
   c. If B was threatened with mere economic harm, he could not sue for duress.
   d. B can't claim duress unless the threats are made against family members.

6. In cases involving undue influence,
   a. a party must show that a person close to them has threatened them
   b. there is no presumption of undue influence in a solicitor–client relationship where the client raises the issue of undue influence
   c. undue influence may arise where one party puts moral pressure on another
   d. where there is a solicitor–client relationship, it is necessary to show that the client is disadvantageously affected by the contract

7. An unconscionable transaction is one that
   a. when brought before the court makes a judge very angry
   b. is governed by both common law and statute
   c. is subject to the defence that the suffering party behaved recklessly or foolishly and made a bad bargain
   d. b and c

8. A mistake by one party to a contract is likely to lead to a remedy where
   a. the mistake is in respect of a fundamental term of the contract and the other party knows of the mistake
   b. the mistake is in respect of minor contract provisions
   c. the mistake was due to the carelessness or negligence of one party
   d. the mistake is in respect of motive or intention of the party making the mistake

9. If A contracts with B and undertakes certain payments that A thinks are legally required, when in fact the payments are not required, which of the following statements is *incorrect*?
   a. If the mistake is a mistake of law there is no remedy for A.
   b. Mistakes of law or fact may well result in a remedy for A.
   c. If A had been negligent in researching what was required, there is unlikely to be a remedy.
   d. Rectification rather than rescission is a likely outcome.

10. If I wish to rely on a defence of *non est factum* to void a contract,

   a. I must have a disability that prevents me from reading or understanding what the document is

   b. I need only be ignorant of the terms or be confused about the effect of the contract

   c. I need to show there was misrepresentation or fraud

   d. none of the above

11. Zeus offered to give Europa to Mercury. Both of them thought Europa was a cow, but it turned out to be a grampus, which looks like a cow, but is worth far less. This is an example of

   a. a unilateral mistake

   b. undue influence

   c. *non est factum*

   d. a mutual mistake

12. A mistake about the subject matter of a contract may result in a contract remedy if

   a. the mistake is about a term or condition that is fundamental or important to the contract

   b. a reasonable person would have considered the term or condition important

   c. the party who suffered as a result of the mistake considered the term or condition important

   d. a and b

Short Answer

1. A seller says, "We will have zoning permission" during negotiations for the purchase of a building lot. Explain whether this is a misrepresentation if

   a. the seller knew permission would never be granted,

   b. the seller had no idea whether permission would be granted but made the statement anyway, or

   c. the seller believed permission would be granted.

2. Give an example of a situation where a misrepresentation is also a term of the contract.

3. What is the effect on the remedies available to the victim of a misrepresentation that has become a term of the contract?

4. In what circumstances can duress be used to rescind a contract?

5. How does undue influence differ from duress in terms of circumstances where it can be used, and in terms of remedies?

6. How does unconscionability differ from duress and undue influence?

7. Suppose a party to a contract makes a mistake about how the law applies to a contract. Should this mistake be treated differently from a mistake of fact? Why or why not?

8. What are the consequences if a party makes a mistake in the identity of the subject matter of a contract? How are the consequences different from those where the mistake is about the quality of the subject matter? Is the distinction meaningful? Why or why not?

9. What are the consequences if a party makes a mistake about whether the subject matter of a contract exists? If the subject matter does not exist, does it matter if it ceases to exist before the contract is made, at the time the contract is made, and after the contract is made? Explain.

10. In what circumstances will the plea of *non est factum* succeed?

11. What are the effects of a unilateral mistake by a party to a contract if the unmistaken party is aware of the mistake or ought to be aware of the mistake? Would your answer be different if the unmistaken party has no idea that the other party has made a mistake? Why or why not?

12. How does a common mistake differ from a mutual mistake? How and in what circumstances are the consequences of mutual mistake different from those of common mistake?

13. There are a number of possible remedies in cases of misrepresentation or mistake. Explain the result of the following remedies:

   a. rescission

   b. damages for breach of contract

   c. rectification

14. Provide an example of

   a. a material misrepresentation

   b. an innocent misrepresentation

   c. a fraudulent misrepresentation

15. Henry asks Roger if the bike he is selling is roadworthy. Describe the contractual defect, if any, in the following situations:

  a. Roger says nothing. The bike is in front of them.

  b. Roger, who is an expert on bikes, says nothing, and Henry knows little about them. The bike is in front of them.

  c. Roger says it is roadworthy, but hasn't checked whether it is. It turns out not to be roadworthy.

  d. Roger's grandmother tells Henry she will cast an evil spell on Henry if he doesn't buy the bike. Henry believes that Roger's grandma can cast evil spells, and out of fear buys the bike.

Apply Your Knowledge

1. Puccini bids on a load of Edam cheese being sold by Rossini. Puccini requires a regular grade of Edam for his gourmet shop. Rossini has dealt with Puccini before and knows the nature of Puccini's business. Rossini is also told how to package the cheese, but he is not told precisely what grade of Edam Puccini wants. Rossini sells and delivers it. The price is quite a bit lower than the usual price for a load of Edam. On delivery, Puccini discovers that it is a grade of Edam suitable only for processing into a cheese spread. Puccini seeks to rescind the contract and get his money back on the ground that there was a mistake as to the identity of the subject matter.

  Develop and present arguments to support Puccini's position and arguments to support Rossini's position. You may wish to share this exercise with another student, with one of you taking Rossini's position and one of you taking Puccini's.

2. Charlie, a fruit merchant, contracts with Camille to purchase from her a load of mangoes currently being shipped to Vancouver. Charlie and Camille are unaware that the mangoes spoiled along the way and were sold off very cheaply by the captain of the ship. The subject matter of the contract, the load of mangoes, ceased to exist before the parties entered into their agreement and there can be no contract. Would it make a difference if the mangoes spoiled *after* the contract was entered into? What remedies might be available to the parties in this situation? Is the law on mistake of any help here? Consider remedies for breach of contract.

3. Oscar wants to sell his piano. Leslie wants to buy a new piano and thinks Oscar's is new. Oscar doesn't know that Leslie thinks she is buying a new piano; he thinks she is looking for a second-hand one. The objective view of the reasonable person might be that the condition of the piano provides reasonable support for Leslie's mistake, and that there was no evidence to prevent Oscar from being mistaken about Leslie's intent. If so, it might be argued that the parties had not reached a consensus and there was no contract.

  Develop arguments to support Oscar's position and Leslie's position on the basis that the mistake is

  • a unilateral mistake of Leslie's, and

  • a mistake as to the identity of the subject matter of the contract.

Contractual Rights

5

Introduction 114

Privity of Contract 114

Assignment of a Contract 121

Chapter Summary 125

Key Terms 125

Review Questions 125

LEARNING OUTCOMES

After completing this chapter, you should be able to:

- Explain the principle of privity of contract and describe the statutory exceptions that permit third parties to enforce rights under a contract.

- Understand under what circumstances vicarious performance is acceptable under a contract.

- Define "trust" and distinguish between express and implied trusts.

- Distinguish between novation and assignment, as they relate to contracts.

- Distinguish between equitable and statutory assignments.

Introduction

The general rule in contract law is that only the parties to an agreement are bound by the obligations in the contract and are entitled to enforce those obligations. There are, however, a number of exceptions to this rule. This chapter discusses those exceptions, which include vicarious performance (or "contracting out"), novation, express trusts, implied trusts (resulting trusts and constructive trusts), and equitable and statutory assignments of contracts. In these situations, third parties may be liable under the original contract and may be able to enforce rights to which they were not originally entitled.

Privity of Contract

privity
the relationship that exists between the parties to a contract

As the term suggests, **privity** involves being privy to, or a party to, a contract. Only the parties to a contract may claim the benefits of the contract or incur any liability under the contract. This may seem self-evident, but some contracts purport to confer benefits on third parties, or third parties may wish to be substituted for one of the parties. In those cases, the third parties may wish to enforce the contract.

The general rule is that a third party who is a "stranger" to the contract may not claim any benefits or incur any liability from the contract because of the lack of privity.

EXAMPLES

Lack of Privity

- Connor and Julian own adjoining properties. Connor enters into a contract with Maya whereby Maya agrees to rent Connor's property and build a motel on it. Julian would greatly benefit from this, since he owns and operates a restaurant on the adjoining property. However, Maya fails to fulfill the contract and does not build the motel. Despite the fact that Julian will suffer as a result of Maya's breach of contract, he cannot enforce the contract because he is not a party to it—he lacks privity. Only Connor can enforce the contract.

- The homeowners in a certain neighbourhood decide they want to form a residents' association. All of them enter into a contract that states that if any of the homeowners in the neighbourhood fails to cut his or her grass and lets it grow past a certain length, then any other member of the group may cut the grass and the offending homeowner will be obligated to pay a fee of $100 to the member who cut it. Some time after the contract is formed, Brian buys a house and moves into the neighbourhood. Brian doesn't cut his grass and Raffi goes over one Saturday morning and cuts it for him. Raffi then sends a bill to Brian for $100. Brian is not obligated to pay the $100 because he was never a party to the contract and cannot incur any liability under it.

Contract Made on Behalf of a Person Is Binding on That Person

Cordeiro v. Banks, [2012] OJ No. 503 (Sm. Cl. Ct.)

Facts

The defendant Banks bought a house. It needed to be cleaned thoroughly. He mentioned this to his real estate agent, who said she could take care of it. She hired the plaintiff, whose services she had used in the past in various circumstances. The defendant found the price excessive, and he also argued that he had no obligation to pay the defendant as she had no privity of contract with him.

Decision

While the real estate agent retained the plaintiff's services, it was clear to all that she did so on behalf of the defendant, contracting as his agent so that as principal, he was bound by the real estate agent's actions.

Practical Tip

If you allow someone to make arrangements for goods or services for you, you will be bound by the contract even though you do not directly communicate with the other party, so you should consider communicating directly with the other party if you wish to be in control of the terms of the agreement, or give explicit instructions to your agent.

Statutory Exceptions to the Requirement of Privity

The doctrine of privity can be rationalized in terms of the lack of consideration. The third party paid or received no consideration for the contract so he or she cannot enforce it, nor be bound by it. However, statutes can impose liability or confer benefits on third parties despite the lack of consideration. A few examples of statute law are as follows:

- The law of partnership states that a partner may enter into a contract on behalf of the partnership and that the contract will impose liability and be binding on all the partners.
- In real property law, contracts that impose restrictions on the use of real property are binding not just on the parties to the contract but also on all subsequent owners of the property, even though they were never parties to the original contract, provided that these interests are registered on title. Such restrictions might be the granting of a right of way or a restriction on the height of any building constructed on the property.
- The parties to an insurance contract are the policyholder and the insurance company. However, many insurance contracts, or policies, such as those for life insurance, name a third party as a **beneficiary**. If the insurance company will not honour the policy, it may be enforced by the beneficiary.

Apart from statutory exceptions to the general rule, there are a number of other means by which third parties may assert rights under a contract.

beneficiary
a person who is entitled to the benefits of an agreement entered into between two or more other parties

Novation

A third party may replace one of the parties to a contract by forming a new contract. The result of **novation** is the termination of the old contract and the substitution of the new contract. The new party has the benefits and liabilities of the contract, and the old party no longer has any rights or obligations. There is no difficulty with privity of contract with novation, because the third party becomes a contracting party. The requirements of novation are as follows:

- The new party must assume complete liability.
- The other party must accept the new party *in substitution for* the old party, not *in addition to* the old party.
- The other party must accept the new contract in substitution for the old contract.
- The other party must accept that the new contract terminates the old contract.
- The new contract must be made with the consent of the old party.

EXAMPLE

Novation

Busy Bees Cleaners Inc. agrees to provide office cleaning services to Sharif, Wasserman, and Powell under a long-term contract. The owners of Busy Bees decide to retire and close down the business before the end of the contract. However, they recommend another company, Action Clean Ltd., to replace them. After negotiations, Sharif, Wasserman, and Powell enter into a new contract with Action Clean under the same terms and conditions as their contract with Busy Bees. In doing so, there has been novation. Busy Bees is released from its obligations under the old contract, and the new contract with Action Clean is substituted for the old contract.

Vicarious Performance

As a general rule, a party to a contract must perform his or her obligations under that contract. He or she cannot get a third party to perform those obligations without the consent of the other party. Nevertheless, there are situations in which a party might wish to have a third party do some or all of the work under a contract. This is called **vicarious performance**, and it is permissible in limited circumstances.

A party may employ a third party to perform his or her obligations when the performance required is not of a personal nature. If the work could be performed equally well by another person, the party may "contract out" the work. However, the original party to the contract remains responsible if the work is not done properly. If the work to be done is of a personal nature, the party may not hire another to perform the contract.

Assumption of Mortgage by Purchaser Does Not Amount to Novation

National Trust Co. v. Mead, [1990] 2 SCR 410

This case is a leading Canadian case on the subject of novation.

Facts

Remai Construction Ltd. obtained a mortgage from the plaintiff, National Trust, to finance the construction of a condominium building. Remai sold a unit to Mead, who assumed an obligation to pay the mortgage. The question later arose as to whether the assumption of the mortgage amounted to novation, where Mead replaced Remai in all respects.

Decision

There was no novation in this case, and Remai was still subject to some contract liabilities. A clause permitting the plaintiff to release Remai cannot be construed as a total release and substitution of Mead. A number of other clauses clearly indicated that National Trust had no intention of fully releasing Remai. On balance there was evidence that the plaintiff intended to rely on both or either to pay the mortgage.

Practical Tip

For novation to occur, the contract must not only clearly indicate who the substitute parties are, but also clearly indicate that the former parties are no longer responsible for both the liabilities that arose before novation and those that arise after novation.

It is important to look at the common practices in the business or industry in question to determine whether vicarious performance is acceptable. Vicarious performance is common in a number of trades and industries, including shipping, building construction, dry cleaning, transportation, repair of goods, and manufacturing.

Vicarious Performance

- Saroj takes her car to Maurice for repair. Maurice agrees to fix her car, which needs engine repair and body work. Maurice does the engine repair himself, but sends the car down the street to Alain for the body work. When Saroj gets her car back, she finds that the body work was not done properly.

  In this case, vicarious performance is common and acceptable. Saroj needs the work done; presumably she does not care who does it. However, Maurice is responsible for the poorly done body work even though he did not do it himself. Saroj may sue him for breach of contract. Maurice may then in turn sue Alain for breach of contract.

- Glass Hammer Productions Ltd. hires Roberto Forte, a famous opera singer, for a concert. Roberto is feeling poorly on the day of the performance, so he sends his protégé, Bruno Pelizzari, to sing in his stead.

  In this case, the nature of the performance of the contract is personal, and vicarious performance is not acceptable. Glass Hammer Productions is not required to accept a substitute for the performer it hired.

CASE IN POINT

Vicarious Performance Permissible Where It Makes No Difference Who Performs the Service

Tru-Wall Group Ltd. v. Stadium Corp. of Ontario Ltd., [1995] OJ No. 2610 (Ct. Jus. (Gen. Div.)); 57 ACWS (3d) 536 (SC)

Facts

Tru-Wall, the applicant, entered into an agreement to lease a box in the SkyDome stadium (now the Rogers Centre). Under the lease agreement the respondent had the right to supply various services. The respondent sold or subcontracted to SDC its rights to supply various services. The applicant claimed that the services were such that they could not be vicariously performed, and as the respondent could not provide the services and was in breach of its obligations, the applicant was entitled to terminate the lease.

Decision

The application was dismissed. Vicarious performance of an assignor's contractual burdens or obligations should be permitted where it could make no difference to the beneficiary or recipient. In this case, one could not see how the arrangement involving SDC and the respondent could be said to have affected the services the applicant had contracted for. And if the services were not satisfactory, the respondent was ultimately responsible. If SDC faltered, the respondent was not excused from liability, so the applicant was not deprived of a remedy should one be required.

Practical Tip

While vicarious performance is implicitly permissible in certain circumstances, it is always possible to include a term in the contract barring or limiting vicarious performance.

Express Trusts

trust
a legal entity created by a grantor for a beneficiary whereby the grantor transfers property to a trustee to manage for the benefit of the beneficiary

settlor
a person who creates a trust by transferring property to a trustee for the benefit of a third party

trustee
a person who holds property in trust for, or for the benefit of, another person

express trust
a trust that arises as a result of an agreement, usually in writing, that is created in express terms

A strict rule that only the parties to an agreement can enforce it has the potential to lead to unfair results. If a contract conferred a benefit on a third party, and the parties to the agreement were unwilling to enforce it, the third party would be prohibited from enforcing the agreement. The law of trusts developed to deal with this situation. A **trust** is created by contract where property is transferred from one person (the **settlor**) to another for the benefit of a third party. The law of trusts allows the person who is to receive the benefit of the contract, the beneficiary, to enforce the contract against the person who is to administer the property for his or her benefit, the **trustee**. A trust that is declared in clear and unequivocal terms, usually in writing, is called an **express trust**.

EXAMPLE

Express Trust

Gwyn wants to create a trust for her son, Sean, in case she dies before he turns 18 years of age. In her will, she directs that all of her estate is to be invested for the benefit of Sean until he is 18 years old, and she names her sister Bethan as the trustee. After Gwyn dies, the property is transferred to Bethan. However, instead of administering the trust for the benefit of Sean, Bethan spends the money on herself.

Sean is not a party to the trust agreement—Gwyn and Bethan are the only parties. However, the law of trusts allows Sean to enforce the agreement because he is the beneficiary of the trust.

Implied Trusts

In other cases, the parties to a contract may create a benefit for a third party without expressly calling it a trust or without using language in the contract that would allow the third party to enforce the contract. In those cases, the third party must argue that a trust was created by inference or implication. The courts will examine the terms of the contract and the acts of the parties to determine whether the true intent of the contract was to create a trust. This can be a difficult argument to make because the courts are reluctant to impose a trust unless there is clear evidence that the parties intended to create a trust. When the courts find that a trust can be inferred from the contract, it is called an implied trust. In recent years, courts in Canada and England have developed the law of implied trusts particularly with respect to the concepts of the **resulting trust** and the **constructive trust**. The beneficiary of these types of trusts may enforce the terms of the implied trust. Note that this is an area that continues to evolve, and in the past there has been some confusion in cases about how these two types of implied trusts differ from each other, and in what circumstances they are to be applied.

Resulting Trust

A resulting trust arises where, on the evidence, there appears to be an intent to create a trust by the person who buys property in the name of another, where there is no contract or document that expressly states that the property is held in trust. In this situation, the property is deemed to be held in trust for the purchaser, with the titleholder as trustee. Resulting trusts often also arise where the terms of an express trust cannot be fully carried out, and there is no provision to deal with the situation in the trust itself. For example, if several people give money under an express trust to A to be used for B's education and B dies, there is a resulting trust in favour of the original donors. A is not free to keep the money but must return it to the donors.

> **EXAMPLE**
>
> **Resulting Trust**
>
> Luis was in danger of going bankrupt. He sold his house to his brother, Geraldo. There was an understanding between the brothers, not put in writing, that once Luis's finances were on a sound footing, Geraldo would transfer the property back. There was a falling out between the two brothers, and Geraldo stated that he was keeping the house as it was now registered in his name. Luis applied to the court, which held that there was a resulting trust, in that Geraldo was holding the property for the benefit of Luis, so that Luis was the true owner.

Constructive Trust

Unlike a resulting trust, a constructive trust does not depend on evidence of the parties' intention to create a trust. Instead, it rests on an assessment of the fairness with which parties are treated considering all of the surrounding circumstances. In

resulting trust
an implied trust, as distinguished from an express trust, where the legal titleholder is presumed to be holding property for a beneficiary in circumstances where a common intent can be implied

constructive trust
an implied trust, as distinguished from an express trust, where the person with legal title to property is unjustly enriched, the other party suffers a deprivation, and there is no legal reason for permitting one side to benefit disproportionately. A constructive trust does not depend on the intent of the parties.

particular, the court is most likely to find that there is a constructive trust where one party is unjustly enriched, the other suffers a deprivation, and there is no legal justification or reason for permitting one side to benefit disproportionately.

EXAMPLE

Constructive Trust

Natasha and Evelyn form a partnership. The partnership agreement states that if either of them should die, then her share of the profits of the partnership should be paid to her husband. Evelyn dies and Natasha refuses to pay the profits to Evelyn's husband, Luis. Luis is not a party to the partnership agreement. The partnership agreement did not set up an express trust. He would have to argue that it is a constructive trust that had been created in his favour. If successful, Luis would be able to obtain a share of the profits.

CASE IN POINT

Constructive Trust and Common-Law Spouses

Pettkus v. Becker, [1980] 2 SCR 834

This is a leading case in the development of the law regarding constructive and resulting trust in Canada.

Facts

Pettkus developed a successful beekeeping business over many years on property owned by Pettkus. Becker, through her hard work in the business, also contributed substantially to the value of the common enterprise. Pettkus and Becker were not married but lived as husband and wife from 1955 to 1974, except for a three-month separation in 1972. When the relationship terminated in late 1974, Pettkus regarded all of the property as his. Becker commenced an action seeking a declaration of entitlement to one-half interest in the lands and a share in the beekeeping business.

At trial Becker was awarded 40 beehives without bees, together with $1,500 representing earnings from those hives for 1973 and 1974. The Ontario Court of Appeal awarded Becker one-half interest in the lands owned by the appellant and in the beekeeping business. Pettkus appealed.

Decision

The appeal was dismissed. The Court could find no evidence of any kind that would justify a finding of a resulting trust—there was no oral agreement between Pettkus and Becker that there was a joint intention to share equally in the assets and proceeds of the beekeeping business. Indeed, there was no evidence that Pettkus ever intended to share the value of the business or the gain from it with Becker, and in support of this

there was no evidence that Pettkus was committed to marriage or a permanent relationship.

However, a constructive trust could apply in this case. The requirements were all present: the unjust enrichment of Pettkus, a corresponding deprivation for Becker, and the absence of any juristic reason to justify Pettkus's enrichment. The facts showed that Becker believed that she had some interest in the beekeeping business, and this belief was reasonable. Becker put in 19 years of unpaid labour, getting little in return, thereby satisfying the first two requirements for a constructive trust—enrichment and deprivation, with a causal connection between the two. In the circumstances, Pettkus knew or ought to have known that a sizable contribution of the kind made by Becker required compensation. Where one person in a relationship tantamount to spousal prejudiced herself in reasonable expectation of receiving an interest in property, and the other in the relationship freely accepted benefits conferred by the first person in circumstances where he knew or ought to have known of that expectation, it would be unjust to allow the recipient of the benefit to retain it.

Practical Tip

Couples who plan to live together without marrying are wise to negotiate a cohabitation agreement dealing with property issues. Such negotiations will often expose unanticipated expectations: Pettkus would have revealed that he wanted to share nothing, and Becker might have ended the relationship and found herself another bee farmer with more generous views.

Assignment of a Contract

In a commercial context, a contract is a thing of value that can be treated as an asset. For example, you may buy furniture from Fly By Night Furniture on a conditional sale contract, where you agree to pay the purchase price plus interest over an extended period of time. Fly By Night, as **assignor**, can then sell or assign the contract to a finance company, the **assignee**, who has the right to stand in the shoes of Fly By Night and collect all of the money that you, the party charged under the contract, still owe Fly By Night after the **assignment** takes place. This assignment differs from novation because no new contract is formed, and your consent is not required.

While assignments are common business transactions now, at one time the courts would not recognize them. The assignee gained no rights under the contract because of the lack of privity of contract, and therefore could not enforce the contract. However, the courts now recognize equitable and statutory assignments. They still do not recognize the assignment of contracts for personal services, which may be neither vicariously performed nor assigned to a third party.

assignor
a party who assigns his or her rights under a contract to a third party

assignee
a party to whom rights under a contract have been assigned by way of an assignment

assignment
a transfer by one party of his or her rights under a contract to a third party

Equitable Assignments

To avoid the privity of contract rule in dealing with assignments, the concept of an *equitable assignment* developed. This allows for assigning contractual rights under some circumstances. Equitable assignments have certain characteristics that can make them cumbersome to deal with, but they have some advantages as well. An equitable assignment can be verbal or in writing, and it can be a partial assignment of the assignor's rights or a complete and absolute assignment of all of the assignor's rights.

To allow an assignee to enforce a contract by equitable assignment, the following requirements must be met:

- All the parties must be brought before the court. This means that in any action to enforce the contract the assignor must be a party, even if he or she no longer has any interest in or rights under the contract.
- The court must be satisfied that the intention of all parties (but not the party to be charged) is to assign the contractual rights.
- The party to be charged must have notice of the assignment before the assignee can enforce the contract against him or her.

TIP

You can always include a term in the contract prohibiting assignments if you wish to prevent contract rights from being assigned.

Statutory Assignments

The widespread practice of assigning contracts and the inconvenience of having to make the assignor a party to any actions to enforce the contract led to the development of the statutory assignment. All the common-law provinces have legislation that recognizes the assignment of contractual rights. Statutory assignments have different requirements than equitable assignments. They do not replace equitable assignments, so in deciding how to enforce a contract that has been assigned, it is necessary to determine whether it is a statutory or an equitable assignment.

An assignee to a statutory assignment may enforce a contract without involving the assignor if

- the assignment of rights is absolute and unconditional;
- the assignment is in writing and signed by the assignor; and
- express notice of the assignment, in writing, is given to the party to be charged.

Note that the party to be charged does not have to consent to the assignment—he or she must only be given notice of the assignment. The assignment is effective against the party to be charged as of the date that he or she receives the notice. If the assignor has assigned the same contract to two different assignees, either accidentally or fraudulently, the assignee who first gives notice to the party to be charged is entitled to enforce the contract.

Defences and Assignments

All assignments, either equitable or statutory, are subject to any "equities" that exist between the original parties to the contract up until the time of notice. These equities might include rights that arise because of fraud, duress, or undue influence on the part of the assignor at the time the contract was entered into. For example, if the creditor uses duress to force a debtor to enter into a contract, the debtor can use duress as a defence if the creditor tries to enforce the contract. If the creditor assigns the contract, the debtor can claim duress as a defence to payment under the contract in an action by the assignee. Even though it was not the assignee who used duress, the assignee takes the assignment subject to all the conditions that existed between the original parties up until the time notice of the assignment is given to the party to be charged. The assignee can be in no better a position than was the assignor. Defences such as fraud, duress, and undue influence are discussed in more detail in Chapter 4, Contractual Defects.

> **EXAMPLE**
>
> **Equities**
>
> Pierre is employed with Auto Leasing Corp. As part of the terms of his employment, he is entitled to the use of a car. Pierre leases a car from his employer. He signs an agreement that states that he is not required to make any lease payments while he is employed with Auto Leasing Corp. If his employment with Auto Leasing Corp. ceases for any reason, Pierre must start making the lease payments himself. Auto Leasing Corp. experiences business problems and stops paying its employees. In an effort to raise capital, it assigns all its car leases, including Pierre's lease, to United Financing Ltd. At the time of the assignment, it owes Pierre $8,000 in unpaid wages. Auto Leasing Corp. then goes out of business. Pierre's employment is terminated, and United Financing Ltd. wants Pierre to make the payments under the lease. They give him notice of the assignment and demand payment.
>
> The equities that exist between the original parties, Pierre and Auto Leasing, at the time of the assignment include the wages owed to Pierre. Because United Financing

takes the assignment of the lease subject to any equities that exist between the original parties until the time that the notice is given, Pierre can claim a setoff and deduct the $8,000 owed to him by Auto Leasing from the money he owes to United Financing under the lease.

In addition, if the assignor owes money to the party to be charged under this or another contract, the party to be charged can claim the defence of **setoff** and deduct this debt from the moneys now owed to the assignee under the contract. This creates some risk for the assignee in taking an assignment, and assignees usually require some form of assurance from the assignor that no equities or setoffs exist that would interfere with enforcement of the contract.

> **setoff**
> in an action for debt, a defence where the debtor admits that he or she owes a debt to the creditor but also claims that the creditor owes a debt to him or her, and uses this to cancel or reduce the debt owed to the creditor

CASE IN POINT

Notice of Assignment Must Be Given to Party to Be Charged

Maxium Financial Services Inc. v. Bhagvati, [2012] OJ No. 521 (Sm. Cl. Ct.)

Facts

The defendant leased a hot water heater from Ozz Comfort Solutions. In 2007, Ozz assigned its rights in the lease to the plaintiff. In 2010, the plaintiff claimed the defendant defaulted on lease payments. There was no evidence offered by the plaintiff to show that the defendant ever received notice of the assignment as required by law. The plaintiff claimed that a "buyout quote" it sent late in 2010 constituted notice of assignment. If so, it came long after the apparent assignment in 2007.

Decision

Of the buyout notice as notice of assignment, the court stated:

The Buyout Quote appears on Ozz documentation with that company's name or logo appearing in the top left corner. It purports to describe a "Buyout Quote" although the meaning of that term is not apparent. The quote is stated to have an expiry date of August 10, 2011. It then sets out some figures based on $1,022.53, plus tax, an administration fee and additional charges, for the total of $1,363.57. It then states "Please note that this is only a Quote and not an invoice. Please inform us of your intention to buyout at least 7 days prior to the above noted Due Date. Cheques should be made payable to Maxium Financial Services Inc." A mailing address is then provided.

One can only speculate on the meaning which the defendant might have taken from this Buyout Quote if he received it. It could have been interpreted as irrelevant junk mail. If the recipient understood it to be connected to his prior lease with Ozz, but did not intend to purchase the hot water tank, or saw it after the expiry date, the document could have been meaningless to him.

The inscrutability of the Buyout Quote is remarkable. The court cannot be sure what that document is. The court can only be sure of what it is not.

Neither the assignee nor the assignor had given proper notice of the assignment to the defendant. Accordingly, the assignment was ineffective, so the plaintiff had no right to demand payment from the defendant. The claim was dismissed.

Practical Tip

If you are sending out a notice of assignment, make sure it clearly indicates what contract right is being assigned and to whom, including details of where and how payments are to be made. Send the notice by registered mail or courier so that you know it has been received.

Assignments by Operation of Law

Some assignments occur automatically when certain events occur. These assignments are governed by statutes that set out the duties of the assignor. For example, when a person goes bankrupt, all of his or her contractual rights are assigned to the trustee in bankruptcy. When a person dies, all contractual rights are assigned to the estate trustee with a will (if the person died with a will) or the estate trustee without a will (if the person died without a will). Similar provisions exist for situations where a person becomes incapable of managing his or her affairs due to a mental disability.

CASE IN POINT

No Equity for Setoff Where Party Acknowledges Assignment

RPG Receivables v. Krones Machinery, 2010 ONSC 2372 (CanLII)

Facts

Krones had contracts with Kennedy for the supply of machinery for a number of Krones' projects. Kennedy assigned its accounts receivable on invoices it had sent to Krones to RPG. Kennedy delivered a notice of assignment to Krones, which Krones executed and acknowledged. Krones subsequently did not make all of the payments on assigned receivables, claiming that it had overpaid on previous invoices rendered by Kennedy prior to the assignment, and that it was entitled to set the overpayment off against amounts now due to RPG under the assignment from Kennedy. RPG argued that there was no right in the original contract between Kennedy and Krones to set off for overpayment, and that therefore RPG was entitled to payment in full.

Decision

Setoff was not available to Krones in this case, as there was no right to it in the original contract between Krones and Kennedy. Krones could not obtain greater rights on an assignment by Kennedy than it had against Kennedy in the first place, unless it negotiated them with the assignee, RPG. When Kennedy assigned the debt to RPG, there was no right between Krones and Kennedy to set off overpayments against amounts due on invoices. And if Krones could not make this claim against Kennedy, it could not subsequently argue that the assignee, RPG, would be subject to the equities if Kennedy was not.

Practical Tip

If you are acknowledging an assignment to a stranger of a contract you have with the assignor, it is a good idea to check that all your pre-assignment rights have been honoured by the assignor before acknowledging the assignment.

CHAPTER SUMMARY

As a general rule, a third party who is not a party to a contract cannot incur any liability or claim any benefit under that contract due to lack of privity of contract. However, some statutes provide an exception to this rule, as in contracts of insurance or contracts that involve partnerships. A third party may gain rights under a contract by novation, where the third party is substituted for one of the parties and a new contract is formed. Contracts that do not require personal services may be vicariously performed by a third party.

Parties to a contract may create a trust, which expressly confers a benefit on and may be enforced by a third party. Parties may also enter into a contract that confers a benefit on a third party by implication or inference and that the third party can argue is a constructive trust. Third parties may also acquire rights and liabilities under a contract by way of an equitable assignment or a statutory assignment. Assignments are subject to the equities that existed between the original parties to the contract.

KEY TERMS

assignee, 121
assignment, 121
assignor, 121
beneficiary, 115
constructive trust, 119

express trust, 118
novation, 116
privity, 114
resulting trust, 119
setoff, 123

settlor, 118
trust, 118
trustee, 118
vicarious performance, 116

REVIEW QUESTIONS

True or False?

_____ **1.** For novation to successfully occur, the other party must accept the new party.

_____ **2.** Vicarious performance is possible where the service provided by the party seeking to subcontract is deemed to be personal.

_____ **3.** A beneficiary is a person who holds another person's property in trust for that other person.

_____ **4.** Consuela donated a large sum to a trustee for a charity to cover damage to a local landmark. Before any of the money could be spent, the trustee discovered that the damage was covered by insurance, and none of the sum collected needed to be used. In the circumstances, there is a resulting trust, and Consuela is entitled to get her money back.

_____ **5.** Sturdy Used Cars Ltd. sold Albert a Rustmobile with a 30-day guarantee. Albert is paying for the car on an installment plan. Sturdy assigned its rights to the installment payments to Shady Financial Services. Sturdy never gave notice of the assignment to Albert. Albert can refuse to pay Shady Financial Services.

_____ **6.** An assignee to a statutory assignment may enforce the contract without involving the assignor, even if the assignment is not in writing.

_____ **7.** The party to be charged must consent to an assignment.

Multiple Choice

1. Edward has agreed to purchase a sculpture from Michelangelo. Maisie really likes Michelangelo's work and would love to buy this sculpture.

   a. No problem. Maisie can just offer a higher price than Edward had agreed to pay, and she can have the sculpture.

   b. She can agree with Edward to purchase his right to buy the sculpture and have Edward's contract rights assigned to her.

   c. She has no right to acquire this particular sculpture under any circumstances, as Michelangelo can choose to whom he wishes to sell.

   d. None of the above.

2. Sihar and Reamy are in a business partnership. Reamy buys a new desk for the office.

   a. If Reamy doesn't pay the seller, he can be sued for the purchase price.

   b. The seller can sue Sihar for the purchase price if the seller is not paid.

   c. The seller can sue only the partnership business, but not Reamy and Sihar personally, for non-payment of a partnership debt.

   d. a and b

3. Abdul buys a life insurance policy from Fly By Night Insurance. He names Bibi as his beneficiary on the policy.

   a. When Abdul dies, Bibi, who was unaware of the policy, can collect under the policy because a beneficiary can enforce the policy despite the usual privity of contract rule.

   b. When Abdul dies, Bibi cannot collect because she is not a party to the contract.

   c. Bibi can collect only if she were added as a party to the insurance contract.

   d. None of the above.

4. Under the doctrine of novation,

   a. the former party must be removed from the contract entirely

   b. novation creates a new contract that replaces the old contract

   c. both post-novation parties must accept the new contract

   d. all of the above

5. Michelangelo is a famous painter and sculptor. Lucretia has hired him to paint her portrait.

   a. Michelangelo cannot contract this work out to Maurizio, an unknown sculptor.

   b. Michelangelo can contract the work out if he feels like it to anyone he chooses.

   c. Lucretia, who is famous, and whose patronage by being painted will enhance Michelangelo's career, can assign her right to have her portrait painted to Buffone, her servant.

   d. a and c

6. Vicarious performance

   a. means a substitute person may perform a contract on behalf of a party

   b. is generally not permitted on shipping, building construction, and dry-cleaning contracts

   c. releases the original party from liability for any breaches by the subcontractor

   d. none of the above

7. Seung-Hui by contract makes an arrangement in writing to give a capital sum to Junghoo, to be used as Junghoo determines, for the benefit of Taeg Sang.

   a. This is an implied trust.

   b. This is an express trust.

   c. This is a parallel trust.

   d. All of the above.

8. Abel and Susanna lived together for 20 years in a common-law relationship. They worked together and built a business, all of the assets of which were in Susanna's name. When they separated, Susanna claimed that all the assets were hers because they were in her name.

   a. Abel can successfully challenge Susanna using the doctrine of constructive trust.

   b. Abel can successfully challenge Susanna using the doctrine of resulting trust.

   c. If the property is in Susanna's name it is hers and Abel has no right to it.

   d. Abel can successfully challenge Susanna using the doctrine of crenellation.

9. Jotham assigns the amounts Yanna owes him for work previously done, to Pia.

   a. If Pia wants to enforce rights against Yanna, Pia must be made a party to the lawsuit.

   b. Yanna must have notice of the assignment if the contract is to be enforced against her.

   c. a and b

   d. none of the above

10. An assignee takes subject to the equities.

   a. This means the assignee is entitled to equitable remedies when enforcing the contract.

   b. This means the assignee is subject to the liabilities the assignor had under the contract with the other party.

   c. This means the assignee is responsible for enforcing equitable rights.

   d. a and c

Short Answer

1. Explain the doctrine of privity of contract. What is the rationale for its existence?

2. What are the requirements of novation?

3. Define vicarious performance.

4. Describe the difference between a novation and an assignment of a contract.

5. What are the requirements of an equitable assignment?

6. What are the requirements of a statutory assignment?

7. Under what circumstances do assignments occur as an operation of law?

8. Describe the risks the assignee assumes when taking the assignment of a contract.

9. What is a setoff, and when may it be used?

10. How would you distinguish between an implied and express trust?

11. Under what circumstances might a resulting trust arise?

12. Under what circumstances might a constructive trust arise?

Apply Your Knowledge

1. Sturdy Tires Ltd. manufactures tires and sells them to wholesalers. Sturdy Tires has an agreement with all its wholesalers that they will not sell the tires for less than the list price except where they are selling to approved dealers. In that case, the wholesalers may sell at a reduced price as long as they obtain an agreement in writing from the dealers that the dealers will not sell the tires below the list price.

   Sturdy Tires sells tires to Selkirk & Sons Inc., a wholesaler. Selkirk & Sons then sells the tires at a reduced price to Doucet Auto Limited, an approved dealer. Despite the agreement with Selkirk & Sons, Doucet holds a promotion and sells the tires for less than list price. Sturdy Tires then brings an action to prevent Doucet from selling its tires for less than list price. Will Sturdy Tires be successful in its action? Why or why not?

2. Peter is an elderly man who owns a hardware store. Because of his failing health, he can no longer run the business. He wants to sell it to his nephew, Jonathan, who often helps out in the store. Jonathan cannot afford to buy the business outright, so a contract is agreed upon whereby the business will be transferred to Jonathan. In exchange, Peter will be kept on as a consultant for the rest of his life, and Jonathan will pay Peter a monthly sum. The contract also states that when Peter dies, Jonathan will continue to pay the monthly sum to Peter's widow, Lesia.

   Jonathan pays the monthly sum to Peter while he is alive, but after Peter's death he refuses to pay the sum to Lesia. Can Lesia enforce this contract? Why or why not?

3. Sarah has a champion Siamese cat named Editrix. She decides to breed it with a superchampion, on the theory that she can make a great deal of money starting up a line of superchampion Siamese cats. She conducts a lot of research and discovers that Karl Clambitt, of Karl's Cattery, is one of the world's most renowned cat breeders. He has great expertise and an eye for good matches that produce genetically superior offspring. His apparent judgment and knowledge convinces Sarah that he is the right person to oversee this breeding enterprise. She brings Editrix to him and they sign an agreement in which he promises to use his skill and ability to achieve Sarah's goals.

   Karl, however, decides he needs a vacation and ships Editrix over to a colleague to carry out the breeding operation. The colleague, Freda Feline, is new to the business, having just retired as an accountant. Her operation is not particularly secure, and one evening a pack of raccoons climbs over the fence of her cattery. One of the raccoons takes a fancy to Editrix, and several weeks later Editrix gives birth to what may best be described as "catcoons." They have the worst physical features and least desirable traits of both animals, howling incessantly at a high pitch, snarling at anyone who comes near, and eating out of garbage cans.

Sarah finds out about all this and is furious. She tells Karl he can take the catcoons and stuff them in his ear. Tell Sarah what her contract rights are.

4. Dixon & Flagel Ltd. manufactures chemicals. Calder's Chemical Supply Inc. is one of its customers. To finance the purchase of its chemical inventory, Calder's enters into inventory financing agreements with Dixon & Flagel for each order of chemicals. On February 1, Dixon & Flagel delivers an order to Calder's. Under the inventory financing agreement, Calder's is to pay Dixon & Flagel the sum of $14,000 over a period of six months for the chemicals.

On February 10, Calder's discovers that some of the chemicals are defective and demands a refund in the amount of $6,500. On March 1, Dixon & Flagel assigns the contract to Capital Financing Corp. Capital Financing gives Calder's notice in writing of the assignment on March 5. On March 15, Dixon & Flagel delivers another order of chemicals to Calder's. The cost of the second order is $8,000, to be paid over six months. When delivering the second order, Dixon & Flagel damages Calder's loading dock, which costs Calder's $1,500 to repair. Calder's refuses to pay for any of the chemicals until Dixon & Flagel pays the demanded refund and pays for the damage to the loading dock. What options do the parties in this situation have?

Contract Interpretation

6

LEARNING OUTCOMES

Introduction 130	After completing this chapter, you should be able to:
Contract Provisions: Representations, Terms, Conditions, and Warranties 131	• Describe the goal of contract interpretation.

Introduction 130

Contract Provisions:
Representations, Terms,
Conditions, and Warranties 131

The Search for Certainty:
The Parol Evidence Rule, Its
Exceptions, and Rectification 134

Exclusion and Penalty Clauses 139

Frustration 148

Chapter Summary 156

Key Terms 156

Review Questions 156

After completing this chapter, you should be able to:

- Describe the goal of contract interpretation.

- Distinguish among representations, terms, conditions, and warranties.

- Explain the parol evidence rule and describe the exceptions the courts have developed with respect to the relevance and admissibility of outside evidence in interpreting a written contract.

- Understand the legal rules relating to exclusion (exemption) and penalty clauses.

- Explain the concept of frustration as it relates to contracts, and the common-law and statutory remedies that apply.

Introduction

Every contract case that comes to court does so either because one party disagrees with the other about what the contract provisions mean, or because he or she knows very well what the provisions mean and seeks to escape the consequences of that meaning. In either situation the case will turn on the court's interpretation of the language of the agreement. Over the centuries, the courts have established rules about classifying contract provisions to determine their consequences, resolving ambiguity or uncertainty, and determining the consequences of attempts to use language to limit the negative consequences of a contract for a party.

The primary aim of the court is to interpret contracts so as to find and give effect to the intention of the parties—that is, to make the contract work. In doing this the court may pay some attention to commercial realities, but generally will not use the rules of interpretation to remake a bad bargain. Instead, it will try to interpret a contract to salvage it, in whole or in part, and make it work as it thinks the parties intended. Where a provision is found to be so incoherent as to be impossible to interpret in a reasonable way, the court may determine it to be void for vagueness but will try to save the balance of the contract. Only as a last resort will the court declare a whole contract void because its meaning and purpose are uncertain, or because the original purpose is impossible to carry out.

This does not mean a court will never intervene to declare a contract to be void or voidable. It may do so where one or both parties have made a major mistake about an important element of the contract. Mistake and its effects are discussed in Chapter 4, Contractual Defects. Where contract performance becomes impossible because of circumstances beyond the control of either party, the court may find that the contract is frustrated, and bring it to an end. The court will also intervene where one side has engaged in fraud, misled the other party, or exercised some kind of undue influence arising from the nature of the relationship or the relative bargaining positions of the parties. These issues are discussed in Chapter 3, Protecting Weaker Parties, and in Chapter 4, Contractual Defects.

In this chapter, we will introduce some of the major concepts used by courts to interpret contracts:

- *Classifying contract provisions:* We will examine how the courts classify and interpret representations, terms, conditions, and warranties in a contract in terms of the effect those provisions have on the rights and responsibilities of the parties.

- *Assessing evidence to prove the meaning of a provision:* We will look at the search for certainty and the way in which the courts assess evidence using the parol evidence rule to decide the meaning of an unclear term or provision.

- *Interpreting exclusion and penalty provisions:* We will examine how the courts interpret exclusion and penalty clauses—provisions that seek to enhance or limit liability and damages under a contract when there is a breach.

- *Determining frustration:* Last, we will examine how courts determine when and how a contract may become frustrated so that it has become impossible to perform due to circumstances beyond the control of either party.

Contract Provisions: Representations, Terms, Conditions, and Warranties

As a contract is being made, the parties may make a number of statements to each other. Some will be statements that are made in the course of negotiations, and some will be statements that are terms agreed to in the contract itself. It is not always clear whether a statement is part of the negotiating process or part of the contract itself. And when we determine that a statement is part of the contract, we have to then determine what the effect of the contract statement means in terms of consequences for the parties, particularly if there is a breach of contract.

We must first consider whether a statement is a **representation** or a term of the contract. If a statement is a representation, it is not a part of the contract that either party has agreed to. Instead it is classed as a statement made by one party during negotiation of the contract. Representations are important in contract law because some misrepresentations may permit the party who is misled to avoid the contract. To have this effect, a representation must be a statement of fact, not opinion, and must be material; that is, a **material representation** is one that induced the other party to enter into the contract. Misrepresentation is discussed in more detail in Chapter 4, Contractual Defects.

representation
a statement made to induce someone to enter into a contract

material representation
a statement of fact, not opinion, made by one party, of sufficient weight to induce the other party to enter into the contract

---

EXAMPLE

Representation

Alphonse is looking for a load of Freestone peaches for his jam factory. Freestone peaches have the right texture, and it is crucial that the peaches be of that type. Bertrand has a warehouse full of peaches he wants to sell. Alphonse asks Bertrand, "Are these Freestone peaches?" If Bertrand says "yes," that is a material representation. If Bertrand says, "I think so," that is merely his opinion and not a material representation. If Bertrand says, "Peaches have lots of vitamins," that is not a material representation because the presence or absence of vitamins is not important to Alphonse in making peach jam. It would not influence him in deciding whether to enter into a contract with Bertrand.

If a statement related to a contract is not a representation, it may be a **term**. A term is part of the contract itself, an element of what one party or the other has promised. Terms fall into two categories.

1. If the term of the contract is essential or goes to the root of a contract, it is called a **condition**.

2. If the term is a minor or subsidiary term of the contract, it is called a **warranty**.

Whether a term is a condition or a warranty determines what the effect will be if it is breached. A breach of condition is considered so serious as to destroy the value

term
a provision of a contract; terms are either conditions or warranties

condition
an essential term of a contract, the breach of which denies the innocent party the benefit of the contract, or defeats the purpose of the contract

warranty
a minor term of a contract, the breach of which does not defeat the purpose of the contract

Reliance on Material Representation

Hirsch v. duBrule, [2006] A J No. 1712 (Prov. Ct.)

Facts

The plaintiff was a young woman with thinning hair. She decided to purchase a hair replacement system from the defendant. In the course of discussions, the defendant represented to her that he would be able to match her hair, or that even if he could not exactly match her hair, he would provide her with a hair replacement system she would be happy with. The contract itself, however, contained, among others, the following two clauses:

10. I [the Plaintiff] acknowledge that the Company's literature, and consultation were, and are, intended to familiarize me with the basic methods of hair replacement available today and, in particular, the unique attributes of the Company's method. I realize that the Company's statements describing the benefits and attributes of the System using the method are accurate when related to the average client but are not necessarily accurate with respect to each individual client. …

14. This document alone contains my entire agreement with the Company. Any promises, inducements, or agreements not set forth in this agreement, whether oral or written, shall have no force or effect.

Decision

The court found that the initial statement made by the defendant was a pre-contract representation and that it strongly influenced the plaintiff to purchase the hair replacement system. The court also found that the hair replacement was not a good match and that it failed to meet the promise in the pre-contract representations.

The question then was whether the two clauses overrode any representations made. On their face they clearly did. However, the court held that where a disclaimer clause in a contract clearly contradicts a pre-contract representation, then the disclaimer clause or any clause limiting liability must be clearly brought to the attention of the other party. If it is not, then the contract provision is of no effect. Consequently, the plaintiff was entitled to rescission of the contract and the return of the price paid.

Practical Tip

If you make representations, you may avoid being bound by them if you qualify them. Statements such as "To the best of my knowledge," "As far as I can tell," or "So far as I know" may assist if you made some attempt to inform yourself and if the representations were not fraudulent. Also, putting disclaimers in large type and simple language in a written contract can help support an argument that you brought the disclaimer to the other party's attention.

of the contract for the victim of the breach so that he or she is deprived of most or all of the value of the contract. If the breach is one of warranty only, it is adjudged less serious, and the remedies may be more restricted than would be the case for breach of condition. Determining whether a term is a condition or a warranty is not always easy. You have to examine the contract as a whole, as well as the context in which the agreement was made, including what representations and statements the parties made during negotiations. What may be a breach of condition in one case may be a breach of warranty in another, depending on the circumstances. The effects of breach of condition and breach of warranty are discussed in more detail in Chapter 8, Breach of Contract and Remedies.

EXAMPLE

Conditions and Warranties

Mai Ling signed an agreement to purchase the latest model of a Zephyr sports car. The model she chose was fast and manoeuvrable, and this was important because she drove from Toronto to Montreal every weekend to visit her boyfriend. She chose green for the exterior colour. The car that was delivered was a different model from what she ordered, although it was green. This would be a breach of condition because the car itself, the subject matter of the contract, was quite different from what she bargained for. Had the right model been delivered but in the wrong colour, the colour would likely have been a breach of warranty, because the colour was not her primary concern.

If Mai Ling had contracted to have her house painted and chose green, and the house was painted purple, the difference in colour would amount to a breach of condition. Here, colour would be a key and essential part of the contract, rather than a subsidiary consideration.

CASE IN POINT

Breach of Warranty Does Not Void the Contract

Herron v. Hunting Chase Inc., 2001 ABQB 1134 (CanLII), 2003 ABCA 219 (CanLII)

Facts

The plaintiffs agreed to sell shares of their company, Chase Manufacturing, to the defendant Hunting. The agreement provided that the plaintiffs' retained earnings would be $200,000 at the time of closing, and that Hunting would pay the plaintiffs certain bonuses.

At closing, the retained earnings did not total $200,000 and Hunting did not pay the bonuses. The plaintiffs sued, seeking payment of the bonuses pursuant to the agreement. Hunting argued that the fact that the plaintiffs had failed to retain the $200,000 excused it from having to pay the bonuses. The trial judge agreed. He found that Herron's failure with respect to the retained earnings was a breach of an essential condition, not a mere breach of warranty, and this entitled Chase to repudiate or rescind the contract. The plaintiffs appealed.

Decision

The appeal was allowed on several grounds. On the issue of whether the breach was one of condition or warranty, the court held that it was a breach of warranty so that the breach of the retained earnings provision was not one that entitled the defendants to repudiate the contract. That being the case, as the contract was not void, on the separate issue of the bonuses, Hunting should have paid the bonuses and Hunting was therefore liable to the plaintiffs for the amount of the bonuses.

Practical Tip

In drafting a contract, you may wish to identify specific terms as being conditions or warranties, and spell out the consequences for breach of both, including clauses to limit liability.

Terms of a Contract

Warranty	Condition
• term of lesser importance (minor or subsidiary)	• important term that is essential and goes to the root of the contract
• breach does not defeat the purpose of the contract	• breach deprives the injured party of most or all of the value of the contract
• if breached, injured party can sue for damages, but the contract is not over	• if breached, injured party can sue for damages, and the contract is ended
• injured party must still perform his or her obligations	• injured party is discharged from the contract
• example: agreement for sale of home—warranty that the basement is dry, with no leaks	• example: agreement for sale of home—conditional on being zoned as a two-family residential property

The Search for Certainty: The Parol Evidence Rule, Its Exceptions, and Rectification

Where an oral contract exists, you can imagine how the parties might get into a disagreement about the terms, each party relying on his or her memory as to what was agreed to and remembering the terms of the contract differently. However, when the contract is in writing, it is reasonable to expect that a dispute about its terms can be settled by looking at what is written, and by giving the language used in the contract its plain and ordinary meaning when interpreting the terms. It is also reasonable to say that if the contract is in writing, the parties should not be able to drag in other evidence, oral or written, to contradict the written terms of the agreement.

parol evidence rule
if a contract is in writing and is clear, no other written or oral evidence is admissible to contradict, vary, or interpret the agreement

This is the approach that the common law takes in interpreting written contracts. The approach is expressed in the **parol evidence rule**, which states that if the contract is in writing and the language of the written agreement is clear and unambiguous, then no other oral or written evidence can be used to interpret, vary, or contradict the terms of the written agreement. The court interprets the agreement by looking only at its written terms, and does not consider other evidence because it is not relevant to determining what the contract means.

Where a court finds that the language of a contract is unclear or ambiguous and applies the parol evidence rule, it has to consider whether there is evidence outside the written agreement that is relevant to interpreting the agreement. As a result of considering this outside evidence, the courts have developed several exceptions to the parol evidence rule where outside evidence may be deemed to be relevant and admissible in interpreting a written contract. These exceptions are as follows.

Exceptions to the Parol Evidence Rule

Exception	Explanation
Ambiguous contract language	If a term is unclear or uncertain, external evidence can be used to interpret it.
Essential collateral agreement	A contract separate from the one being considered that has some impact on the interpretation of the contract being considered can be introduced into evidence.
Essential implied term	Where a contract that by custom or convention contains a term that has been inadvertently left out, a party may produce outside evidence of custom or convention to show that a term has been left out by mistake.
Condition precedent existing outside the contract	If the parties agree that there is a condition precedent to the performance of the contract, then a party may introduce external evidence of the condition precedent where it is not specifically referred to in the contract.
Rectification	Where a term agreed to in negotiations is inadvertently omitted from the written document, a party may ask to have that term included by way of rectification, or correction of the document, provided • a mistake has been made in recording the intention of the parties, • there is evidence of a common intention, and • there is clear and cogent evidence of the mistake.

Ambiguous Contract Language

Where it can be shown that the language of the written agreement is unclear or ambiguous, so that the meaning of a term or provision is not certain, oral evidence or other written evidence may be used to assist in interpreting the agreement.

EXAMPLE

Ambiguous Language

A contract for membership in a professional organization has a term that says, "All members who are doctors and lawyers may vote at membership meetings." Fred argues that it is clear that a member must be a doctor *and* a lawyer to vote. Ginger argues that the language is ambiguous and that it could also mean members who are members of either the medical or the legal profession may vote. Ginger, by arguing that the language is ambiguous, may introduce evidence to show that only 2 of 700 organization members are members of both professions and that, in context, Fred's interpretation is nonsensical. Ginger, having argued ambiguity, is entitled to present evidence from outside the contract to resolve the alleged ambiguity. If the court decides that the evidence is relevant to proving that point, the evidence will be admitted to assist in interpreting the meaning of the contract notwithstanding the parol evidence rule.

Essential Collateral Agreement

A collateral agreement is a separate and independent contract with valuable consideration that could be enforced independently of the main contract or that has some impact or effect on the main contract, but is not specifically referred to in it. In this case, the court, by giving effect to the collateral contract, will modify the main contract, despite its written terms.

EXAMPLE

Essential Collateral Agreement

Alberto agrees to purchase a boat from Marina's Marina. He decides he wants a fire control system installed in the boat. The contract for the purchase of the boat is in writing and sets out a price for the boat. It also states that "a fire control system is to be added," with the price to be added to the purchase price. Alberto and Marina then agree on the fire control system to be installed by Marina. Marina presents an invoice setting out the cost of the equipment plus labour for installation. Alberto says that he is not paying for the labour. He says that the contract for the purchase of the boat included the addition of the cost of the parts for the system, not its installation. Marina argues that the cost is the cost of the parts and includes the cost of installation. If the court finds the original purchase agreement unclear as to what "a fire control system is to be added" means, it may permit Marina to introduce evidence of the collateral agreement to provide and install the fire control system, in order to determine the meaning of the disputed term in the main contract.

Essential Implied Term

If the parties use a form of contract that by custom of a trade or by convention usually contains a term that has been inadvertently left out, a party may be able to use oral and written evidence of the custom or convention to show that an implied term of the agreement has been left out.

EXAMPLE

Essential Implied Term

Kris orders a load of grade A lumber from the building supply company to be delivered to a lot where Kris is building a house. The lumber is loaded on the truck but gets rained on and warps prior to delivery. Kris complains about the quality. The building supply company says, "You ordered grade A lumber, you got grade A lumber. The contract didn't say anything about the state of the goods on delivery." If it is a custom of the building supply business to deliver supplies as ordered in good condition, Kris may be able to use oral or written evidence to show that this is an implied term of the written contract and that the court should "read" the implied term into the written agreement.

Condition Precedent Existing Outside Contract

Parties to a contract may also separately agree that the contract does not have to be performed until after a particular event, called a **condition precedent**, has occurred. If so, a party who claims that he or she is not obliged to honour the written contract because the condition precedent has not occurred may advance oral and written evidence of non-performance of the condition precedent to contradict the terms of the written agreement.

condition precedent
an event (or non-event) that must occur (or not occur) before a contract can be enforced

---

EXAMPLE

Condition Precedent

Ivan and Nan agree by written contract that Ivan will sell his car to Nan for $3,000. Nan tells Ivan before she signs that first she will have to see if she can borrow the money from the bank; if she cannot borrow the money, she says she will not be able to buy the car. Ivan orally agrees and Nan signs. Nan is unable to borrow the money, and Ivan says she is bound by the written contract. Nan may be able to contradict the written terms of the contract by producing written or oral evidence that there was a condition precedent that makes the written sale contract unenforceable.

Rectification

Rectification is an equitable remedy available to alter the terms of a written agreement where a mistake has been made in the document. It is available in circumstances where the common law might not permit altering the written terms.

The right to this remedy arises where the parties to the contract have held long negotiations and have reached an agreement that is reduced to a written document where a mistake was made recording the terms. Consequently, the effect of the contract is quite different from what was intended by the parties. Rectification does not alter the intention of the parties. Rather, it ensures that the wording of the written agreement accurately corresponds to what the parties intended to do. Rectification is a powerful remedy and is used with caution, because the courts watch carefully to ensure that it is not simply a cover for trying to undo a bad bargain. The court's focus is not on interpreting the terms of the contract (as is the case when the parol evidence rule is used) but on whether the terms the parties agreed to, whatever they are or however they are interpreted, are accurately reflected in the written contract.

For a party to successfully invoke the remedy of rectification, the party has to show the following with strong and clear evidence:

- *A mistake in recording the intentions of the parties.* The mistake must be clear and unambiguous. It must also be a mutual mistake—that is, both parties are mistaken, and both are mistaken in the same way. Some cases of unilateral mistake give rise to rectification but only in unusual circumstances, such as where a deed of gift has been used and the promisor unilaterally dictates the terms of the contract.

- *Formation of a common intention.* In Canada and England, even if no prior contract has been concluded to show that a mistake has been made, if there is strong and convincing evidence that the parties achieved a position where they had a common intention, that suffices for rectification where that common intention is not reflected in the final contract document.[1]

- *Clear and cogent evidence of a mistake.* There must be clear and convincing proof of a mistake in expressing the parties' intention. The evidence may be written or oral. The standard of proof required appears to be more than the usual civil standard in contract cases of proof on a balance of probabilities. The standard of proof may be as high as the criminal law standard of proof beyond a reasonable doubt, but there is some difference of opinion among commentators on whether the standard is as strict as that.[2] Clearly, if the case turns on oral evidence, the court is likely to scrutinize this evidence with great care to ensure that a claim for rectification is not an attempt to remake a bad bargain.

Remember that since this is an equitable remedy, it is subject to the usual equitable bars or defences. Delay by the party claiming rectification may be seen as evidence of insincerity. Negative effects on third parties who are not party to the agreement but who rely on it may act as a bar to rectification. Attempts to carry out the agreement may be seen as accepting it as it stands, and rectification may then be refused. Also, if the parties cannot be restored to their original positions before making the agreement, rectification may be refused.

EXAMPLE

Request for Rectification

Woodlot Canada Ltd., in Newfoundland, enters into an agreement to ship lumber to Woodhouse Ltd., in England. There have been complex negotiations involving exchanges of faxes and emails, and eventually a formal written agreement is prepared and signed by both parties. The price agreed to is £40,000, as reflected in the negotiation correspondence. When the contract is printed, the price is listed as $40,000. Woodlot immediately applies to have the contract rectified. Woodlot argues that both parties intended the price to be in British pounds sterling (£), not dollars, that the recording of the price in the written contract as a dollar amount was a mistake in recording the terms of the contract, and that the evidence, in the form of negotiation correspondence, clearly indicates that the price should have been expressed in pounds sterling.

---

1 This is the statement of the law on this issue in the English Court of Appeal case *Joscelyne v. Nissen*, [1970] 2 QB 86 (CA). This decision has been followed in Canada.

2 G.H.L. Fridman, *The Law of Contract in Canada*, 3d ed. (Scarborough, ON: Carswell, 1994), 830-32.

Parol Evidence Admissible for Rectification of Ambiguous Terms

Certus Developments Inc. v. Strategic Equity Corp., 2006 ABQB 645 (CanLII)

Facts

The plaintiff, Certus, purchased certain lands from the defendant, Strategic Equity, in a commercial mall development. The transaction included a grant to the plaintiff of a right of way and easement over certain of the defendant's lands, to permit vehicles to come and go, and to permit use of parking areas by the plaintiff or its agents. At issue was whether Certus could construct parking facilities for its own use on the lands granted by easement. The defendant said the contract clearly did not contemplate more than the use of existing parking areas by the plaintiff, none of which was for its exclusive use. The plaintiff said that the contract was ambiguous on that issue, and extrinsic evidence should be allowed to prove the plaintiff's position, as an exception to the parol evidence rule.

The defendant pointed to section 1 of the agreement, which granted an easement to Certus "to pass and re-pass over the Easement Area on foot or by vehicle as may be reasonably required for purposes incidental to or necessary for ingress to and egress from the Certus Lands," an easement "not exclusive to Certus." Rather, under section 1, Strategic Equity "retains the right … to pass and re-pass over the Easement Area on foot or by vehicle as may be reasonably required for purposes incidental to or necessary for ingress to and egress from the Premier Lands and for the use, without charge, of all parking stalls located on the Easement Area." The defendant submitted that the agreement spoke for itself, and extrinsic evidence to vary or contradict the agreement was inadmissible, and the contract did not entitle Certus to build its own private parking on the lands subject to the easement.

Certus countered that the language of the agreement was ambiguous. In that regard, it noted that, regardless of section 1 of the agreement regarding Strategic Equity's retained rights of access, section 3 said that "for the better enjoyment of the easement granted to Certus, at its own expense Certus may construct from time to time … improvements upon the Easement Area," such as parking facilities. Thus, Certus submitted that the extrinsic affidavit evidence filed was admissible and was sufficient to interpret the agreement given the possible conflict of sections 1 and 3.

Decision

The court found that the terms of the contract were ambiguous and admitted affidavit evidence to clarify the terms, but found that the affidavit evidence was not credible and was of no real help to the plaintiff in support of its claim that it had a right to build its own parking facilities on the easement lands.

Practical Tip

Ensure that all terms of a contract regarding the parties' rights are set out clearly and unambiguously. Otherwise, outside evidence may be admissible to help interpret any terms that are unclear.

Exclusion and Penalty Clauses

Exclusion (Exemption) Clauses

Sometimes a party will insist on including in a contract an **exclusion clause**, also called an **exemption clause**, that protects that party from liability for negligence in performing contractual obligations or for failing to carry out contractual obligations. For example, most parking lot contracts include a clause that states that the lot owner is not liable for damage to your car or its contents, or for theft of the car or contents, however the damage is caused. In other contracts, the clause limits liability. For example, if you buy a roll of film that includes developing the pictures you take, the contract is likely to include a clause that says if the company loses or damages

exclusion/exemption clause
a clause in a contract that limits the liability of one of the parties

the film or fails to develop it, it is liable only for the cost of the film, even if you are a professional photographer and your pictures are worth thousands of dollars. Generally, a party to a contract who wishes to limit liability for negligent conduct or for conduct where that party is liable though not at fault may limit liability, provided both parties agree to a limited liability clause in the contract. It is clear, however, that fraud by the party relying on an exclusion clause will not be excluded no matter what the clause says. An exclusion clause may not apply to other breach situations, although the law in this area in Canada has recently changed, and will be discussed later in this section.

Notice of an Exclusion Clause

For an exclusion clause to operate, the party relying on it must be sure to bring the clause to the other party's attention and notice. The act of giving notice must include reasonable steps to draw the clause to the other party's attention. If, for example, the clause is buried in fine print on the back of the contract, even if the other party has accepted the contract and it is otherwise binding on him or her, he or she may be able to show that the placement of the clause does not constitute reasonable steps to bring it to his or her attention. These clauses are often inserted by the party relying on them in printed form contracts or documents that are separate from but part of the contract, such as parking lot, film-processing, and dry-cleaning receipts. In these cases, the courts have required that the party relying on the clause demonstrate that the other party knew the clause was there or had ample opportunity to know it was there. For example, if a parking lot posts a large, illuminated sign that sets out the liability exclusion in plain language in large print right where you drive into the lot and pay, that may be a reasonable way of giving the necessary notice. So may printing the clause on the contract in plain language and in larger print of a different colour from that of the rest of the contract. Where the exclusion clause is referred to on the contract but posted elsewhere—for example, on a receipt—that may be insufficient to constitute proper notice of the clause.

Generally, the courts will carefully examine how notice was given. They are reluctant to permit a party to contract out of his or her own negligence, particularly where bargaining power is unequal, as it often is with printed form contracts, where negotiation of the terms at the time you park your car, for instance, is simply impractical.[3] However, where the contracting parties have roughly equal bargaining power, where there is time to consider the terms carefully, and where both parties are independently advised, the courts are more likely to let the clause stand on the ground that, with equality of bargaining power, the exclusion clause is not unilaterally imposed on one party by the other.

The courts have also made it clear that notice must be given before the contract is entered into, not afterward.[4] However, express notice need not be given in every

---

3 *Browne v. Core Rentals Ltd.* (1983), 23 BLR 291 (Ont. HC); *Tilden Rent-A-Car Co. v. Clendenning* (1978), 83 DLR (3d) 400 (Ont. CA).

4 *Campbell v. Image*, [1978] 2 WWR 663 (BC Co. Ct.); *Mendelssohn v. Normand Ltd.*, [1970] 1 QB 177.

case, particularly where both parties are relatively sophisticated and are experienced with the type of contract in question, or are knowledgeable about the practices and conventions in a particular trade. For example, in one case an owner of goods sued when the goods were damaged by the shipper. The evidence showed that the plaintiff had worked in the shipping industry and was familiar with the standard form shipping contract, which contained a standard exclusion clause. The court held that while the plaintiff was not given express notice of the clause, he certainly was aware of the existence of the clause and what it meant from his experience in the industry.[5]

Strict Interpretation

If the court is satisfied that the party relying on the clause gave appropriate notice, the court may interpret the clause narrowly against the person relying on the clause. In particular, the ***contra proferentem* rule** of interpretation may be used so that the party relying on the exclusion clause must show strict compliance with the contract. For example, if a parking lot contract excludes liability for theft or damage to the car by the parking lot company, but damage is done by an employee and not by the company, the clause might not operate to exclude liability. For that to happen, the clause would also have to include a phrase that excluded liability caused by the owner or by the negligent acts of employees. Similarly, if such a clause had been drafted, it would not exclude liability if the damage was intentionally done by the employee, because only negligence is excluded. The clauses are construed narrowly against the person who inserted them in the contract and relies on them.

When an employee or agent of the contracting party relying on an exclusion clause causes harm, it is clear that there must be explicit language to cover the act if the party relying on the clause is to escape liability. If the clause does not cover employee or agent negligence, then the contracting party who is the principal or employer is liable for the employee's or agent's negligence. What is not so clear is whether the employee is protected by the employer's exclusion clause if the employer's contract covers employee negligence when the employee is not a party to the contract. Normally, strangers do not acquire rights under a contract because they are not parties and because they gave no consideration. Therefore, while the employer may not be liable for an employee's negligence, an employee may have to deal with personal liability issues if his or her acts caused damage to the employer's customer.

The courts, while acknowledging the need for strict construction of exclusion clauses, are uneasy about a result where liability is shifted from the employer to the employee, who is least likely to be able to bear the financial burden of covering the loss. The courts have dealt with employee liability in two ways. First, they have relied on agency law, where the employer is seen as an agent of the employee, contracting on the employee's behalf as well as his or her own, when employee acts are covered by the exclusion clause. This effectively prevents the injured party from pursuing either the employer who prepared the contract or the employee on whose behalf the employer negotiated the exclusion clause.[6] Second, in Canada, the Supreme Court

> **TIP**
>
> If you are drafting an exclusion clause, use larger print, use a different colour, place the clause in a text box, or otherwise visually draw the attention of the other party to the clause—these are explicit and visible signs of having given the party notice.

> *contra proferentem* rule
> a rule used in the interpretation of contracts when dealing with ambiguous terms according to which a court will choose the interpretation that favours the party who did not draft the contract

---

5 *Captain v. Far Eastern Steamship Co.* (1978), 97 DLR (3d) 250 (BCSC).

6 *New Zealand Shipping Co. v. A.M. Satterthwaite and Co.*, [1974] 1 All ER 1015 (PC).

has focused on the special nature of the employer–employee relationship and the way in which that relationship should be affected by the exclusion clause.

In *London Drugs Ltd. v. Kuehne & Nagel International Ltd.*,[7] the corporate defendant stored a transformer for the plaintiff. The defendant's contract excluded liability for any amount over $40 unless the plaintiff paid a surcharge. The plaintiff declined to pay the surcharge. The defendant's employees, in moving the transformer, damaged it. The plaintiff sued the corporate defendant and its employees. The trial court held that the corporate defendant was protected by the exclusion clause and was liable for $40, but, strictly interpreting the clause, the employees were liable for the full amount of the plaintiff's loss on the ground that they were not covered by the clause. In the Supreme Court of Canada, the majority held that the employees were covered by the exclusion clause, allowing for a relaxation of the strict construction rule for third parties who are agents of the contracting party relying on the clause. Iacobucci J, however, focused on the special relationship of employer–employee and the common interest both have in performing the employer's contractual obligations. In the view of Iacobucci J, if the customer knows that the employer's obligations are to be carried out by employees and the contract has a term limiting liability of the employer for work to be done by employees, it is not sensible to uphold the strict privity of contract rules, which will result in employees shouldering the whole liability burden. In these circumstances, the customer has notice of the risks that he or she is running as a result of the exclusion clause. However, before an employee can shelter under the clause, the clause must extend explicitly to employees and the employee must show that he or she was acting in the course of employment and engaged in providing the very services covered by the contract between the employer and the employee. The effect of this decision is to create a narrow protective right for third parties and a limited exception to the normal privity rules.

Exclusion Clauses, Fundamental Breach, and Tercon v. British Columbia

In England, the courts developed a limitation of the application and operation of exclusion clauses in circumstances where the exempted conduct or act amounted to more than a breach of a minor term, but was a fundamental breach of the contract, where the breach went to the "root" or "heart" of the contract. Determining whether a breach was fundamental was not always easy. If you contracted to ship goods and the shipper negligently allowed them to be destroyed, you could argue that the contract was about shipping goods and their destruction was a fundamental breach, since the subject matter of the contract had been lost. Similarly, where the goods were slightly damaged in transit, it would be hard to argue that the breach was more than minor. The problem with fundamental breach is that it is difficult to determine where the line between these two extremes lies: where a breach goes from minor—where exclusion clauses apply—to major—where the breach is so enormous that the exclusion clause cannot be relied on.

---

7   *London Drugs Ltd. v. Kuehne & Nagel International Ltd.* (1992), 97 DLR (4th) 261 (SCC). See in particular the decision of Iacobucci J. For a further discussion of this case see Fridman, *supra* footnote 2, at 586-88.

The courts in Canada and England have gone back and forth on the effect of fundamental breach on an exclusion clause, and the fortunes of fundamental breach have waxed and waned accordingly. The impact of fundamental breach and its effect on exclusion clauses was weakened considerably as a result of the decision of the Supreme Court of Canada in *Hunter Engineering Co. v. Syncrude Canada Ltd.*[8] After a major review of the cases and the issue, the Court was split, taking two different approaches: one approach applied the doctrine of fundamental breach and considered whether the breach undermined the entire contract so as to go to the root of the contract, in which case the exclusion clause did not apply; the other approach found fundamental breach to be an artificial doctrine that creates unnecessary complexities and uncertainty in the law. If unfairness resulted from applying an exclusion clause, it would be better to simply address the matter as an issue of unconscionability.[9] As a result of the Court's split in this case, the future of fundamental breach became very uncertain.

That uncertainty came to an end with the decision of the Supreme Court of Canada in *Tercon Contractors Ltd. v. British Columbia (Transportation and Highways)*,[10] in which the Supreme Court abandoned fundamental breach altogether as a tool for determining whether a party could rely on an exclusion clause. The facts of the case are set out in the Case in Point below.

The problem with fundamental breach was put succinctly and clearly by Binnie J:

> On this occasion we should again attempt to shut the coffin on the jargon associated with "fundamental breach." Categorizing a contract breach as "fundamental" or "immense" or "colossal" is not particularly helpful. Rather, the principle is that a court has no discretion to refuse to enforce a valid and applicable contractual exclusion clause unless the plaintiff (here the appellant Tercon) can point to some paramount consideration of public policy sufficient to override the public interest in freedom of contract and defeat what would otherwise be the contractual rights of the parties.

As an alternative to using fundamental breach as a method of determining whether an exclusion clause was enforceable, the Court set out a three-part analytic scheme:

1. *Does the exclusion clause apply to the circumstances of the case?* The court must determine whether, as a matter of interpretation, an exclusion clause applies to the circumstances established by the evidence of what the parties intended—is the breach one that is contemplated by the exclusionary clause?

2. *If the clause applies, was it unconscionable?* If the exclusion clause does apply, the second issue is whether the exclusion clause, considering all of the circumstances, was unconscionable and therefore invalid at the time the

---

8   *Hunter Engineering Co. v. Syncrude Canada Ltd.* (1989), 57 DLR (4th) 321 (SCC).

9   For a more detailed review of the fortunes of the doctrine of fundamental breach in recent case law, see Fridman, supra footnote 2, at 588-600.

10   *Tercon Contractors Ltd. v. British Columbia (Transportation and Highways)*, 2010 SCC 4 (CanLII).

Public Policy Consideration Prevents Enforceability of Exclusion Clause

Tercon Contractors Ltd. v. British Columbia (Transportation and Highways), 2010 SCC 4 (CanLII)

Facts

The province of British Columbia solicited expressions of interest for the design and construction of a highway. This resulted in six teams making submissions. The province subsequently decided to design the highway itself. Tercon and Brentwood had been shortlisted. The province had chosen Brentwood, but Brentwood turned out to be working in a joint venture with an unqualified bidder, so that its bid technically did not meet the requirements for the province's tendering contract. The province had therefore breached its own tendering contract by awarding the construction contract to an unqualified applicant. This and related conduct by the province constituted a breach of the implied contractual duty of fairness to bidders. Tercon sued to recover its tendering costs, and the province defended by relying on a broad exclusion clause.

At trial, the court found that the province had acted in a cavalier and grossly unfair manner, and that the unfair and improper conduct by the province was not contemplated by the parties to the tendering contract. The province, deprived of any reliance on the exclusion clause, was ordered to pay Tercon's damages for breach of the tendering agreement. The Court of Appeal set aside the decision, holding that the exclusion clause was clear and unambiguous and barred compensation for all defaults.

Decision

The Supreme Court of Canada allowed the appeal. Clear language would have been necessary to exclude liability for breach of the implied obligation, particularly in the case of public procurement. The Court rejected the idea that the exclusion clause contemplated improper conduct such as that engaged in by the province, particularly where the conduct struck at the heart of the integrity of a public tendering process.

Practical Tip

Draft exclusion clauses carefully, making sure to address in detail all conduct that may be contemplated. Note, however, that no matter how carefully drafted, such clauses may not protect you against unconscionable behaviour or behaviour against which public policy would not justify protection.

contract was made. The equitable doctrine of unconscionability in contract formation applies where one party takes unfair advantage of the lack of bargaining power of the other party. Finding the balance between unconscionability and hard bargaining is not easy, as the cases seem to often turn on a judge's subjective view of the circumstances surrounding the formation of a contract. You may wonder whether the problems with fundamental breach described by Binnie J are going to re-emerge in determining whether an exclusion clause is unconscionable.

3. *If the exclusion clause is held to be valid at the time of contract formation and applicable to the facts of the case, the court may consider whether the clause should be enforced based on public policy considerations.* The party seeking to avoid enforcement of the exclusion clause must demonstrate an abuse of freedom of contract that outweighs the public interest in the court enforcing contracts as made by the parties. The court noted that conduct approaching serious criminality (though not outright criminal) and obvious fraud are examples of conduct that would override freedom of contract and render an exclusion clause inoperable. As with the second step, this appears to open the door to subjective judgments about when public policy considerations would override freedom of contract.

Exclusion Clause

JoAnn parks her car in Wanda's Parking Lot. The following is printed on the back of the parking receipt: "Wanda is not responsible for loss or damage to your car due to the negligence of Wanda or her employees." Linh, one of Wanda's employees, loses her temper and wilfully bashes in the windshield of JoAnn's car. JoAnn sues Wanda for damaging her car. Wanda says she is not liable because she is exempt as a result of the liability clause.

The clause may not operate if JoAnn can show that she had no notice of the clause and that printing it on the back of the ticket did not constitute a reasonable step in bringing the clause to her attention before the contract was made. JoAnn may also argue that even if she had notice, the clause has to be construed narrowly—it exempts Wanda and her employees from negligence, but Linh's act was wilful and is not covered by the exclusion. JoAnn could also argue that even if Wanda is exempt, Linh is not because she was not a party to the contract and could not benefit from the exclusion. Against this, Linh might argue that if Wanda is covered Linh might also be, since Wanda could have excluded herself and, acting as Linh's agent, could have bargained an exclusion for Linh, as well. Alternatively, Linh could argue on the basis of Iacobucci J's reasons in *London Drugs* that JoAnn had notice that Wanda's employees would carry out Wanda's contractual obligations and that employees such as Linh are specifically covered by the clause. This argument might fall apart, of course, because Linh's wilful conduct was outside the exclusion clause in any event.

Penalty Clauses

Clauses in a contract that determine in advance the manner and amount of compensation to the injured party in the event of a specific type of breach are called penalty clauses or compensation clauses. The courts interpret these clauses very carefully, reserving the right to ultimately decide on damages to be awarded.

Penalty clauses are used in a variety of situations and usually take one of three forms.

- A clause that provides a very low amount of compensation for a specific harm done. This may be seen as an exclusion clause rather than one providing a penalty or compensation.
- A clause that prohibits the parties from suing for breach of contract to obtain damages and allows instead substitution of other goods or repairs.
- A clause that provides for the payment of a specific sum or forfeiture of a performance bond or other security, where the sum is expressed as a pre-assessment of the parties' loss from non-performance. This is sometimes referred to as a **liquidated damages clause**, where an amount is agreed to that will presumably cover the actual loss that is likely to occur.

A penalty clause that provides for a clearly inadequate amount for a loss is really an exclusion clause and is subject to controls imposed by the courts discussed in the

penalty clause
a term in a contract that imposes a penalty for default or breach

liquidated damages clause
a term in a contract that attempts to reasonably estimate the damages that will be suffered if the contract is breached

preceding section. A clause that limits the right to sue for damages and provides alternative remedies is also subject to court scrutiny on the issue of whether the clause provides adequate compensation. If a court finds that the clause provides inadequate remedies, the injured party may be able to sue for damages despite the clause.

The type of penalty clause that has attracted much court attention is one that provides for liquidated damages on breach. Here the issue is whether the amount forfeited really is designed to compensate for damages or whether it is in the nature of a penalty. If the amount is a real pre-estimate of damages made in good faith, the court will allow the clause to stand. However, if the amount claimed is out of proportion to the damages likely to be sustained, the court may perceive it as a penalty. If the court sees it as a penalty, the court is also likely to see it as a threat or form of coercion and is likely to prevent the party benefiting from the clause from relying on it. This type of compensation clause often sets out an amount to be paid "as liquidated damages and not as a penalty." The courts are not deceived by this phrase, or deflected from determining whether the amount really can be construed as damages or whether it constitutes a penalty. If it is determined to be a penalty, the court may provide relief to the party who is required to pay. The question whether a specific amount constitutes damages or a penalty must be determined on the facts of a particular case. Some reference points are as follows:

- If the amount is extravagant and unconscionable with regard to the maximum loss that could possibly follow from the breach, the clause is likely to be seen as a penalty clause.
- If the obligation requires payment of a certain sum and stipulates that if that sum is not paid, a much greater sum must then be paid, the clause is likely to be seen as a penalty clause.
- If there is only one event that triggers payment, the sum is likely to be seen as liquidated damages.
- If one sum is payable on any of several events occurring, some serious and others trifling, there is a presumption that the sum is a penalty. However, this may not be the case where it is difficult to prove or project the actual losses for any of the events.[11]

Generally, if the court determines that a sum is a penalty, it will not enforce the clause whether the clause withholds a payment or compels one to be made. The burden of proving a penalty lies with the person who alleges that it is a fact. However, where the court finds that the sum is a penalty, it may not interfere if the clause is not unconscionable or if it is protected by statute.[12] Where a clause has been found to require court intervention, the court may substitute a reasonable amount for the sum set out in the clause. It is not clear whether a clause that is found to be a penalty clause is simply void or not, but there are cases where the court has granted relief from forfeiture by relieving a party from having to pay the penalty, particularly where the clause has been found to be unconscionable.

---

11 *Dunlop Pneumatic Tyre Co. Ltd. v. New Garage & Motor Co. Ltd.*, [1915] AC 79 (HL).

12 *Dimensional Investments Ltd. v. R*, [1968] SCR 93.

EXAMPLE

Penalty Clause

Khan wants to have a marina showroom built by Fly By Night Construction. Khan is anxious to have the showroom completed and open by the Victoria Day weekend, because his most profitable season begins then. Based on past experience, he figures he will average about $10,000 a week in sales. Khan insists that Fly By Night substantially complete the building so that it can be opened by the Friday of the Victoria Day weekend. He also insists on a penalty clause in case the building is not completed on time, with Fly By Night paying $30,000 to Khan for each week after the deadline until the building is substantially completed. Fly By Night is three weeks late and objects to the clause, saying it is a penalty and not liquidated damages. The amount claimed is 200 percent more than the actual estimated damages and could be seen as a penalty, although Khan could argue that it is reasonable because actual losses are hard to estimate, and there may be other ancillary costs to Khan as well that cannot be anticipated. If Fly By Night is successful, the court could set an appropriate amount for damages, relieving Fly By Night of the obligation to pay a penalty.

CASE IN POINT

Penalty Amounts to Usurious Interest Rate

Garland v. Consumers' Gas Co., [1998] 3 SCR 112

Facts

Garland brought a class action against Consumers' Gas on the ground that its penalty for late payment violated the usury provisions of the *Criminal Code*. The penalty was imposed as a flat fee if payment was made after the due date. The fee was not subject to simple or compound interest, and had been approved by the utility's regulatory body after extensive hearings. Evidence showed that the fee was not onerous if the gas bill was paid long after it was rendered, but if the bill was paid only a few days after it was due, the late fee could amount to an interest rate of upwards of 60 percent, contrary to the *Criminal Code*. In this case it would also be well above the amount of any damages sustained by the gas company as a result of late payment.

Decision

The trial court dismissed Garland's action, and the Court of Appeal dismissed his appeal. However, a majority in the Supreme Court of Canada granted Garland's appeal and ordered a new trial. "Interest" in the *Criminal Code* is very broadly defined and can include penalties for late payment as in this case. However, not every late payment that goes beyond damages is necessarily a matter for the criminal law. The Court also noted that late payers were not encouraged to delay payments to reduce the impact of the penalty clause, and there was statistical evidence to show that most late payers paid up relatively quickly, resulting in the late payment charge on its face being not just a penalty, but possibly usurious.

Practical Tip

Some contracts include a clause such as "paid as damages and not as a penalty" in an attempt to avoid the court finding the sum to be punitive. This is unlikely to work if a party challenges it: the court will assess whether the payment approximates damages, so it would be wise when using such a clause to provide for a fair and reasonable amount.

Frustration

doctrine of frustration
of contract
a legal doctrine that
permits parties to a
contract to be relieved of
the contractual obligations
because of the occurrence
of some event beyond
their control that makes
it impossible for them to
perform the contract

A contract may become impossible to perform through no fault of either party. In some situations the court invokes the **doctrine of frustration of contract**, declaring that the contract has been frustrated and that the parties to it should be relieved of their obligations under it. The doctrine of frustration began to develop only in the 19th century. At common law, before this time, parties who made promises were expected to remain bound to carry out the terms of the agreement no matter what. The contractual promise was seen as absolute, and impossibility of performance did not excuse the obligation of performance unless the parties explicitly provided for a termination of the contract because of impossibility. For example, if Mona engaged a famous portraitist, Leon, to paint her portrait, the contract might set out what would happen if Leon died before finishing the painting. In this situation, the parties might decide to terminate the contract, because Mona may not have wished to have a lesser painter complete it, and Leon might not want his estate to be bound by an obligation to find someone to complete the work.[13]

However, by the 19th century, in cases where no explicit provision was made to terminate because of impossibility of performance, the courts in some circumstances began to imply terms permitting termination on the ground of impossibility. This marked the beginning of the development of the doctrine of frustration of contract, in which the courts held that in some circumstances the occurrence of certain events beyond the control of the parties made it impossible to perform the contract.

Factors Affecting Frustration of Contracts

The following are some of the situations that can lead to a finding that a contract has been frustrated:

force majeure
a major event that the
parties to a contract did not
foresee or anticipate that
prevents performance of
the contract and thus terminates the contract; such
an event—for example, a
natural disaster or war—is
outside the control of the
parties and cannot be
avoided with due diligence

- The impossibility arises from an act of some third party.
- The impossibility arises from some natural or external force: fire, flood, earthquake, weather, or other **force majeure**.
- The impossibility cannot be prevented by the parties and is beyond their control.
- The impossibility is not, directly or indirectly, brought about by the party who is arguing that the contract has been frustrated.
- The impossibility is caused by the death or serious physical incapacity of a party where a personal attribute of that party was required to perform the contract—for example, where the party was obliged to compose a piece of music and had been chosen for his or her particular skills.
- The impossibility is caused by the subject matter of the contract ceasing to exist—for example, where a theatre is leased for a concert, burns down, and is no longer available.

---

13 *Paradine v. Jane* (1647), 82 ER 897.

- The impossibility is caused by a change in the law that is not contemplated by the parties.
- The impossibility is caused by serious delay that is not caused by or contemplated by the parties.

Frustration Based on Implied Term Theory

The courts used two approaches to develop the law of frustration of contract:

- the assumption of an implied term of the contract permitting termination, and
- the construction of the purpose of a contract to decide whether the contract could be terminated because the purpose could not be fulfilled.

In the implied term approach, the term can be seen as a condition precedent to performance of a contract. For example, if A rents a theatre from B for a performance and the theatre burns down so that it is impossible for A and B to carry out their contractual obligations, the court might see the existence of the theatre as an implied condition precedent to performance of the contract by either party, even though the parties made no explicit provision for this possibility.[14] In other cases, other suitable terms have been implied to deal with the frustration of a contract by the occurrence of some event neither party explicitly contemplates, but which clearly makes impossible the performance of the contract the parties agreed to.

The implied term approach rests on the idea that the contract the parties agreed to, by its nature, must have assumed or implied certain things or situations to exist in order for the contract to be performed. If the contract cannot be performed because some intervening event makes it impossible through no fault of the parties, then the contract can be seen to be frustrated because performance is no longer possible. The test for determining whether there is an implied term requiring discharge due to frustration is an objective "reasonable person" test rather than what the parties say they contemplated. If the contract has express terms for termination because of frustration, the courts will not imply a term for a situation not covered by the express term. In this situation, the courts hold that the parties, having directed their minds to include express terms, must have excluded any other basis for finding that the contract has been frustrated.[15]

Frustration Based on Construction Theory

Another approach the courts took in developing the doctrine of frustration was determining that a contract had become frustrated or impossible to perform because the very basis or purpose of the contract had ceased to exist; what remained

---

14   *Taylor v. Caldwell* (1863), 122 ER 309; *Appleby v. Myers* (1867), LR 2 CP 651. These cases were followed in Canada, starting with the Supreme Court of Canada decision in *Kerrigan v. Harrison* (1921), 62 SCR 374.

15   Fridman, supra footnote 2, at 640.

CASE IN POINT

Implied Term Approach Used to Relieve Party from Contractual Obligation Due to Frustration

Kerrigan v. Harrison, 1921 CanLII 6, 62 SCR 374

Facts

Kerrigan purchased two lots on Lake Erie from Harrison. As part of the sale, Harrison promised access to the lots via a road named Harrison Place, which ran along the lake. As the result of a storm, the shore was badly eroded and the road collapsed and disappeared into the lake. Kerrigan sued Harrison for damages and for an order requiring the repair of the road.

At trial, the defendant was ordered to restore the road or replace it with a new one that served the same purpose. On appeal to the Ontario Court of Appeal, the court held that Lake Erie was Crown property, and that as a result of erosion, the road and the land it stood on were in the lake and were therefore now Crown property, so that Harrison had no power or obligation to do anything.

Decision

The Supreme Court of Canada ruled in favour of Harrison, but focused on the doctrine of frustration: the parties had contemplated only that the specific road, Harrison Place, would provide a right of way, and it was an implied term that it would continue to exist; when it ceased to exist through no fault of either party in a situation not contemplated by them, Harrison's obligations to provide a right of way to Kerrigan were at an end.

Practical Tip

Where nature may play a role in the continued existence of the subject matter of a contract, although the courts may imply a term that the subject matter exists, you may wish to include a term that addresses the remedy, or lack thereof, should the subject matter be destroyed.

was not the contract the parties had agreed to or contemplated. In these cases, the courts subjectively tried to determine what the parties' "purpose of the adventure" or "common object of the agreement" was. Finding the common purpose of the parties involved a subjective analysis of what the parties actually said the contractual purpose was. If intervening events made fulfilling the contractual purpose impossible so that there was a radical change in the obligations of the parties, then the contract could be deemed to be frustrated, and the parties then would be relieved of their obligations to continue.[16]

The cases indicate that courts in both Canada and England are now more inclined to follow the construction theory. G.H.L. Fridman sets out some sound reasons why this should be so. His comments about the need to be realistic and practical rather than formulaic and overly abstract in interpreting contract problems apply to all areas of contract law, not just to the doctrine of frustration:

> What, then, is the purpose behind replacing the "implied term" theory ... by the "construction theory," with its emphasis on a radical change in the obligation? The answer seems to be the desire by courts to escape from ... the need for fictions, replacing them by a more realistic approach that provides an explanation of what

---

16   *Davis Contractors Ltd. v. Fareham Urban District Council*, [1956] AC 696 (HL); *Capital Quality Homes Ltd. v. Colwyn Construction Ltd.* (1975), 61 DLR (3d) 385 (Ont. CA).

the courts are truly performing rather than an explanation that employs such facile expressions and notions as "implied terms." To imply a term in order to resolve the issue is obviously legal sleight-of-hand, concealing what is really being done. To inquire into the true nature of the contractual obligation, for the purpose of discovering whether it is in conformity with that obligation that it can validly outlast and survive the change of circumstances that has occurred is more direct, honest, open, and rational. Such an approach is consistent with what has been happening generally in the law of contract, namely, the realization that contracts cannot be understood and interpreted except by reference to the surrounding circumstances.[17]

Distinguishing Between Impossibility and Frustration

In some cases the terms "impossibility" and "frustration" are used interchangeably, but they are not quite the same. "Impossibility" refers to situations where performance is physically or legally impossible. "Frustration" includes situations where performance is physically or legally possible but the results would be very different from the purpose of the contract that the parties had contemplated. Today, cases that deal with contract frustration have gone beyond the narrower concept of impossibility to include contracts that, while technically possible to perform, are in practical and commercial terms frustrated because the original contract purpose has disappeared.

> **TIP**
>
> In order to avoid frustration-of-contract situations—and also some of the situations that give rise to disputes about mistake in contract—try using a preamble to the contract, with "whereas" clauses setting out the nature and purpose of the contract and other useful background information.

EXAMPLES

Frustrated Contracts

■ Farah wants to buy a load of eggplants for processing. They must be very ripe and bought late in the season. Timothy agrees to supply them. There is an express provision discharging the contract if the goods are destroyed by hail or lightning. Before they can be harvested, there is a violent earthquake that creates a fault line that swallows up and destroys all the eggplants. Farah sues for breach of contract, and Timothy's response is that the contract has been frustrated by the destruction of the eggplants. The earthquake is an act of nature not caused by either party and wholly outside their control. While there is an express term contemplating discharge from frustration, it does not contemplate earthquakes, so that it could be said that the parties did not contemplate or foresee the cause of the destruction. Further, it could be said that the parties, knowing that eggplants are fragile, might have contemplated that the contract could not be carried out if the eggplants were destroyed, so an implied term permitting discharge might be found by a court. On the other hand, because the parties did make express provisions for discharge by frustration, by not including earthquakes it could be argued

---

17   Fridman, supra footnote 2, at 636-37.

that they did not intend to treat the contract as frustrated. However, if one analyzed the contract to determine what the parties intended, it could be said to be the delivery of eggplants. Where that was no longer possible, performance would be radically different from what was originally contemplated, and the contract therefore could be treated as discharged because doing what the parties intended was no longer possible.

■ The Prince of Ptomania is to be crowned king. Lady Hinkle rents rooms from Professor Baloneya along the coronation route at a very high price so that she can watch the coronation procession. Unfortunately, the week before the procession there is a revolution, and Prince Ptomania is overthrown and sent into exile. Baloneya demands payment, saying, "You rented rooms for the day, Hinkle—you have to pay." Hinkle's answer is that Baloneya knew the purpose of the rental, which was why the rent was so exorbitant. Since the purpose of the contract has ceased to exist, Hinkle says she should not have to pay; the contract has been frustrated and cannot be enforced.[18]

Common-Law Remedies for Frustration

At common law, when a contract was terminated because performance was frustrated, the position of the parties was crystallized or frozen. The cases left the loss where it fell at the time of crystallization. If one party had paid a deposit, it could not be recovered. If the other party had done some work, the cost could not be recovered. In this situation there might be a setoff, where a party could apply the deposit in his or her hands to compensate for the work he or she had done. But what of an executory contract? If a party had paid a contract price and the other party had done nothing, a windfall situation would be created for the party who was paid, while the other party was out of pocket with nothing to show for the payment. Furthermore, if money was due in advance and a frustrating event occurred, the money might still have to be paid if the due date occurred before the frustrating event.[19] The unfairness of this situation was addressed by the House of Lords in the case of *Fibrosa Spolka Akcyjna v. Fairbairn Lawson Combe Barbour Ltd.*[20] The court held that where there was a total failure of consideration due to frustration of the contract, parties were entitled to recover moneys paid before the crystallizing event, although the court did not allow the party who made the expenditures to carry out his or her obligations to recover money for those expenditures. While some later cases seem to be more flexible, allowing recovery on the basis of what is just and reasonable whether there was total failure of consideration or not,[21] the case law does not create much order or certainty. It has been left to the legislature to do what is necessary to create clear rules for compensation when a contract is frustrated.

---

18 For a similar decision, see *Krell v. Henry*, [1903] 2 KB 740 (CA).

19 *Chandler v. Webster*, [1904] 1 KB 493.

20 *Fibrosa Spolka Akcyjna v. Fairbairn Lawson Combe Barbour Ltd.*, [1943] AC 32 (HL).

21 *Cahan v. Fraser* (1951), 4 DLR 112 (BCCA).

Purpose of Contract Relevant to Determining Whether It Is Frustrated

Capital Quality Homes Ltd. v. Colwyn Construction Ltd., [1975] OJ No. 611; (1975), 61 DLR (3d) 385 (Ont. CA)

Facts

The plaintiff, Capital Quality Homes, had entered into an agreement with the defendant, Colwyn, to buy a large lot that had been divided into 26 parcels on which the plaintiff intended to build individual homes. At the time that the contract was entered into, the land was not subject to subdivision control, but just prior to the sale closing, the *Planning Act* was amended so that the lands could no longer be subdivided into 26 lots. The defendant argued that the plaintiff had purchased a piece of land, and that the defendant could convey it, so that the transaction was valid, and that land purchases were not subject to the doctrine of frustration, as the land could be conveyed. Whether the land could be later subdivided was neither here nor there. The plaintiff argued that both parties understood and contemplated that the land was being conveyed for the purpose of subdivision, and that as the legislative amendment had not been contemplated by the parties, the contract should be treated as frustrated. The trial judge held that the contract was frustrated and that the plaintiff was entitled to be returned to its pre-contract position with the return to it of the deposit.

Decision

The Court of Appeal upheld this decision; it decided that the doctrine of frustration could not be fixed or limited by mechanical or arbitrary rules, so that contracts involving the sale of land could be subject to the doctrine of frustration. The court noted that the doctrine was flexible, and instead of searching for implied terms, one should look at the contract as a whole to determine what the parties intended and then decide, as a result of the frustrating act, whether there was still a contract capable of fulfillment as originally contemplated by the parties. In this case, both parties knew this was a contract for the sale of land to be divided into 26 parcels; when that was no longer possible, the original purpose was gone and the contract was properly held to be frustrated.

Practical Tip

Including a clear statement of the purpose of a contract may help a party to argue frustration of contract where a change in the law makes performance impossible.

Apportioning Losses for Frustration at Common Law

Zora wants to build a house along a clifftop for the scenic view. She hires Tariq Contractors Ltd. to design and build the house. Tariq has completed the design and bought some custom building supplies when Zora is notified by the municipality that the zoning for the property is being changed to prevent her from building any structure on the land. She has paid Tariq a deposit of about 15 percent of the value of the work done and the materials supplied by Tariq.

At common law, once the contract is frustrated, the parties' positions are crystallized, and the losses lie where they fall. Tariq could keep the deposit but has to absorb losses for the work done and the materials supplied. Zora loses her deposit and is left with the vacant land.

Legislation Governing Frustration of Contracts

An act to deal with frustrated contracts was passed in England in 1943 and became the model statute for frustrated contracts legislation in all provinces except British Columbia and Nova Scotia. Ontario's *Frustrated Contracts Act* is typical of this kind

specific goods
specific, identifiable chattels that have been singled out for contract purposes

of legislation.[22] British Columbia has a modified form of the statute that is used in the other provinces.[23] Nova Scotia still relies on the common law. Where the contract concerns the sale of **specific goods**, except in British Columbia, the subject matter may be covered by the provincial *Sale of Goods Act* rather than by the common law or the provincial *Frustrated Contracts Act*.

Frustrated Contracts Act

The Act covers most but not all contracts. Among the exclusions are

- contracts governed by a specific statute that has frustration provisions, on the basis that a specific statute overrides the provisions in a general statute, such as the *Frustrated Contracts Act*;
- contracts where the parties have created express terms to deal with frustration;
- certain contracts for the carriage of goods by sea;
- insurance contracts;
- contracts for the sale of goods when the goods cease to exist before the contract is entered into without fault by either party and before risk passes to the buyer (this is likely to be a case of mistake, rather than frustration); and
- contracts where the goods cease to exist after the contract is entered into without fault by either party and before risk passes to the buyer.

The operation of the legislation is triggered when a contract that is governed by the law of the province where the *Frustrated Contracts Act* is in operation has become impossible to perform or has been frustrated, and the parties have been discharged from the further performance of the contract because of frustration or impossibility. The Act does not create rules for deciding *when* a contract is frustrated—that is still left to the case law. What the statute does is to regulate post-contract collapse recovery:

- Money that is paid before discharge is recoverable.
- Debts accrued but not yet paid are not to be paid.
- Total failure of consideration is not required. Even if some value was obtained, the contract can be terminated for frustration and parties may receive compensation.
- Where a party has incurred expenses to carry out the contract, the party may be allowed to keep part or all of a deposit paid by the other party, or to recover some or all of the expenses.
- The court is given a reserve power to apportion losses and benefits so that if one party receives some benefit, where failure of consideration is not total, he or she will have to pay the other side a reasonable amount for that benefit.

---

22   *Frustrated Contracts Act*, RSO 1990, c. F.34.

23   *Frustrated Contract Act*, RSBC 1996, c. 166. Discussion in the text is based on the legislation in other provinces.

Sale of Goods Act

Where there is a contract for the sale of specific goods and the goods are destroyed after the contract was made but before risk passes to the buyer, either party may back out of the agreement. If the goods are not specific goods, are not destroyed, or are subject to express terms, or the risk has passed to the buyer, the parties have to look to the *Frustrated Contracts Act* or to common law for relief.

CHAPTER SUMMARY

The role of the court is to try to find and give effect to the intention of the parties to a contract when there is a dispute about its meaning or its consequences. The initial step is to classify contract statements. Representations, if factual and if they induce a party to enter into an agreement, may allow the injured party to avoid a contract if the representation is incorrect. Where there is a dispute about a term, if the term is a condition, it is deemed to be a serious provision affecting the principal purpose of the contract. If it is a warranty, it is deemed to be a subsidiary or minor provision for which the consequences for breach are less serious.

Where a contract is in writing, the courts normally interpret the words of the agreement and will not look at oral evidence of what the parties intended. However, where the language of the agreement is ambiguous, the court may use the parol evidence rule to hear oral or written evidence about what the parties intended. Where the terms of the written agreement are clear, but are the result of a mistake, the court may invoke the equitable remedy of rectification to correct the mistake.

Where parties have attempted to exclude liability, the court may intervene to relieve a party from the effects of an exclusion clause where one party has exempted himself or herself from liability or imposed a clause requiring one party to pay damages to the other for failure to meet contract terms. The courts interpret exclusion clauses strictly and limit their application. Damage or penalty clauses are also closely examined to see whether the fixed damage amount bears some resemblance to the actual damage done, and is not a penalty.

Sometimes a contract becomes impossible to perform through the happening of an event that is no fault of either party. In this kind of situation, the courts may hold that the contract is frustrated, relieving both parties of the obligation to continue performance from the time of the frustrating event, although both sides may have to bear their own losses and benefits under the contract from the time of frustration.

KEY TERMS

condition, 131
condition precedent, 137
contra proferentem rule, 141
doctrine of frustration of contract, 148
exclusion/exemption clause, 139

force majeure, 148
liquidated damages clause, 145
material representation, 131
parol evidence rule, 134
penalty clause, 145

representation, 131
specific goods, 154
term, 131
warranty, 131

REVIEW QUESTIONS

True or False?

_____ 1. Rectification is a remedy available to alter the terms of a written agreement where a mistake has been made in the document.

_____ 2. A warranty is a term of a contract, but a condition is not.

_____ 3. A party may avoid being bound by a representation that includes a qualification such as "So far as I know."

_____ 4. Stepan and Ali negotiate a contract for Ali to paint Stepan's house. Ali includes a clause that says he is not liable for damage to the property, however caused. The clause is written in small print, and Ali does not draw it to Stepan's attention. Stepan can argue that Ali should not be able to rely on the clause because it was not drawn to his, Stepan's, attention.

_____ 5. The *contra proferentem* rule of interpretation allows the courts to imply terms into the contract.

_____ 6. The *Frustrated Contracts Act* governs post-contract collapse recovery.

Multiple Choice

1. Idris asks Bihar, a peach wholesaler, whether the peaches she is selling are suitable for making jam. Bihar says, "I think so." Idris goes ahead and buys a bushel of peaches.

   a. Bihar's statement is a material representation.
   b. Bihar's statement is a condition.
   c. Bihar's statement is a warranty.
   d. Bihar's statement is a statement of opinion.

2. In the situation above, if Bihar was asked by Idris if the peaches were Freestone peaches and Bihar said yes, Bihar's answer would be

   a. a representation
   b. a warranty
   c. an offer
   d. a condition

3. The following is an exception to the parol evidence rule.

   a. the doctrine of *res ipsa loquitur*
   b. essential collateral agreement
   c. essential implied term
   d. b and c

4. Harrison and Benedek have been negotiating over the sale of a powerboat. There have been lengthy negotiations by email, and a price is agreed to of US$14,000. The printed contract records the price, in error, in Canadian dollars.

   a. Tough—the deal is in Canadian dollars as that is what the contract says.
   b. Evidence of the actual price can be introduced using the emails to rectify the error in the contract.
   c. As the parties have not reached agreement on price, there is no contract.
   d. None of the above.

5. Victoria's Secret Laundry's customer contracts contain a clause that says if it loses or damages any of the customer's garments, its liability for damages is limited to the price charged to the customer for doing the laundry, a cost of about $1.

   a. This is a penalty clause.
   b. This is a *contra proferentem* clause.
   c. This is an exclusion clause.
   d. a and c

6. At common law, if a contract was frustrated,

   a. the parties were entitled to recover expenditures made before the occurrence of the events that caused frustration
   b. each party absorbed any costs incurred up to the point where the contract was frustrated
   c. the party relying on the doctrine of frustration could not be the party who directly or indirectly caused the contract to be frustrated
   d. a and c

7. Suliman agrees to sell his car to Arturo for $2,000. The day before the car is delivered to Arturo, it is hit by lightning and destroyed. The contract is deemed to be frustrated as the purpose of the contract was for the sale of a car, and the car no longer exists through no fault of either party.

   a. This is an example of the construction theory of frustration of contracts.
   b. This is an example of the implied term theory of frustration of contracts.
   c. a and b.
   d. None of the above.

Short Answer

1. Why is distinguishing among representations, conditions, and warranties important?

2. What is the parol evidence rule, and what is its purpose?

3. In what circumstances can oral and other written evidence be used to interpret a written contract?

4. What is the effect of rectification on an agreement?

5. In what circumstances can a party to a contract successfully obtain the remedy of rectification?

6. Why is fundamental breach no longer the basis for barring the application of an exclusion clause? What has replaced it?

7. What are penalty clauses? What forms do penalty clauses take?

8. When might a court intervene with respect to the application of a penalty clause?

9. What sort of events give rise to a frustrated contract? What sort of events will not give rise to a frustrated contract?

10. Describe the theory of implied term and the theory of construction of a contract as they are used in frustration of contract cases. Which approach are courts likely to use now, and why?

11. What is the difference, if any, in the meaning of "impossibility" and "frustration" as those terms are used in frustration cases?

12. To what extent were the problems with common-law remedies overcome by

    a. the *Fibrosa* case,

    b. the *Frustrated Contracts Act*, and

    c. the *Sale of Goods Act*?

Apply Your Knowledge

1. Leah owns a motorboat specially equipped for fishing. In addition to the outboard engine, it has special seats, trolling rigs, and an electronic fishfinder. She offers to sell the boat with the motor to Tranh for $20,000. They also agree that the special seats, trolling rigs, and electronic fishfinder will be included for $2,000. The written agreement refers to the sale of a boat and motor with "fishing equipment" for $22,000, with a deposit of $2,000. Before the sale is completed Leah decides she would like to keep the fishfinder. When Tranh objects, Leah tells him they agreed to sell only what was specifically in the written agreement, and that the fishfinder is not included. Assess Tranh's chances of obtaining the fishfinder, and discuss his alternative remedies.

2. Extreme Skiing Company, a company that specializes in ski trips, offers a heli-skiing trip that involves a helicopter ride to a remote mountain slope. The price of $1,000 per person, which includes hotel, meals, and helicopter transportation, is advertised in a skiing magazine. In response to the advertisement, Allyson calls Extreme Skiing and agrees over the telephone that she and Matthias will join the trip. Extreme Skiing's representative says he will mail the enrollment forms to Allyson and Matthias. Allyson agrees that she and Matthias will meet the trip operators at the hotel the day before the trip. Two weeks before the trip date, Allyson and Matthias receive and complete the enrollment forms. They mail the forms back to Extreme Skiing along with the payment price. These are received by the company one week before the trip.

Allyson and Matthias go to the designated hotel the day before the trip. As they and the other eight participants assemble in the hotel lobby, the trip operators hand out forms entitled "Standard Release and Waiver of Liability" and ask each participant to sign one. The form states that Extreme Skiing is not responsible for any losses or damages suffered by the participants for any reason, including negligence on the part of the company.

Allyson and Matthias are reluctant to sign the form but are told that unless they do so they will not be allowed to go on the trip. Finally they sign the form. The next day, all the participants are taken by helicopter to the ski slope.

During the course of the ski trip, there is an avalanche and Allyson suffers a broken leg as a result. Matthias also loses all of his ski equipment. An investigation reveals that there had been an avalanche warning about the area into which the participants were flown, and that Extreme Skiing ought to have been aware of this warning.

What contract issues arise in this fact situation?

3. Employees of a contracting party need and deserve protection when damage occurs and an exclusion clause is invoked. Explain why employees might need protection and how the courts have approached this issue. (You may want to read *London Drugs Ltd. v. Kuehne & Nagel International Ltd.* (1992), 97 DLR (4th) 261 (SCC).)

4. Cleopatra wants to buy a load of grapes to make into wine. Antony agrees to supply what is required. Cleopatra inspects one of several of Antony's vineyards in Italy and likes what she sees. She specifies that the grapes should be selected from "those located on Antony's property" and that risk will pass to the buyer on delivery to Cleopatra at her processing plant in Alexandria. Antony accepts these terms. There is express provision discharging the contract if the grapes are destroyed by hail or go down in a sinking ship. Before they can be harvested, a severe heat wave ripens them too early. The grapes are good for nothing but vinegar. Cleopatra sues for breach of contract and Antony claims the contract is ended due to frustration. Set out arguments for and against each party's position.

Discharge of Contract

7

LEARNING OUTCOMES

Introduction 160

Discharge by Performance 160

Discharge by Agreement 163

Discharge as of Right 167

Discharge by Operation of Law ... 168

Chapter Summary 169

Key Terms 169

Review Questions 169

After completing this chapter, you should be able to:

- Explain what tender of performance and tender of payment mean.

- Describe the requirements of a waiver of a contract.

- Explain the effect of a material alteration of a contract.

- Explain the term "accord and satisfaction" as it relates to contract law.

- Distinguish between the terms "condition precedent" and "condition subsequent."

- Explain when contracts are discharged by operation of law.

Introduction

Once a contract has been **discharged**, the obligations under that contract are cancelled, and the contract itself is **null and void**.

Contracts may be discharged

- by performance,
- by agreement,
- as of right,
- by operation of law,
- by frustration, or
- by breach.

Frustration was discussed in Chapter 6, Contract Interpretation, and breach is discussed in Chapter 8, Breach of Contract and Remedies.

Discharge by Performance

The most common way to discharge a contract is by performing the obligations under the contract. Performance may consist of performing services, paying money, delivering goods, and so on. Offering to perform the obligations under a contract is called **tender of performance**. For the contract to be discharged, both parties must tender performance. However, if one party tenders performance and the other party does not accept it, the refusing party is in breach of the contract unless he or she has a valid and lawful reason for refusing to accept performance. At that point, the party who tendered performance need not attempt to tender performance again and may sue the other party for breach of contract. In addition, one party must not interfere with, hinder, or prevent the other party from tendering performance. Any hindrance can be treated by the tendering party as refusal and breach of contract.

EXAMPLE

Tender of Performance and Refusal

Susan and Tanya have a contract whereby Tanya has agreed to buy Susan's crop of tomatoes for an agreed-upon price. However, when the crop is ready, the price of tomatoes has dropped and Tanya no longer wants to buy Susan's tomatoes. She now wants to buy her tomatoes at a lower price from another farmer. Susan delivers the tomatoes to Tanya, but Tanya refuses to accept them. Susan has tendered performance, but Tanya has refused to accept it. Tanya is in breach of contract.

Note that tender of performance must be within the exact terms of the contract. If the performance tendered does not comply with the terms of the contract in any way, the other party need not accept it. Performance must be exactly as specified in the contract and must occur on the right date, at the right time, and in the right place.

EXAMPLE

Non-Complying Performance

Willem and Thomas have a contract whereby Thomas has agreed to buy 1,200 litres of molasses from Willem. The contract states that the molasses must be delivered in 80 15-litre containers. Willem delivers the molasses in 100 12-litre containers. Because the tender of performance does not comply with the terms of the contract, Thomas is not obligated to accept it. Even though the total amount of molasses delivered (1,200 litres) is correct, Willem did not perform his obligations and is in breach of contract.

Where the performance required of a party is the payment of money, this is called *tender of payment*. The precision required for the tender of performance also extends to the tender of payment. To comply with the terms of the contract, payment must be tendered either in **legal tender** or in the method specified in the contract, if any. If the contract states that payment must be made by way of certified cheque, delivery of an uncertified cheque will not constitute performance, and the receiving party need not accept it. If the contract does not specify a form of payment, legal tender must be used. The *Currency Act*[1] states that legal tender consists of notes (also called bank notes or bills) issued by the Bank of Canada and all coins issued by the Royal Canadian Mint. However, tender of payment using coins is subject to some restrictions. Section 8(2) of the *Currency Act* states:

legal tender
notes (bills) issued by the Bank of Canada and coins issued by the Royal Canadian Mint, subject to certain restrictions

> A payment in coins ... is a legal tender for no more than the following amounts for the following denominations of coins:
>   (a) forty dollars if the denomination is two dollars or greater but does not exceed ten dollars;
>   (b) twenty-five dollars if the denomination is one dollar;
>   (c) ten dollars if the denomination is ten cents or greater but less than one dollar;
>   (d) five dollars if the denomination is five cents; and
>   (e) twenty-five cents if the denomination is one cent.

Section 8(2.1) goes on to state:

> In the case of coins of a denomination greater than ten dollars, a payment ... may consist of not more than one coin, and the payment is a legal tender for no more than the value of a single coin of that denomination.

Therefore, paying a debt with a truckload of pennies is not performance and need not be accepted by the creditor. However, unless the contract states otherwise, payment in Canadian notes is always legal tender. The amount tendered must also be the exact amount, as a party is not obligated to make change. Therefore, offering a $1,000 bill to pay a $10 debt (especially when the party knows that the other will not be able to make change) is not proper tender of payment.

TIP

You can avoid problems in tendering by specifying in the contract how tender of payment is to be made—whether by certified cheque, money order, electronic transfer, or cash.

---

1   *Currency Act*, RSC 1985, c. C-52.

Specified Form of Payment Unavailable

American Chicle Co. v. Somerville Paper Box Co., [1921] OJ No. 240, 50 OLR 517 (SC)

Facts

The defendant owned land in Ontario that it mortgaged, and the mortgagee (creditor) assigned the mortgage to the plaintiff. The mortgage contained a provision that the mortgage should be paid off and void "on payment in *current gold coin* at the option of the mortgagee of $75,000 of lawful money of Canada with interest thereon" and "the mortgagor covenanted [agreed] with the mortgagee that the mortgagor will pay the mortgage money and interest and observe the above proviso."

In an action for foreclosure the question raised was whether the plaintiff was entitled to receive gold coin in payment of the mortgage money, or payment of so much Canadian or United States currency as would purchase gold coin to cover the principal and interest owing. Gold coin was at the time of the trial, and had been since the beginning of the First World War, unprocurable in Canada, but it could be obtained from the United States Treasury at the current rate of exchange.

Decision

Under the *Currency Act*, the right of the mortgagee was limited to requiring payment in gold coins made in Canada for currency purposes. However, because government regulations made Canadian gold coins unavailable, the defendant was unable to procure gold coins, and its contract to pay therein was suspended while that state of affairs existed. The plaintiff was not entitled to payment in gold, but would have to accept the amount due paid in Canadian currency.

Practical Tip

When creating a contract, you should take care not to insist on a form of payment that cannot reasonably be made. Otherwise, you may have to accept some other form of payment.

In the business world, large sums of money are rarely paid in cash. Cheques and electronic transfers of funds are the preferred forms of payment. Using cash is inconvenient and creates potential security problems. Despite the common practice of using forms of payment other than legal tender, it is important to remember that unless the contract states otherwise, a party to a contract is not obligated to accept any form of payment *except* legal tender. This fact can be used by unscrupulous parties to get out of a contract to which they would otherwise be bound.

If a debtor tenders payment in the correct form, on the right date, and at the right time and place, but the creditor refuses it, the debtor still has the obligation to pay the creditor. However, the debtor is not obligated to try to make another attempt at

Tender of Payment

Paolo agrees to sell his kayak to Allison for $2,500. They agree that Allison will pick up the kayak the following day. Later the same day, Paolo gets an offer of $2,900 from Renée. Paolo wants to sell the kayak to Renée instead. Allison hears about this and shows up at Paolo's the next day with payment in cash. Paolo cannot refuse the tender of payment. However, if Allison had arrived with a cheque, even a certified one, Paolo would be able to refuse payment because a cheque is not legal tender.

payment. In addition, even though the money remains outstanding, the creditor might be prohibited from charging interest on the debt after the date of tender. If the creditor tries to sue the debtor for payment after the date it was originally tendered, a court could use its discretion to punish the creditor by awarding the costs of the litigation to the debtor.

Of course, it would be foolish for a party to refuse a reasonable form of payment for the sole reason that the form was wrong, apart from any other lawful reason for refusing the tender of payment. If a debtor tries to make payment in the form of a certified cheque and the creditor refuses it because it is not legal tender, the creditor is within his or her rights, and the debtor still has the obligation to pay the creditor. However, the creditor might still be prohibited from charging interest on the debt after the date of tender; if the creditor tried to sue the debtor for payment, he or she might face the same cost consequences.

Discharge by Agreement

The parties to a contract may agree between themselves not to proceed with the contract before the terms of the contract are fully performed. This is a **waiver**, and it discharges the contract. By agreeing to a waiver, neither party can insist on the performance of the other party's obligations. If neither party to the contract has performed any of the terms of the contract, then there is a mutual release of the parties from their obligations. This mutual release constitutes consideration for the waiver, and it is enforceable. If one of the parties has performed his or her obligations but the other has not, then the waiver lacks consideration. To be enforceable, other consideration should be present, or the waiver should be in writing and under seal. A waiver must be voluntary and cannot be imposed by one party on another.

waiver
a voluntary agreement to relinquish a right, such as a right under a contract

TIP

If you agree to a waiver of a contract, it is wise to record in writing the terms of the agreement to waive the contract rights and obligations.

EXAMPLE

Waiver

Margit agrees to build a garage for Ramesh for $5,000. Before Margit begins construction, Ramesh tells her that he has changed his mind and he does not want a new garage after all. At this point, if both Margit and Ramesh agree, they can each waive the other's obligations under the contract and the contract is discharged. Margit is under no obligation to agree but may do so voluntarily if she wishes. The consideration for the waiver is the mutual release of their obligations: Margit from her obligation to build the garage, and Ramesh from his obligation to pay $5,000. Such a waiver would be enforceable. If Margit has already built the garage and Ramesh then states that he no longer wants it, then any agreement by Margit to forgo payment would be without consideration and unenforceable.

CASE IN POINT

Waiver of Time Requirement Lasts for Reasonable Period of Time and Can Be Retracted

Saskatchewan River Bungalows Ltd. v. Maritime Life Assurance Co., [1994] 2 SCR 490

Facts

In 1978, Maritime issued an insurance policy on the life of MF to the respondent Saskatchewan River Bungalows Ltd. (SRB). SRB mailed a cheque for the annual premium in July 1984, but the cheque was never received or deducted from SRB's bank account. Maritime then sent a notice to SRB agreeing to accept late payment by a given date in September, but SRB did not respond. In November, Maritime wrote a letter advising SRB that the premium due remained unpaid and that "this policy is now technically out of force, and we will require immediate payment of $1,361 to pay the July 1984–85 premium." Finally, in February 1985, Maritime sent a notice of policy lapse to SRB, indicating that evidence of insurability (medical evidence) would now be required—in effect, a new policy would have to be created.

SRB was unaware of the November letter asking for the late payment, or the February letter cancelling the policy, until April 1985. It then began to search for the lost premium cheque. It was not until July 1985 that SRB sent a replacement cheque. It was refused.

The person insured on the policy was by then terminally ill and uninsurable. He died in August. Maritime rejected SRB's claim for benefits under the policy on the ground that it was no longer in force.

Decision

The plaintiff was not entitled to any of the benefits under the policy. The demand for payment in the November letter was a clear and unequivocal expression of Maritime's intention to continue coverage upon payment of the July premium and as such constituted a waiver of the time requirements for payment under the policy. However, there are situations where a waiver is retractable, and this is one. A waiver can be retracted if reasonable notice is given. The November letter did that. But a notice requirement is not required where, as here, there was no reliance on the waiver by the insured. (The insured was not aware of Maritime's waiver until it opened the November letter in April 1985.) The February policy lapse notice was effective. In any event, once SRB opened its mail in April 1985, it clearly became aware of Maritime's intention in the November letter to retract its waiver. Even if a reasonable notice requirement were imposed, it was adequately met by the respondent's failure to tender a replacement cheque until July 1985. Maritime had no obligation to accept the replacement cheque, and the policy lapsed.

Practical Tip

It is important to keep careful track of accounts payable and receivable.

---

material alteration
a change in a contract that changes its legal meaning and effect; a change that goes to the heart or purpose of the contract

The parties to a contract may voluntarily decide to alter or amend the terms of the contract. If they change only minor terms, the contract itself remains intact. However, if the changes amount to a **material alteration** of the terms of the contract, the original contract is discharged and a new contract (the altered contract) is substituted. It is often difficult to determine whether the terms that have been altered are only minor or are material or substantial terms. To make this decision it requires examining the effect of the alterations. If the alterations change the effect, meaning, or purpose of the contract, they may be material alterations. The alterations must go to the heart or root of the contract. If so, the original contract is discharged, and a new contract has been substituted for the original.

The parties to a contract may also agree that a new contract will be substituted for an existing contract. If the new contract is between the existing parties, it is a *substituted agreement*. If the new contract involves the substitution of a new party, it is *novation*. In either case, the original contract is discharged. Novation is discussed in Chapter 5, Contractual Rights.

In some cases, a party to a contract may find that he or she is unwilling or unable to fulfill his or her obligations under the contract and wants to terminate the contract. The other party may be willing to allow the contract to be terminated upon the payment of a sum of money or some other compensation. For example, if a supplier of goods finds that it cannot deliver the goods requested by a buyer, it may offer to substitute other goods. If a party who had agreed to supply services finds that he or she cannot complete the job, the other party may be willing to accept payment of money as compensation for the delay and expense of finding someone else to complete the work. This form of compromise is called **accord and satisfaction**. There is a distinction between accord and satisfaction and the material alteration of terms or a substituted agreement, which is found in the intent of the parties. With accord and satisfaction, the primary intent of the parties is to discharge the existing contract. In the case of a material alteration of terms or a substituted agreement, the primary intent of the parties is to form a new contract.

In the case of *British Russian Gazette & Trade Outlook Ltd. v. Associated Newspapers Ltd.*,[2] the court stated:

> Accord and satisfaction is the purchase of a release from an obligation arising under contract … by means of any valuable consideration, not being the actual performance of the obligation itself. The accord is the agreement by which the obligation is discharged. The satisfaction is the consideration which makes the agreement operative.

> **TIP**
>
> It is difficult to tell whether alterations to a contract's original terms are minor or material alterations. Often the process is informal and the parties are not directing their minds to these issues, as in the example at left. If there is no formal amending agreement to the original contract, it is a good idea to keep track of changes by way of correspondence, emails, and other written records so as to avoid a situation where the other party tries to back out claiming failure of performance, when in fact there was a mutual intention to change what had been agreed to.

accord and satisfaction

a means of discharging a contract whereby the parties agree to accept some form of compromise or settlement instead of performance of the original terms of the contract

EXAMPLE

Material Alteration

In November, Ibrahim orders a camper from Bayshore RV Ltd. The camper is to be of a certain size, have a custom layout, and have various custom luxury fittings for the interior. The contract states that the camper will be ready no later than the following May. Over the next few months, Ibrahim keeps changing his mind about what he wants. He changes the fittings, the size of the camper, and the layout. When Bayshore finally has the camper ready, it is nearly July, two months after it was supposed to be ready. Ibrahim refuses to take delivery, claiming that Bayshore is in breach of contract.

Bayshore argues that the changes made to the original contract were not just cosmetic: Ibrahim ordered a different-sized camper with a different layout. Therefore, the alterations were material, the original contract had been discharged, and a new contract had been substituted. The new contract makes no mention of a delivery date, so Bayshore is not in breach of contract.

---

2   *British Russian Gazette & Trade Outlook Ltd. v. Associated Newspapers Ltd.*, [1933] 2 KB 616, at 644 (CA).

Both Parties Must Agree to Extension of Time of Original Contract

GMAC Leaseco Corporation v. Grzegorz Jaroszynski, 2012 ONSC 1005 (CanLII)

Facts

GMAC had leased a vehicle to the defendant. The vehicle was stolen, the lease went into default, and GMAC sued for the deficiency. Lease payments were drawn from the defendant's bank account under an agreed payment plan. However, the lease had been twice extended without the defendant's knowledge or agreement.

Decision

The lease extensions constituted a material variation of the contract without the defendant's consent. Therefore, the defendant was not liable for any of the payments due under the lease extensions, and was entitled to the return of funds drawn out of his account after the end of the original lease term.

Practical Tip

Once the time period of a contract has expired, if you wish to extend it and continue to receive payments, make sure you have the other party agree to the extension in writing.

Discharge by Agreement Difficult to Determine

Sirisena v. Oakdale Village Homes Inc., 2010 ONSC 2996 (CanLII)

Facts

The plaintiffs agreed to buy a new home from the defendant. They agreed to pay a $25,000 deposit and $7,823 for upgrades, and the closing date was to be October 26, 2006. By a letter dated May 31, 2006, the defendant advised the plaintiffs that the closing date was to be extended by 120 days to February 23, 2007, the maximum first extension that the defendant could impose unilaterally under the contract. The plaintiffs wanted a closing date in the summer, so the parties entered into an amending agreement that replaced the original October 26, 2006 closing date with a closing date of July 27, 2007.

The defendant then sent yet another letter, dated January 22, 2007, setting a new closing date of October 30, 2007 and offering to terminate the agreement with a full return of the deposit. The defendant claimed the January 22, 2007 letter was sent to the plaintiffs in error, taking the position that no such offer to terminate had been made.

The plaintiffs meanwhile sent a letter stating that they wished to terminate the agreement on the strict understanding that their $25,000 deposit and $7,823 for extras would be released with interest.

The defendant took the position that the amending agreement reset the contractual right of the defendant to extension periods, arguing the plaintiffs were therefore contractually obliged to accept a closing long after the July 27, 2007 closing date in the amending agreement.

Decision

The plaintiffs were entitled to a return of the deposit and upgrade fees. The defendant's January 22, 2007 letter amounted to an anticipatory breach of the agreement, particularly the agreed-upon closing date of July 27, 2007. The plaintiffs were entitled to accept the breach and terminate the agreement.

Practical Tip

Determining whether the facts support discharge by agreement can be difficult. Rather than an exchange of letters or emails, have both parties sign a discharge agreement that clearly sets out the discharge terms.

Parties may also discharge a contract by **merger**. If the parties enter into a verbal agreement that they later commit to writing, they have actually formed two contracts. The first is the verbal contract, and the second is the written contract. If the terms of the contract are identical, the first contract is merged with or absorbed into the second contract. The first contract is thereby discharged. If the terms of the contracts are not identical, then either novation or the material substitution of terms has occurred.

merger
the discharge of one contract by its replacement with, or absorption into, an identical contract

Discharge as of Right

The terms of a contract can allow one or both parties to discharge or terminate the contract. This is an **option to terminate**. This is also a form of discharge by agreement, as the option is included in the contract by the agreement of the parties. Ordinarily, the option must be exercised before the complete performance of the contract, and exercising the option is usually subject to certain terms. For example, a contract of employment may be terminated by the employer upon reasonable notice to the employee. A mortgage may be terminated by the mortgagor upon payment of the outstanding principal, plus an interest penalty, to the mortgagee. The exercise of the option to terminate does not depend on any event—the party with such a right may exercise it at will.

option to terminate
a term in a contract that allows one or both parties to discharge or terminate the contract before performance has been fully completed

A contract may provide that one or both parties have the right to terminate the contract if some event in the future does or does not occur. This is called a **condition precedent**. For example, someone buying a house may make the agreement to purchase conditional upon obtaining financing. If the financing is not obtained, he or she is not required to purchase the house. Someone buying a business may make the purchase conditional upon receiving a favourable audit of the financial statements of the business. If the auditor's report is negative, the purchase need not be completed. If a certain area of land is currently being considered for rezoning, a land developer may wish to purchase the property only if the rezoning application is *not* approved. If the rezoning application is approved, the developer has no obligation to purchase the property. These are all conditions precedent that may be included in the terms of the contract. The contract does not come into existence before the fulfillment of the condition precedent. The parties cannot withdraw their offer and acceptance, but they incur no obligation to perform the contract until the condition is fulfilled. The obligation to perform is, in effect, postponed. However, if one of the parties decides to terminate the contract before the fulfillment of the condition, he or she is in breach of contract.

condition precedent
an event (or non-event) that must occur (or not occur) before a contract can be enforced

A condition precedent must be distinguished from a **condition subsequent**, which is a future event that, if it occurs, terminates or discharges an existing contract. In the case of the condition precedent, the contract does not come into existence until the event occurs. With a condition subsequent, the contract exists and performance is required, but the contract may be discharged if the event occurs. For example, a contract to attend an outdoor concert may contain a term that states that the ticket price is refundable if the concert is cancelled due to weather conditions. In a contract to construct a building, the building plans may be subject to approval by the owner

condition subsequent
an event that, if it occurs, will terminate an existing contract

at various stages through the ongoing construction. Failure to obtain approval from the owner, or the withholding of approval by the owner, will terminate the contract.

A contract may also provide that in the event of a natural disaster or an "act of God," strike or lockout, war, or insurrection, the contract is terminated. This kind of a condition subsequent, when written into a contract, is often referred to as a *force majeure* clause and is commonly found in contracts for the transport of goods and for construction. To rely on a *force majeure* clause, the events in question must be beyond the control of the parties to the contract and not able to be avoided through the exercise of **due diligence**.

due diligence
the attention and care that a reasonable person would exercise with respect to his or her concerns; the obligation to make every reasonable effort to meet one's obligations

Discharge by Operation of Law

The *Bankruptcy and Insolvency Act*[3] provides that upon being released or discharged from bankruptcy, all of the contracts under which the bankrupt had any obligations are discharged. There are some exceptions to this, which include obligations to pay child support and to repay student loans.

All of the provinces have statutes of limitations that limit the time period within which actions to enforce contractual rights may be commenced. The Ontario *Limitations Act, 2002*,[4] for example, states that a proceeding shall not be commenced in respect of a claim after two years from the date the claim was discovered. The time limits imposed by these statutes are inflexible—it is impossible to enforce a contract if the action is brought outside these time limits. So if a contract is breached, and you want to sue, you have to do so within two years of the breach. Any lawsuit after that time will be barred by the *Limitations Act*.

This does not actually discharge the contract, which remains valid and binding. However, the obligations under the contract can no longer be enforced, so that the effect is the same as if the contract had been discharged.

doctrine of laches
a common-law doctrine that states that the neglect or failure to institute an action or lawsuit within a reasonable time period, together with prejudice suffered by the other party as a result of the delay, will result in the barring of the action

The time limits imposed by the various limitations statutes are a statute codification of the common-law **doctrine of laches**, which is based on the premise that failure to bring an action for the enforcement of contractual rights within a reasonable time may result in prejudice to the other party. If this is the case, the action will be barred and the courts will refuse to hear the action or enforce the contract. The *Limitations Act* does not replace the doctrine of laches. The difference between the two is that the limitations statutes impose specific time limits, while the doctrine of laches relies on the concept of a "reasonable" time limit. Therefore, it is theoretically possible to bring an action within the time limits imposed by the limitations statutes but still be barred by the doctrine of laches if the court thinks that a reasonable time limit is shorter than that specified in the statute.

The doctrine of laches simply bars the enforcement of the contract; it does not discharge it. However, the effect is the same as with the limitations statutes. If the contract is unenforceable, it is the same as if it had been discharged.

---

3   *Bankruptcy and Insolvency Act*, RSC 1985, c. B-3.

4   *Limitations Act, 2002*, SO 2002, c. 24, sched. B, s. 4.

CHAPTER SUMMARY

Once a contract is discharged, it is null and void. Contracts are most commonly discharged through performance of the obligations under the contract. Performance usually takes one of two forms: performing an action (for example, delivering goods or performing services) or paying money. The act of offering to perform the obligations under a contract is called tender of performance or tender of payment. The performance must comply exactly with the terms of the contract, or the tender need not be accepted by the other party. Once all obligations are performed, the contract is discharged.

Parties to a contract may also agree to discharge it. If this occurs before performance of the contract, this is called a waiver, and the contract is discharged. If the parties agree to materially alter the terms of the contract, a new contract is formed and the original contract is discharged. If the parties agree that the terms of the contract will not be fulfilled and a compromise or settlement is reached instead, this is called accord and satisfaction, and the original contract is discharged. If the parties enter into a verbal contract that is later put in writing, the original verbal contract merges with the written contract and is thereby discharged.

The terms of a contract may also provide that one or both parties have the option to terminate or discharge the contract, usually upon terms such as notice or the payment of money. The terms of a contract may also include a condition precedent, the occurrence of which is necessary before the contract becomes enforceable. If the condition precedent is not fulfilled, the contract is discharged. Another term of a contract may be a condition subsequent, the occurrence of which will discharge the contract.

A contract may be discharged by the operation of law, such as through the operation of the *Bankruptcy and Insolvency Act*, or be in effect discharged, such as through the operation of the *Limitations Act* or the doctrine of laches.

KEY TERMS

accord and satisfaction, 165
condition precedent, 167
condition subsequent, 167
discharged, 160
doctrine of laches, 168

due diligence, 168
legal tender, 161
material alteration, 164
merger, 167
null and void, 160

option to terminate, 167
tender of performance, 160
waiver, 163

REVIEW QUESTIONS

True or False?

_____ **1.** If a contract is discharged by frustration, one party may sue the other for breach.

_____ **2.** If I have contracted to deliver 30 litres of maple syrup in 10 3-litre bottles, and deliver 30 litres in 15 2-litre bottles, I have successfully tendered performance.

_____ **3.** Unless the contract states otherwise, payment in Canadian bank notes is always legal tender.

_____ **4.** Morris builds a shed for Aram under a contract. Aram then says he has changed his mind because he lost his job, and Morris says, "OK, I understand." Morris has waived his contract rights.

_____ **5.** Accord and satisfaction is the result when one contract is joined to a later one.

_____ **6.** A condition precedent is a term of a contract, the occurrence of which is necessary before the contract becomes enforceable.

_____ **7.** Once a term of a contract is waived, the waiver cannot be retracted.

Multiple Choice

1. George agrees to buy a sofa from Couch Potato Ltd. George then discovers that he can get a better deal elsewhere. When Couch Potato tries to deliver the sofa, George refuses delivery.

   a. This is an example of discharge by frustration.

   b. This is an example where one party has made a tender of performance.

   c. Couch Potato Ltd. has done everything necessary under the contract to be entitled to sue for breach of contract.

   d. b and c.

2. Dorcas contracted to supply Titmuss with a new red Zitmobile coupe. When Titmuss comes to pick up the car, the only one available is bright blue. Titmuss made it clear that the car had to be red.

   a. Titmuss can sue for breach as this is non-complying performance.

   b. Titmuss can waive the requirement that the car be red and accept delivery.

   c. Titmuss can refuse delivery of the car.

   d. All of the above.

3. Puffnagel contracted to purchase a painting from Bob. The contract stated that payment must be made by certified cheque.

   a. Even though the contract specifies the terms of payment, under the *Currency Act*, Puffnagel can pay in cash.

   b. Puffnagel can pay only by certified cheque.

   c. Puffnagel could substitute a money order for the certified cheque as it offers the creditor the same protection and security.

   d. None of the above.

4. If a contract does not specify the form of payment,

   a. a party can pay in cash or by cheque

   b. the other party can refuse payment by cheque

   c. the other party cannot refuse payment in cash

   d. b and c

5. Gregoire agrees with Tamara that she will supply Orix to Gregoire and bill him monthly. He doesn't pay for January and February. Tamara sends Gregoire a letter saying that if he doesn't pay what is owing within 30 days, she will cease making further deliveries.

   a. If Tamara, after sending the letter, then makes a delivery the next day, she may have waived her objection and is still bound to perform the contract, even if he doesn't pay in 30 days.

   b. If Tamara, after sending the letter, makes a delivery 45 days from the day she sent the letter, she has waived her objection and is still bound to perform the contract.

   c. a and b.

   d. None of the above.

6. Zainab orders a fence to be built from cedar in her yard by Sergei, to be completed by April 1. She then indicates she wants it built from stone, and wants to add a trellis on top. Sergei agrees. He doesn't finish until mid-May, and Zainab refuses to pay, arguing that Sergei is in breach of the contract to build the fence by April 1.

   a. Zainab is right—the changes were all minor and Sergei missed the deadline.

   b. The changes were major, but the delivery date is a term of the contract, so she doesn't have to pay.

   c. The changes are major and material, so the old delivery date is not relevant.

   d. None of the above.

7. Nils has contracted to build a barn for Moise. Under the terms of the contract, the roof was to be slate. Nils is unable to find enough slate to do the roof and offers to do it in cedar, with a discount on the price.

   a. If Moise accepts Nils's offer, this is described as novation.

   b. If Moise accepts Nils's offer, this is described as accord and satisfaction.

   c. If Moise accepts Nils's offer, this is a material alteration creating a new contract.

   d. a and c.

8. If Amir wants to buy a house and inserts a term that he only has to complete the contract if he can obtain financing of the purchase price,

   a. this is called a condition precedent

   b. this is called a condition subsequent

   c. this is called merger

   d. none of the above

9. Annabel contracts to supply 40 bushels of organic barley to Magda by October 1. In late August there is a violent tornado, and the whole field of barley is destroyed.

   a. Too bad for Annabel—because she has failed to deliver the barley, she is liable for breach.

   b. Annabel is liable because she could have taken steps to prevent the loss of the barley.

   c. Annabel is not liable because the loss was caused by events beyond her control and was not avoidable by the exercise of due diligence.

   d. Annabel is liable because, though the loss was due to events beyond her control, she didn't include a clause in the agreement absolving her from liability if such an event occurred.

10. Maurizio and Horace entered into a verbal agreement. Later they put their agreement in writing.

   a. If the terms of the verbal agreement are the same as the written one, the contract only takes effect when it is reduced to writing.

   b. If the terms of the verbal agreement are the same as the written one, there are two contracts that have merged into one.

   c. If the terms of the written agreement are not identical to the verbal agreement, then novation or a material substitution of terms has occurred.

   d. b and c

Short Answer

1. In what ways can a contract be discharged? What is the effect of discharging a contract?

2. Define "legal tender." When is legal tender required for the tender of payment?

3. If one party tenders a truckload of coins in the exact amount due as payment on a contract price of $500, does the other side have to accept payment in that form? Why or why not?

4. If a creditor refuses to accept tender of payment, is the debtor freed from the obligation to pay? Explain. What might be the effect of a creditor refusing tender of payment?

5. Define a "waiver." What is the consideration for a waiver? What should you do in a case where there is no consideration for a waiver?

6. What is the material alteration of the terms of a contract? What is its effect on the contract?

7. Describe the difference between accord and satisfaction and material alteration of the terms of a contract.

8. Describe when merger of a contract might occur. What is the difference between merger and a substituted agreement?

9. Define "condition precedent." Does a contract that is subject to a condition precedent exist before the fulfillment of the condition precedent? Why or why not?

10. Define "condition subsequent."

11. Under what circumstances can a contract be discharged or rendered unenforceable by the operation of law?

12. How does the doctrine of laches differ from the *Limitations Act* in how it affects a contract?

Apply Your Knowledge

1. Nils and his wife, Wanda, enter into a contract with Robert whereby Robert agrees to invest $50,000 in their custom furniture manufacturing business in exchange for a share of the business and its profits. Shortly after entering into this contract, Nils dies and the business has to be shut down. Wanda is left with no source of income, enormous debts, and five children. Out of the goodness of his heart, Robert offers to accept the sum of $10,000 instead of the anticipated profits, even though shutting down the business constitutes a breach of the terms of the contract. How would you characterize Robert's action? What danger does Wanda face in accepting this generous arrangement? What can Wanda do to protect herself?

2. Creative Designers Ltd. agrees to redecorate Carmen's home for the sum of $20,000. The services are to include completely redecorating the living room, den, and dining room. The work is to start on May 1 and be completed no later than August 1. After work begins, Carmen changes her mind about the colour of the paint she wants in the den and the type of carpet she wants in the living room. She also wants Creative Designers to redecorate the hall and the foyer. Creative Designers agrees to make all the changes. However, the work is not complete on August 1. Carmen claims that Creative Designers is in breach of contract. What arguments could Creative Designers make?

3. Northern Sawmills Inc. contracts to supply The Building Depot Ltd. with a shipment of its first-quality hardwood. The Building Depot wants Northern Sawmills' lumber because it has access to the best-quality hardwood in the area. To obtain the same quality lumber from any other source would be much more expensive. However, Northern Sawmills finds that it cannot deliver the hardwood as promised. It is out of first-quality hardwood but has lots of second-quality hardwood. What options are available to the parties in this case?

4. The catcoons in Chapter 5 have ended up with Sarah. They are still obnoxious, with the worst qualities of both cats and raccoons, but as they are a bit of a novelty, Sarah has discovered that she may be able to sell them to people with too much money and not enough sense, who want to have a unique, one-of-a-kind animal. Explain the outcome in the following contract situations:

a. Sarah agrees to sell catcoon 1 for $20,000 to Bob Bigbucks when it reaches the age of seven weeks. At six weeks, Sarah finds she can't stand the animal and she shows up at Bob's to deliver and demands her money. Bob wants out of the contract. Can he get out? Explain.

b. Catcoon 2 is sold to Norris Nouveauriche on the same terms. Nothing is said about the form of payment in the contract, and Norris wants to pay by cheque. Can he? Explain.

c. Catcoon 3 is sold by Sarah to Dora Muchodinero on the same terms as before. Dora has decided that a catcoon destroying her Louis Quatorze living room suite isn't such a great idea. She offers Sarah $2,000 to cancel the contract. Explain whether she is entitled to cancel.

d. Catcoon 4 is to be sold to Avery Avaricious on the same terms as the others. When Avery hears that catcoon 3 is also available for sale, he offers to take both animals if Sarah will give him half price on the second one. Sarah agrees to come back the following week with both catcoons and complete the deal. When she returns the next week, Avery has changed his mind and is only willing to take catcoon 4. What arguments might the parties make to support their positions?

Breach of Contract and Remedies

8

Introduction 174

Method of Breach 174

Nature of Breach 176

Remedies 177

Choice of Remedies 191

Chapter Summary 194

Key Terms 194

Review Questions 194

LEARNING OUTCOMES

After completing this chapter, you should be able to:

- Describe the kinds of activities that amount to breach of contract and the various consequences for breach of contract.

- Explain the concept of repudiation, both express and implied.

- Identify the various remedies available for breach of contract.

- Identify the circumstances in which damage awards are made and explain the obligation to mitigate damages.

- Identify under what circumstances specific performance and injunctions are awarded.

- Explain the differences among rescission, restitution, and discharge.

- Explain the impact of exclusion clauses on a contract.

Introduction

breach of contract
failure, without legal
excuse, to perform any
promise that forms
part of a contract

This chapter discusses the actions and non-actions that constitute **breach of contract** and the remedies that are available to the injured party.

When one party to a contract fails or refuses to fulfill his or her obligations under the contract without legal excuse, this is considered a breach of contract. However, different types of breaches have different consequences. The method of the breach must first be established, and then the nature or seriousness of the breach must be examined. Then, the remedies available to the injured party can be determined. The injured party may be able to

- claim compensation for damages suffered as a result of the breach;
- declare that the contract has been discharged, thereby releasing the injured party from his or her obligations;
- compel the party in breach to perform the obligations; or
- apply a combination of all three.

Method of Breach

repudiate
to renounce or reject
an obligation

**express repudiation/
express breach**
the failure or refusal to
perform the obligations
under a contract when
they become due

A party to a contract may **repudiate** the contract, thereby breaching the contract. The most common form of repudiation is failing or refusing to perform the obligations of the contract when they become due. This form of repudiation is known as **express repudiation** or **express breach**. The repudiation must be clear, unambiguous, and explicit. It may take the form of an actual declaration of refusal, or simply a failure to perform.

> **EXAMPLE**
>
> **Express Repudiation or Express Breach**
>
> Samuel promises to deliver a load of gravel to Northwest Contracting Limited on a certain day. On that day he fails to deliver the gravel as promised. In the alternative, on the day of delivery, he telephones Northwest Contracting and states that he cannot deliver the gravel as promised.

anticipatory breach
an express repudiation that
occurs before the time of
performance of a contract

If the repudiation occurs before the date of performance, it is an **anticipatory breach**. Again, the repudiation must be clear, unambiguous, and explicit.

> **EXAMPLE**
>
> **Anticipatory Breach**
>
> Samuel promises to deliver a load of gravel to Northwest Contracting Limited on a certain day. Before that day, he discovers that the company that supplies his gravel has increased its price, with the result that if Samuel delivers gravel to Northwest at the agreed-upon price, he will lose money. Samuel calls Northwest before the day of delivery to say that he will not be delivering the gravel.

Refusal to Perform Amounts to Express Repudiation

Canada Egg Products Ltd. v. Canadian Doughnut Co. Ltd., [1955] SCR 398

Facts

By a contract in writing entered into in February, Canada Egg agreed to sell to Canadian Doughnut a quantity of powdered egg yolk and egg albumen. It was provided that initial deliveries were to begin July 15 and that if the powder was not satisfactory, or not in accord with the specifications, it was to be returnable within 14 days of delivery.

On May 7, Canada Egg notified the respondent that the contract was not valid and that it would not make delivery. Despite the notice, Canadian Doughnut continued negotiating for delivery until June 1 when, because of Canada Egg's continued refusal to deliver the order other than a small quantity of albumen, Canadian Doughnut, without notifying Canada Egg, made the purchases elsewhere. On June 25, Canadian Doughnut brought an action for a declaration that a valid contract had been entered into and claimed damages for an express repudiation by Canada Egg.

Decision

The Supreme Court of Canada held that the refusal by Canada Egg on May 7 to perform the contract, which it never retracted, constituted in the circumstances a continuing refusal and an express repudiation of the contract. The commencement of a lawsuit by Canadian Doughnut was sufficient notice of its acceptance of the appellant's continuing and express repudiation, even if there was on June 1 another and independent act of repudiation by Canadian Doughnut when it sought to buy the supplies elsewhere. The acceptance of Canada Egg's breach by Canadian Doughnut was made within a reasonable time, justifying Canadian Doughnut's claim for damages.

Practical Tip

Hindsight is wonderful. In this case it is easy to identify acts of express repudiation and anticipatory breach by Canada Egg, but it took three levels of court and a lot of time and legal fees for Canadian Doughnut to clarify what its rights were in the face of a breach. In situations like this, it is wise for you, if you were in Canadian Doughnut's position, to make clear to the other party that you consider its acts to be express repudiation and anticipatory breach, as the case may be, and to outline the consequences. It is also a good idea not to muddy the waters, in the face of such a breach, by continuing to try to get the other side to perform.

More difficult is the situation where one party repudiates the contract by implication. **Implied repudiation** is a form of anticipatory breach, since it occurs before the performance date. The innocent party must ascertain, from the actions or statements of the other party, that he or she does not intend to perform the obligations under the contract when the time for performance arrives. The innocent party is in a difficult position. The party who appears to be repudiating by implication may still perform the contract as specified when the time comes. However, if he or she does not, the innocent party may suffer increased damages as a result of the delay in waiting to address the situation. Further, if the innocent party assumes that the other party intends to breach when that is not the case, the innocent party may take steps that result in a breach on his or her part. Because the very nature of implied repudiation relies on speculation and inference, misunderstandings may occur.

implied repudiation
repudiation that is not express and must be implied or deduced from the circumstances

> **EXAMPLE**
>
> **Implied Repudiation**
>
> Dawn enters into a contract with Emil to paint his house. Two weeks before the day she is supposed to start work, Emil finds out that she has sold all of her painting equipment to one of her competitors. Clearly, without her painting equipment, Dawn will be unable to perform her obligations under the contract. Emil might want to treat this as an implied repudiation of the contract. However, if Dawn buys new equipment before the day she is supposed to start painting, she could still perform her obligations. On the other hand, if Emil waits to find out what Dawn will do, he may not be able to find a replacement for her in time to have his house painted.

However, in some cases the nature of the implied repudiation is such that there can be no misinterpretation. This includes situations where the implied repudiation makes performing the contractual obligations impossible.

> **EXAMPLE**
>
> **Implied Repudiation That Is Certain**
>
> Lindsey and Scott enter into a contract whereby Lindsey agrees to sell Scott her laptop. Before the date that Lindsey is supposed to deliver the laptop to Scott, he finds out that she has sold it to someone else. While this is still a case of implied repudiation, because of the certainty that Lindsey will be unable to deliver the laptop to Scott on the agreed-upon date, Scott may treat this as a breach of contract.

Nature of Breach

Once it has been established that a contract has been breached, the nature or effect of the breach must be examined. The nature of the breach is determined primarily on the basis of its seriousness. A term of a contract that is essential or goes to the root of the contract is called a condition. A minor or subsidiary term is called a warranty. It is important to examine the contract as a whole and in context to determine whether any given term is a condition or a warranty. For instance, in a contract to buy a car, the make and model of the car would be a condition, while the colour of the car might be a warranty. The delivery of a car of the correct make and model, but the incorrect colour, would be breach of a warranty but not breach of a condition. However, in a contract to paint a house, the colour of the paint might be a condition. In such a case, painting the house the wrong colour would be a breach of a condition. A breach of a condition must wholly deprive the innocent party of the benefit he or she expected to receive under the contract. The distinction between a breach of warranty and a breach of condition is important in determining what remedies are available for the breach.

Avoiding Communication Regarding Contractual Obligations May Amount to Implied Repudiation

Neretlis v. Meade, [2005] OJ No. 638 (SC)

Facts

Neretlis sued the defendant, Meade, for specific performance of a written agreement of purchase and sale of Meade's house. Shortly after the agreement was signed, Meade engaged in conduct that indicated he had no intention of completing the sale or performing the contract. He did not hire a lawyer or respond to Neretlis's lawyer's communications. When Neretlis and his lawyer came to his home to tender, Meade made sure he was not there. Meade pleaded *non est factum* and coercion. He claimed that he had a concussion at the time he signed the contract and did not know what he was signing. In addition, he claimed that his real estate agent coerced him into signing the agreement.

Decision

The court ruled in favour of Neretlis. Meade knew he was signing a listing agreement with the real estate agent. The reasonable inference that was made from Meade's behaviour was that he had no intention of closing the sale. The claim of *non est factum* was unsuccessful. The court found that Meade did not have a concussion, but a contusion, which did not prevent him from dealing with contractual matters. The evidence indicated that Meade knew that he had signed an agreement of purchase and sale and regretted it. In addition, there was no evidence of coercion. Neretlis came into court with clean hands—this was an objectively fair transaction and there was no evidence that it caused hardship to Meade. An order for specific performance was justified.

On the issue of implied repudiation, Low J had this to say:

I am ... satisfied that there was an implied repudiation by the defendant of the contract and thus anticipatory breach. The express declaration, however construed, the failure to prepare a deed, the fact that the defendant did not retain a solicitor, the fact that he ignored Mr. Phillips' communications concerning the closing—these lead to the reasonable inference that the defendant had no intention of closing the sale and, in my view, it is the only reasonable inference to be drawn in the circumstances.

Practical Tip

Failing to reply to communications and evading meeting with the other party will not get you out of a contract, nor will unsubstantiated claims of ill health or coercion at the time of signing. Think carefully before you sign.

Remedies

The remedies available in the event of breach of contract include

- damages,
- specific performance,
- injunction,
- rescission,
- restitution,
- discharge, and
- *quantum meruit.*

Damages

The most common remedy for breach of contract is the award of damages. Damages are a sum of money to compensate the injured party. The intent of the court in making such an award is, as far as possible, to put the injured party into the position that he or she would have been in had the contract been fully performed. This is a popular remedy because with most contracts it is easy to translate the non-performance into monetary loss. Unless there is some compelling reason to award some other form of relief, the court will only award damages.

EXAMPLE

Monetary Loss from Non-Performance

Catherine agrees to sell her lawnmower to Suzanne for $100. Suzanne takes the lawnmower and gives Catherine a cheque. However, the cheque is returned NSF. The contract has clearly been breached. The loss suffered by Catherine is the sum of $100, and an award of damages in the amount of $100 (plus, perhaps, interest on that sum) would fully compensate her.

---

liquidated damages
damages that are easily determined from a fixed or measurable standard, or can be assessed by calculating the amount owing from a mathematical formula or from circumstances where no subjective assessment has to be made

unliquidated damages
damages that cannot be fixed by a mathematical or measured calculation but require information from a source outside the contract

consequential damages
secondary damages that do not flow from the breach of contract but from the consequences of the breach, such as loss of future profits

expectancy damages
damages that are based on a loss of expected profits

lost opportunity damages
damages that are based on a longer-term loss of business

It is important to distinguish between **liquidated damages** and **unliquidated damages**. Liquidated damages are easily ascertainable, usually by examining the terms of the contract and applying some form of mathematical calculation using a known or agreed formula or method of calculation. In this situation, anyone using a simple calculator should come up with the same results. If, for example, the contract specified payment of the sum of $4,000 but only $1,500 was paid, applying the mathematical formula $4,000 − $1,500 = $2,500 calculates the liquidated damages. However, sometimes the damages are not so easy to calculate because the breach of a contract can have far-reaching consequences. **Consequential damages** do not flow directly from a breach of contract but from the consequences of the breach. These damages are, in a sense, one step removed from the breach itself. Consequential damages include those based on a loss of expected profits, often referred to as **expectancy damages**, and damages based on a longer-term loss of business, often referred to as **lost opportunity damages**.

Consequential damages are often unliquidated. Unliquidated damages cannot be easily calculated with a mathematical formula and usually require information that is outside the contract itself. For example, in calculating damages for loss of profit, it might be necessary to look at evidence from other, similar contracts or at the particular industry as a whole to determine the actual loss suffered. In other cases, it may be necessary to hire an appraiser, an accountant, or some other expert to assist in calculating the damages.

If the consequences of the breach were reasonably foreseeable by the parties at the time that the contract was performed, the party in breach may be liable for all the losses that flow from the breach, including consequential damages. The injured party must prove that the damages were reasonably foreseeable at the time that the contract was made. The party in breach will want to argue that the damages claimed by the injured party are too "remote" and could not have been reasonably foreseen.

Reasonably Foreseeable Damages

Tents R Us Ltd. contracts to buy a load of grommets from Trusty Parts Inc. for the sum of $7,500. Trusty Parts fails to deliver the grommets, and Tents R Us is forced to buy them from another manufacturer for $8,500. Clearly, the damages immediately suffered amount to $1,000. However, Tents R Us needed the grommets to finish making a shipment of tents due to Backpacker's World Limited, for which Tents R Us expected to earn $15,000 in profits. Because of the breach by Trusty Parts, Tents R Us cannot deliver the tents on time and so loses its anticipated profits.

The consequential damages suffered include the lost profits of $15,000. In addition, the failure to deliver the tents on time to Backpacker's World, a long-time customer of Tents R Us, has damaged the relationship between the two companies. Backpacker's World will no longer do business with Tents R Us, so the long-term losses include the future loss of business from Backpacker's World. The damages might then include loss of anticipated profit over the next few years, amounting to many thousands of dollars. To claim all of these damages, Tents R Us must prove that Trusty Parts knew or ought to have known that these consequences would reasonably flow from its failure to perform its obligations under the contract. The damages claim for loss of profit over the next few years is clearly unliquidated and requires some form of external evidence to support it.

It is often difficult to accurately calculate the losses suffered by the injured party as a result of a breach. To address this problem, some parties include a clause in the contract that sets out the damages to be paid in the event of a breach. If this clause is a genuine attempt to calculate in advance the loss that might be suffered, it is referred to as a liquidated damages clause. Such a clause provides incentive to the parties to comply with the terms of the contract. The courts usually uphold such a clause, even if the actual damages suffered are greater or less than the clause provides for. However, this clause must be distinguished from a penalty clause, which provides for a payment of damages far in excess of the actual damages that could be suffered or that makes no genuine attempt to correlate the damages payable with the damages suffered. The courts often ignore penalty clauses and instead calculate the damages award based on the actual loss. Whether a clause is a liquidated damages clause or a penalty clause is often difficult to determine and is decided on the facts of each case.

Duty to Mitigate

The injured party has a duty to **mitigate** his or her losses. He or she is not entitled to remain inactive in the face of the other party's breach of contract, but must take positive, reasonable steps to minimize the loss suffered as a result of the breach, though not extraordinary steps. Failing to mitigate losses may result in a court not awarding compensation for the full loss suffered. Compensation will be limited to those damages that could not have reasonably been avoided.

mitigate
to take steps to minimize or reduce the damages one will suffer as a result of another's breach of contract

CASE IN POINT

Mitigation Required for Consequential Damages Claim

Wingold Construction Co. Ltd. v. Kramp, [1960] SCR 556

Facts

Wingold was constructing a commercial building. After putting in the foundation, it required sand fill on which it could then pour a concrete floor. Kramp was in the process of preparing a lot for construction. On the lot was a sand hill, which Kramp needed to remove. Both parties inspected the sand hill and agreed on a price per load to be delivered to Wingold. In effect, Wingold bought the sand hill from Kramp, and Kramp began delivery. Partway through the delivery process, Wingold started to complain about the quality—that there was clay mixed in with the sand. Nevertheless, Wingold did not refuse deliveries at that point. But at a later date, Wingold refused to accept further deliveries and obtained the rest of the sand it needed from another source. Wingold then sued, arguing that the goods delivered were not in accordance with the contract and that Kramp was in breach of its warranty. Wingold claimed not only damages for the difference between the price Wingold had paid for sand from other sources and that under the contract, but also consequential damages, including the cost of trying to work with and use the sand delivered by Kramp and the cost of its removal.

Decision

The Supreme Court of Canada agreed that Wingold was entitled to damages for breach of warranty for the difference in value of goods at the time of delivery and the value they would have had if they had met the standard required by the warranty. But because Wingold continued to accept deliveries after it discovered the goods were not up to the warranty standard, it could not then also claim consequential damages. It had a duty to mitigate—to take steps to limit its loss once it had discovered the breach, and this it did not do.

Practical Tip

In situations where consequential damages are likely, it will be easier to prove that the damages were reasonably foreseeable if the victim of the breach promptly indicates in writing to the party in breach what the consequences of the breach will be or are likely to be. It is also important that the victim of the breach take reasonable steps to mitigate the damage, rather than let damages mount up.

EXAMPLE

Mitigation and Losses

André contracts to sell his computer to Teresinha. She breaches the contract by refusing to complete the transaction. André can claim against Teresinha the full purchase price of the computer as the damages he suffered as a result of her breach. However, if he takes no steps to mitigate his loss by trying to sell his computer to someone else, he may be denied recovery of the full amount of his loss. If he is forced to sell the computer at a lower price than the one Teresinha contracted to pay, he will be able to claim as his damages the difference between the price he would have received from Teresinha and the price he did receive. However, if he is lucky enough to sell the computer for more than the price Teresinha had contracted to buy, André will not be able to recover any damages against her because he suffered no loss. Even though she is clearly in breach, she would suffer no consequences.

Specific Performance

In some cases, damages cannot adequately compensate the injured party. In those cases, **equitable remedies** may be available. An example of an equitable remedy is specific performance, which requires the party who is in breach to perform his or her obligations under the contract. If this party refuses to comply and perform, he or she will be in contempt of court and could be subject to quasi-criminal penalties such as fines or imprisonment. **Specific performance** is usually available only when the contract is for the sale of unique goods or real property.

Real property is ordinarily considered unique because no two parcels of land are identical. If a buyer expects to buy land and the vendor breaches the contract by failing to complete the transaction, it is not possible for the buyer to take an award of monetary damages and replace the land that is lost. If the buyer can prove that he or she was ready, willing, and able to complete the transaction and fulfill all his or her obligations under the contract, the court can compel the vendor to complete the transaction through an order for specific performance.

If the contract is for the sale of unique goods, specific performance may be an available remedy. However, this is less common than with real property. The goods must be so rare and unique that the disappointed buyer cannot readily find the same or similar goods from another source; examples include antiques, works of art, and rare coins or stamps.

Specific performance is not available for contracts that involve personal services performed by an individual, such as in an employment contract. In such a case, the courts are unlikely to force an individual to provide personal services, as this would amount to a form of servitude. Monetary damages are considered adequate compensation.

Because specific performance is an equitable remedy, certain restrictions are placed on the party asking for the remedy. Equity requires that this party come to court with "clean hands"—that is, free of any unethical behaviour. If a party does not have clean hands, he or she will be denied the equitable remedy and will be awarded monetary damages. Equitable remedies can also be denied if the injured party was partly at fault or contributed to the breach of contract in some way, or if he or she delayed for an unreasonable length of time in pursuing a remedy for the breach. These restrictions apply to all equitable remedies.

equitable remedies
remedies developed by the court of equity that are based on fairness instead of the strict application of common law

specific performance
a remedy requiring the party who is in breach of a contract to perform his or her obligations under the contract

EXAMPLE

Unclean Hands

Hisham, Kamal, and Salwa were business partners. Hisham leaves the partnership and then sues Kamal and Salwa. He claims that as part of the mutual agreement to dissolve the partnership, he should be allowed to take certain client contracts with him. Kamal and Salwa claim in their defence that Hisham has tried to steal customers from the partnership by spreading untrue stories about the remaining partners' business practices. If the defence allegations are true, Hisham would likely be unable to claim specific performance, because his actions in defaming his former partners leave him with "unclean hands." However, he might still be able to claim legal remedies such as damages (subject to any counterclaims by his former partners).

CASE IN POINT

Unethical Behaviour Bars Remedy of Specific Performance

David Cooper Investments Ltd. v. Bermuda Tavern Ltd., 2001 CanLII 3639 (ON CA)

Facts

David Cooper Investments sued Bermuda Tavern on a contract to purchase the tavern. David Cooper owned David Cooper Investments, and David's brother Irving owned the Bermuda. Irving was having financial difficulty and was indebted to the bank. He made an arrangement with the bank that he would sell the Bermuda to raise cash, but he also needed cash right away. His brother David loaned him the money at no interest. Irving put the Bermuda on the market and negotiated with a potential buyer, Pratt, but no deal was reached. David then, without Irving's knowledge, started negotiating with Pratt, falsely representing that he had authority to sell the Bermuda. Both the bank and David put further pressure on Irving to pay what was owed to them. Irving agreed to sell the Bermuda to David (at a low price), and David had made a deal with Pratt to sell it to him (at a higher price). Prior to closing, Irving found out about David's resale to Pratt and refused to close the deal with David. David sued Irving for specific performance. Irving argued that David had acted in bad faith, and in breach of confidence and fiduciary duty to Irving.

Decision

David, while not acting in a very brotherly manner, was not liable for breach of confidential information regarding the resale to Pratt, as David was acting on his own and not on Irving's behalf—it was not a joint venture with Irving, so there was no fiduciary relationship.

However, although the contract was enforceable and Irving had breached the contract, the court awarded damages, refusing specific performance to David. Thus, Irving was free to sell the Bermuda for the best price he could get. David did not come to the court with "clean hands"—he had put undue pressure on Irving when Irving was vulnerable, and he lied to Irving and to Pratt.

Practical Tip

It is unwise to mislead a party to a contract in any way, especially if that party is vulnerable or desperate. Though damages may be awarded, equitable remedies, such as specific performance, may be denied.

Injunctions

injunction
a court order that prohibits someone from doing some act or compels someone to do some act

prohibitory injunction
an injunction that directs a person not to do a certain thing

mandatory injunction
an injunction that commands a person to do a certain thing

negative covenant
a promise in a contract to refrain from doing a certain thing

An **injunction** is another form of equitable remedy. Injunctions govern the behaviour of a party, either to prohibit certain actions or to compel certain actions. A **prohibitory injunction** directs a person not to do a certain thing. A **mandatory injunction** commands a person to do a certain thing. The most important considerations for the court in determining whether to grant an injunction are whether the injured party could be adequately compensated by damages instead of an injunction, and whether it is fair and just to grant the request for the injunction. The court will not grant an injunction if the injured party could be adequately compensated by an award of damages, or if it would be unfair to, or cause irreparable harm to, the party in breach. Also, a court will set a higher standard for a mandatory injunction than it will for a prohibitory injunction.

The courts most often grant a prohibitory injunction when the contract contains an express provision that is a promise by one party that it will not do a certain thing. This is also known as a **negative covenant**. If the party then commits the prohibited act, the injured party could then apply to the court for an injunction to stop it.

Negative Covenant

Chem-Products Ltd. rents land from Pristine Properties Inc. The rental agreement contains a negative covenant that Chem-Products will not use the land to store certain chemicals. If Chem-Products then uses the land to store these chemicals, one of the options available to Pristine Properties is to ask the court for an injunction prohibiting Chem-Products from doing so.

While it is helpful to have a negative covenant in the contract, it is not necessary to have such a covenant before the court will grant a prohibitory injunction. A contract may include an implied promise that could be used as the basis for a prohibitory injunction.

Implied Promise

Assume that in the above example, Pristine Properties carries on business on the property adjacent to Chem-Products. Chem-Products dumps garbage on the property and emits loud sounds from the property at all hours of the night and day, which adversely affect the business next door. Pristine Properties can make a request for a prohibitory injunction. Although there may not be a specific negative covenant in the contract prohibiting garbage dumping and noise, the court may recognize an implied promise not to interfere with Pristine Properties' business. This would be true even if there was no statutory remedy available to Pristine Properties (for example, municipal noise bylaws).

A mandatory injunction, while it is not the same as specific performance, can often have the same effect. Courts are less willing to grant mandatory injunctions in circumstances where they would not grant specific performance, as in contracts involving personal services performed by an individual. However, the courts have granted mandatory injunctions in cases "to prevent the breach of an agreement under which the plaintiff obtained from the defendant exclusive rights to the manufacture and distribution in two provinces of certain patent and proprietary remedies, [and] to prevent the improper termination of an automobile franchise agreement."

Injunctions can be a very powerful remedy but, because the litigation process can be long and time-consuming, a lawsuit in which a party is seeking an injunction may take years to come to trial. By then, the behaviour that the injured party sought to prohibit may have done irreparable damage. In such a case, a party may seek an **interlocutory injunction**, also called an **interim injunction** or temporary injunction. This allows the injured party to prevent ongoing damage from occurring while awaiting the trial and final determination of the matters in dispute. At trial, the injured party will usually ask for the injunction to be made permanent.

interlocutory/interim injunction
a temporary injunction granted by a court before the final determination of a lawsuit for the purpose of preventing irreparable injury

CASE IN POINT

No Injunction Where Damages an Adequate Compensation

Siemens Canada Ltd. (c.o.b. Siemens IT Solutions and Services) v. Sapient Canada Inc.,
[2009] OJ No. 3739 (SC)

Facts

The plaintiff, Siemens, was a subcontractor on a computer systems contract that Sapient had entered into to install a computer system for Enbridge. After some disagreements, Sapient terminated Siemens' contract and locked Siemens out of the project facility and stopped it from doing any further work on the contract. Siemens brought a motion for a preliminary injunction prior to trial. Siemens asked that Sapient be restrained by a prohibitive injunction from terminating Siemens' contract, and also asked that Sapient allow Siemens access to the worksite, return certain items, and provide access codes. These latter requests were clearly for injunctive relief that was mandatory.

Decision

The motions judge decided that the injunction requested was mandatory and that the evidence did not meet the higher standard for a mandatory injunction. Even if it were determined to be a prohibitory injunction, Siemens did not meet the test for a prohibitory injunction either. First, there was little evidence of irreparable harm. If the contract was wrongly terminated, Siemens could be compensated by damages. Further, the risk of harm to Sapient by permitting Siemens to re-enter the premises and re-introducing it as part of the project at this late date would be so disruptive as to outweigh any risk Siemens might be subjected to. The injunction was therefore refused.

Practical Tip

Siemens might have benefited from incorporation of a negative covenant into its subcontract with Sapient to make it easier to obtain the prohibitory injunction it sought upon a contract dispute arising, as it did here.

Rescission

rescission
the cancellation, nullification, or revocation of a contract; the "unmaking" of a contract

Rescission is both a common-law remedy and an equitable remedy, although the term is used most commonly to refer to the equitable remedy. The purpose of rescission is to put the parties in the position they would have been in had the contract never been made. This is in contrast to the purpose of damages, which is to put the parties in the position they would have been in had the contractual obligations been performed.

void contract
a contract that does not exist at law because one or more essential elements of the contract are lacking; an unenforceable contract

Common-law rescission may be available to a party if the contract is **void** or **voidable** at his or her option. This would be an option with a void contract, such as a contract in which one party is a minor, or with a voidable contract, where the terms of the contract allow one party to avoid it as of right or upon the occurrence of some event. In these cases, that party has the right to rescind the contract without having to resort to the court for a remedy. The right to rescind a contract is different from the right to terminate or discharge a contract. A contract that is discharged is terminated or ended. A contract that is rescinded never existed.

voidable contract
a contract that may be avoided or declared void at the option of one party to the contract; once it is declared invalid no further rights can be obtained under it, but benefits obtained before the declaration are not forfeit

Equitable rescission can be granted by a court only as a remedy for a breach of contract by the other party. The intent is to restore the parties to their original positions. There is some similarity between common-law and equitable rescission, but equitable rescission is broader and is available in more circumstances. However, those circumstances must be exceptional. Again, the courts will not award an equitable remedy, including the remedy of rescission, where damages would adequately compensate the injured party. In restoring the parties to their original positions, the courts will order that moneys and property that had been exchanged be returned and that both parties be relieved of their obligations under the contract.

Rescission is awarded most often in cases that involve fraud, misrepresentation, or duress. Rescission can also be granted in cases that involve mistake, which is discussed in more detail in Chapter 4, Contractual Defects.

There are some restrictions on granting rescission in addition to the usual restrictions on equitable remedies. First, rescission cannot apply to part of a contract. If rescission is granted, the whole contract is rescinded. Second, it must be possible to restore the parties to their original positions (for example, the property that was the subject matter of the contract has not been destroyed or has not diminished substantially in value due to use). Third, the rescission cannot prejudice any innocent third party (for example, a third party who has purchased the property that is the subject matter of the contract).

> **EXAMPLE**
>
> **Rescission**
>
> Lina buys a refrigerator from Arnold's Appliances for $750. When the refrigerator is delivered and installed, Lina discovers that the freezer section of the refrigerator does not work. She wants to return the refrigerator and get her $750 back. She is asking for rescission. Arnold's Appliances offers to refund half the purchase price to compensate her for the non-functioning freezer. Arnold's Appliances is offering damages. In such a case, the court would likely award the remedy of rescission, since a refrigerator with a non-functional freezer section is of little value to Lina, and she could not be adequately compensated by an award of damages.

> **CASE IN POINT**

Damage Award May Be Available If Case for Rescission Due to Misrepresentation Fails

Xiaoyan Wu v. Xiaoming Yao, 2011 ONSC 3937 (CanLII)

Facts

Wu and Yao decided to go into the restaurant business together as equal partners. Yao had previous restaurant experience and Wu put up much of the capital and worked in the venture. The restaurant operated for six months but, for a variety of reasons, it did not do well. Six months into the operation, Wu took legal action against Yao, as she suspected Yao had misrepresented certain aspects of the business and its finances. Wu sued for misrepresentation and asked for rescission of the partnership agreement, and for damages flowing from Yao's alleged misrepresentation.

Decision

On the evidence, Wu failed to establish that there was misrepresentation that would render the partnership agreement void. Wu therefore was not entitled to rescission. Wu was awarded damages for breach of a provision of the partnership agreement where Yao was responsible for purchase of equipment to run the restaurant. But this was set off against rental payments Yao had made, reducing Wu's damages to $7,300.

Practical Tip

Though you may not be able to make a case for rescission based on misrepresentation, mistake, or other grounds, you may still be awarded damages for breach of contract.

Restitution

restitution
a remedy in which one
seeks to rescind a contract;
if granted, restitution
restores the party, as
far as possible, to the
pre-contract position

Restitution is an equitable remedy, the purpose of which is to restore the parties, as much as possible, to the position in which they would have been had no contract ever been made. Often, restitution can be accomplished by the remedy of rescission, discussed above. In some cases, however, simply rescinding the contract might not restore the parties to their pre-contract positions, because it could allow the party in breach to retain the benefits obtained under the contract, such as earned profits. In such cases, some form of compensation or recovery is necessary. Restitutionary recovery is based on the idea that the party in breach must disgorge to the injured party any benefits he or she gained under the contract before its rescission, where it would be unjust for him or her to retain such benefits. This must be distinguished from damages. The measure of damages is the amount of the loss of the injured party. The measure of restitutionary recovery is the amount by which the party in breach was unjustly enriched under the contract. Under the **unjust enrichment doctrine**, a party who breaches a contract at the expense of another should not be permitted to benefit from his or her wrongdoing. Therefore, a person who has been unjustly enriched at the expense of another can be required to make restitution in the form of payment of money. However, an exception exists for parties who are not parties to a contract but who are enriched as a result of a breach of that contract.

**unjust enrichment
doctrine**
the principle that a person
should not be permitted
to inequitably gain a
profit or benefit at the
expense of another

CASE IN POINT

Restitution Unavailable Where Unjustly Enriched Party Is Not Bound by the Contract

Elgin North Auto Body Ltd. v. Norman, [2011] OJ No. 4292 (Sm. Cl. Ct.)

Facts

Connors bought a 1998 BMW in 2004. Shortly after he bought it he transferred title to the car to Norman as security for a debt he owed her. At this point Norman was the owner of the car, although Connors still had possession and use of it. Connors was then involved in an accident and without saying anything to Norman, he took the car for repair to Elgin. Elgin completed the repairs and invoiced the insurer, which issued a cheque to Elgin. However, Norman found out about the accident and the repairs. As the registered owner, she would have accepted the insurance money and not repaired the car. She demanded the insurer pay her the money. The insurance company stopped payment on the cheque to Elgin and paid her. Elgin sued both Norman and Connors. Connors did not defend and judgment was entered against him. Norman, however, filed a defence—Connors, who had possession of the car and later disposed of it, had arranged the repairs without her knowledge or consent, and she denied that Elgin had any claim against her.

Decision

The action against Norman was dismissed. Elgin had no claim against Norman as she did not take the car in for repairs or authorize Connors to do so. It is clear she had no contract with Elgin. She had a reasonable belief, as owner of the car, that she was entitled to the insurance proceeds. Further, Elgin's claim for restitution failed as she received no benefit from the work done by Elgin, which, in any case, she did not request.

Practical Tip

It is a good idea for a business contracting with an apparent agent to verify that the agent has authority to bind the principal.

Discharge

In some circumstances, an injured party may choose to treat a contract as having been **discharged** as a result of breach by the other party. This is most common in cases where the injured party has not yet completed performance of his or her obligations under the contract. If this common-law remedy is available, the injured party no longer has any obligations under the contract and may treat the contract as being at an end. The injured party may then claim damages for breach of contract. The party in breach cannot compel the injured party to perform his or her obligations under the contract and cannot claim damages for non-performance by the injured party. However, an injured party who chooses to treat a contract as having been discharged may not claim remedies that are incompatible with this remedy, such as specific performance or rescission. In addition, an injured party who continues to accept the benefits of a contract after becoming aware of the breach may later be prohibited from claiming that the contract has been discharged by the breach and may be restricted to claiming damages only.

discharged
released, extinguished; a discharge of a contract occurs when the parties have complied with their obligations or other events have occurred that release one or both parties from performing their obligations

CASE IN POINT

Remedy of Discharge Requires Party to Act in Good Faith

G & K Services Canada Inc. v. Domingos Meat Packers Ltd., 2010 ONSC 5990 (CanLII)

Facts

G & K agreed to supply certain products to Domingos. In May 2005, after the contract had been in effect for a number of years, Domingos wrote to G & K giving notice that it was terminating the contract for failure by G & K to deliver the goods as contracted for. Further, Domingos stated that the quality of the goods delivered did not meet the requirements set out in the contract. G & K had the right under the contract to take steps to remedy deficiencies before the contract could be terminated. G & K responded by taking various steps to remedy the defects and asked for feedback and other responses, which Domingos did not provide. Notwithstanding G & K's efforts to provide a remedy, Domingos terminated the contract, effectively claiming a remedy for breach of contract by discharging the contract. G & K sued Domingos for breach of contract based on what it alleged to be Domingos' unlawful termination of the contract. At issue was whether Domingos was free to discharge the contract by giving notice of termination.

Decision

G & K was successful in its lawsuit and was entitled to damages for breach of contract by Domingos. A clause in the contract allowed G & K to attempt to remedy any deficiencies. G & K resolved virtually every deficiency raised, asked for feedback from Domingos, and was met with silence. In the circumstances, it could not be said that Domingos had the right to walk away from the contract. A party seeking to use the discharge remedy must exercise the remedy in good faith and not act capriciously or arbitrarily. Having discharged the contract in bad faith, Domingos was liable for damages to G & K.

Practical Tip

If you wish to seek a discharge of a contract based on the other party not fulfilling his or her obligations, you must fulfill all your obligations under the contract and act in good faith.

Quantum Meruit

quantum meruit
an equitable doctrine that states that no one should unjustly benefit from the labour and materials of another; under those circumstances, the law implies a promise to pay a reasonable amount, even in the absence of a contractual term for price; loosely translated as "as much as is deserved"

The doctrine of **quantum meruit** is most commonly relied on in two situations: first, where the contract is silent as to the consideration for the goods or services and, second, where the contract has been partially performed and the value of the performance must be determined.

If one party requests goods or services from another whose occupation it is to provide such goods or services, payment is understood and expected. That person may deliver such goods or services without a price being discussed. Nevertheless, this is not a situation of a gratuitous promise; payment is expected by both parties, and only the amount of the consideration has not been specified.

Even though the consideration is not specifically mentioned in the request, an agreement of this type will not fail for lack of consideration. The law will imply a promise to pay in a request for goods or services.

Where there is no mention of price, the implied promise is for payment of what the services are reasonably worth, or payment for *quantum meruit*. However, parties who have negotiated a contract that contains a term as to the price to be paid for the goods or services cannot later rely on the doctrine of *quantum meruit* to get a better price. *Quantum meruit* can be relied on only where the contract is silent as to the amount (quantum) of the consideration.

In determining what goods or services are reasonably worth, the courts look to the prices charged by similar suppliers and fix the contract price accordingly.

The remedy of *quantum meruit* is also available when the injured party has partly performed his or her obligations under the contract at the time of the repudiation by the other party. *Quantum meruit* is considered a quasi-contractual remedy. The injured party is entitled to compensation for the work performed even if it was not completed. The terms of a contract usually do not include a valuation of partially completed work. The doctrine of *quantum meruit* allows the injured party to obtain a valuation of, and compensation for, the work performed. The injured party must show that it was in fact the other party who repudiated the contract or made the completion of the contract impossible. This remedy is not available when the injured party has completed his or her obligations under the contract, in which case the appropriate remedy is damages.

EXAMPLE

Quantum Meruit

Cameron hires Deborah to renovate his kitchen for the sum of $5,000. Deborah has completed approximately 75 percent of the job when Cameron decides that he no longer wants the renovations and refuses to pay her or to let her finish. Deborah must prove that Cameron repudiated the contract, and because she did not complete the contract, she must claim the remedy of *quantum meruit* for compensation for the work done. Since she completed 75 percent of the contract, she is entitled to claim 75 percent of the contract price, or $3,750.

Quantum Meruit Award Where Contract Price Not Clear

Marine Clean Ltd. v. PC Forge, 2009 CanLII 10677 (ON SC)

Facts

Marine Clean provided a quote to provide industrial cleaning services to Forge. Marine Clean provided the service and invoiced Forge 18 months after the work started. While a quote had been given, it was not clear that it had become part of the contract. The invoice amount was much higher than the quote. Marine Clean argued that the work was greater than it had been led to expect, which delayed completion and increased costs. Marine Clean maintained that the work was done skillfully. Forge maintained that the invoice price was too high. Marine Clean sued on its invoice.

Decision

Marine Clean's claim was allowed in part. The actual contract price was not clear, and as the parties disagreed as to what it was or should be, the judge resorted to the doctrine of *quantum meruit* to assign a just price, as it was clear that there was a contract for services and that the services were performed. In this case, many of the invoiced items were not supported by documentation, and the project was not completed in a timely manner, which led to an increase in overall costs. In the circumstances, the court ordered Forge to pay half of the amount of the invoice as reasonable payment.

Practical Tip

If it is difficult to determine a precise price before work is done, set out in the contract the method to be used to determine an appropriate price. In contracts where performance occurs in stages, as in construction or renovation contracts, it may be useful to insert a schedule indicating the monetary value of the work completed at various stages, so that if a *quantum meruit* claim has to be made, it can be easily quantified.

Substantial Performance

Quantum meruit is normally not available to the party who repudiates a contract. However, the doctrine of **substantial performance** may be available. This doctrine recognizes that performing contractual obligations that do not entirely meet the terms of the contract but nevertheless confer a benefit on a party is of value and must be taken into consideration in determining the damages recoverable by the party claiming injury for non-performance and by the party claiming compensation for the partial performance.

substantial performance
performance of contractual obligations that does not entirely meet the terms of the contract but nevertheless confers a benefit on a party

Substantial Performance

Tony agrees to build a cottage for Marijke for $40,000. Tony builds the cottage but fails to complete the porch according to Marijke's design. Marijke claims that Tony has breached the contract and refuses to pay him the $40,000. Tony can argue the doctrine of substantial performance because he has substantially complied with the terms of the contract. A court would likely award Marijke damages to compensate her for the porch and deduct these damages from the amount of money it would order Marijke to pay Tony. If, for instance, it would cost Marijke $4,000 to have someone else complete the porch according to her design, she would be ordered to pay Tony the remaining $36,000.

Exclusion Clauses

Many modern contracts include an exclusion clause, also known as an *exculpatory*, *exemption*, or *limitation* clause. The purpose of such a clause is to limit, exempt, or exclude the liability of one party for breaching the contract. In a standard form contract—a contract that is preprinted and whose terms are non-negotiable—the exclusion clause favours the party who drafted the contract. Such a contract is also known as an **adhesion contract**.

Exclusion clauses are widely used by vendors because they allow a vendor to protect itself against liability and transfer any risk to its buyers. This is common where the vendor is not the manufacturer of the product but just the distributor, or in cases where the vendor is financing only the purchase of goods or equipment, such as with a financing or leasing company. If the product is faulty, the buyer then has the option of pursuing the manufacturer for a remedy. However, the exclusion clause prevents the buyer from seeking remedies against the vendor. In most cases this will mean that the buyer must still pay the vendor for the faulty product, although it may make a claim against the manufacturer for compensation.

The problem with exclusion clauses is that they are usually found in contracts where there is unequal bargaining power between the parties. The buyer is often unaware of the existence of the clause in the contract before signing it. Even if the buyer is aware of the clause, he or she may not understand its implications. In many cases, the buyer, even if objecting to the clause, has no choice but to sign the contract as is if he or she wants to buy the goods, since the vendor is unwilling to change the terms of its contract. An ordinary consumer simply does not have the bargaining power to negotiate the terms of such a contract. However, the courts have traditionally been wary of such onerous clauses, especially in contracts in which one party has little or no bargaining power. As a result, the courts have developed an approach that prevents many exclusion clauses from being used in circumstances that are unfair to the weaker party.

One requirement developed by the courts is that of **adequate notice**. In most cases, the courts assume that a party who signs a contract intends to be bound by the terms of the contract, even if he or she did not read the contract before signing it. However, if the contract contains a clause that is unexpected and unfair and that could not reasonably be expected to be found in a contract of that nature, the party who wishes to rely on the clause must bring the clause to the other party's attention and explain its legal implications before the contract is signed. If there is no notice of the existence of the clause, the court will not uphold the clause. The onus is therefore on the party relying on the clause to prove that the other party had adequate notice of it.

Another requirement developed by the courts is that the clause must be strictly interpreted. Exclusion clauses are usually drafted in very broad terms in an attempt to apply to the maximum number of possible situations. The courts have attempted to balance the notion that parties should have the freedom to contract (even if that means entering into contracts that are foolish) with the notion that allowing parties to evade responsibility under a contract is unfair. As a result, the courts apply the *contra proferentem* rule, which requires that a term of a contract, such as an exclusion

---

adhesion contract
a standardized contract for goods or services offered to consumers on a non-negotiable or "take it or leave it" basis, without offering consumers the opportunity to bargain over the terms of the contract

adequate notice
the requirement for a party who wants to rely on an exclusion clause in a contract to bring the clause to the other party's attention and explain its legal implications before the contract is signed

clause, be interpreted strictly. In the event of any ambiguity, or where there may be more than one interpretation of the term, the court must favour the interpretation of the term that favours the party who did *not* draft the clause. This rule is applied to all areas of contract interpretation but is of great importance in interpreting exclusion clauses.

TIP

In order to meet adequate notice requirements for an exclusion clause, consider printing the clause in a font that will be eye-catching and attract the reader's notice and attention, or require the reader to sign that he or she has read and accepts the terms—the latter is a common approach used with computer software downloads.

EXAMPLE

Exclusion Clause

Chester wants to lease a tractor from Farmco Equipment Rentals. Farmco presents Chester with a standard form contract, and draws his attention to the following standard exclusion clause:

> The lessee acknowledges that the lessor has made no representation or warranty with respect to the equipment, its condition, or fitness for purpose. The lessee shall unconditionally and without setoff pay the rent stipulated even if the equipment does not operate as intended by the lessee, or at all, or totally fails to operate or function. The lessor shall not be liable to the lessee for any loss, cost, expense, or damage caused directly or indirectly by the equipment or for any loss of business or other damages whatsoever.

Chester signs the contract, and the tractor is delivered to his farm. The next day, the tractor's engine stops working. Because Chester was given adequate notice of the clause and the wording of the clause was unambiguous, he is unlikely to succeed in a suit for breach of contract against Farmco.

Over the years, the courts have refused to uphold exclusion clauses for a variety of reasons. For example, the courts have stated that a clause that exempts a party from liability under the contract does not exempt the party from liability in tort. In other cases, if the party did not perform the terms of the contract exactly as agreed upon, the courts have stated that the exclusion clause does not apply because a different contract has been performed than that originally agreed upon. The result has been that exclusion clauses have become longer, broader, and more detailed in an attempt to prevent the ambiguity that might lead to applying the *contra proferentem* rule.

If the breach is a breach of a condition or a breach of a warranty and (1) adequate notice was given of the clause, and (2) the clause is carefully drafted and the *contra proferentem* rule does not prevent the application of the clause, the courts will uphold the application of the exclusion clause and relieve the party in breach from liability.

Choice of Remedies

The remedies available to an injured party depend in part on the method of breach and the nature of the breach. In the case of *anticipatory breach*, the injured party has the option of waiting for the date on which the performance is due. If the other party fails to perform on that date, the anticipatory breach becomes an *express*

Clear Exclusion Clause with Adequate Notice Binding

Cejvan v. Blue Mountain Resorts Ltd., [2008] OJ No. 5442 (SC)

Facts

Cejvan sued Blue Mountain for damages for injuries he sustained in an accident on Blue Mountain's ski hill. While snowboarding down a marked hill, he saw what he thought was a natural jump off the trail, and took it. Unfortunately, he hit three steel pipes that were covered with snow, as was the warning sign about the pipes. A ski patroller had noticed that the pipes and warning sign were covered but she took no steps to clear them. Cejvan sued Blue Mountain, alleging negligence. Blue Mountain argued that the exclusion and waiver clause on the lift ticket and Cejvan's contributory negligence in his going off the groomed trail absolved it of liability.

Decision

Cejvan's action was dismissed. Blue Mountain was clearly negligent, as its employee knowingly failed to clear the snow around the pipes so that a snowboarder or skier could have seen and avoided them. However, Blue Mountain was not liable to Cejvan because of the contractual exclusion of liability and waiver clause, of which he had ample notice and which was very clear: The clause stated that "[the] ticket holder assumes all risk of personal injury ... resulting from any cause whatsoever including ... negligence on the part of BMR and its employees." The increased risk due to the negligence of Blue Mountain might not have been covered by a general exclusion clause, but in this case, there was clear exclusion of liability due to Blue Mountain's negligence in the clause itself.

Practical Tip

If you wish to rely on an exclusion clause, make sure it is clearly worded, specifies all the risks contemplated, and comes to the attention of the other party prior to entering into the contract.

---

breach or *express repudiation*, and the injured party may proceed according to the nature of the breach. However, the injured party also has the option of claiming a remedy as soon as he or she learns of the anticipatory breach.

If the nature of the breach is the breach of a *warranty*, or a minor term of the contract, the injured party may not choose to treat the contract as having been discharged or to rescind the contract. If the term breached is a warranty, the court will usually award damages to compensate the injured party. This means that the injured party must still comply with his or her obligations under the contract. However, if the breach is a breach of a *condition*, or a major term of the contract, the injured party may choose to treat the contract as having been discharged or may rescind the contract. The injured party also has the choice of treating a breach of a condition as a breach of a warranty and accepting the lesser remedy of damages. However, the injured party does not have the option of treating a breach of a warranty as a breach of a condition.

The availability of equitable remedies to the injured party depends on the facts of each case. While the courts will look at the nature of the breach in determining whether to grant an equitable remedy, the primary considerations are still whether common-law remedies will adequately compensate the injured party and whether the injured party has come to court with "clean hands."

Summary of Remedies

Remedy	Purpose/Characteristics	Availability
Damages	• to put the injured party in the position he or she would have been in had the contract been fully performed • injured party must still comply with his or her obligations under the contract	• available for breach of warranty • available for breach of condition at the option of the injured party (other remedies are available)
Specific performance	• party in breach must perform his or her obligations under the contract • failure to comply amounts to contempt of court (fine or imprisonment possible)	• usually only available for sale of unique goods or real property • not generally available for contracts for personal services • only available if innocent party comes to court with "clean hands"
Injunction	• prohibitory injunction directs a person not to do a certain thing • mandatory injunction commands a person to do a certain thing	• may be available as an equitable remedy where a contract has been breached • not available if injured party could be adequately compensated by damages • not available if it would be unfair to, or cause irreparable harm to, the party in breach
Rescission	• to put the parties in the position they would have been in had the contract never been made	• available where contract is void (e.g., contract with a minor) or voidable (at option of a party where the terms of the contract allow) • available for breach of a condition (major term of the contract)
Restitution	• to put the parties in the position they would have been in had the contract never been made (same as rescission)	• available when rescission of the contract might not restore the parties to their pre-contract positions because it could allow the party in breach to retain benefits obtained under the contract (unjust enrichment)
Discharge	• injured party no longer has any obligations under the contract and may treat the contract as being at an end • damages may also be available • party in breach cannot compel injured party to perform his or her obligations and cannot claim damages for non-performance by the injured party	• available for breach of condition
Award based on *quantum meruit*	• determines compensation for goods or services to prevent one party from unjustly benefiting from the labour and materials of another	• available where the contract is silent as to the consideration for the goods or services • available where the contract has been partially performed and the value of the performance must be determined

CHAPTER SUMMARY

A party may breach a contract through an express or implied repudiation by failing to perform the contract obligations. A party may also commit an anticipatory breach by communicating his or her intention to repudiate the contract before the time or date set for performance. A party may commit a breach of a condition (a breach of a term that goes to the root of the contract) or a breach of a warranty (a breach of a minor term of the contract). Exclusion clauses are often found in adhesion contracts, which are preprinted contracts, the terms of which are usually non-negotiable. Such a clause must be brought to the attention of the weaker party and will be strictly interpreted by the courts.

In the event of a breach of contract, the injured party is most commonly entitled to an award of damages to compensate for the loss flowing from and consequential to the breach. Damages are intended to put the injured party in the position that he or she would have been in had the contract not been breached. An injured party may also claim the equitable remedies of specific performance, injunction, rescission, or the quasi-contractual remedy of *quantum meruit*. In the event of a breach of a condition, the injured party is ordinarily entitled to claim rescission, discharge, or damages. However, in the event of a breach of a warranty, the injured party is usually restricted to an award of damages.

KEY TERMS

adequate notice, 190
adhesion contract, 190
anticipatory breach, 174
breach of contract, 174
consequential damages, 178
discharged, 187
equitable remedies, 181
expectancy damages, 178
express repudiation/express breach, 174
implied repudiation, 175

injunction, 182
interlocutory/interim injunction, 183
liquidated damages, 178
lost opportunity damages, 178
mandatory injunction, 182
mitigate, 179
negative covenant, 182
prohibitory injunction, 182
quantum meruit, 188
repudiate, 174

rescission, 184
restitution, 186
specific performance, 181
substantial performance, 189
unjust enrichment doctrine, 186
unliquidated damages, 178
void contract, 184
voidable contract, 184

REVIEW QUESTIONS

True or False?

_____ 1. Claus ordered goods from Kai Wen. Kai Wen failed to deliver. As a result, Claus was unable to supply his customers with those goods. Claus can sit back and let the damages he sustained from loss of sales continue to increase and then sue Kai Wen for all his losses.

_____ 2. In order to obtain an order for specific performance, you must show that you have behaved ethically and properly in the circumstances surrounding your claim.

_____ 3. The purpose of rescission of a contract is to put the person who seeks to rescind in the same position he or she would have been if the contract had never existed.

_____ 4. Deva hired Boris to do customized repair work on her sailboat. Boris does all the work except for one minor piece. Deva is only obliged to pay him if he does all of the work for which he was contracted.

_____ 5. Exclusion clauses will be subjected to much more scrutiny by the courts than other provisions of the contract.

_____ 6. The remedy of discharge is available for breach of a warranty.

_____ 7. Failure to comply with an order for specific performance will give rise to damages.

Multiple Choice

1. Ariel has contracted to supply widgets to Beatrice. The day before deliveries are to begin, Ariel tells Beatrice that she will not be able to supply the widgets.
   a. This is an example of anticipatory breach.
   b. If Beatrice finds a new supplier at a lower cost, she can't sue Ariel.
   c. Beatrice can sue Ariel for specific performance.
   d. a and b

2. Ali hired FlybyNight Renovations to install a new kitchen in his home. Ali later discovers that FlybyNight is selling off its equipment to a used equipment company.
   a. This is an example of anticipatory breach.
   b. This is an example of mandatory breach.
   c. This is an example of implied repudiation.
   d. a and c

3. A term of a contract that, if breached, wholly deprives the innocent party of the benefit of the contract is called
   a. a breach of term certain
   b. a breach of warranty
   c. a breach of condition
   d. none of the above

4. The following is an example of liquidated damages:
   a. damages for loss of future earnings caused by a breach of contract
   b. damages for personal injury caused by a breach of contract
   c. damages for failure to repay a contract debt
   d. a and b

5. A party who has breached a contract
   a. is liable for reasonably foreseeable losses of the innocent party
   b. may be liable for consequential damages
   c. will be liable for damages that are not too remote
   d. all of the above

6. Cosimo de Medici agreed to buy an antique bowl from Antonio's Antiques. Antonio then tells Cosimo that he decided to sell the bowl to someone else for more money.
   a. Cosimo can sue only for damages.
   b. Cosimo has to mitigate his damages by trying to buy a similar bowl somewhere else.
   c. Cosimo may obtain an order for specific performance.
   d. None of the above.

7. Moab hires Abel Realty to sell his house. One of the contract conditions is that Erik, an agent employed by Abel whom Moab dislikes, has no involvement of any kind in the transaction. Moab discovers that Erik found the buyer and is therefore entitled to a commission. Moab refuses to pay the commission.
   a. Moab will likely be able to obtain an injunction to prevent Erik from participating in the deal.
   b. Moab can sue only for damages.
   c. Moab's condition is unreasonable and the courts will not enforce it.
   d. The contract is void and Moab should rescind it.

8. Walid bought a new Zipmobile. He has had the car for three months and it is clearly a lemon. He wishes he had bought something else. Walid should
   a. claim damages for the defective car
   b. obtain a mandatory injunction requiring the seller to furnish a new automobile
   c. claim rescission, returning the car and getting his money back
   d. none of the above

9. Restitution
   a. will restore the parties to their pre-contact positions
   b. will require a party who has been unjustly enriched to disgorge any profit
   c. is an equitable remedy
   d. all of the above

10. A party may rely on the doctrine of *quantum meruit* where
    a. a gratuitous promise has been made
    b. the parties have been silent as to the precise price
    c. the contract has been partly performed and the value of part performance must be determined
    d. b and c

Short Answer

1. What options are available to the innocent party in the event of anticipatory breach?

2. Explain the difference between breach of a condition and breach of a warranty.

3. What is the purpose of damages?

4. Define "consequential damages."

5. What is the test for determining the remoteness of consequential damages?

6. When is an injunction available? What are the different types of injunctions? Explain the difference in the standards to obtain these different types of injunctions.

7. Describe the duty to mitigate. What is the result of a failure to properly mitigate damages?

8. What is the difference between rescission and restitution?

9. With what conditions must a party comply to claim an equitable remedy?

10. Under what circumstances is the remedy of specific performance available? When will specific performance not be awarded?

11. What conditions must be present for the courts to enforce a claim for *quantum meruit*?

12. Explain the purpose of an exclusion clause. What must be proved by the party seeking to uphold an exclusion clause?

Apply Your Knowledge

1. Sylvie, a scientist, enters into a contract with Central Hospital to perform research for them exclusively for a period of two years. However, during that time, Central Hospital discovers that Sylvie is also working on a research project for another hospital. What remedies are available to Central Hospital? What factors would the court take into consideration in determining what remedies to grant to Central Hospital?

2. Nicholas, a carpenter, contracts with Alexandra to build an addition to her house for $15,000. When he has completed all the work except the installation of two windows, he refuses to complete the contract. Can Alexandra discharge the contract? Can she rescind the contract? Is Nicholas entitled to be paid anything for his work? Why or why not? What remedies are available to Alexandra?

3. Gilbert bought a vacuum cleaner from Sullivan Cleaning Machines one month ago. During that time, the vacuum cleaner has broken down eight times, and Gilbert has been able to use it only once. Gilbert wants to return the vacuum cleaner and get his money back. Sullivan Cleaning Machines says that the vacuum cleaner can be repaired and has offered to repair it at no cost. However, Gilbert says that he has returned the vacuum cleaner twice for repairs but the problem has not been solved. The contract also states that Sullivan Cleaning Machines is not liable for any defects in the vacuum cleaner and that it makes no warranties as to the condition or fitness for purpose of the vacuum cleaner. The company further states that the customer shall be entirely responsible for the cost of any repairs. What remedies are available to Gilbert? What remedy would you recommend? What arguments would Sullivan Cleaning Machines make? What remedy would a court be likely to award?

4. Elite Manufacturers Ltd. has prepared a contract bid for a lucrative contract with Bijou Theatres Inc. to construct its new multiplex theatre. Elite Manufacturers Ltd. is told by an inside source at Bijou Theatres that it has a very good chance of getting the contract because none of the other bidders has much experience in building theatres. The bid must be submitted by noon on January 15. Elite Manufacturers contracts with Express Courier Co. to deliver the bid package. Express Courier advises that it can deliver the package by 10:00 a.m. on January 15. The courier slip, which is filled out and signed by an employee of Elite Manufacturers, states in very fine print on the back, "Carrier's liability for loss, damage, destruction, or injury to a shipment shall not exceed the lesser of $1.50 per pound or $50." Unfortunately for Elite Manufacturers, the bid is not delivered on time and the company does not win the contract. Discuss the issues that arise in this case with respect to breach of contract, and render a decision.

5. Murgatroyd Holdings hired Khan Environmental to repair the malfunctioning heating and air conditioning system in one of its buildings. Khan indicated that the estimated cost of the repairs would be $40,000 based on a preliminary inspection, but that the unit would have to be taken apart to discover the extent of the problem. Khan indicated that the price might be higher than the estimate after the unit was taken apart, depending on what

parts and work were needed. Murgatroyd said it would pay the estimated price and that Khan was to go ahead with the work as described in its letter. Khan did so, and disassembled the unit. When it did so, it found further parts that had to be replaced, and invoiced Murgatroyd separately for $10,000. Murgatroyd paid the $40,000 but refused to pay the invoice for $10,000.

a. What argument might Murgatroyd make to support its refusal to pay the $10,000?

b. What might Khan argue in reply?

Electronic Contracts and E-Commerce

9

Introduction 200

The Legislative Framework
for E-Commerce 201

E-Commerce Issues: Problems
and Solutions 207

Chapter Summary 220

Key Terms 220

Review Questions 220

Appendix: Electronic Commerce
Act, 2000 223

LEARNING OUTCOMES

After completing this chapter, you should be able to:

- Explain the general approach taken by e-commerce legislation to contracts on the Internet.

- Describe the provisions of e-commerce legislation as they relate to mode of delivery, timing, and location of e-contract documents.

- Describe what shrink-wrap, click-wrap, and browse-wrap agreements are, and explain how the issues of notice and consent are affected by these three types of agreements.

- Understand how the electronic format, generally, influences consent.

- Explain the similarities and differences between pen-and-ink signatures and e-signatures, and distinguish between the two types of digital code systems.

- Describe what electronic agents are, and explain how this new technology is treated in e-commerce and under the traditional law of principal and agent.

- Describe how jurisdiction is determined for online contracts, having regard to both legislation and traditional common-law concepts.

Introduction

e-commerce
commercial transactions using the Internet; sometimes used interchangeably with e-contracts

The emergence of electronic business transactions, known as **e-commerce**, has raised many questions involving contract law. Existing contract principles and rules address some of these matters, and legislation has been enacted in most jurisdictions to clarify the law and create stable, predictable modern business relations. The common-law rules regarding offer and acceptance discussed in Chapter 2 have been addressed in the new legislation. The questions raised by e-commerce include:

- Do the advances in electronic communication require changes to the law of contract?

- Do we need to regulate these e-commerce transactions differently from other contracts?

- If a contract is or must be in writing, how do you sign an electronic contract?

- Where a computer program engages in an online transaction on behalf of a website, without supervision or oversight, how are errors corrected and who is liable for the actions of the computer program?

- When and how is an online contract formed?

- If there is a dispute about an online contract, how do we determine which court has jurisdiction?

e-contracts
contracts where the entire contracting process takes place on the Internet; sometimes used interchangeably with e-commerce

- How do you cancel an **e-contract**, or repudiate one if you have made an error?

These questions are clearly very important for the smooth running of modern business transactions. In 2011, there were 2.3 billion Internet users in the world, approximately 32.7 percent of the world's total population. Since 2000, Internet use has grown 528.1 percent.[1] Much of this traffic is made up of e-commerce, involving trillions of dollars in transactions.

In this chapter, we address the questions above and other e-contract questions. Although the case law on e-contracts is sparse, it appears that contract law does not have to be reinvented to meet the demands of e-commerce. Rather, we will see that contract principles and rules that you are familiar with can be applied to solve disputes and resolve issues involving e-contracts. There are two reasons for this. First, the courts favour adaptation of existing rules of law to novel situations. This has long been a hallmark of our legal system and should come as no surprise. Second, most jurisdictions have followed a UN-sanctioned international model for creating a statute to govern e-commerce that is designed to avoid making issues more complicated than they need to be. Ontario, for example, has enacted the *Electronic Commerce Act, 2000*. As you will see, many of the questions at the beginning of this chapter can be resolved by reference to various provisions of the *Electronic Commerce Act, 2000*. The Act is reproduced as an appendix to this chapter.

---

1   Internet World Stats, April 2012, http://www.internetworldstats.com/stats.htm.

The Legislative Framework for E-Commerce

Legislation on e-commerce has generally focused on issues of legal enforceability of e-commerce contracts, and the authentication of electronic documents, contracts, and records. Legislators have approached the job of creating e-commerce statutes in a variety of ways, but they can be reduced to three different general approaches. As e-commerce began to grow in the last decade of the 20th century, the earliest legislative responses used a very specific approach, enacting strict guidelines regarding the use of specific technologies. This was not a very productive approach, as computer technology changed rapidly and this type of legislative response, narrowly focused as it was, quickly became obsolete and irrelevant.

A second type of response granted basic legal recognition to all electronic authentication of e-documents, but gave special benefits to approved authentication techniques. This approach, however, was too narrow, focusing as it did on authentication issues only—that is, are the senders and receivers who they say they are, and is the contract verifiable?

The third approach is sometimes referred to as an enabling approach. It does not prescribe either specific technologies or specific procedures. Rather, it takes a minimalist approach to facilitate the process of creating legally valid and binding contracts—in effect making e-commerce work as fluidly and seamlessly as possible.

Canada has opted for the third approach. The federal government and all provinces and territories of Canada have passed e-commerce statutes. All of these statutes are based on a model statute developed by the Uniform Law Conference of Canada in 1999.[2] This, in turn, was heavily influenced by the United Nations model e-commerce legislation, which set out basic international e-commerce standards. This model has been followed in much of the rest of the world.[3] The net result is that Canadian e-commerce legislation, and the Ontario legislation in particular, mirrors the minimalist approach taken in most of the rest of the world, and is designed to facilitate e-commerce.

Overview of the Ontario Electronic Commerce Act, 2000

The Act establishes rules for commercial, consumer, and public transactions made by electronic means, including those made by use of an electronic agent, such as a computer program that can collect and store information, and that can act and make decisions without human review or oversight. The Act also provides for ways in which a person can "sign" an electronic document so that the electronic signature functions for legal purposes like a signature on a paper document (s. 1).

---

2   "Uniform Electronic Commerce Act," June 20, 2012, http://www.ulcc.ca/en/poam2/index.cfm ?sec=1999&sub=1999ia.

3   "UNCITRAL Model Law on Electronic Commerce (1996)," June 20, 2012, http://www.jus.uio.no/ lm/un.electronic.commerce.model.law.1996/doc.html.

Application

The Act applies to the provincial Crown and to provincial public agencies, including municipalities (ss. 1–2).

Electronic Documents

Generally, the Act makes electronic documents and document forms equivalent to analogous paper documents for most purposes, as long as the electronic document

- maintains the integrity of the original paper document as to form and content,
- can be retained, stored, retrieved, and reviewed by the recipient, and
- meets the standards set out in the Act.

If the document meets these requirements, it will be deemed to meet the requirements for documents in writing pursuant to the *Statute of Frauds* and under other statutes where documents in writing are required, unless expressly prohibited (ss. 4–10).

EXAMPLE

E-Document That Is Equivalent to a Paper Version

Thieu has agreed to guarantee Sergei's debt to Nina of $1,000. Thieu uses a word-processing program to create an electronic version of the debt guarantee. It is laid out like a paper guarantee and has the same content elements. Thieu signs the document using an electronic signature of the simple kind, his typed name, and sends the document to Nina by email. Nina is able to download the document, store it, and retrieve it if she needs to review it later. The electronic document will therefore be acceptable as equivalent to a paper document and will meet the requirements of the *Statute of Frauds*.

Electronic Signatures

Electronic signatures may be used in place of written signatures. While the Act does not set out specific technological requirements, to be valid and acceptable, an electronic signature must

- reliably identify the person using it;
- create a reliable association of the electronic signature with the document to which it is attached;
- meet any prescribed requirements as to method of signature or prescribed technology requirements, if any—for example, encryption requirements imposed by a party; and
- where a seal is to be affixed to a document, meet the previously discussed signature requirements as well as any prescribed seal equivalency requirements (s. 11).

Public Bodies Conducting Business

Public bodies may conduct business using electronic systems and documents, provided that the body has given its express consent and that the Act or another statute does not prohibit the use of electronic documents (ss. 14–18).

Offer and Acceptance

Offer and acceptance or other contract-related communication may be expressed by use of electronic documents or electronically transmitted information unless the parties agree otherwise (s. 19).

EXAMPLE

Electronic Offer and Acceptance

Griselda calls Marisol and offers to sell Marisol her bike for $100. Marisol says she needs to think about it. The next day, she sends Griselda an email stating that she accepts the offer. Because the parties did not specify the mode of communication for acceptance, Marisol's electronic acceptance is valid.

Electronic Agents

An electronic transaction may use an **electronic agent** that completes or performs a transaction electronically without supervision or oversight by an individual, but the Act makes a transaction with an electronic agent unenforceable in the following circumstances:

- the individual makes a material error in electronic information or in an electronic document used in the transaction;
- the electronic agent does not give the individual an opportunity to prevent or correct the error and the individual promptly notifies the other party;
- consideration is received as a result of an error and the individual fails to return or destroy the consideration in accordance with the other party's instructions; and
- the individual, in the case of an error, benefits materially by receiving the consideration.

electronic agent
a computer program or other electronic means that can act (or respond to acts or documents) without review or oversight by an individual at the time the act or response occurs

EXAMPLE

Use of an Electronic Agent

Howard wishes to buy his textbooks online at 2:00 a.m. He goes to the Texts R Us website to make his purchases. There is no one overseeing the transaction from the seller's end, and an electronic agent handles the entire transaction. Howard looks through the online catalogue and selects the books he needs. He lists them on a web page called "the shopping cart." The page also has conditions of sale, including information about the cost of shipping, taxes, and returns. All of this is set out on a summary page showing the items purchased along with the total cost. The website asks him to review the transaction and sets out the terms, to which he must click "I Agree" if he wishes to complete the transaction. When he clicks, the transaction is complete, and Texts R Us will courier his purchases to him and debit his credit card, which he uses to pay. The site gave him the opportunity to review the purchase prior to its completion, so this is a valid electronic agent under the Act. If Howard had made an error, he would have had to notify the seller promptly, and the website should allow him to do this. If Howard wished to cancel the order because of a material error, he also would have to return the books if they were delivered, and the seller must refund payment, returning the parties to their pre-contract positions.

When E-Communications Are Deemed to Be Sent and Received

The Act has clear rules about *when* communications are deemed to be sent and received, although parties may opt out of these rules and adopt their own. These rules have obvious applications in determining when offers and acceptances have been sent or received. The importance of the timing of offers and acceptances is discussed in Chapter 2. Different rules apply depending on the situation:

- *Where the parties are using different systems:* Electronic information is deemed to be sent electronically when it is beyond the sender's control.

- *Where the parties are using the same system:* The information is deemed to be sent when the information becomes capable of retrieval by the addressee.

- *Where the addressee has a designated system (one the addressee has designated for this type of communication, such as a website order system):* Electronic information is deemed to be received electronically once it becomes capable of retrieval.

- *Where the addressee does not have a designated system (or one that is ordinarily used for particular types of communication):* Information is deemed to be received when the addressee becomes aware of the communication and is able to retrieve it (ss. 22(1)–(3)).

EXAMPLE

When an E-Communication Is Deemed to Be Sent and Received

Agnes and Joyce have been negotiating over the sale by Agnes of a painting. They have been communicating by email using their email accounts. Neither has designated a particular system for this kind of communication. (If one of the parties conducted sales on a website, requiring the other to use the site to make a purchase, that would be a designated system.) Joyce sends an email to Agnes saying, "Will you accept $300 for the painting?" Once Joyce has sent the email, and it is in Agnes's inbox ready to be retrieved, it is deemed to be sent. It is also deemed to be received when it is in Agnes's inbox and Agnes becomes aware that it is there and is able to retrieve the email from Joyce.

Where E-Communications Are Deemed to Be Sent from and Received

The Act sets out clear rules about *where* an e-communication is deemed to be sent from and received. Where there is an alleged breach of contract or other issue involving the transaction, the location may be important in determining which court has jurisdiction over the parties. This can be an issue where a party's office is in one place, but the computer that sends communications is located halfway around the world.

- Electronic communications are *deemed to be sent* from the sender's place of business.
- Electronic communications are *deemed to be received* at the addressee's place of business.
- If the parties have more than one place of business, then the one most closely related to the e-transaction is *deemed to be the place of business*. But if there is no e-transaction, the principal place of business is deemed to be the place of business.
- If a party does not have a place of business, then the person's *habitual residence* will be used to determine location.
- The parties may contract out of these provisions and create their own rules (ss. 22(4)–(7)).

EXAMPLE

Where an E-Communication Is Deemed to Be Sent from and Received

In the previous example, Joyce and Agnes are deemed to be sending their emails to each other from their respective places of business (or their homes, if this transaction is not related to either of their businesses), even though their Internet service provider (ISP) running their email and its server may be in another country. If this was a business transaction and each had branch offices, then the one most closely related to the negotiations would be deemed to be the place of business for each of them.

Other Provisions

SHIPMENT OF GOODS

There are special rules governing electronic communications involving the shipment of goods, because both common law and statute law relating to the shipment of goods assign great importance to shipment documentation. Generally, contracts for shipping goods may be created electronically, as can almost any communication connected with the shipping contract—for example, monitoring a shipment or signing for receipt of goods. There is a requirement that documents of title, if electronic, meet reasonable standards of reliability. As with other parts of the Act, these standards are not prescribed and are left to be determined as a question of fact. Nor is the technology to be used prescribed (s. 23).

ELECTRONIC FORMS

If there is authority in a statute to prescribe forms, or the manner of submitting them, this includes the power to prescribe electronic forms and provide for electronic submission of them. If a form is prescribed by an act, the *Electronic Commerce Act* permits regulations to be made to create electronic versions of those prescribed forms. If a law prescribes a particular manner of communicating information, the Act authorizes regulations to be made to create an electronic means of communicating information (ss. 24–25).

STATUTORY OVERRIDE

The *Electronic Commerce Act* is of general application, and does not override any law that expressly authorizes, prohibits, or regulates the use of electronic documents or communication. Nor does the Act override any requirement that information be posted and displayed in a particular way. For example, if a notice, by law, must appear in a newspaper, then the Act does not override this provision, although electronic posting is not prohibited by this provision (s. 26).

FREEDOM OF INFORMATION AND PRIVACY LEGISLATION

The Act does not limit or override the provisions of provincial freedom of information and privacy legislation that are intended to protect the privacy of individuals or to provide rights of access to information held by public bodies. For example, if documents could be accessed electronically, they cannot be made available if it results in an invasion of privacy covered by freedom of information and protection of privacy legislation (s. 27(1)).

Where a document is covered by freedom of information and protection of privacy legislation, and that document is in a non-electronic form or was created and communicated non-electronically, the Act does not authorize a public body to destroy a non-electronic document where its retention is required by law or its destruction is in accordance with a schedule established by law (s. 27(2)).

BIOMETRIC INFORMATION

The Act does not apply to the use of biometric information used as a signature (for example, the recording of the scanning of a fingerprint or determination of DNA), unless another statute permits it or the parties to a transaction involving biometric information expressly consent to its use (s. 29).

DOCUMENTS NOT SUBJECT TO THE ACT

The Act does not apply to the following documents: wills; trusts created by wills; powers of attorney; negotiable instruments such as cheques, bills of exchange, and promissory notes; and registerable land transactions. The Act also does not apply where another statute specifically sets out a system or procedure for conveying information or data electronically. An example is the registration of a security agreement under the *Personal Property Security Act*, which can be done electronically following a specific system using specialized software. The Act also does not apply to anything done under the *Election Act* or the *Municipal Elections Act, 1996* (ss. 30–31).

REGULATIONS

The Act sets out the power to make regulations. As of the date of writing, no regulations have been made. The power to make regulations includes the power to designate bodies that are or are not public bodies, to prescribe classes of documents to be covered under the Act, and to create requirements with respect to seals and signatures on documents (s. 32).

E-Commerce Issues: Problems and Solutions

The Ontario *Electronic Commerce Act, 2000* (and similar legislation in other parts of Canada) has provided a basic framework for creating valid and enforceable contracts electronically, leaving the technology choices up to the parties. This approach has resulted in minimal change to statute and common law, including the law of contracts. Nevertheless, legal issues have arisen, often having to do with the impact of technology on e-commerce processes involved in creating contracts, assenting to their terms, verifying that assent, correcting errors, and determining jurisdiction to decide e-commerce disputes. We turn below to a discussion of some of these issues.

Shrink Wrap, Click Wrap, and Browse Wrap: Has a Contract Been Formed?

While it is clear that legislation facilitates the formation of electronic contracts, it does not speak specifically to the consequences of the ways in which terms can be presented to a party in the formation of a contract, and how the process might be policed or controlled. There are three main types of electronic transactions that have attracted attention involving the presentation of contract terms.

The first type is a **shrink-wrap contract**. Here, you buy the product on the Web and have it shipped to you; the product is often encased in plastic packaging moulded or shrunk to fit the box, hence the name. After opening the package, you find that there are additional contract terms that you did not see and may not have been aware of when you bought the product. In some cases, instead of being inside the packaging, binding terms may be printed and enclosed as part of the documentation accompanying the package when it is shipped and delivered to you. While shrink-wrap contracts are common in e-contract situations, they predate the use of Internet contracts and are certainly still available by purchasing from a store.

The second type is a **click-wrap contract**. Here, when you purchase something on a website, you are given the opportunity, before the transaction is completed, to read through terms of the contract on the website. You are required to click or otherwise indicate agreement with those terms before the transaction can continue and be completed. There is no actual requirement that you read the posted terms; the only requirement is that you click to acknowledge that you agree with them, whether you read them or not. If a purchaser refuses to agree, the transaction is not completed.

shrink-wrap contract
a transaction where there are additional terms or conditions inside the packaging or in documentation furnished after the purchase; the purchaser does not see these additional terms until after the transaction is completed

click-wrap contract
an electronic transaction where the purchaser sees the terms and must click on an icon that indicates the purchaser has agreed to the terms before the transaction is completed; also called a "click-through" agreement

browse-wrap contract
an electronic transaction where the purchaser is able to click and see the terms of a contract on a website, but is not required to read or agree to them to complete the transaction

The third type is a **browse-wrap contract**. While browsing a website, you may see a notice containing terms and conditions that state that they bind anyone using the website or the services offered on it. You do not have to click or otherwise indicate to those controlling the website that you have seen, read, or agree to the terms. The mere use of the website raises the presumption of agreement; you do not actually have to see the terms and conditions.

Shrink-Wrap Agreements

Shrink-wrap agreements, on their face, appear to violate the common-law rules of contract by imposing binding terms on a party that the party did not agree to when entering into a contract to purchase goods. Surprisingly, this does not appear to be the case. Courts in Canada and elsewhere have held that if the seller gives notice, prior to the completion of the purchase, that there are additional binding terms on the inside of the package, then those terms are binding, even though the buyer cannot see those terms until after the purchase is completed. The fact that you cannot know the actual terms without opening the package or taking delivery of it after ordering it on the website, even though you had notice that there are additional terms, does not seem to have bothered the courts. In the US case of *ProCD, Inc. v. Zeidenberg*,[4] the Federal Court referred to a shrink-wrap contract as a "rolling contract," holding that the contract was not complete at purchase, as one would normally assume, and that having been given notice of additional terms, the consumer was bound by them if he or she then proceeded to purchase the item, even though the consumer had not seen them before he or she took delivery.

In *Systemshops*, the issue was whether there was any notice at all. (See the Case in Point below.) As this case demonstrates, failure to give notice of additional terms may be fatal to the claim by the party relying on a shrink-wrap agreement.

But a further problem concerns the adequacy of notice. Some websites may technically provide notice, but do so in such a way that notice is deemed to be inadequate, which is an issue in situations involving not only shrink wrap, but also browse wrap and, to some extent, click wrap. Consider the observations of a US court considering the evidence of the adequacy of notice given on a website in a case involving a web-based shrink-wrap agreement:

> This license agreement is not set forth on the homepage but is on a different web page that is linked to the homepage. However, the visitor is alerted to the fact that "use is subject to license agreement" because of the notice in small gray print on gray background. Since the text is not underlined, a common Internet practice to show an active link, many users presumably are not aware that the license agreement is linked to the homepage. In addition the homepage also has small blue text which when clicked on, does not link to another page. This may confuse visitors who may then think that all colored small text, regardless of color, do not link the homepage to a different web page.[5]

---

4   *ProCD, Inc. v. Zeidenberg*, 86 F.3d 1447 (7th Cir. 1996).

5   *Pollstar v. Gigmania Ltd.*, 170 F.2d 974 (ED Cal. 2000).

A Valid Shrink-Wrap Agreement Requires Notice of Terms

North American Systemshops Ltd. v. King, [1989] AJ No. 512, 68 Alta. LR (2d) 145 (QB)

Facts

King had purchased a computer program on a disk from the plaintiff, North American Systemshops. The plaintiff discovered that King had breached copyright by making multiple copies of the program, which the plaintiff argued was prohibited by the terms of the licence agreement that was shrink-wrapped inside the package containing the program purchased by King. King argued that the licence terms did not apply to him because he had no notice of them prior to purchase.

Decision

The plaintiff's action was dismissed. The copyright claim failed because the plaintiff failed to establish it had actual ownership of the copyright, but the court also held that the licence was not binding on the defendant. The licence statement was in the inside back cover of a booklet that came shrink-wrapped with the product, but the user would not have to refer to the booklet for general use. The plaintiff gave no other notice on the outside of the packaging, or elsewhere prior to purchase, that there were additional binding terms.

Practical Tip

If you are including additional terms inside a shrink-wrap package, it is wise to put notice of these terms in large, clear print on the outside of the package. The notice should indicate that there are additional terms inside that are binding on the purchaser. Better yet, indicate what these additional terms relate to—a user licence agreement, for example.

Click-Wrap Agreements

The click-wrap agreement appears to be a better way of providing notice of terms because it requires the user to click "I Agree" before the transaction can be completed. Courts have generally upheld such transactions, as the purchaser had the opportunity to read and agree to all the terms prior to completing the transaction.

Browse-Wrap Agreements

With a browse-wrap agreement, the operator of the website provides the user the opportunity to read the terms governing the transaction but does not require the user to click to indicate agreement prior to the purchase. Courts seem to be split on the enforceability of a browse-wrap agreement. Some courts have held that browse wrap does not create a contract. There needs to be some manifestation of assent on the user's part, and there is no specific act indicating this assent. The only act by the user is to download a product or complete an order, and that is a more ambiguous indicator of assent than with a click-wrap agreement. Other courts, however, have held that browse-wrap agreements are arguably enforceable if the notice of terms is sufficiently clear so as not to be easily overlooked. This approach follows the approach taken in shrink-wrap agreements, which are deemed to be valid if there was adequate notice of additional terms.

CASE IN POINT

Read the Terms Before You Click on "I Agree"

Rudder v. Microsoft Corp., 1999 CanLII 14923 (ON SC)

Facts

Rudder claimed that Microsoft had breached its agreement, and proceeded to sue in Ontario. Microsoft countered that the dispute was to be determined in the US courts because the sales agreement contained this term, which the purchaser agreed to by clicking on the website his agreement to all terms. Rudder claimed that the terms were not clearly presented because he could read the agreement only one computer screen at a time. He said that he scanned through the terms, paying attention only when he came to the cost of the subscription, at which point he clicked on the "I Agree" button on the agreement. There were two opportunities during registration to withhold agreement, and a notice that subscribers were bound by the entire agreement, whether or not they read it. The terms were all in the same font size, although some clauses were in capital letters.

Decision

Rudder's case was dismissed. There was no factual basis to claim the forum clause amounted to being in fine print. The term was presented no differently from the rest of the multiple printed pages, which a person was obliged to read one page at a time. The notice that the agreement was binding was clear and unequivocal.

Practical Tip

The courts will apply the common law of contracts to electronic transactions, so despite the tedium of scrolling through the terms in an electronic format, you should check them carefully before clicking on "I Agree," because you will likely be bound by them.

Does the Electronic Format Influence Consent?

In many of the shrink-wrap, click-wrap, and browse-wrap cases, the courts appear to pay very little attention to the environment in which individuals engage in e-commerce or the way in which Internet sites, as a medium, influence behaviour. There is an assumption in most cases, as in the Cases in Point cited in this chapter, that a transaction on the Internet is no different from one on paper. But academic commentators have noted that paper and electronic media are indeed different, that electronic media may have a psychological effect on the viewer that paper does not have, and that these differences may require regulation of content and presentation of electronic formats.[6] Consider these examples:

- A 13-year-old boy bought $3 million worth of goods through the eBay™ website just by clicking an icon on several online auctions.
- An auction on eBay™ for what at first appeared to be the sale of a Playstation® console reached $300, even though the box for the Playstation®, and not the Playstation® console itself, was the item for sale. The seller had written "sell Playstation box at …" This was ambiguous enough that on a quick read-through, one might assume that a Playstation® console was for sale.

---

6   Vincent Gautrais, "The Colour of E-Consent" (2003-4) 1 U.O.L.T.J. 189-212.

CASE IN POINT

Adequacy of Notice in a Browse-Wrap Agreement

Kanitz v. Rogers Cable Inc., 2002 CanLII 49415 (ON SC)

Facts

The plaintiffs had subscribed for high-speed Internet access from the defendant. When the computer program was downloaded and installed on the plaintiffs' computers, they were provided with a user agreement. The agreement indicated that it could be amended from time to time by Rogers, and that notice would be given by email, ordinary mail, or a posting on the Rogers website. Rogers did amend the agreement and gave notice on its website. The plaintiffs continued to use Rogers, arguably accepting the contract amendments. The plaintiffs claimed otherwise, and that notice was inadequate.

Decision

The notice was deemed adequate. Had the plaintiffs taken the time to go to Rogers' website, they would have seen a notice that the user agreement had been amended. The plaintiffs continued to use Rogers' service subsequent to the posting of the notice and the amended user agreement. Under the terms of the user agreement, they were deemed to have accepted the amendments. The amendments were easily accessible on the Rogers website and were clearly identified by a bold heading within the amended user agreement. There was, therefore, adequate notice given to customers of the changes to the user agreement, which then bound the plaintiffs when they continued to use the defendant's service.

Practical Tip

Read online contracts carefully and note links to other documents and to information about future notices of amendments. You may wish to download and print all contractual documents concerning the transaction before you agree to the contract if you think you are more likely to read them from a printed version.

- On an adult website, the client "signed" a contract containing a clause that was reasonably hidden from the viewer, providing that the local Internet connection to the site would be subject to long-distance charges, to be paid by the client. About 50,000 people in North America signed up without reading the clause in question.[7]

Internet users expect the purchase process to be a quick one, but often it is not. As a result, they will often skim through or ignore contract terms and click the "I Agree" icon in order to simply complete the transaction as quickly as possible. In having to examine a transaction one screen at a time, it is difficult to check one part of a transaction against another, as one may wish to do for a transaction on paper. Ask yourself how often you read the terms of use or other terms before you click the "I Agree" icon. The contract terms are often in smaller print in a dull and formalistic layout, very long, and in legalese rather than in user-friendly language. Contractual terms are often found at the bottom of a web page and may be overlooked entirely. These online transactions are usually complex, involving a succession of steps with requests for information. Material on a monitor may be distracting—with moving images, for example, that make reading difficult. Perhaps regulation as to content and presentation of electronic formats would, in fact, be a worthwhile legislative initiative. To date, though, there seems to be no movement beyond academic discussion.

---

7   Ibid. See also footnotes 8 and 9, infra.

Summary: Electronic Transactions

	TYPE OF AGREEMENT		
	Shrink-Wrap Agreement	**Click-Wrap Agreement**	**Browse-Wrap Agreement**
Location of Terms	• The product is delivered encased in plastic packaging, moulded or shrunk to fit the box. • Terms in addition to those on the website appear inside the packaging or in the accompanying documentation. The purchaser would not have seen these terms at the time of formation of the contract.	• Before the transaction is completed, the purchaser is given the opportunity to read through all the terms of the contract on the website. • The purchaser is required to click "I Agree" to indicate agreement to the terms, or the transaction cannot be completed.	• The terms of the contract are available to be read somewhere on the site. • The purchaser is not required to click on a button or otherwise indicate agreement to the terms. The purchaser may not even see them.

Adequacy of Notice	• If there is notice on the website that there are additional binding terms on the inside of the package, then those terms are binding.
	• It is advisable to indicate what the additional terms relate to.
	• It is also wise to put notice of these additional terms in large, clear print on the outside of the package.
		• If the purchaser clicks "I Agree," then the purchaser is likely bound to those terms, regardless of whether there is a large amount of material to read, or whether it is in fine print.	• There is conflicting case law:
			  – Some courts have held that there needs to be some manifestation of assent on the purchaser's part, and there is no specific act indicating this assent, aside from downloading or completing an order form.
			  – Other courts, however, have held that these agreements are enforceable if the notice of terms is sufficiently clear so as not to be easily overlooked.

Hyperlinks and Contract Formation

hyperlink
text or image on a web page that, when clicked on, takes the user to a linked page

A **hyperlink** is composed of words on a website, usually in a different colour from other text, and often underlined. (A hyperlink may also be applied to an image such as a photo or icon.) When the hyperlink is clicked on, it leads to a document other than the one on which the hyperlink appears. Is a hyperlinked document part of the transaction or document in which the hyperlink appears, or is the linked document external to the document or transaction in which the hyperlink appears and completely separate from it? The issue has been raised in several cases, but there does not appear to be a uniform answer to this question. Because this issue has not yet been settled by the courts, users should keep in mind that the second document may be considered part of the first document, even if it contains additional terms, and drafters should ensure that notice of the link is clear and obvious.

The Supreme Court of Canada was asked to consider the effect of a hyperlink in another case, this one involving a claim for libel. Though this is not a contracts case, the issue raised is of interest as it relates to commerce and liability on the Internet. (See the Case in Point below.)

Click on the Link to Get the Whole Picture

Dell Computer Corp. v. Union des consommateurs, 2007 SCC 34, [2007] 2 SCR 801

Facts

Dell advertised a hand-held computer on its website. Due to an error on the site, it posted two different prices. Dumoulin attempted to order at the lower price and Dell refused to process Dumoulin's order. With the help of the Union des consommateurs, Dumoulin filed a motion for authorization to institute a class action suit against Dell. Dell invoked an arbitration clause contained in the terms and conditions of the sale. One of the issues concerned the location of the arbitration clause. There was a hyperlink in the main contract form on the website that linked to other terms and conditions on a separate linked document.

Decision

The Supreme Court of Canada held that the arbitration clause was not an external one within the meaning of the Quebec *Civil Code*. If it had been a paper contract and the arbitration clause had been physically separate, the clause would likely have been seen as an external document and presumably not part of the contract. The Court held that the traditional test of physical separation under the *Civil Code* could not be transposed in the context of e-commerce. Because the hyperlink appeared in the main contractual document and was easily accessed, it could not be said to be separate from the contract, and the link itself was notice to Dumoulin that there was further material to consider.

Practical Tip

Be sure that attention is carefully drawn to any hyperlink to another document that contains important information that you consider to be part of the main document.

As we have seen, if a link appears in a contract, the reader is expected to click, read, and be bound by the terms if the reader proceeds. But apparently, from the case above, if you are posting a hyperlink in a document you create to a document you did not create, you have no responsibility to check the linked document or accept any responsibility for the contents. While these cases can be distinguished on their facts and the legal issue considered, they do not lead to a clear picture of when a hyperlink can be relied on to legally link two documents.

E-Signatures

Section 11 of the *Electronic Commerce Act, 2000* clearly permits and contemplates electronic signatures. The Act requires that a signature reliably identify the signer and reliably be connected to the document signed. However, the Act does not say how this should be done. Given the Act's technological neutrality, this is not surprising, but it does give rise to problems of identification and verification where any electronic symbol may suffice as a signature, because there is no assurance that the transmitter of a series of symbols is who he or she claims to be. So, if I simply type my name in a message to you, I use the letters of my name, but anyone could be sending it and you would have no way of knowing whether it was me or someone else.

The issue of electronic signatures arose in *Zundel*. (See the Case in Point below.) While *Zundel* is not a contract case, it is a good example of the types of security issues that can arise regarding the simple use of one's name or other identifier entered directly into electronic communications. To address this problem, there are

CASE IN POINT

Responsibility for Website Content Posted Under a Person's Name

Zundel, Re, 2005 FC 295 (CanLII)

Facts

Ernst Zundel is a well-known Holocaust denier. In deportation proceedings, the contents of a website he maintained were considered in evidence, and there was an issue of whether he was responsible for content posted in his name on the site. One of the Zundel website documents presented to the court bore Zundel's electronic signature in the form of his name printed at the bottom of the article on the site; Zundel claimed he never put his name at the bottom of the article on the website. On further questioning, he admitted that he agreed with the content of the article and that he would not do anything to distance himself from it.

Decision

The court decided that the electronic signature was affixed to the documents with his authorization. Zundel's evidence was considered to be internally inconsistent. He claimed that his wife posted articles on the website under the name of Ernst Zundel, that she had full authority over the website, and that he had no control over what was posted. However, he then admitted that he agreed with the content. The court found that if he had disagreed with the content, he would never have allowed anyone to use a website bearing his name to disseminate information and propaganda worldwide.

Practical Tip

If you are operating a public website where employees are authorized to enter information on it, make sure to check the website regularly and use a log-in security system so that you can monitor who adds and changes entries.

---

symmetric cryptosystem
a form of electronic signature that uses an alphanumeric code known to both sender and recipient that allows the recipient to verify who the sender is

asymmetric cryptosystem (public key encryption)
a form of electronic signature consisting of a private and public key; the sender controls both and sends them as the signature on a document; the recipient can access the public key to unlock the private key to decrypt the document and verify the signature, but the codes in the private key are not revealed to the recipient

PIN
a personal identification number used in a symmetric cryptosystem to identify one party electronically to another party

two digital code systems in common use by those engaged in e-commerce. The first is referred to as a **symmetric cryptosystem**, and the second as an **asymmetric cryptosystem** (also called **public key encryption**).

The symmetric cryptosystem is the simpler of the two systems and involves the use of a single alphanumeric code known to both the sender and the receiver. An example of this type of code is the password you use to access your email. You indicate to the email service provider what your password is, and when you later use it to open your account, the email server recognizes the password as yours and lets you access your mail. Another example is the personal identification number (**PIN**) that you use with a credit or debit card at a cash machine or in stores, and for online banking. Both you and the bank know the number, and the bank recognizes you as the person getting cash from your account, using the credit or debit card, or transferring funds. Symmetric encryption is secure if only you and a trusted recipient know the code, and if neither your system nor the other party's has been hacked, but it is problematic where it is used for secure communications involving several parties, where some may not be trustworthy or even known to you.

A more secure system is asymmetric encryption. This is much more complicated than symmetric encryption. To put it simply, the person creating the signature has two keys or codes, a private key and a public key. You sign a document using the private key known only to you and shared with no one, including any recipient. It will encrypt the document and in the process act as a signature for you, because only you have the private encryption key. When you send the encrypted message, the recipient will receive the private key and the public key, which the recipient can use to decrypt the document, and in the process identify you as the signer. The keys are related in

Safety of Handwritten Versus Electronic Signatures

Newbridge Networks Corp, Re, [2000] OJ No. 1346, 48 OR (3d) 47 (SC)

Facts

Newbridge proposed a procedure for shareholders and others to vote on stock option issues by using an electronic voting system. Some of the parties involved challenged the proposed procedure.

Decision

Justice Farley noted "for most intents and purposes and on balance the electronic procedure envisaged is a safer and more reliable system than is that which relies on the mails or other delivery systems. Password integrity has been built in." When a voter signs electronically using a password, it is far easier to verify than the usual pen-and-ink signature would be if challenged. This does not mean that electronic signatures are guaranteed to be secure, though, because someone can obtain and use a password without authorization. The following are some interesting comments of Farley J on the traditional signature:

My signature at the present time looks usually something like an ultra-squiggle. However, my signature may vary from time to time—in fact signature to signature. In generic terms my signature may be depicted as something like "xxxx" but it may vary and be "xxx," "xx," or "xxxxxx." I give an illustrative anecdote. Some years ago I was a witness to a document which was to be filed in a South Carolina land registry office. That office returned the document explaining that the signature >ultra squiggle< did not accord with my print name "J. M. Farley" and that it should be re-executed. Tilting at windmills or the bureaucracy in a foreign land is never truly productive. I re-executed my signature in a more legible squiggle as "J. M. Farley" as I may have signed it a half century ago in grade school. Both >ultra squiggle< and grade school squiggle "J. M. Farley" were my signatures on that document as I intended those writings to be my signature. If I execute an electronic signature, that too is my signature as I intend it to be my signature (and the recipient is so advised of that intention in the context).

Practical Tip

If you are using an electronic signature or a password, it is better to encrypt it, and it is of vital importance that it be kept secure. If you are using an ink signature on paper and verification is crucial, consider having the document notarized or having it witnessed by someone who would be trusted to verify your signature, such as a bank manager or licensed professional.

---

that what the private key can do by encrypting a message, the public key can undo, but the public key cannot reveal the internal contents of the private key to the addressee. Even here there may be security issues: while the public key can open a message sent using the private key, there is no guarantee that the user of the private key is who he or she claims to be. This problem could be addressed by having a single certifying authority that both sender and receiver could rely on to ensure that a digital signature belongs to the person using it. While there are a variety of certifying bodies used to certify that websites are what they say they are, there is no single body in Canada authorized by statute to certify symmetric or asymmetric encryption keys.

If the purpose of signing a contractual document is to verify the content of the document and signify agreement to its terms, then electronic signatures purport to do the same thing as ink signatures on paper. While electronic signatures may be quicker and easier to verify than signatures in ink on paper, they are still not foolproof. Issues involving their misuse will have to be resolved in ways similar to cases involving the misuse of ink signatures on paper—by searching for evidence that verifies the authenticity of the signature—but instead of calling in handwriting experts, parties to disputes about electronic signatures will be calling in computer security experts.

Electronic Agents

The *Electronic Commerce Act, 2000* contemplates the use of electronic agents. These are computer programs that select or gather information or documents, or complete or perform a transaction electronically, without supervision by an individual. The Act recognizes that, unlike other contract situations, you cannot ask for clarification from an electronic agent, and the Act addresses this concern in a situation where an individual makes a material error and wants to correct it. A material error is one that is not minor or trivial. The electronic agent must provide a reasonable opportunity for the individual to prevent or correct the error, but the individual must act promptly once the error is discovered. For example, most websites offering goods or services will provide a summary page where the user is asked to check the details of the transaction, and an opportunity is provided to correct any obvious errors before he or she completes the transaction. If an error is discovered after the contract is made, the parties are expected to return the consideration, in effect returning the parties to their pre-contract positions.

The situations contemplated here mirror the contract law of mistake, but the Act goes further and is simpler. The type of mistake the individual makes is not categorized beyond being classed as material. Also, it does not matter whether the electronic agent recognizes or identifies the error, but it does require the individual to do so and act promptly to correct the error. If the electronic agent makes an error, it is not afforded the same rights as the individual.

The correction of errors an individual makes is not the only legal issue that arises with electronic agents. There is also the question of whether the person who directs or uses an electronic agent is liable for things the electronic agent does when there is no actual oversight or overt control of the process. It is clear that those who operate or use electronic agents are responsible for what those agents do, and that the normal rules of agency law apply. If you use an electronic agent to, on your behalf, enter into contracts, search websites, download information, or do other things, you as a principal are liable for the acts your agent made on your behalf and at your direction. The fact that you were not aware of the specific details of the electronic agent's activity will not provide a defence because you "instructed" the electronic agent to do certain things, so you will have to accept the consequences of the agent's actions.

Jurisdiction Over E-Contracts: Statutory and Common Law

Jurisdiction in contract disputes refers to the question of which court has jurisdiction to resolve the dispute, and which law applies. If the parties all reside in Ontario, the goods contracted for are in Ontario, and the breach occurs in Ontario, there is no real issue about jurisdiction—the Ontario courts would have jurisdiction because everything about it that determines jurisdiction is connected to Ontario. But suppose you are located in Ontario and order goods manufactured in China on the Internet from a service provider located in the United Kingdom, and the goods are shipped from a subsidiary of the manufacturer located in Malaysia. Which country's courts will have jurisdiction, and which country's laws will apply? Statute law answers only some of the jurisdictional questions. Most of the answers are left to the

CASE IN POINT

Principal Liable for Acts of Electronic Agent

Century 21 Canada Limited Partnership v. Rogers Communications Inc., 2011 BCSC 1196

Facts

Century 21, a real estate broker, maintained a website where users could obtain details of properties listed for sale by the broker. Rogers, through a subsidiary, ran a website that featured real estate listings. The Rogers site used a search engine as an electronic agent to access the Century 21 site and comb it, looking for properties within certain parameters, and would then post the details obtained from the Century 21 site on its own website. Century 21 sued Rogers for trespass and unauthorized use of its materials. There was evidence that browse-wrap terms of use posted on the Century 21 site precluded the kind of activity Rogers' subsidiary was engaged in. One of the defences advanced by Rogers was that its search engine automatically checked the Century 21 site and downloaded information, and that no employee of Rogers was involved in the process, so it did not have notice of the terms of use and could not be liable for violating them.

Decision

The court rejected the idea that the use of an electronic agent such as a search engine relieved Rogers of responsibility. The court noted that the search engine had to be programmed by an individual, and that the user of a tool such as an electronic agent has to accept responsibility for what the tool does. Liability is not avoided simply because the act is automatic, or because the search engine was unaware of the conditions of use.

Practical Tip

Be very careful when setting the parameters on an electronic agent so that you limit its selections to what is necessary. Also remember to create opportunities for those dealing with the electronic agent to ensure that it is not encroaching on others' legal rights and not creating liability for wrongdoing.

common law, but the common law on determining international jurisdictional disputes can be extraordinarily complex—and adding in e-commerce as a factor increases that complexity. The location of the website content provider, the host server, any intermediaries, and the end users and their servers and intermediaries are all added factors that have to be considered to determine jurisdiction.

Statutory Determination of Jurisdiction

The *Electronic Commerce Act, 2000* makes a modest contribution to determining jurisdictional issues. Sections 22(4)–(7) provide that electronic information or documents are deemed to be sent from the sender's place of business to the recipient's place of business. If there is more than one place of business for a party, then the one most closely related to the document or transaction is deemed to be the place of business. If there is no place of business, then the party's habitual residence is deemed to be the place of business. Note that this definition speaks to a physical location rather than an address on the Internet or the place where computers, service providers, or websites are actually located. Section 22 addresses only one piece of the jurisdictional picture: it can help to resolve any dispute about where a communication or document was sent from and received, but we need to look at this in the context of the common-law tests.

Territorial Jurisdiction: Applying the Common Law

At common law, in e-commerce cases, the courts try to determine jurisdiction on a reasonable basis, which in Canada has led to a "substantial connection" test (see the Case in Point on *Braintech* below). The test examines all relevant factors to see which jurisdiction is most closely connected to the transactions. Although *Braintech* deals with libel rather than e-commerce, it illustrates how Canadian common law on jurisdiction can be applied to cases involving Internet communication.

In the United States, the test is slightly different. A defendant cannot be brought before the court unless he or she has minimal contacts with the jurisdiction so as not to offend "traditional notions of fair play and substantial justice."[8] For example, a product may be offered on the Internet, and consumers in hundreds of locations might purchase it. If it turns out the product is defective, should the offeror have to defend hundreds of lawsuits in different jurisdictions where the purchaser's address may be the only connection to a particular jurisdiction? The answer to this question should be "no."[9]

Jurisdiction Over the Parties: Applying the Common Law

Questions about e-commerce jurisdiction are generally answered by applying the usual common-law test—that is, finding a substantial connection to a jurisdiction. But the courts also have to determine whether specific parties are actually involved in a dispute within their jurisdiction. This issue has been raised in e-commerce cases because of the number of parties that may have a connection to an Internet transaction. In Canada, the Supreme Court of Canada has distinguished between active and passive e-commerce participants. A service provider that merely acts as a conduit of information transmitted by others, with no specific knowledge of the contents transmitted, will generally not be liable with respect to the content transmitted.[10] An Internet service provider would have to have some kind of active involvement to attract liability. For example, if it undertook to block pornography sent by its servers and failed to do so effectively, a service provider could attract liability even though it was not the author of the offending material.

---

8 *International Shoe Co. v. Washington*, 326 US 310, 66 S. Ct. 154 (1945).

9 For an excellent discussion of jurisdiction and other legal issues in the context of Internet communications from which much of this analysis of jurisdiction is taken, see R. Orpwood, "Electronic Contracts: Where We Have Come from, Where We Are and Where We Should Be Going" (2008) 1:3 Int'l. In-House Counsel J. 455.

10 *Society of Composers, Authors and Music Publishers of Canada v. Canadian Assn. of Internet Providers*, 2004 SCC 45 (CanLII).

Determining Jurisdiction in Disputes Involving Internet Communication

Braintech v. Kostiuk, 1999 BCCA 169 (CanLII)

Facts

Braintech claimed that Kostiuk used the Internet to transmit and publish defamatory information about Braintech. The information was posted through a discussion group or bulletin board. Braintech carried on business in Texas and obtained a default judgment against Kostiuk in the state of Texas. It then commenced an action to enforce the judgment in British Columbia. Kostiuk was a non-resident of Texas and had no place of business in Texas. It was not alleged that there was any commercial activity by Kostiuk in Texas or that anyone in Texas had read the alleged libel. Kostiuk did not defend the British Columbia action, and judgment was obtained against him. Kostiuk appealed and asked that the action in British Columbia to enforce the Texas decision be dismissed on the ground that, on the facts, there was no connection to Texas on which jurisdiction of the Texas courts could be established.

Decision

The appeal was allowed. The trial judge erred in failing to consider whether there were any contacts between the Texas court and the parties that could amount to a real and substantial presence. British Columbia was the only natural forum, and Texas was not an appropriate forum.

Where an e-commerce transaction occurs, liability may fall on the seller, the content provider, the service provider, other Internet intermediaries, the purchaser, or the purchaser's service provider. Given the number of participants, an examination of which jurisdiction has a substantial connection, based on the facts of each case, is crucial.

Practical Tip

When contemplating litigation involving e-commerce, or any communications over the Internet, consider the facts carefully to determine which jurisdictions are connected to the factual issues. Where there is a choice, exercise it on the basis of which jurisdiction is most convenient for you in terms of cost, effort, and whether the law in one jurisdiction favours your particular legal situation more than another jurisdiction. If you have the opportunity, insert a clause in the contract identifying which court will have jurisdiction over disputes.

CHAPTER SUMMARY

In Canada, electronic commerce is regulated to some extent by statute law at both the provincial and federal levels. All Canadian statutes, such as the Ontario *Electronic Commerce Act, 2000*, follow the enabling approach, which minimally interferes with the process of creating and validating electronic contracts—allowing for adaptation to evolving technology—and generally follows the common law regarding the creation of contracts. The common law continues to operate with respect to offer, acceptance, consent to terms, formality requirements, and the use of contracting agents in much the same way as it does for contracts not involving electronic communication.

Nonetheless, some new legal issues, or old legal issues in an electronic context, have arisen. Issues of consent and contract formation commonly arise from the presentation of contracts on the Internet, and particularly with shrink-wrap, click-wrap, and browse-wrap agreements. In general, the cases indicate that if a party is given notice of terms, even if all terms are not disclosed immediately, then a party using the Internet for a transaction will be bound. In considering the notice issue, the courts have paid little attention, so far, to the way in which electronic presentation may obscure the presentation of terms, and notice of them. The impact of hyperlinks on the presentation of contract terms has raised the issue of whether, and in what circumstances, the law will view a linked document as part of the main document or transaction in which the hyperlink appears.

Electronic signatures, under both statute and common law, are viewed as equivalent to pen-and-ink signatures. Validation of either kind of signature can be problematic, though advances in e-signature technology make e-signatures generally more secure and easier to validate than their pen-and-ink counterparts. Also, the use of electronic agents is permitted, provided an individual can correct errors made with an agent. Otherwise, the ordinary law of agency appears to apply, and principals are bound by the acts of their agents, electronic or otherwise.

Electronic commerce has resulted in complex questions concerning where a transaction occurred and which courts have jurisdiction over disputes. Legislation provides one piece of the answer in determining where the place of business of a party to an e-transaction is located, but much of the answer will still be based on the common law, where jurisdiction is based on a substantial connection to a jurisdiction determined on all of the facts. In considering these issues, including who may be liable, the law distinguishes between passive and active participants, the former being Internet service providers that merely act as conduits, without overseeing the content of what they are transmitting.

KEY TERMS

asymmetric cryptosystem
   (public key encryption), 214
browse-wrap contract, 208
click-wrap contract, 207

e-commerce, 200
e-contracts, 200
electronic agent, 203
hyperlink, 212

PIN, 214
shrink-wrap contract, 207
symmetric cryptosystem, 214

REVIEW QUESTIONS

True or False?

_____ **1.** All documents created as e-documents under the *Electronic Commerce Act, 2000* are automatically equivalent to the written documents under the *Statute of Frauds*.

_____ **2.** Graziella runs an antique sales operation in London, England, with branches in Paris and Rome. She has a website that is hosted and run from an ISP in Kazakhstan. Maurice, in Toronto, orders an antique chair from Graziella online from her London store. Graziella's place of business, according to the *Electronic Commerce Act, 2000*, is deemed to be Kazakhstan.

_____ **3.** Contracts for the carriage of goods are governed by special rules under the *Electronic Commerce Act, 2000*.

_____ **4.** An asymmetric cryptosystem is a code to identify you as a sender, as in the case of a bank card password, known only to you and the bank.

_____ **5.** The *Electronic Commerce Act, 2000* does not apply to the use of biometric information as an electronic signature.

_____ **6.** The *Freedom of Information and Protection of Privacy Act* and the *Election Act* are not subject to the provisions of the *Electronic Commerce Act, 2000*.

Multiple Choice

1. Canadian e-commerce statutes can best be characterized as
   a. taking a technologically specific approach
   b. recognizing approved authentication techniques
   c. taking an enabling approach
   d. none of the above

2. An electronic agent under the *Electronic Commerce Act, 2000*
   a. can collect and store data
   b. can make decisions without human oversight or intervention
   c. creates contracts that are always binding on individuals using the electronic agent
   d. a and b

3. An electronic signature under the *Electronic Commerce Act, 2000*
   a. is always binding and is the equivalent of an ink signature
   b. does not have to identify the person using an e-signature
   c. cannot be used to seal a document
   d. none of the above

4. Lin sends a contract acceptance by email to Sunil. They use different email systems and neither has designated a system for this type of communication.
   a. Lin is deemed to have sent it when she clicks the "send" button on her email system.
   b. Sunil is deemed to have received it when it arrives in his inbox.
   c. Sunil is deemed to have received it when he becomes aware that the message is in his inbox and he can retrieve it.
   d. a and c.

5. Gorus goes online to buy a canoe. In small print several pages into the website, there is a brief message that additional terms may apply to any canoe purchase, and there is a hyperlink to the additional terms. Gorus doesn't see the message about additional terms and clicks on the icon for "complete purchase."
   a. This is a click-wrap agreement.
   b. This is a browse-wrap agreement.
   c. This is a shrink-wrap agreement.
   d. None of the above.

6. On the facts in question 5 above, Gorus might advance the following argument as a successful defence:
   a. Shrink-wrap agreements are illegal.
   b. Notice of additional terms must be set out clearly and they were not in this case.
   c. Gorus has to indicate that he has read all the terms of the contract before they apply.
   d. None of the above.

7. A certifying authority
   a. is required under the provisions of the *Electronic Commerce Act, 2000*
   b. is used to verify and confirm encryption keys
   c. a and b
   d. none of the above

8. Morris, who lives in Toronto, ordered goods from a website maintained by a service provider in Vancouver for a company based in Florida. The goods were delivered to Toronto from Florida but were manufactured in Belize. They were found to be defective when received by Morris in Toronto. The court least likely to have jurisdiction is
   a. Vancouver
   b. Toronto
   c. Florida
   d. Belize

9. Mirella ordered a book online. On the website, terms and conditions were set out in legalese, with an icon marked "I Agree" that she had to click on in order to complete the transaction.

   a. If she clicks on the "I Agree" icon, she is bound by the terms.

   b. The terms must be in plain language in order to be binding.

   c. She is not bound if she didn't read the terms before she clicked on the "I Agree" icon.

   d. None of the above.

10. The following documents are subject to the *Electronic Commerce Act, 2000*:

    a. a contract for the purchase of services

    b. a will

    c. a contract for the purchase of goods

    d. a and c

Short Answer

1. What is the approach to e-commerce taken by the Ontario *Electronic Commerce Act, 2000*?

2. What does the Act apply to?

3. Does the Act make all electronic documents automatically equivalent to paper ones? Explain.

4. Are electronic signatures the equivalent of pen-and-ink signatures? Explain.

5. Can you make and accept offers electronically? Are there any limitations that apply?

6. What is an electronic agent? Give an example.

7. Are transactions with electronic agents always enforceable? Explain.

8. When is electronic information deemed to be sent and received? Use examples to explain.

9. Does the Act cover every e-transaction in Ontario? Describe any limitations.

10. Explain what is meant by shrink-wrap, click-wrap, and browse-wrap agreements.

11. What contract issues do shrink-wrap, click-wrap, and browse-wrap transactions raise?

12. How do we determine which court has jurisdiction over an electronic transaction case?

Apply Your Knowledge

1. Read the Case in Point on *Rudder v. Microsoft Corp.* on page 210 of the text. This case was decided in 1999, prior to the passage of the *Electronic Commerce Act, 2000*. Is there anything in the Act that might have resulted in a different decision from the one made in this case? Explain.

2. Consider whether acceptance has been communicated and a contract formed in the following examples:

   a. Allan emails Betty on Monday and offers to sell her his car for $3,000. She emails him back the same day and accepts his offer. Allan does not check his email.

   b. Allan phones Betty and offers to sell her his car for $3,000. She tells him that she will get back to him. She emails him the same day, accepting his offer. He uses his email only for work and doesn't check it. Betty doesn't phone him back, so he sells the car to Charles.

   c. Allan meets Betty and offers to sell her his car for $3,000. She cannot decide immediately, so Allan tells her to email him before Wednesday, although he usually uses his email address only for work. On Tuesday Betty emails him her acceptance.

3. The chapter opened by posing the following questions. Provide brief answers to these questions, using examples to explain your answers.

   a. Do the advances in electronic communication require changes to the law of contract?

   b. Do we need to regulate these e-commerce transactions differently from other contracts?

   c. If a contract is or must be in writing, how do you sign an electronic contract?

   d. Where a computer program engages in an online transaction on behalf of a website, without supervision or oversight, how are errors corrected and who is liable for the actions of the computer program?

   e. When and how is an online contract formed?

   f. If there is a dispute about an online contract, how do we determine which court has jurisdiction?

   g. How do you cancel an e-contract, or repudiate one if you have made an error?

Appendix: Electronic Commerce Act, 2000

SO 2000, c. 17

General

Definitions

1(1) In this Act,

"electronic" includes created, recorded, transmitted or stored in digital form or in other intangible form by electronic, magnetic or optical means or by any other means that has capabilities for creation, recording, transmission or storage similar to those means and "electronically" has a corresponding meaning;

"electronic agent" means a computer program or any other electronic means used to initiate an act or to respond to electronic documents or acts, in whole or in part, without review by an individual at the time of the response or act;

"electronic signature" means electronic information that a person creates or adopts in order to sign a document and that is in, attached to or associated with the document;

"public body" means,

   (a) any ministry, agency, board, commission or other body of the Government of Ontario,

   (b) a municipality or its local board, or

   (c) an entity that is designated as a public body by a regulation made under clause 32(a).

Extended meaning of "legal requirement"

(2) In this Act, a reference to a legal requirement includes a reference to a provision of law,

   (a) that imposes consequences if writing is not used or a form is not used, a document is not signed or an original document is not provided or retained; or

   (b) by virtue of which the use of writing, the presence of a signature or the provision or retention of an original document leads to a special permission or other result.

Crown

2. This Act binds the Crown.

Use, etc., of electronic information or document not mandatory

3(1) Nothing in this Act requires a person who uses, provides or accepts information or a document to use, provide or accept it in an electronic form without the person's consent.

Implied consent

(2) Consent for the purpose of subsection (1) may be inferred from a person's conduct if there are reasonable grounds to believe that the consent is genuine and is relevant to the information or document.

Same

(3) Subsection (2) is subject to section 14 (public bodies).

Payments

(4) For greater certainty, subsection (1) applies to all kinds of information and documents, including payments.

Functional Equivalency Rules

Legal recognition of electronic information and documents

4. Information or a document to which this Act applies is not invalid or unenforceable by reason only of being in electronic form.

Legal requirement that information or document be in writing

5. A legal requirement that information or a document be in writing is satisfied by information or a document that is in electronic form if it is accessible so as to be usable for subsequent reference.

Legal requirement to provide information or document in writing

6(1) A legal requirement that a person provide information or a document in writing to another person is satisfied by the provision of the information or document in an electronic form that is,

(a) accessible by the other person so as to be usable for subsequent reference; and

(b) capable of being retained by the other person.

Additional rules, public bodies

(2) Subsection (1) is subject to section 16.

Legal requirement to provide information or document in specified non-electronic form

7(1) A legal requirement that a person provide information or a document in a specified non-electronic form to another person is satisfied by the provision of the information or document in an electronic form that is,

(a) organized in the same or substantially the same way as the specified non-electronic form;

(b) accessible by the other person so as to be usable for subsequent reference; and

(c) capable of being retained by the other person.

Additional rules, public bodies

(2) Subsection (1) is subject to section 16.

Legal requirement re original documents

8(1) A legal requirement that an original document be provided, retained or examined is satisfied by the provision, retention or examination of an electronic document if,

(a) there exists a reliable assurance as to the integrity of the information contained in the electronic document from the time the document to be provided, retained or examined was first created in its final form, whether as a written document or as an electronic document; and

(b) in a case where the original document is to be provided to a person, the electronic document that is provided is accessible by the person so as to be usable for subsequent reference and capable of being retained by the person.

Integrity and reliability

(2) For the purposes of clause (1)(a),

(a) the criterion for assessing integrity is whether the information has remained complete and unaltered, apart from the introduction of any changes that arise in the normal course of communication, storage and display;

(b) whether an assurance is reliable shall be determined in light of all the circumstances, including the purpose for which the document was created.

Additional rules, public bodies

(3) Subsection (1) is subject to section 16.

Exception, *Personal Property Security Act*

(4) Despite subsection (1), control of an electronic document does not constitute possession of the original document for the purposes of the *Personal Property Security Act*.

Whether information or document is capable of being retained

9. For the purposes of sections 6, 7 and 8, electronic information or an electronic document is not capable of being retained if the person providing the information or document prevents or does anything to hinder its printing or storage by the recipient.

Whether information or document is provided

10(1) For the purposes of sections 6, 7 and 8, electronic information or an electronic document is not provided to a person if it is merely made available for access by the person, for example on a website.

Same

(2) For greater certainty, the following are examples of actions that constitute providing electronic information or an electronic document to a person, if section 6, 7 or 8 is otherwise complied with:

1. Sending the electronic information or electronic document to the person by electronic mail.

2. Displaying it to the person in the course of a transaction that is being conducted electronically.

Legal requirement that document be signed

11(1) Subject to subsections (3) and (4), a legal requirement that a document be signed is satisfied by an electronic signature.

Endorsement

(2) For greater certainty, subsection (1) also applies to a legal requirement that a document be endorsed.

Reliability requirements

(3) If the document is prescribed for the purposes of this subsection or belongs to a class prescribed for those purposes, the legal requirement is satisfied only if in light of all the circumstances, including any relevant agreement, the purpose for which the document is created and the time the electronic signature is made,

(a) the electronic signature is reliable for the purpose of identifying the person; and

(b) the association of the electronic signature with the relevant electronic document is reliable.

Other requirements

(4) If the document is prescribed for the purposes of this subsection or belongs to a class prescribed for those purposes, the legal requirement is satisfied only if,

(a) the electronic signature meets the prescribed requirements, if any, as to method; and

(b) the electronic signature meets the prescribed information technology standards, if any.

Additional rules, public bodies

(5) Subsection (1) is subject to section 17.

Seal

(6) The document shall be deemed to have been sealed if,

(a) a legal requirement that the document be signed is satisfied in accordance with subsection (1), (3) or (4), as the case may be; and

(b) the electronic document and electronic signature meet the prescribed seal equivalency requirements.

Legal requirement re retention of written documents

12(1) A legal requirement to retain a document that is originally created, sent or received in written form is satisfied by the retention of an electronic document if,

(a) the electronic document is retained in the same format as the one in which the written document was created, sent or received, or in a format that accurately represents the information contained in the written document; and

(b) the information in the electronic document will be accessible so as to be usable for subsequent reference by any person who is entitled to have access to the written document or who is authorized to require its production.

Same, electronic documents

(2) A legal requirement to retain a document that is originally created, sent or received electronically is satisfied by the retention of an electronic document if,

(a) the electronic document is retained in the format in which it was created, sent or received, or in a format that accurately represents the information contained in the document that was originally created, sent or received;

(b) the information in the electronic document that is retained will be accessible so as to be usable for subsequent reference by any person who is entitled to have access to the document that was originally created, sent or received, or who is authorized to require its production; and

(c) where the electronic document was sent or received, information, if any, that identifies its origin and destination and the date and time when it was sent or received is also retained.

Previously retained electronic documents

(3) A legal requirement described in subsection (2) is satisfied despite non-compliance with clause (2)(c) if the electronic document was retained before the day this Act comes into force.

Legal requirements re one or more copies

13. If the use of electronic information or an electronic document is otherwise permitted, a legal requirement that a copy of information or of a document be provided or that one or more copies of information or of a document be provided to the same person at the same time is satisfied by the provision of a single version of electronic information or of an electronic document.

Public Bodies

No implied consent

14. For the purposes of subsection 3(1), the consent of a public body is given only by an explicit communication that is accessible to the persons likely to seek to communicate with the public body about the matter or purpose in question.

Power to use electronic means

15(1) If a public body has power to create, collect, receive, store, transfer, distribute, publish or otherwise deal with information and documents, it has power to do so electronically.

Express provision

(2) Subsection (1) is subject to any provision of law that expressly prohibits the use of electronic means or expressly requires them to be used in specified ways.

References to writing or signing

(3) For the purposes of subsection (2), a reference to writing or signing does not in itself constitute an express prohibition of the use of electronic means.

Consent of other persons

(4) Nothing in this Act authorizes a public body to require other persons to use, provide or accept information or documents in electronic form without their consent.

Additional conditions, provision of electronic information or documents

16. When information or a document is to be provided to a public body, a legal requirement mentioned in section 6, 7 or 8 is satisfied by the provision of electronic information or an electronic document only if,

(a) the electronic information or document meets the information technology standards, if any, of the public body;

(b) the public body acknowledges receipt of the information or document in accordance with its own acknowledgment rules, if any; and

(c) the conditions in section 6, 7 or 8, as the case may be, are also satisfied.

Additional conditions, electronic signatures

17. A legal requirement for a signature that is to be provided to a public body is satisfied by an electronic signature only if,

(a) the electronic signature meets the information technology standards, if any, of the public body; and

(b) the electronic signature meets the requirements as to method and as to reliability of the signature, if any, of the public body.

Electronic payments

18(1) Subject to subsection (2), a payment to or by a public body may be made in electronic form in any manner specified by the public body.

Same, Minister of Finance

(2) A payment into or out of the Consolidated Revenue Fund may be made in electronic form in any manner specified by the Minister of Finance.

Electronic Transactions and Electronic Agents

Formation and operation of electronic contracts

19(1) An offer, the acceptance of an offer or any other matter that is material to the formation or operation of a contract may be expressed,

(a) by means of electronic information or an electronic document; or

(b) by an act that is intended to result in electronic communication, such as,

(i) touching or clicking on an appropriate icon or other place on a computer screen, or

(ii) speaking.

Contracting out

(2) Subsection (1) applies unless the parties agree otherwise.

Legal recognition of electronic contracts

(3) A contract is not invalid or unenforceable by reason only of being in electronic form.

Involvement of electronic agents

20. A contract may be formed by the interaction of an electronic agent and an individual or by the interaction of electronic agents.

Errors, transactions with electronic agents

21. An electronic transaction between an individual and another person's electronic agent is not enforceable by the other person if,

(a) the individual makes a material error in electronic information or an electronic document used in the transaction;

(b) the electronic agent does not give the individual an opportunity to prevent or correct the error;

(c) on becoming aware of the error, the individual promptly notifies the other person; and

(d) in a case where consideration is received as a result of the error, the individual,

(i) returns or destroys the consideration in accordance with the other person's instructions or, if there are no instructions, deals with the consideration in a reasonable manner, and

(ii) does not benefit materially by receiving the consideration.

Time of sending of electronic information or document

22(1) Electronic information or an electronic document is sent when it enters an information system outside the sender's control or, if the sender and the addressee use the same information system, when it becomes capable of being retrieved and processed by the addressee.

Contracting out

(2) Subsection (1) applies unless the parties agree otherwise.

Presumption, time of receipt

(3) Electronic information or an electronic document is presumed to be received by the addressee,

(a) if the addressee has designated or uses an information system for the purpose of receiving information or documents of the type sent, when it enters that information system and becomes capable of being retrieved and processed by the addressee; or

(b) if the addressee has not designated or does not use an information system for the purpose of receiving information or documents of the type sent, when the addressee becomes aware of the information or document in the addressee's information system and it becomes capable of being retrieved and processed by the addressee.

Places of sending and receipt

(4) Electronic information or an electronic document is deemed to be sent from the sender's place of business and received at the addressee's place of business.

Contracting out

(5) Subsection (4) applies unless the parties agree otherwise.

Place of business

(6) If the sender or the addressee has more than one place of business, the place of business for the purposes of subsection (4) is the one with the closest relationship to the underlying transaction to which the electronic information or document relates or, if there is no underlying transaction, the person's principal place of business.

Habitual residence

(7) If the sender or the addressee does not have a place of business, the person's place of habitual residence is deemed to be the place of business for the purposes of subsection (4).

Contracts for the Carriage of Goods

Acts related to contracts for the carriage of goods

23(1) This section applies to anything done in connection with a contract for the carriage of goods, including, but not limited to,

(a) furnishing the marks, number, quantity or weight of goods;

(b) stating or declaring the nature or value of goods;

(c) issuing a receipt for goods;

(d) confirming that goods have been loaded;

(e) giving instructions to a carrier of goods;

(f) claiming delivery of goods;

(g) authorizing release of goods;

(h) giving notice of loss of, or damage to, goods;

(i) undertaking to deliver goods to a named person or a person authorized to claim delivery;

(j) granting, acquiring, renouncing, surrendering, transferring or negotiating rights in goods;

(k) notifying a person of terms and conditions of a contract of carriage of goods;

(l) giving a notice or statement in connection with the performance of a contract of carriage of goods; and

(m) acquiring or transferring rights and obligations under a contract of carriage of goods.

Use of electronic documents

(2) A legal requirement that an act referred to in subsection (1) be done in writing or by using a written document is satisfied if the act is done electronically.

Exception, documents of title

(3) Despite subsection (2), if a right is to be granted to or an obligation is to be acquired by a particular person, and there is a legal requirement that this be done by the transfer or use of a written document, the legal requirement is satisfied by the use of one or more electronic documents only if they are created by a method that gives a reliable assurance that the right or obligation has become the right or obligation of that person.

Standard of reliability

(4) For the purposes of subsection (3), whether an assurance is reliable shall be determined in light of all the circumstances, including the purpose for which the right or obligation is conveyed and any relevant agreement.

Reverting to writing

(5) If one or more electronic documents are used to do an act referred to in clause (1)(j) or (m), no written document used to do the same act with respect to the same goods is valid unless,

    (a) the use of electronic documents has been terminated with respect to the act and the goods, unilaterally or by agreement; and

    (b) the document in writing that replaces the electronic document contains a statement of the termination.

Same

(6) The replacement of the electronic documents by a document in writing described in subsection (5) does not affect the parties' rights or obligations.

Rule of law re written document

(7) No rule of law is inapplicable to a contract of carriage of goods by reason only that the contract is set out in or evidenced by one or more electronic documents rather than by written documents.

Forms

Authority to prescribe, approve or provide form

24(1) Authority to prescribe, approve or provide a form includes authority to prescribe, approve or provide an electronic form and to prescribe requirements for its electronic signature.

Authority to prescribe or approve manner of submitting form

(2) Authority to prescribe or approve the manner of submitting a form includes authority to prescribe or approve that it be submitted electronically.

Statutory form

(3) If a form is set out in an Act, the Lieutenant Governor in Council has authority to make a regulation under that Act prescribing an electronic form that is substantially the same as the form set out in the Act and prescribing requirements for its electronic signature; the prescribed electronic form may be substituted for the statutory form for all purposes.

Communication of information

25(1) If a provision of law requires a person to communicate information otherwise than by means of a form, the Lieutenant Governor in Council has authority to make a regulation prescribing electronic means that may be used to communicate the information and prescribing requirements for electronic signature of the information.

Same

(2) For the purposes of subsection (1),

    (a) if the provision of law forms part of an Act, the regulation prescribing electronic means is made under that Act; and

    (b) if the provision of law forms part of a regulation, the regulation prescribing electronic means is made under the same Act as that regulation.

Application of Act

Preservation of other laws re electronic documents

26(1) Nothing in this Act limits the operation of any provision of law that expressly authorizes, prohibits or regulates the use of electronic information or electronic documents.

Other requirements continue to apply

(2) Nothing in this Act limits the operation of a legal requirement for information to be posted or displayed in a specified manner or for any information or document to be transmitted by a specified method.

References to writing or signing

(3) A reference to writing or signing does not in itself constitute a prohibition for the purpose of subsection (1) or a legal requirement for the purpose of subsection (2).

Preservation of other laws re privacy, access to information

27(1) Nothing in this Act limits the operation of the *Freedom of Information and Protection of Privacy Act*, the *Municipal Freedom of Information and Protection of Privacy Act*, or any other provision of law that is intended to,

    (a) protect the privacy of individuals; or

    (b) provide rights of access to information held by public bodies and similar entities.

No premature destruction of non-electronic documents

(2) This Act does not authorize a public body or similar entity to destroy a document whose retention is

otherwise required by a provision of law or a schedule for the retention or destruction of documents, where the document,

(a) is in a non-electronic form; and

(b) was first created by or on behalf of the body or entity, or communicated to it, in that non-electronic form.

Legal requirements to which Act does not apply

28. This Act does not apply to legal requirements that are prescribed or belong to prescribed classes.

Biometric information

29(1) This Act does not apply to the use of biometric information as an electronic signature or other personal identifier, unless another Act expressly provides for that use or unless all parties to a transaction expressly consent to that use.

Definition

(2) In subsection (1),

"biometric information" means information derived from an individual's unique personal characteristics, other than a representation of his or her photograph or signature.

Election Act and *Municipal Elections Act, 1996*

30. This Act does not apply to anything done under the *Election Act* or the *Municipal Elections Act, 1996.*

Documents to which Act does not apply

31(1) This Act does not apply to the following documents:

1. Wills and codicils.

2. Trusts created by wills or codicils.

3. Powers of attorney, to the extent that they are in respect of an individual's financial affairs or personal care.

4. Documents, including agreements of purchase and sale, that create or transfer interests in land and require registration to be effective against third parties.

5. Negotiable instruments.

6. Documents that are prescribed or belong to a prescribed class.

Exception: documents of title

(2) Except for section 23 (contracts for carriage of goods), this Act does not apply to documents of title.

Regulations

Regulations

32. The Lieutenant Governor in Council may, by regulation,

(a) designate entities or classes of entities as public bodies for the purposes of clause (c) of the definition of "public body" in subsection 1(1);

(b) prescribe documents or classes of documents for the purposes of subsection 11(3) (reliability requirements for electronic signatures);

(c) prescribe documents or classes of documents, requirements as to method for electronic signatures and information technology standards for the purposes of subsection 11(4);

(d) prescribe seal equivalency requirements for electronic signatures for the purposes of subsection 11(6);

(e) prescribe legal requirements or classes of legal requirements for the purposes of section 28;

(f) prescribe documents or classes of documents for the purposes of paragraph 6 of subsection 31(1).

33. Omitted (provides for coming into force of provisions of this Act).

34. Omitted (enacts short title of this Act).

Contract Preparation and Drafting

10

Introduction	232
Preparing to Draft a Contract	232
Drafting a Contract	234
Structure of a Contract	247
Contract Administration	254
Chapter Summary	258
Key Terms	258
Review Questions	258
Recommended Texts on Interpretation and Drafting	261
Appendix: Sample Contracts	262

LEARNING OUTCOMES

After completing this chapter, you should be able to:

- Understand how to gather and organize client information.

- Describe what is required in an outline of a contract.

- Explain the steps in preparing a draft contract.

- Explain what is meant by "plain language" and describe the various vocabulary issues that can arise in drafting a contract.

- Describe the various components of a typical contract.

- Explain the steps involved in the signing, revising, and storing of an agreement.

Introduction

In the preceding chapters you have learned how to interpret contracts and how contracts can be used to achieve a variety of purposes. In this chapter you will learn how to organize client information to prepare a contract and how to draft a simple contract. If you are working as a law clerk, be sure to have the supervising lawyer review the material you prepare. If you are working independently—for example, as a contract administrator or a paralegal—be careful not to exceed your reach. If you are entering an unfamiliar area or dealing with a difficult drafting problem, ask for help and advice. Even when you are sure of yourself, let a colleague review and critique your work.

Preparing to Draft a Contract

You should take a number of steps before you begin drafting a contract, including obtaining facts, directions, and instructions, and organizing information. Once that is done, a draft is prepared, reviewed, and revised before it is presented to the other party. It will then be further revised as the parties reform and refine their positions during negotiations. Follow the step-by-step procedure described below to prepare a contract draft, but don't be too rigid about it—occasionally, circumstances will require you to modify your procedures.

1. Obtain Instructions

Get all of the necessary facts, including relevant documents, such as collateral contracts or floor plans for a lease of commercial space. If there is an existing file on the matter, read it, particularly the correspondence, which may identify and highlight many of the important issues. Be sure you understand both the client's and the other party's goals. For example, your client may want to lease commercial retail space for 5 years with a right to renew for a further 10 years at a predetermined rent. Obviously, a standard commercial lease won't be enough to achieve these goals, and you will have to give thought to how to craft provisions that will do what the client requires.

2. Use a Checklist to Review Facts

Often a contract that was previously drafted to deal with a similar situation (called a *precedent*) or a checklist from a text can help you ensure that you have obtained all of the relevant facts and identified all of the legal issues. Many firms maintain files of previously used contracts that can be used as precedents or models for the work you are doing. There are also texts, such as *O'Brien's Encyclopedia of Forms*, published by Canada Law Book, that provide commercial legal documents and contract precedents. Take care with precedents, though, because a precedent will rarely fit your case exactly; as well, a precedent should not be used as a substitute for hard, critical thought about the facts and issues in your case. The cautious use of precedents in connection with drafting the contract is discussed later in this chapter.

3. Identify and Research Legal Issues

Once you have identified legal issues, you may need to do some research to see how the case law has dealt with fact situations similar to yours. For example, if you are trying to provide for a right to renew a lease at a predetermined rent, you may need to look at law that deals with this kind of provision to see how the other side may seek to escape or limit the right of renewal so that you can block those escape routes with appropriate contract language.

4. Continue to Obtain Further Instructions and Clarification from the Client

As you research the facts and the law, you may discover problems that the client and the supervising lawyer did not anticipate. Do not hesitate to flag problems and obtain further directions and instructions.

5. Prepare a Pre-drafting Outline

This document should set out client goals, list all relevant facts, identify obligations of the client and the other party, and identify qualifiers of those obligations: conditions precedent, exclusions, warranties, guaranties, dispute settlement mechanisms, and so on.

6. Identify Terms to Be Defined

As you review the facts and legal issues, identify those terms that need to be specifically defined in the contract. Remember that you do not need to define words where the ordinary dictionary meaning is used or where the words are used in their ordinary context. "Time," for example, does not usually require a definition. But if the contract contemplates events across several time zones, it may be necessary to define "time" in terms of an applicable time zone.

7. Create Contract Categories, Headings, and Subheadings

Do not try to immediately draft provisions of the contract without first preparing an outline. Identify legal issues and create contract categories to organize the facts and legal issues. From these categories, create headings to be used in the contract.

8. Create a Logical Sequence of Headings and Subheadings

Sequence the headings and subheadings in a logical way. In doing this you are creating an outline that can also form the basis for a table of contents for the contract. Try to do this without referring to a precedent, and use the precedent later to see if you have missed anything. You may want to write out the categories and headings on index cards, shuffle them at random, and start to lay them out, organizing and reorganizing them into a sequence that seems logical and coherent. The sequence should use a logical approach, but most commonly, important matters come first: price and primary obligations of the parties followed by representations, conditions precedent, contract administrative matters, definitions, schedules, and appendixes. If there appear to be too many headings, determine whether some can be logically grouped as subheadings of a main heading.

You are now ready to prepare a first draft of the contract.

Drafting a Contract

Preparing the First Draft of a Contract

Here are some suggestions to help you prepare the first draft.

Be Prepared to Write the First Draft in One Sitting

Writing the first draft in one sitting gives you some assurance of consistency and that you have included all of the necessary information.

1. Review Precedents Carefully

If you have a precedent, review it carefully and critically for appropriate language. Check to see whether the language used has been judicially interpreted. For whom was the precedent used: a client in the same position as your client or someone in the same position as the other party? Look at the precedent as though it came from the other party and examine it critically in that context, being prepared to reject or modify unsuitable provisions and to add suitable ones.

Remember that there are benefits to using precedents: they provide you with checklists, you may be able to use wording someone else has crafted that has withstood judicial challenge, and you may be alerted to legal issues or problems you had not anticipated. But you must be careful—you may spend hours looking for a precedent that "fits" your facts. This is unlikely to happen, and you may end up with a precedent that is too general. Don't be lulled into following a precedent that seems to be close to what you want—read it carefully and do not simply leap at it without thinking critically about it. Beware of including words, terms, or phrases that you do not understand—remember to research before you look at and adopt a precedent. Use the precedent to check your draft to see that important provisions have not been omitted and that appropriate language has been used—that is, that unnecessary jargon and ambiguity have been avoided.

2. Draft the Provisions of the Agreement

Using the headings and subheadings from your outline in an appropriate sequence, draft the necessary provisions, taking care to include all necessary facts and cover all necessary issues. If you seem to have too many headings, be prepared to reduce the number of headings and create more subheadings. If there are too many long, cumbersome clauses under a heading, consider creating more headings and subheadings.

3. Revise the Draft

If you mark a hard copy of the draft, use a red pencil so you can easily spot corrections. Enter the corrections from the hard copy of each draft after each revision. This will ensure that you always have a clean copy of the latest revision. Drafts should be given to the supervising lawyer and discussed with the client. Do not delete or throw out earlier drafts. Instead, number and date them. As revising continues through the period of negotiations with the other party, the content of a revision may become important if there is a disagreement as to what was decided, or, if after the contract is completed, there is a dispute about the meaning of a term. Previous revisions may show how a particular term was drafted and what it was meant to do. The drafts may even become evidence in interpreting the contract under exceptions to the parol evidence rule.

4. Check for Internal Consistency

Check to see that terms and expressions are used as they are defined and are internally consistent throughout the document.

5. Check Cross-References

Ensure that any cross-references are accurate as to content and paragraph and sub-paragraph numbers. If, in your first draft, paragraph 3 makes a reference to a term in paragraph 7, make sure that the referenced paragraph is still paragraph 7 in your fourth or fifth draft.

6. Check Against the Client's Instructions

Has the client changed or modified his or her instructions? Does the draft reflect the client's instructions? It is a good idea to have any instructions, amendments, or modifications in writing, with a copy in your file.

7. Proofread the Draft

Proofread for style, punctuation, and grammar. Eliminate unnecessary legal jargon and replace it with simple, clear language. Edit for brevity and simplicity of language. First drafts are often wordier than they need to be and can often be edited down, becoming clearer in the process. Check for ambiguous language and inconsistent or contradictory language or provisions.

8. Have Others Review the Draft

Give each draft to the supervising lawyer and also to the client to ensure that the document reflects the client's goals and instructions.

Common Language and Drafting Problems

When you draft a contract, whether you have a precedent or not, exercise great care with the language. While plain language drafting makes the job easier than it used to be, you should be aware of a number of common writing problems. While some of the more common problems are identified below, you will still need to be familiar with and be prepared to use standard texts on interpretation and drafting. Several are listed at the end of the chapter.

Structure and Purpose of a Legal Sentence

All sentences consist of a *subject*, the person or thing being discussed, and a *predicate*, the part of the sentence that says something about the subject. Other words may modify the subject and the predicate. Legal sentences have the same structure and observe the same rules of English grammar as other sentences.

Legal sentences, however, follow certain conventions that are different from those used in other writing because legal sentences have a specific purpose—they create rights and obligations. These conventions are as follows:

- The subject consists of an identifiable legal person, *the legal actor*, who will be taking legal action.
- The predicate consists of a verb, object, and other modifying words, *the legal action*, which describes the legal action to be taken by the legal actor, creating rights, grants of power or authority, obligations, duties, and liabilities.

Using the Active Voice

Generally, the legal actor who is performing the legal action must be identified so that everyone reading the document knows who is to act. This is done by using the active voice so that the reader knows who is to receive a benefit or perform an obligation. Since contracts are about who is to perform obligations and receive benefits, identifying the actors is very important. There are times, however, when you may not be able to identify the actor or when you will want to maintain uncertainty. For example, the phrase "the premises may be entered" may be used if you do not wish to be too specific as to who may enter. In these situations, using the passive voice is appropriate. The passive voice is also appropriate in **recitals**, definition clauses, and other sentences in contracts where rights and obligations are not being created.

recital
a part of a contract, at the beginning, that recites facts that establish the background of the parties and their purpose in entering into the contract

---

EXAMPLES

Using Passive and Active Voice

- *Appropriate use of the passive voice* "Omissions in the contract are considered extra to the contract and are not included in the contract price." Since no rights or obligations are created, this is an appropriate use of the passive voice.

- *Inappropriate use of the passive voice* "Rubbish shall be removed from the work site at the end of each working day." Because an obligation is created here, who is to remove the rubbish is important, but we are not told who has this responsibility.

- *Appropriate use of the active voice* "The building contractor shall remove rubbish from the work site at the end of each working day." Here, the person who is to perform the obligation is identified.

Using the Present Tense

Generally, unless there is a specific reason to do otherwise, a legal sentence should be written in the present tense. The contract is presumed to be speaking from and after the time it is written, in which case the present tense makes this clear. As well, the present tense is appropriate to the state of events at the time the contract is operating.

There are times when other tenses should be used. A form of the past tense should be used to describe actions that precede in time the current action; this makes clear that conditions precedent, for example, must be performed before the current obligation is undertaken or the right is conferred. Where an obligation is to be performed in the future, use a form of the future tense.

EXAMPLES

Using Present and Future Tense

- *Using the present tense for a constant present obligation*   "The contractor *is* to keep the site clear of rubbish at all times."

- *Using a form of the past tense (present perfect) for a condition precedent to a current obligation*   "If the contractor *has not cleared* the site of rubbish at the end of the working day, the contractor is to pay the site owner for the cost of removing the rubbish."

- *Using the future tense for an obligation to be performed in the future*   "On the anniversary of the signing of this agreement, the husband *will pay* to the wife the sum of $10,000."

Fact Situation or Context

The subject of a legal sentence tells you who is to act, and the predicate says what he or she is to do. The fact situation, or context,[1] tells you in what circumstances the action in the predicate will take place. At times the context is implicit and clear, but at other times specifying the context can simplify meaning. If there are a number of obligations to be performed in a specific situation, stating that situation, and following it with a list of obligations in subparagraphs can simplify and shorten the document, since the context need not be repeated for each of the obligations. The fact situation can be quite complex, containing conditions precedent and other terms that may affect verb tense.

---

1   The English legal writer Coode, in his original and complex analysis, divided sentences into four parts: subject, predicate, case, and condition. The Canadian authority on drafting, Elmer A. Driedger, reduces these to the "fact situation" in which an obligation operates. The authors of this book, great believers in simplicity, prefer the Driedger approach.

Fact Situation with List of Obligations

Once the contractor has begun work on the site, in order to ensure that the site is a safe workplace, the contractor shall

a. remove all rubbish from the site at the end of the working day,

b. erect safety barriers to keep trespassers off the site, and

c. erect and maintain a lighting system to illuminate the site during hours of darkness.

Provisos

In traditional drafting, the writer who is dealing with an obligation or right that is to be limited in some circumstances will often use phrases like "provided that" or "provided always that." Most commentators today believe that these kinds of phrases should be avoided. Usually, "provided that" can be replaced by "if," "except that," "except if," or a new sentence. The result is likely to be a clearer sentence. The kinds of provisos used in traditional drafting often lead to ambiguity, and the phrases used to create these provisos are part of an archaic writing style that makes little, if any, grammatical sense.

Provisos

- *Old style* "The contractor is responsible for maintaining a safe work site, *provided always that* the building owner is not in breach of his obligations."

- *New style* "The contractor is responsible for maintaining a safe work site *except if* the building owner is in breach of his obligations." This version is clearer and simpler.

Misusing "And" and "Or"

"And" and "or" have different meanings in different contexts, which can cause confusion for drafters. "And" can have the following meanings:

- *Joint* "Betty *and* Carlos"—both together, but neither alone.
- *Several-inclusive* "Betty *and* Carlos"—either of them or both together. This version can also use an "or": "Betty *or* Carlos or both of them."
- *Several-exclusive* "Betty *and* Carlos"—either of them, but not both together.

Context can sometimes make the meaning clear. For example, "The contractor shall pay cleaning and disposal expenses" would be given a several-inclusive meaning, since the contractor could pay cleaning expenses, if incurred, and disposal expenses, if incurred, or both sets of expenses, if both are incurred. It is wise to include enough sentence modifiers in the predicate to eliminate any ambiguity and make the meaning clear.

The phrase "and/or" is sometimes used to prevent the reader from assuming that "and" means a joint option and "or" means exclusively one option. This can lead to uncertainty and difficulty in interpretation. For example, consider the following provision: "If the owner has to clean the site, he is entitled to sell and/or lease the contractor's bulldozer on the site to defray the cleanup costs incurred." On its face, this permits the contractor to sell and lease the bulldozer, which is not possible. Because the intention is to give the owner the opportunity to do one thing or the other, but not both, it would be best to make this clear by using "or" in place of "and/or."

EXAMPLES

Using "And" and "Or"[2]

1. "contractor's tools that are intended to be used for excavation *and* cleaning"

This could mean

- "contractor's tools that are intended for excavation and contractor's tools that are intended for cleaning," creating two separate and exclusive categories of tools. If this meaning is intended, this version should be used.

- "contractor's tools that are intended for doing *both* excavation and cleaning," creating one class of tools to perform both functions. If this meaning is intended, the original phrase 1 can be used, although it could be made even clearer by using this version.

2. "contractor's tools that are intended to be used for excavation *or* cleaning"

This could mean

- "contractor's tools that are intended to be used either for excavation or for cleaning *but not both*." If this meaning is intended, then this version should be used.

- "contractor's tools that are intended to be used for excavation or cleaning *or both*." If this meaning is intended, the original phrase 2 can be used, although for greater clarity this version could be used.

3. "contractor's tools that are intended to be used for excavation, *and* contractor's tools that are intended to be used for cleaning"

This could mean

- "*both* contractor's tools that are intended to be used for excavation and contractor's tools that are intended to be used for cleaning" in a joint sense—that is, both together and not either one separately, if the sentence containing the phrase is mandatory or in command form. If this is the case, this version should be used.

- "contractor's tools that are intended to be used for excavation, *or* contractor's tools that are intended to be used for cleaning, *or both*," in the

---

2 This set of examples is based on the approach used in F.R. Dickerson, *The Fundamentals of Legal Drafting* (Boston: Little, Brown, 1965).

sense that either could be used, or both could be used, if the sentence containing the phrase is permissive and grants options. If this is the case, this version should be used.

4. "contractor's tools that are intended to be used for excavation *or* contractor's tools that are intended to be used for cleaning"

This could mean

- "contractor's tools that are intended to be used for excavation or contractor's tools that are intended to be used for cleaning, *but not both*." If this is the intended meaning, this version should be used.

- "contractor's tools that are intended to be used for excavation or contractor's tools that are intended to be used for cleaning, *or both*." If the intention is to be permissive and permit either or both to be used, then the original phrase 4 can be used, although for greater clarity this version could be used.

Expressing Time

When expressing periods of time in contracts it is important to be precise about when a time period begins and ends. Here are some helpful drafting conventions.

"FROM" A GIVEN DATE

There is no clear answer from the cases whether the date from which a time period runs is included or not, so very clear language should be used.

EXAMPLES

Using/Not Using "From"

- *Ambiguous* "from the 16th of July to ... ." It is not clear whether July 16 is included in the time period or not.
- *Unambiguous* "for a period of 10 days after July 16th." This version clearly indicates that the period begins on July 17.

"ON" A GIVEN DATE

If the word "on" is used to mark the beginning of a period of time, the date is included. "On and after" or "on and from" do not add to or clarify the meaning and should not be used.

EXAMPLE

Using "On"

"Interest on the principal amount begins to run, calculated daily, on May 1" means that interest will be calculated daily beginning with interest for May 1 and for all the following days of the interest period.

"WITHIN" A PERIOD OF TIME

When an event is to occur within a particular time period, the last day of the period is usually excluded from the time period. This is exactly opposite to what is required under the Ontario *Rules of Civil Procedure*,[3] where the first day of a period for doing something is excluded and the last day is included. To avoid difficulties, use language that clearly states what you intend.

EXAMPLE

Using "Within"

"The contractor shall be responsible for cleaning the work site within a period of two days, commencing on the day after the last work is done on the site by the contractor."

"BETWEEN" IDENTIFYING THE START AND END OF A PERIOD

Do not use the word "between" because it creates ambiguity. Many cases have excluded both the first date and the last when "between" was used, but the rulings are not consistent. To avoid difficulties, use very clear language to indicate whether the first or the last dates are included or excluded.

EXAMPLES

Using/Not Using "Between"

- *Ambiguous* "Between July 16, 2012 and August 1, 2012, the debtor may prepay the amount owing without payment of interest." It is not clear whether the period includes July 16 and August 1.
- *Unambiguous* "After July 16, 2012 and before August 1, 2012, the debtor may prepay the amount owing without payment of interest." The period is clearly defined as starting and including July 17, and ending on July 31.

"UNTIL," "BY," OR "FROM/TO" A DATE

Using these expressions to establish the beginning or end of a period often leads to questions about whether the beginning and end dates are included or excluded. For example, the phrase "by July 31" is usually interpreted to mean the performance of the event *before* that date. To avoid ambiguity, if something may be done until a specific date, it is best expressed by writing "until and including" the date or "until but excluding" the date, depending on your purpose. It is advisable to avoid "from July 1 to July 10," since it is not clear whether July 1 and 10 are included or excluded. Instead, your intention can be expressed clearly by writing "commencing on July 1 and ending on July 10, both days included" (or excluded, if that is what you intend).

---

3   *Rules of Civil Procedure*, RRO 1990, reg. 194, rule 3.01(1)(a).

DAY, MONTH, YEAR

A day is presumed to be 24 hours, running from midnight to 11:59:59 p.m. If you wish to have a day start or end at a fixed hour, set out the time: "on July 31, before 4:00 p.m." If you wish a whole day to be included, you can define it as a "clear day" or simply a "day." If you use the word "time" rather than "day," the interpretation is that the event is to occur at a specific time during the day. A "month" usually refers to a lunar month of four weeks. The term "calendar month" is often used, but its meaning is unclear: in some cases it has been deemed to refer to a period between a day in one month to the same day in the next month—for example, from July 6 to August 6—in other cases it has been held to mean that the month ends on the same day as it began, which can lead to a conclusion that July 1 and August 1 are in the same month. The best way to avoid these problems is either to define precisely what you mean by "month" in the definition section of the contract or to use a more precise measure of time, such as a day. A "year" means 12 calendar months, calculated from January 1 or some other chosen date. It includes 365 days, or 366 in a leap year. Fractions of days are not taken into account except by astronomers.

EXPRESSIONS OF AGE

Defining a time period by the age of a person leads to ambiguities about whether the age that starts and ends the period is included or excluded. It is also not clear when the event of being a particular age actually occurs. Precision of language is required here.

EXAMPLE

Using Age to Define a Time Period

- *Ambiguous* "When the employee is more than 60 years old." Is the person more than 60 on the day after her 60th birthday or on the day of her 61st birthday? Either is plausible.
- *Unambiguous* "When the employee has passed the day of her 60th birthday" or "When the employee has passed the day of her 61st birthday," depending on what you intend.

Misusing "Shall" and "May"

"Shall" is often used improperly to convey a sense of what is to happen in the future, to address inanimate objects, to give directions, and to declare a legal result. It is properly used to convey a command to do something or to abstain from doing something. To convey a sense of the future, use "will." If you want to create an option or permit something rather than require it, use "may."

Using "Shall" and "May"

- *Inappropriate use of "shall": conveying a sense of future* "The contractor shall complete the work by 4 p.m. July 31, or he *shall* forfeit his performance bond." This should be written as "The contractor shall complete the work by 4 p.m. July 31, or he *will* forfeit his performance bond." Note that the first part of the sentence is a command to do something, while the second part indicates what is to happen in the future.

- *Inappropriate use of "shall": addressing inanimate objects* Do not write "The performance bond *shall* contain provisions that … ," since this expresses a command to a thing that cannot act. Instead, write "The performance bond *must* contain provisions that … ."

- *Inappropriate use of "shall": giving directions* Do not use "The contractor shall complete form A" if this is a direction that occurs when an event occurs. Instead, use "The contractor must complete form A," or "The contractor is to complete form A."

- *Inappropriate use of "shall": declaring a legal result* Do not use "Excavate *shall* mean …" where the phrase is a declaration of a legal result—in this case, a definition. Instead, use "Excavate means … ."

- *Appropriate use of "shall"* "The contractor *shall* clean the work site." This phrase uses "shall" appropriately, since it contains a command to the contractor to do something.

- *Appropriate use of "may"* "The contractor *may* use a subcontractor to clean the work site." This provision is permissive, giving the contractor an option.

Rules of Construction and Interpretation

If there is a dispute about what the contract language actually means, judges resort to a number of rules of construction to interpret the disputed language.

Lists

Take care when drafting lists as part of a contract, since two contradictory rules may cause mayhem. The **ejusdem generis** rule may result in words in the list being defined as being confined to the category or thing described by the first word in the list. The rule of **expressio unius est exclusio alterius** has a different effect, requiring an interpretation that the things included imply that other things not specifically mentioned in the list are excluded. Neither rule may reflect what you intended.

EJUSDEM GENERIS

This rule provides that general words following specific words are confined to the class or category of the specific words. You can avoid the problems caused by this rule by using appropriate wording. For example, if you have given a list of tools but do not wish to restrict the general meaning of "tools," use a phrase at the end of the

ejusdem generis
a rule of contract construction that requires that general words following specific words take their meaning from the specific words and are confined to the same category as the specific words

expressio unius est exclusio alterius
(Latin) "to express one thing and exclude another"; a rule of contract construction that requires that the use of one word implies the exclusion of another

list such as this one: "or any other tool, *whether of the same kind of tool previously listed or not.*"

EXPRESSIO UNIUS EST EXCLUSIO ALTERIUS

This rule means that the inclusion of one thing implies the exclusion of those things not listed. If you want to avoid the application of this rule to a list, use a phrase like "construction equipment, *including but not limited to* bulldozers, back hoes, graders ... ." Do not use "for greater certainty but not so as to restrict the generality of the foregoing." This phrase, besides being wordy, is used in s. 91 of the *Constitution Act, 1867,*[4] where it has been given a variety of interpretations, some of them contradictory.

Recitals

Recitals can set out the history and context of an agreement, the principles that guide the parties, or the reasons why they are agreeing to do certain things. Recitals can be important and useful in interpreting ambiguities or uncertainties in the contract. Be sure that descriptions of consideration and other important terms are in the main body of the contract and not in a recital, and avoid using phrases in a recital that describe nominal consideration, such as "for two dollars, and other valuable consideration." These only confuse the interpretation of the contract. If there is a conflict between the contents of the recitals and the main body of the contract, the latter generally prevails.

Headings

Be careful with the language you use in headings in the body of the contract. In some cases, headings have been used to help interpret the terms of the contract.

Mathematical Concepts

Occasionally you will have a formula in a contract, often to calculate something such as sales commissions, bonuses, or increases in payment that are tied to inflation. Mathematical concepts are not always easy to express in language. Where you have described a formula or method of calculation, include written formulas or describe the calculation method step by step. Give examples in an appendix of how the formula works. If necessary you can include the formula as an appendix too, but reference the appendix in the relevant contract provision so that it becomes a part of the contract.

Inappropriate Use of "Legalese"

In drafting contracts you may feel that you need to use legal jargon to make effective legal documents. Some people maintain that clients expect to see legalese, that legalese is more accurate than ordinary language, that jargon employs necessary

---

4 *Constitution Act, 1867,* 30 & 31 Vict., c. 3 (UK).

technical terms or **terms of art** that are essential to a contract, and that your employers expect you to use legal jargon.

Is legalese necessary, and should you be using it? The short answer is that since the 1980s in Canada and other parts of the common-law world there has been a substantial movement away from the use of legalese and toward **plain language drafting** for contracts and other legal writing. Law schools, law societies, bar associations, leading law firms, and judges have all endorsed a movement to clearer language. For example, since 1990 the Law Society of Upper Canada has taught the plain language approach to bar admission students in legal writing courses, as well as in continuing education courses for practising lawyers. Large banks and corporations have also shifted over to plain language documents, particularly for consumer contracts.[5] Legislative bodies have required certain contracts to be drafted in plain language to be enforceable. For example, British Columbia requires plain language to be used in consumer motor vehicle leases. New York State has long required insurance contracts to be in plain language.

Still, there are concerns about plain language drafting, often from older lawyers. Some argue that if a document is in plain language, clients may think they can do the work themselves. However, clients pay for expertise and for results, and surveys indicate that the public thinks that legal drafting in the old style results in hard-to-read documents that are meant to confuse a layperson.[6]

Another concern expressed about plain language is that it is not as precise or accurate as the older style of legal writing. Again, the evidence does not support this assertion. There have been a number of studies of statutes and contracts that have been redrafted with no loss of precision or specificity of meaning. In many cases, redrafted documents are shorter, clearer, more precise, easier to understand, and less time-consuming to master.[7] In fact, there have been judicial comments that many traditionally drafted documents are anything but clear—their writers use so much jargon that it is impossible to determine what the documents mean. In one case, a judge commenting on notice of a liability exclusion clause relied on by a courier company said: "Notice cannot be said to be reasonable, in my view, when the clause is neither legible nor capable of comprehension."[8]

Another criticism of plain language is that it ignores necessary technical legal terminology and terms of art. Technical terms and terms of art that have been judicially defined in previous case decisions do need to be used, but legal terms of art and

terms of art
words, phrases, or technical terms that have a fairly precise, specific legal meaning, often as a result of being interpreted and defined in previous court decisions

plain language drafting
the modern style of drafting legal documents that employs plain, ordinary language and emphasizes clarity, precision, and brevity

---

5   The plain language approach is sometimes referred to as the "Chase Manhattan" style after the Chase Manhattan Bank in New York pioneered the use of plain language documents.

6   In a Plain Language Institute (Vancouver) survey, 57 percent of the public responded that legal documents are poorly written and hard to read. Quoted in the Law Society of Upper Canada, *Legal Writing: 42nd Bar Admission Course, Phase 1*, Summer 1999, *Instructors Manual*, 12-21.

7   Ibid., at 12-22. The Law Reform Commission of Victoria (Australia) reported that in a redraft of one piece of legislation, the length was cut by half with no loss in accuracy or precision. Further, the amount of time taken by lawyers and students to comprehend the material when they were tested was cut by one-third.

8   Ibid., referring to *Aurora TV and Radio Ltd. v. Gelco Express Ltd.* (May 10, 1990) (Man. QB (Small Claims), Oliphant J) [unreported].

technical terms take up very little space in most documents. The rest can be written in plain language.

You may also hear that employers require documents to be drafted in the traditional style. In some cases this may be true, and if you are directed by a superior to use a particular format you must follow the directions given. But you are likely to encounter this situation infrequently. Even older lawyers who do not feel they can change their ways often appreciate plain language, as a number of surveys have shown.[9]

Legalese That Can Cause Problems

The following are some of the more troublesome forms of legalese that you are likely to encounter and should avoid.

"SAID" AND "AFORESAID"

Using these terms rarely results in a better-written or clearer legal sentence. The two terms are often used to refer to someone in a document who has already been identified. If, for example, you refer to "the building contractor" for the first time in a document, you do not add clarity or precision by referring to "the said building contractor" or "the aforesaid building contractor" in later paragraphs. Simply writing "the building contractor" is clearer and uses fewer words. If there is more than one contractor, "said building contractor" can create real confusion, because it does not indicate which person you are referring to.

"SUCH"

You will often see a phrase like this one: "to divide the residue of my estate into equal shares for *such* children of mine who survive me." Some drafters use "such" like "said," to identify a person previously identified or described. The solution here is the same as it is for "said": "to divide the residue of my estate into equal shares for *the* children of mine who survive me."

"SAME"

Using "same" just sounds pompous in sentences like "The contractor shall clear rubbish from the work site, and sweep *same*." A better solution is "The contractor shall clear rubbish from the work site, and sweep *it*."

"ANY," "EACH," "EVERY," AND "ALL"

Usually, using the definite article "the" or the indefinite article "a" will suffice. "Any piece of cleaning equipment" can be written as "a piece of cleaning equipment." However, there are times when these words are needed—for example,

- *when an obligation is imposed on a group of individuals* "Each contractor's site manager shall … ," and
- *when a right or power is granted* "Any member may move an adjournment."

---

9 Ibid., at 12-23, referring to S. Harrington and J. Kimble, "Survey: Plain Language Wins Every Which Way" (1987) 66 Mich. B.J. 1024.

COUPLETS AND TRIPLETS

In trying to be precise, traditional writers have often used strings of words rather than simply choosing the right word: "I *give, devise, and bequeath*, the *rest, residue, and remainder* of my estate to my children" can easily be clarified and simplified by "I *give* the *remainder* of my estate to my children." When you are tempted to use a couplet or triplet, usually because you have seen one in a precedent, use the word in the group that best and most clearly reflects your meaning.

LEGAL GOBBLEDYGOOK

Too many contracts contain words that are archaic and that many people today do not understand, or certainly rarely use.

Words to Avoid

Most commentators consider the following terms to be legal gobbledy-gook or nonsense that should not be used:

above-mentioned	henceforth	therewith	wheresoever
afore-granted	hereinafter	to wit	whereof
aforementioned	thenceforth	whatsoever	within named
before-mentioned	thereunto	whereas	witnesseth

Structure of a Contract

Most contracts include certain basic components, although there may be variations depending on the type of contract you are drafting and how complex it is. The basic components include

- identification of the parties,
- recitals,
- terms,
- testimonium and attestation, and
- schedules and appendixes.[10]

Identification of the Parties

The parties to the contract are identified as legal entities showing the capacity in which they contract. The identification of a party may also show the authority the party has to contract—for example, "Jorg Anderson, Litigation Guardian of Sven Anderson."

---

10   The structure of a contract used here is adapted with modifications from "Contract Architecture," part of the Law Society of Upper Canada, *Legal Writing: 42nd Bar Admission Course, Phase 1,* Summer 1999.

If the parties are individuals, they should be identified and described by their names as those names appear on official documents such as birth certificates—for example, "Laurence Michael Olivo." If an individual uses variations of his or her name, those need not be referred to in most cases. However, where an individual is contracting with respect to a sole proprietorship, it is a good idea to link the individual and the name of the sole proprietorship—for example, "Laurence Michael Olivo, carrying on business as 'Olivo Legal Training and Services.'"

Where a contracting party is a partnership, the partners should be named individually along with the name of the partnership—for example, "Laurence Michael Olivo and Jean Fitzgerald, carrying on business as a partnership under the name 'Fly-by-Night Legal Drafting.'" All partners should sign the contract to be sure that each is personally bound to the contract.

Where the contracting party is an artificial person, such as a corporation, government entity, or other artificial body, take care to use the exact name of the entity. The name of the corporation should be *exactly* as it appears in the Articles of Incorporation or in other records of the Corporations branch of the federal or provincial government, depending on which level of government issued the Articles of Incorporation. If the corporation carries on business under a trade name, then that may be included as part of the contracting party's name, but make sure the correct corporate name is used as well—for example, "123456 Ontario Ltd. carrying on business as 'Drafting to the Max.'"

If a government, a government agency or department, a municipality, or an artificial entity created by statute, such as a university, is a contracting party, you need to check the relevant legislation to see what that body is called legally. The official name may bear no relationship to the name it is usually known by. For example, the Ministry of X may be legally described as "The Ministry of X by Her Majesty the Queen in Right of Ontario."

Once you have identified the contracting parties and properly named them, you may also wish to include a short description of each party's capacity, purpose, role, or function—for example, "Laurence Michael Olivo, Author." Avoid pompous and wordy phrases like "hereinafter referred to as the Author." You may see parties described in some contracts as "party of the first part" or "party of the second part." Do not use these terms—they are uninformative and unhelpful. You may want to include the address of each party after the description of the party's capacity, although this is not mandatory. You can also include a title for the agreement. If the contract is for the sale of your bicycle, for example, you can call it a "bicycle sale contract."

EXAMPLE

Identification of Parties

EMPLOYMENT AGREEMENT

BETWEEN:

HAPHAZARD MANUFACTURING LIMITED, Employer

and

GUNTER UFF, Employee

Recitals

Recitals follow the names of the parties and set out background facts and the nature and purpose of the agreement, including references to collateral contracts and other dealings between the parties, events that give rise to the contract, expectations of the parties, and other matters that may be relevant. They should not contain essential terms of the contract, such as consideration, statements of obligations, undertakings, or promises. In older agreements the recitals are preceded by the word "Whereas," although this is no longer considered good drafting practice. Instead, they can be headed by the word "Recitals" or "Preamble" (a "preamble" usually describes the recitals that preface a statute, but the term can be used to preface a contract as well). Each recital can then be numbered (1., 2., 3., etc.) or lettered (A., B., C., etc.).

EXAMPLE

Recitals

PREAMBLE:

1. The Employer wishes to retain the services of the Employee.
2. The Employee wishes to become an employee of the Employer.
3. The Employee therefore agrees to accept the Employer's offer of employment in the position described in Appendix "A" to this Agreement, on the terms described in this Agreement.

Consideration

You need to distinguish between two types of consideration clauses. The first type is a holdover from older contracts drafted in legalese. It is usually found on the first page, after the recitals or preamble. It uses archaic language such as "Now Therefore Witnesseth that for Two (2) dollars of lawful money of Canada and other consideration … ." Leave this consideration clause out altogether, because it adds nothing to the contract except confusion. The second type of consideration clause is the one your contract should include. It appears as a numbered paragraph as one of the terms of the contract dealing with the parties' obligations to each other. This type of clause and how to draft it is discussed below under the heading "Obligations." If you want to avoid having a consideration clause, even as a term of the contract, you may want to have the agreement made under seal, because consideration is then not required. This will affect the form of the attestation clause, which will refer to the contract as being "signed and sealed" and not just "signed." Remember that if you use a seal, the contract may not be subject to the remedy of specific performance.

Terms

This is the body of the contract, sometimes also called the covenants. Set out here the contract provisions, including obligations undertaken by the parties and other substantive matters that are essential to the contract. In setting out the terms or covenants, the most important should go first. The following are generally included.

Obligations

These are promises to do something or to refrain from doing something, and it is here that consideration is usually identified and expressed. Because these clauses are expressed as commands, the use of "shall" or "must" is recommended (save "will" to convey something that is to take place in the future). Keep these clauses short and use simple sentences. If a paragraph turns out to be dense and long, consider using more headings and subheadings, in a logical way, to break up the clause.

EXAMPLE

Obligation

Compensation:

1. As full compensation for the services provided by the Employee, the Employer shall pay the Employee an annual salary of $60,000.00, to be paid in regular installments in accordance with the Employer's usual payment practices. The employer shall make the payments not less frequently than once a month.

Representations

As you will recall from Chapter 4, Contractual Defects, a representation may be made in the course of negotiating a contract and may induce someone to enter into the agreement. But the representation may also be incorporated into the contract as a term that is a promise about the quality of something or about the existence of a particular state of affairs. Often during negotiations one party tries to keep the representations out of the contract, while the other party tries to include them. If the representations are in the contract, the party relying on them has more options for remedies if a representation turns out to be a misrepresentation, even an innocent one. A representation often begins with the phrase "The seller represents that ... ." Consider whether the representation should be open-ended or confined, depending on your position: one side or the other may want to tie a representation to a date and include all parties who may be liable for making the representation; a party may also wish to qualify a representation to certain conditions, as the examples below demonstrate.

EXAMPLES

Representations

- The seller represents that to the best of her knowledge, no urea formaldehyde foam insulation was used in construction of the premises.
- The seller and the guarantor represent that at the time of sale, the seller had clear title to the goods.
- The seller represents that at the time of sale, to the best of his knowledge, the vehicle complied with Canadian and US automobile safety legislation.

Conditions Precedent

A condition precedent is a state of affairs that must exist before a contract can be completed. The contract is suspended until the condition is fulfilled. If it is not fulfilled, then the contract can be made void at the request of one or both of the parties. A condition precedent clause can be identified by phrases like "A condition precedent to …" or "Subject to … ." Commonly, a condition precedent clause is used when a person purchasing a house makes the purchase conditional on being able to finance the purchase by obtaining a mortgage loan. The purchaser tries to make the condition as broad and general as possible, and the seller tries to limit and confine it as much as possible. A well-drafted clause (from the vendor's viewpoint) is one that spells out the limits of the condition with precision and specificity, with time limits by which the condition must be met. It also states for whose benefit the clause is created, what happens if the condition is unsatisfied, and whether and how the condition can be waived.

EXAMPLE

Condition Precedent Clause

A. Performance of the purchaser's obligations is subject to the purchaser being able to obtain a mortgage until and including October 3, 2012 for a principal amount of $60,000 at an interest rate of 5 percent per annum for a term of 5 years, with an amortization period of 25 years, permitting prepayment of principal without penalty or bonus.

B. This condition precedent is for the benefit of the purchaser, who may waive the condition. If the purchaser is not successful in obtaining a mortgage on the terms described in paragraph A, the agreement is terminated.

Statements

In a contract, a statement is something written about the contract itself. It differs from a representation, which is something written about the subject matter of the contract. A statement can be about how the contract is to be interpreted, which law applies or which jurisdiction shall be the place to litigate disputes, or other contract administration matters. There is no magic wording, but each statement should have a separate heading, and the statements should come at the end of the contract, before the testimonium. Some examples of typical statements are set out below.

EXAMPLES

Statements

43. Severability:
The parties agree that if any provision or term of the Agreement is deemed void, voidable, or unenforceable, the remaining terms shall remain in full force and effect.

44. Cancellation of Prior Agreements:
The parties agree that all prior agreements, written or verbal, express or implied, between the parties relating in any way to the employment of the Employee with the Employer are declared null and void and are superseded by the terms of this Agreement.

Definitions

Include a definition section after the contract statements if you need one. You may also place the definitions, in alphabetical order, right after the recitals at the beginning of the contract so that the reader is alerted to them from the start. Define only terms that are being used in a technical way, or where the definition differs from the usual definition of the word or phrase. Do not use illogical definitions—for example, defining "fast" as "slow." If a word is used in more than one way, define both ways, and make a clear reference to where in the contract each definition is being used. In drafting definitions, keep in mind the maxims *ejusdem generis* and *expressio unius est exclusio alterius*. If you want to restrict a definition, use the word "means." If you want to expand the definition, try using "includes." If you want to exclude certain meanings, use "does not include."

EXAMPLES

Definitions

45. **Definitions:**

"paid holiday" includes all statutory holidays, as defined in the Ontario *Interpretation Act*, RSO 1990, c. I.11, as amended, but does not include Easter Monday or Professor Fitzgerald's birthday.

"remuneration" means "net pay after taxes and standard deductions" in paragraphs 7a, 11, 32 and 36, and means "gross pay including bonuses" in paragraphs 7b and 23.

Testimonium and Attestation

The testimonium clause comes at the end of the contract and contains a declaration by the party or parties signing the agreement that the agreement has been signed and, if under seal, sealed, and that a duplicate original has been handed over to the other party. The attestation clause is a declaration that the signing of the document and, if sealed, the sealing of the document have been done in the presence of a witness who signs the declaration. In some cases, the witness may also sign an affidavit of execution. This is required on some documents, such as wills and some real estate documents. An affidavit of execution is similar to the declaration in the attestation clause, except that the affidavit is a sworn statement.

Testimonium and Attestation Clauses

THE PARTIES ACKNOWLEDGE THAT they have signed and delivered this agreement on the dates set out below:

DATED this 7th day of June 20XX.

HAPHAZARD FABRICATIONS LIMITED

Bozenka Paric

Witness

per: *Daniel Duplicitous*

Daniel Duplicitous, President and duly
authorized signing officer of
Haphazard Fabrications Limited

DATED this 7th day of June 20XX

Ishtar Amagediou

Witness

Mortimer Moribund

Employee

Schedules and Appendixes

If lists, formulas, examples of calculations, or collateral agreements are referred to in the body of the contract, they should be reproduced and attached as schedules or appendixes to the agreement after the testimonium and attestation clauses. Make sure the name of the schedule or appendix and its number corresponds to its reference in the body of the document. The same rules about drafting contracts apply, with necessary modifications, to drafting schedules and appendixes, which form part of the contract and need to be clear.

Layout and Format

Use a good word-processing software package to draft contracts. Take care with "canned" contract programs—ones that contain a precedent from which you choose and tack on relevant clauses or fill in blanks. These programs may be fast, but they should be used, if at all, like precedents, to help you refine a draft or an outline after you have thought about and organized the terms and provisions of the contract. Most word-processing software allows you to create an automatic table of contents if you ensure that each paragraph and subparagraph of the contract has a heading or subheading. You should use the automatic numbering or lettering system, so that when you make revisions and amendments, the numbering/lettering sequence is maintained in each draft. Use page numbering on all drafts.

Your aim is also to make the contract easy to read visually. Use a justified left margin, where the words all line up in the same place on the left, and a ragged right margin, where the computer decides when to end a line. Use serif fonts—ones that have short lines on the ends of the letters, such as Times New Roman or Bookman Old Style, since the eye follows these more easily. Font size should be no smaller than 12 points, and line spacing should be one-and-one-half or double spacing.

Make defined terms and headings bold or italic in the text. Cross-references to paragraphs should include the paragraph number and title or heading. A consistent numbering system should be used with paragraphs and subparagraphs and they should be block indented:

   1.
     b)
       iii)

Do not split paragraphs over two pages; end a paragraph on the page on which it starts.

Sample Contracts

Several typical contracts are shown in the appendix to this chapter. In reviewing them, note strengths and weaknesses in drafting. Are the terms clear? Is the contract in legalese or in plain language? Is the layout logical?

Contract Administration

Up to this point in the chapter, we have focused on issues concerning drafting and preparation. But once a written contract is ready to be signed or executed by the parties, there are issues of administration that arise, some of which are discussed here.

How Do the Parties Execute a Contract?

To execute a contract is to sign it. If the contract is to be signed manually on hard copy, the person to be bound, or the attorney (a person with power of attorney to sign contracts on behalf of the person granting the power of attorney), or the person with signing authority for an artificial being (the manager of a limited company, for example) signs the contract using his or her own signature. While a handwritten signature is preferable in the event that forgery becomes an issue, a stamped signature or initial may suffice.

A mark will be used where the person is illiterate and cannot write his or her name. In that case, the person marks an "X" and under it you should state: "Allen Smith, by his mark." It is a good idea to have this type of signature witnessed.

What Needs to Be Done If a Contract Is Under Seal?

If the contract is under seal, as discussed in Chapter 2, Formation of a Contract, ideally the person being bound should sign in addition to affixing a seal, even though signatures are not required in theory. But seals, if they are gummed wafers, do fall off, and even if they stay affixed to the document, they do not identify the person to be bound, so having the person sign the document actually provides backup for the seal. Many people use a gummed wafer as a seal, but you can simply draw a circle and label it "LS" and that will suffice as a seal. Remember that if there is evidence of an intention to seal a contract, even if the seal falls off, evidence of the effort is usually sufficient to prove that the parties intended the document to be under seal—an important feature in a contract lacking in consideration, which, without the seal, would be unenforceable. From a practical point of view, drawing a seal labelled "LS" may be the best protection against problems arising from seals falling off the document. Another protection would be to photocopy the signed agreement, especially the page with the seals and signatures. Although it is not required for a sealed document, you may wish to have a witness to each signature should there later be a dispute about whether a party actually sealed or signed a document.

Can the Parties Use Electronic Signatures?

As you will know from reading Chapter 9, Electronic Contracts and E-Commerce, a contract may be signed electronically on an e-document by simply typing the name of the party to be bound, usually in quotation marks, and often followed by the phrase "signed electronically" in quotation marks or parentheses. In some cases, the parties may use more sophisticated encrypted signature systems, but in the end, it is up to the parties to set the rules for using electronic signatures; electronic signatures generally are deemed to be equivalent to written ones. The Ontario legislation also recognizes electronic equivalents for sealed contracts.

When Do Parties Sign a Contract?

Do the parties have to be present together and sign at the same time? Generally they do not; one party may sign it and his or her lawyer may send it to the other party's lawyer to have the other party sign. This is the usual case where the parties are in different locations, or where they are not anxious to be in the same room—for example, in the case of a separation agreement.

Where on the Document Should the Signatures Appear?

The usual practice is to have the parties sign at the bottom of the last page (sometimes referred to as the "foot" of the document). However, that is not much protection against fraud, as a page may be added or one taken out and another substituted. There are a number of things that are often done to protect against some of the simpler forms of tampering:

- A recital may be inserted just before the signatures, stating that the contract consists of "this and the preceding 9 pages."
- The parties may initial each page, including all appendixes.
- Where there are blank spaces on a page, the drafter may insert a horizontal line below the last printed line higher up on the page, together with a horizontal

line lower down on the page where the text begins again, the two horizontal lines being connected by a diagonal line, looking like a large, hand-drawn "Z."

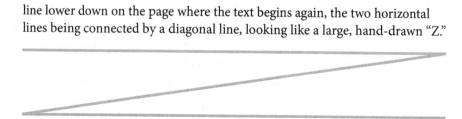

But bear in mind that these techniques will not be much protection against a determined and sophisticated fraudster.

What Form of a Party's Name Should Be Used?

In Canada many people come from abroad and have names for which there is no English or French equivalent. Often such individuals will "Canadianize" their names, or render their names phonetically but using the standard Western alphabet.

The general rule here is to use the standard Western alphabet, and stick to the name you use legally. So if Alessandro Manzoni uses the name Sam Manson, but has Alessandro Manzoni on his driver's licence, his so-called legal name, then that is what he should use. For added certainty, where the parties are identified on page 1, the description can read "Alessandro Manzoni, also known as Sam Manson."

A married woman who normally uses her husband's last name may, in many circumstances, use that name in her signature if that is her normal practice and her other "official documents" reflect that. If her practice is to use her birth name, then she may use it. The type of contract may determine the form used. For example, there is less concern over use of a married name by a woman for a two-week holiday tour than there would be over a contract for the sale of land. If there is some uncertainty as to which form to use, the inclusion of "also known as" in the identification of the parties on page 1 may suffice, either where the parties are named or in a recital at the beginning of the contract.

Who May Be a Witness?

Even where a witness is not required, it is a good idea for the party to be bound to sign the contract with a witness present. The witness then signs next to the signature of the party to be bound. A witness should be someone who has reached the age of majority, is not mentally incapable, and has no conflict of interest with any of the parties to the contract—which usually means the witness has no interest, direct or indirect, in the contract.

A witness is supposed to be able to say that he or she was present when the party whose signature was required signed the contract. The contract cannot be signed, and then be signed later by a witness who was not present and did not see the party sign. In some cases, the witness will also sign an affidavit of execution—an affidavit that says that the witness is over the age of majority and was present and saw the party sign the contract in his or her presence. Affidavits of execution are often required for real estate transactions and for wills, depending on the province.

How Do You Correct Errors After a Document Is Signed?

A document may be amended by drawing a line through an error and writing in the correction, with the parties initialling the change. More substantial changes that go beyond typographical or grammatical errors should probably be dealt with by amending the contract and attaching the amendment as an appendix. Remember that an amendment to an agreement should be subject to the same formalities as the original contract itself—so that a contract under seal should have the attached amendment also executed under seal.

What Do You Need to Do to Safeguard and Preserve the Original Signed Contract?

With the advent of electronic documents, virtually all contracts are word processed. As contracts go through multiple stages as the terms are negotiated, each draft should have a clear, identifying file name, usually using numbers to denote each separate draft. The last draft—the one that is actually final and to be signed—should have the word "final" or some other word or symbol in the file name to identify it as the final product. That way, the file can be easily stored or archived. You may have a separate electronic folder for all final contract copies or you may have a separate file for all documentation for that contract—there is no fixed rule for this, and much depends on how an office is organized, the nature of the business, and the type of contract involved.

It is also a good idea to keep hard-copy files, and to back up the file with the contract onto other disk drives or data storage systems. Hard drives can be damaged, so backups are a good idea.

Remember that many contracts contain private or privileged information. They should be kept securely, perhaps requiring passwords to open the relevant folder or file. Again, office practice will dictate if this should be done, and if so, how.

You may wish to use the contract as a precedent for similar contracts, or wish to share it with colleagues. To avoid breaching confidentiality requirements, it is a good idea to delete the names of the parties and other identifying or confidential information from any copy you make that is going to go outside your office.

If a Client Is Hesitant to Sign a Contract, What Should You Do?

Sometimes a law clerk is asked to oversee contract signing formalities, on the assumption that the client has been advised and is ready and willing to sign. But if the client is unsure or uncertain about the terms or the impact of the contract, you need to call in the lawyer on the file to answer the client's questions and address the client's concerns. Reassuring the client that it is okay to sign, or explaining the provisions of the contract, is something that should be done by a lawyer or paralegal, not a law clerk.

CHAPTER SUMMARY

In order to draft a contract, it is wise to proceed in a methodical way. The drafter begins by obtaining instructions, identifying issues, identifying key terms, and creating headings and subheadings and determining how they should be sequenced. When drafting the contract, use an outline and prepare a first draft in one sitting, using precedents with caution. You should be prepared to revise your draft and proofread it carefully.

In drafting, there are a number of language and drafting problems you should avoid. Use the active and passive voice appropriately and choose the correct tense. Be sure to use words carefully, avoiding some of the more common problems that arise from the use of unclear or ambiguous language. In particular, be careful not to use "legalese" or jargon that you do not understand.

Most contracts, when the draft is complete, should identify the parties and set out recitals, terms, the testimonium and attestation clauses, and the schedules and appendixes, if any.

You also need to know about some of the issues involving administration of a contract, including execution or signing formalities, amendment, and storage of the drafts and final copy.

KEY TERMS

ejusdem generis, 243
expressio unius est exclusio alterius, 243
plain language drafting, 245
recital, 236
terms of art, 245

REVIEW QUESTIONS

True or False?

_____ 1. It is good practice to use a contract precedent verbatim so that you don't introduce errors into the contracts.

_____ 2. If you use the phrase "from the 16th of September to …" it is clear that September 16th is included.

_____ 3. Schedules in a contract are used to set out precisely when the parties' obligations are to be met.

_____ 4. The *expressio unius est exclusio alterius* rule was the precursor to the *ejusdem generis* rule.

_____ 5. Recitals can be important and useful in interpreting ambiguities or uncertainties in the contract.

_____ 6. It is important to include couplets and triplets in a contract to ensure clarity.

_____ 7. An affidavit of execution is required for all formal contracts.

_____ 8. The attestation clause is a declaration that the signing of the document and, if sealed, the sealing of the document have been done in the presence of a witness who signs the declaration.

_____ 9. Using the word "said" is much clearer than using the word "aforesaid."

_____ 10. The term "internal consistency" means that each party's obligations are set out clearly and that their responsibilities don't overlap.

Multiple Choice

1. You should avoid using the passive voice in contract provisions unless
   a. you are directing someone specifically to do something
   b. no rights or obligations are created
   c. anyone can perform an action under the contract, and it doesn't matter who the person is
   d. b and c

2. If you wish to make an action under a contract subject to a condition precedent, you should describe the condition precedent using
   a. the future tense
   b. the present tense
   c. the present perfect tense
   d. any tense you like

3. Where a contract right or obligation is to be limited in some circumstances, the best practice is to introduce the limitation
   a. using the words "provided that"
   b. using a new sentence to introduce the limitation
   c. using the word "except" or "if"
   d. b and c

4. To indicate that Albert is required to do something, you should write
   a. Albert will do …
   b. Albert shall do …
   c. Albert may do …
   d. None of the above

5. If you are drafting a contract with a list, and you intend that the list not include other things not specifically mentioned, your intention is best described by the following rule:
   a. *ejusdem generis*
   b. *expressio unius est exclusio alterius*
   c. *mucio alterus casmacus*
   d. none of the above

6. Recitals
   a. set out the history and context of a contract
   b. are used only as a term in contracts for musical performances
   c. prevail if there is a conflict between the content of a recital and a provision in the body of a contract
   d. a and c

7. Where a contract is required to be under seal,
   a. it will be void if the seals fall off after it is signed
   b. it will be valid if there is some evidence the parties intended it to be sealed
   c. a wax seal and signature are both required
   d. a and c

8. If a partnership is a party to a contract,
   a. it is advisable for all partners to sign in order for all to be bound by the partnership's obligations
   b. it is not advisable to use the name of the partnership in the contract if the partners are named
   c. a and b
   d. none of the above

Short Answer

1. What are the dangers in using a precedent? What are the advantages?

2. When do you need to include a definition section in a contract you are drafting?

3. What is a legal sentence? How does it differ from other types of sentences?

4. What is the "active voice" and why is it important to use it in drafting contracts and other legal writing?

5. What is the "passive voice"? Is it ever permissible to use the passive voice in legal writing? Why or why not?

6. Identify three different meanings that the conjunction "and" can have in a legal sentence.

7. Describe three problems you might encounter in expressing periods of time and how those problems can be solved by using good drafting practices. Use examples in your description.

8. The term "The employee must be more than 65 years old to receive the employer's pension" appears in an employment contract. What problems might you face in deciding when this pension should begin, and how might you eliminate the problems through better drafting?

9. Give examples of when to use the words "shall," "will," and "may."

10. What is the purpose of a recital in a contract?

11. What is plain language drafting? What is legalese? What is the difference between the two? Which is preferred by most writers of contracts, and why?

12. Give an example of inappropriate use of the following words in a legal sentence, and show how you would improve the sentence in each case.

   a. such,

   b. same,

   c. any, each, every, all.

13. If you are acting for a party who wants to minimize the impact of a representation as a term of the contract, what sorts of strategies and drafting techniques might you employ?

14. Explain the difference between a contract representation and a contract statement.

15. Gina is a law clerk who is arranging to have a client come in to sign a commercial lease in a shopping mall.

   a. Gina has set up the appointment for the client to come in but then discovers she has a dental appointment at the same time. She signs her name in the space for a witness next to where the client will sign the contract and leaves instructions for the junior clerk to meet with the client. Is this okay?

   b. The client was born in the Republic of Georgia and his name is Josef Djugashvili. His birth certificate shows his name written in the Cyrillic alphabet. He is generally known in business as Joe Steel but his Ontario driver's licence says Josef Djugashvili. How should he be named in the contract?

   c. This is a commercial long-term lease, and it is to be under seal. What can you use for a seal if Mr. Djugashvili doesn't have a signet ring with his family crest on it, and you have run short of sealing wax?

Apply Your Knowledge

1. TO: Paul Paregoric, Law Clerk
   FROM: Linda Loquacious, Solicitor
   RE: Gregorious Gormand, purchase of "Slumflowers" painting

   Our client, Gregorious Gormand, the well-known gourmet restaurant owner, has arranged to buy a newly discovered Van Gogh painting of some rather drab-looking flowers with a decrepit urban area as background. Our client calls it "Slumflowers," which is, I suppose, an accurate description. The painting is in its original 19th-century frame. The current owner is Tentacle Industries Ltd. The company is in difficulty and has had to liquidate its corporate art collection. Our client knows John Eatem, the president of Tentacle, and they have negotiated the main terms, though not everything is settled. Our client has agreed to purchase this painting for $100,000 in its current condition and in its current frame. Tentacle owes our client $50,000, and the debt will also be considered paid when the painting is delivered and has been accepted by Gormand. Our client is concerned that he not get stuck with something that was painted-by-numbers, so he wants a provision allowing him to have the painting examined and authenticated by an expert before he accepts it. He also wants to hang it in a particular place in his restaurant with museum lighting and wants to be sure it looks right before he finally has to decide to accept it. Our client has also discovered that Tentacle has let the insurance lapse on the painting and wants some provision so that if the painting is destroyed before he finally accepts it, the parties are restored to their pre-contract positions. The seller has said that the painting is original and claims it can trace the painting back through previous owners to Van Gogh himself. Be sure to include something about this in the contract. Our client also wants the painting delivered December 1, 20XX, so that he can hang it in his restaurant just before the busy Christmas season to impress his customers, and use it as a reason to raise the prices on his menu.

   a. Please go through the process of creating categories and headings, and organize the headings into an outline to be used as a table of contents for me to approve.

   b. Once I have approved the outline, please prepare a draft of the contract from our client's perspective.

RECOMMENDED TEXTS ON INTERPRETATION AND DRAFTING

Dick, Robert C. *Legal Drafting*, 3rd ed. Toronto: Carswell, 1995. This standard Canadian work on legal drafting is often referred to by judges and accepted as authoritative. Clear explanations and good examples are used to illustrate concepts.

Fitzgerald, M.F. *Legal Problem Solving: Reasoning, Research and Writing*, 5th ed. Toronto: Butterworths, 2010. This book is a useful introduction to the topic of legal problem solving and is used by law students.

O'Brien's Encyclopedia of Forms, 11th ed. Aurora, ON: Canada Law Book (annual supplements). These volumes provide useful precedent forms for various types of contracts and commercial documents used in Canada.

Saunders, J.B., ed. *Words and Phrases Legally Defined*, vols. 1-5. London: Butterworths, 2007 (annual). This text, and other words and phrases texts and law dictionaries, can be found in the law reference section of most good libraries and all law libraries. It is a good place to start research on how a particular word, phrase, or term has been interpreted by the courts. It is also useful for checking the language used in precedents for the purpose of eliminating inappropriate or archaic language from the contract you are drafting.

Sullivan, R. *Sullivan on the Construction of Statutes*, 5th ed. Toronto: Butterworths, 2008. This is the standard reference work on drafting and interpreting statutes.

Appendix: Sample Contracts

Dog Walking Contract

The parties to this contract and agreement are:

Full Legal Names: _____

Identity / Social Security / Other Number (Specify) _____

Physical Address: _____

(Hereinafter referred to as "the Owner")

AND

Full Legal Names: _____

Identity / Social Security / Other Number
(Specify) _____

Physical Address: _____

(Hereinafter referred to as "the Walker")

The parties choose the above stated addresses as their physical addresses at which legal proceedings may be instituted.

Whereas the Owner wishes to engage the Walker and the Walker agrees to undertake the services under the terms and provisions defined in this Dog Walking Contract as well as the **Owner's Information** sheet, **Pet Information** sheet(s) and the **Veterinary Release Form** which shall all become part of this Contract. Any reference to dogs or pets in this contract shall refer to those specified on the Pet Information sheet(s).

1.   Relationship and Responsibilities

1.1.   It is expressly understood that the Owner retains the services of the Walker as an Independent Contractor and not as an employee. The Walker shall be responsible for his/her insurance and all statutory declarations and payments with regard to income tax and VAT where applicable.

1.2.   The Walker undertakes to perform the agreed-on services in an attentive, reliable and caring manner and the Owner undertakes to provide all necessary information to assist in this performance.

1.3.   The Walker undertakes to notify the Owner of any occurrence pertaining to the dog which may be relevant to the care and well-being of the dog.

1.4.   The Walker will supply and be equipped with a scooper and waste bags and will duly remove the dog's faeces from all public places.

1.5.   The Walker reserves the right to walk other compatible dogs at the same time but undertakes to limit the number of dogs walked with one person to 6 (six).

1.6.   The Owner will provide suitable harnesses, collars and leads as approved by the Walker as well as coats or muzzles if required.

1.7.   The Walker shall not be obliged to perform any other duties except those specified on the Owner's Information sheet and Pet Information sheet.

2.   Compensation

2.1.   The Walker shall be paid the amount of $_____ (_____ dollars) per walk.

2.2.   A monthly retainer of $_____ (_____ dollars) shall be payable in advance and payment of the balance effected within 3 days of receipt of the account for the outstanding balance at the end of every month.

3.   Duration

3.1.   This Dog Walking Contract shall come into effect on the _____ day of _____ 20_____ and shall:

A.   Terminate on the _____ day of _____ 20_____.

OR

B.   Terminate when either party gives 7 (seven) days written notice of termination.

4.   Cancellation or Early Termination

4.1.   Either party may terminate this Dog Walking Contract a minimum of 24 (twenty four) hours prior to the first scheduled visit without incurring penalties or damages.

4.2.   Cancellation by the Owner of scheduled walks with less than 24 hrs notice may be charged at the full rate or rescheduled at the discretion of the Walker.

4.3.   Where the Walker as sole proprietor needs to cancel a scheduled walk due to unforeseen circumstances, he/she may appoint a substitute Walker with the written approval of the Owner and any difference in the fees charged shall be for the account of the Walker.

4.4.   Should any dog become aggressive or dangerous, the Walker may terminate this dog walking contract with immediate effect.

4.5.   Any wrongful or misleading information in the Owner's Information or Pet Information sheets may constitute a breach of terms of this Dog Walking Contract and be grounds for instant termination thereof.

4.6.   Termination under the circumstances described in 4.4 or 4.5 above shall not entitle the Owner to any refunds nor relief of any outstanding payments due.

5.   Liability

5.1.   The Walker will carry liability insurance relative to the services performed for the Owner. A copy of the insurance policy has been made available to the Owner and the Owner acknowledges that he/she is familiar with its content.

5.2.   The Walker accepts no liability for any breach of security or loss of or damage to the Owner's property if any other person has access to the property during the term of this agreement.

5.3.   The Walker shall not be liable for any mishap of whatsoever nature which may befall a dog or caused by a dog who has unsupervised access to the outdoors.

5.4.   The Owner shall be liable for all medical expenses and damages resulting from an injury to the Walker caused by the dog as well as damage to the Owner's property.

5.5.   The Walker is released from all liability related to transporting dog(s) to and from any veterinary clinic or kennel, the medical treatment of the dog(s) and the expense thereof.

6.   Indemnification

The parties agree to indemnify and hold harmless each other as well as respective employees, successors and assigns from any and all claims arising from either party's willful or negligent conduct.

7.   Emergencies

In the event of an emergency, the Walker shall contact the Owner at the numbers provided to confirm the Owner's choice of action. If the Owner cannot be reached timeously, the Walker is authorized to:

7.1.   Transport the dog(s) to the listed veterinarian;

7.2.   Request on-site treatment from a veterinarian;

7.3.   Transport the dog(s) to an emergency clinic if the previous two options are not feasible.

8.   Security

The Walker warrants to keep safe and confidential all keys, remote control entry devices, access codes and personal information of the Owner and to return same to the Owner at the end of the contract period or immediately upon demand.

9.   Relaxation of Terms

No relaxation, indulgence, waiver or release by any party of any of the rights in terms of this agreement on one occasion shall prevent the subsequent enforcement of such rights and shall not be deemed to be a waiver of any subsequent breach of any of the terms.

10.   Whole Agreement

This Dog Walking Contract and Owner's Information sheet, Pet Information sheet(s) and the Veterinary Release Form attached constitute the sole and entire agreement between the parties with regard to the subject matter hereof and the parties waive the right to rely on any alleged expressed or implied provision not contained therein. Any alteration to this agreement must be in writing and signed by both parties.

11.   Assignment

No party may assign any of its rights or delegate or assign any of its obligations in terms of this Dog Walking Contract without the prior written consent of the other party, except where otherwise stated.

12.   Binding Effect

The terms of this Contract shall be binding upon and accrue to the benefit and be enforceable by either party's successors, legal representatives and assigns.

13.   Governing Law

This Contract and Agreement shall be construed, interpreted and governed in accordance with the laws of the State of _____ and should any provision of this Contract be judged by an appropriate court as invalid, it shall not affect any of the remaining provisions whatsoever.

14.   General

The parties agree that any or all parts of this agreement may be submitted to the other party in legible and recordable electronic form and upon acknowledgement of receipt by the receiving party shall become valid parts of the agreement.

Paragraph headings are for convenience of reference only and are not intended to have any effect in the interpretation or determining of rights or obligations under this agreement.

Where appropriate words signifying one gender shall include the other and words signifying the singular shall include the plural and vice versa.

Signed at _____ on this _____ day of _____ 20_____ by the Owner who warrants his/her authority to enter into this agreement.

Owner's Signature: _____

Signed at _____ on this _____ day of _____ 20_____ by the Walker who warrants his/her authority to enter into this agreement.

Walker's Signature: _____

Source: Courtesy of ProDogWalker.com.

Residential Lease

STANDARD FORM OF LEASE
(Residential Tenancies Act R.S.N.S. 1989, c.401)

PARTIES

1. This agreement is made in duplicate between

Landlord

_____
Name

_____
Municipal/Civic Address   PO Box (if applicable)

_____
City   Postal Code

_____
Phone (bus)   Phone (res)

– and –

Tenant(s) _____
                        Name(s)

OCCUPANTS

Other adults or children who will occupy premises _____

Type of Property _____
                        Specify

Only those tenants and occupants named are allowed to live in the premises without written consent of the landlord.

PREMISES

2. The landlord will rent to the tenant and the tenant will rent from the landlord the following premises at Location:

_____
Street   Apt. No.   City / Town

Tenant's mailing address (PO Box if applicable) _____ Postal Code _____

_____

Tenant's Phone # _____ (work) _____ (home)

EMERGENCY CONTACT

Next of Kin _____
            Emergency Contact   Phone # (work)   (home)

☐ The residential premises described above are administered under a public housing program as defined in clause 2(fa) of the Residential Tenancies Act. Program eligibility requirements and rules relating to changes in rent are contained in Schedule "___" attached hereto.

PROPERTY MANAGER OR AGENT

3. The current agent or property manager for the landlord is

_____
Name

_____
Civic Address   Phone # (work)   (home)

4. The current superintendent for the building is

_____
Name

_____
Address

_____
Phone #   Emergency Phone #

WHO TO SERVE

5. All notices to quit or service of documents to the landlord shall be in writing and served in person, by registered mail or by any other means authorized by the Director to

☐ the landlord / owner   (and/or)   ☐ the agent or property manager   or   ☐ the superintendent at the above noted addresses.

LEASE BEGINS

6. The tenancy is to commence or take effect on the _____ day of _____ , 20 ____ and this shall be the anniversary date as defined in the Act.

The term is to run (check one)
☐ from year to year
☐ from month to month
☐ from week to week
and **the tenancy continues until the landlord or the tenant gives proper notice to terminate.**

OR

The tenancy is for a fixed term, beginning on the _____ day of _____ , 20 ____ and ending on the _____ day of _____ , 20 ____ . Any continuation of the tenancy at the end of a fixed term requires the written consent of the landlord. **At the end of the fixed term, the tenancy is finished and the tenant must vacate.**

RENT 7. The tenant will pay rent of $ _____ per _____ by:

(week / month)

☐ Cash   ☐ Pre-authorized automatic withdrawal

☐ Post-dated cheques   ☐ Cheque   ☐ Other

Rent is due on the _____ day of each month/week and is payable to _____.
A late payment fee, if any, shall be charged at no more than 1% per month of the monthly rental.

RENT
INCREASE

The rent may not increase under this lease for 12 months. The rent may be increased on the anniversary date only. The landlord must give a written notice to the tenant of an increase:

(a) 4 months before the anniversary date of a month to month or year to year lease;
(b) 8 weeks before the anniversary date of a week to week lease;
(c) 7 months before the anniversary date of a mobile home lot lease. Note: The Landlord may select a date to be the annual rent increase date for the park. If an annual rent increase date is used notice must be given 7 months before this date. The Landlord must serve the notice of rent increase on the tenants of the mobile home park.

Where the landlord administers a public housing program and the tenant's rent is increased solely on the basis of an increase in income, the restrictions on frequency of rental increases and notice requirements do not apply.

RENTAL
INCENTIVE
(IF ANY)

8. In signing this lease, the landlord has granted to the tenant the following incentives which will remain in effect for the duration of the lease. The tenant is not required to repay or return any rental incentive if he or she terminates the lease before the end of the term in accordance with the provisions of the *Residential Tenancies Act* or sublets the residential premises to a tenant with the consent of the landlord.

_____

_____

RENT
INCLUDES

9. The rent includes:

Appliances	**Utilities**
☐ stove	☐ washer & dryer (coin operated)
☐ fridge	☐ cable service
☐ washer & dryer	☐ heat
☐ dishwasher	☐ water
☐ furniture	☐ hot water
☐ other (define)	☐ electricity
	☐ parking # of spaces _____ space # _____
	☐ facilities to separate recyclables, organics and refuse

The landlord is responsible for providing these services and the deletion of a service is deemed to be a rental increase.

The tenant is responsible for the following:

☐ Lawn care	☐ Late payment charges
☐ Snow removal	☐ Returned cheque charges not to exceed $_____
☐ Garbage removal	☐ Parking @ $ _____ / month # of spaces _____
☐ Tenant Insurance	☐ Locked out charges / keys not to exceed $_____
☐ Separation of recyclables, organics and refuse	

10. Additional obligations

_____

_____

SECURITY
DEPOSIT

11. ☐ A security deposit is not required.
OR
☐ A security deposit of $ _____ (not to exceed 1/2 month's rent) will be deposited for

the tenant by the landlord at _____

Financial Institution / Branch

in a trust account within 3 days of its receipt, and will be returned to the tenant with interest, within 10 days of the termination of this lease. The landlord shall file a claim for unpaid rent and/or damages within 10 days of the termination of the lease if the deposit is not returned.

INSPECTION

An inspection of the premises and the preparation of a written inspection report signed by the landlord and tenant or an electronic inspection report prepared within 7 days of the start of the tenancy and within 7 days of the end of the tenancy is recommended. If a report is prepared it shall form part of the lease.

☐ A form of inspection report is attached to the lease.

☐ An inspection report is not attached.

REASONABLE
RULES

12. The landlord and tenant promise to comply with the statutory conditions set out in Schedule "A". The tenant acknowledges receipt of the rules of the building which are attached hereto as Schedule "____".
Tenants in a public housing program are not permitted to sublet the premises.

| RENTAL ARREARS | 13. | In a monthly or yearly tenancy, where a tenant is in arrears in paying the rent for 30 days or more, the landlord may give the tenant a 15 day written notice to quit the premises. |

In a weekly tenancy, where a tenant is in arrears for 7 days or more, the landlord may give the tenant 7 days written notice to quit the premises.

| SECURITY OF TENURE | 14. | Where a tenant has lived in the premises for 5 years or more, written notice to quit may only be given by the landlord in accordance with the *Residential Tenancies Act*. |

Where a tenant has lived in a mobile home park for 1 year or more, written notice to quit may only be given by the landlord in accordance with the Residential Tenancies Act.

| NOTICE TO QUIT EXCEPT FIXED TERM | 15. | All notices to quit for a tenancy other than a fixed term shall be given in writing in accordance with the following table. |

Type of Tenancy	Notice by Tenant	Notice by Landlord
☐ Mobile Home Lot	at least 1 full month before the end of the tenancy	at least 6 full months before the end of the tenancy
☐ Yearly	at least 3 full months before the anniversary date	at least 3 full months before the anniversary date
☐ Monthly	at least 1 full month before the end of any month	at least 3 full months before the end of any month
☐ Weekly	at least 1 full week before the end of any week	at least 4 full weeks before the end of any week

If a tenant has security of tenure, the landlord must apply to the Director for the notice to quit.

| PUBLIC HOUSING PROGRAM | 16. | Where a landlord administers a public housing program a tenant shall provide income verification in the form as required and the tenant shall not sublet the premises. |

17. This lease is for the benefit of and is binding on the landlord and tenant and their heirs, executors, administrators and assigns.

18. Any or all tenants signing this lease take full responsibility for all of its terms and conditions.

Attachments (Initials required)

1   _____   The tenant has received a copy of the Act and regulations within 10 days from grant, possession or occupancy from the landlord.

2   _____   The tenant has received a copy of the signed lease within 10 days of the date of the signing of the lease.

3   _____   The tenant has read, signed and received the rules and attachments to this lease.

SIGN BOTH COPIES SEPARATELY.
BEFORE YOU SIGN PLEASE READ THE FOLLOWING NOTICE.

TENANTS
GIVING NOTICE

IF YOU WISH TO TERMINATE A YEAR TO YEAR LEASE AT THE END OF THE LEASE TERM, THE LAW REQUIRES THAT YOU MUST GIVE AT LEAST 3 MONTHS WRITTEN NOTICE ON OR BEFORE _____

Notice Date – 3 months prior to anniversary date

OTHERWISE THE LEASE WILL AUTOMATICALLY BE RENEWED FOR ANOTHER YEAR.

IF YOU WISH TO TERMINATE A MONTH TO MONTH LEASE, OR A MOBILE HOME LOT LEASE YOU MUST GIVE AT LEAST 1 FULL MONTH'S WRITTEN NOTICE BEFORE THE EXPIRATION OF ANY SUCH MONTH.

IF YOU WISH TO TERMINATE A WEEKLY TENANCY, YOU MUST GIVE 1 FULL WEEK'S NOTICE BEFORE THE EXPIRATION OF ANY SUCH WEEK.

_____   _____
Date   Landlord

ANY OR ALL TENANTS SIGNING THIS LEASE TAKE FULL RESPONSIBILITY FOR ALL OF ITS TERMS AND CONDITIONS.

_____   _____
Date   Tenant

_____   _____
Date   Tenant

_____   _____
Date   Tenant

SCHEDULE "A"
STATUTORY CONDITIONS

Statutory Conditions

9   (1) Notwithstanding any lease, agreement, waiver, declaration or other statement to the contrary, where the relation of landlord and tenant exists in respect of residential premises by virtue of this Act or otherwise, there is and is deemed to be an agreement between the landlord and tenant that the following conditions will apply as between the landlord and tenant as statutory conditions governing the residential premises:

Statutory conditions

1. Condition of Premises – The landlord shall keep the premises in a good state of repair and fit for habitation during the tenancy and shall comply with any statutory enactment or law respecting standards of health, safety or housing.

2. Services – Where the landlord provides a service or facility to the tenant that is reasonably related to the tenant's continued use and enjoyment of the premises such as, but not so as to restrict the generality of the foregoing, heat, water, electric power, gas, appliances, garbage collection, sewers or elevators, the landlord shall not discontinue providing that service to the tenant without proper notice of a rental increase or permission from the Director.

3. Good Behaviour – A landlord or tenant shall conduct himself in such a manner as not to interfere with the possession or occupancy of the tenant or of the landlord and the other tenants, respectively.

4. Obligation of the Tenant – The tenant is responsible for the ordinary cleanliness of the interior of the premises and for the repair of damage caused by wilful or negligent act of the tenant or of any person whom the tenant permits on the premises.

5. Subletting Premises – The tenant may assign, sublet or otherwise part with possession of the premises subject to the consent of the landlord which consent will not arbitrarily or unreasonably be withheld or charged for unless the landlord has actually incurred expense in respect of the grant of consent. (Pursuant to subsection 6(4) of the Residential Tenancies Act tenants under a housing program shall not sublet the residential premises.)

6. Abandonment and Termination – If the tenant abandons the premises or terminates the tenancy otherwise than in the manner permitted, the landlord shall mitigate any damages that may be caused by the abandonment or termination to the extent that a party to a contract is required by law to mitigate damages.

7. Entry of Premises – Except in the case of an emergency, the landlord shall not enter the premises without the consent of the tenant unless

(a) notice of termination of the tenancy has been given and the entry is at a reasonable hour for the purpose of exhibiting the premises to prospective tenants or purchasers; or

(b) the entry is made during daylight hours and written notice of the time of the entry has been given to the tenant at least twenty-four hours in advance of the entry.

8. Entry Doors – Except by mutual consent, the landlord or the tenant shall not during occupancy by the tenant under the tenancy alter or cause to be altered the lock or locking system on any door that gives entry to the premises.

9. Late Payment Penalty – Where the lease contains provision for a monetary penalty for late payment of rent, the monetary penalty shall not exceed one per cent of the monthly rent.

Statutory conditions re mobile homes

(2) In addition to the statutory conditions set out in subsection (1), there is and is deemed to be an agreement between the landlord and tenant that the following statutory conditions apply as between them in respect of the lease of a mobile home space or a mobile home in a mobile home park:

Statutory conditions respecting mobile homes

1. The landlord shall not restrict in any way the right of a tenant to sell, lease or otherwise part with the possession of a mobile home by the tenant.

2. The landlord shall not receive any compensation for acting as the agent of the tenant in any negotiations to sell, lease or otherwise part with possession of a mobile home space or a mobile home situate in a mobile home park, unless provided for in a separate written agency agreement that is entered into by the tenant

(a) after the tenant enters into the tenancy agreement; and
(b) at the time that the tenant decides he wishes to offer his mobile home for sale or lease or otherwise part with the possession of his mobile home or mobile home space.

3. (1) Except as provided in this condition, the landlord shall not restrict in any way the right of the tenant to purchase goods or services from the person of the tenant's choice.
(2) The landlord may set reasonable standards for mobile home equipment.
(3) Where a person who does not live in the mobile home park and who is offering goods or services for sale

(a) unduly disturbs the peace and quiet of the mobile home park;
(b) fails to observe reasonable rules of conduct that have been established by the landlord; or
(c) violates the traffic rules of the mobile home park,

despite a request by the landlord to discontinue the conduct, the landlord may restrict or prohibit the entry of that person into the mobile home park.

4. The landlord is responsible for compliance with municipal by-laws in respect of the common areas of the mobile home park and the services provided by the landlord to the tenants in the mobile home park.

5. The tenant is responsible for compliance with municipal by-laws in respect of the tenant's mobile home and the mobile home space on which it is located to the extent that the landlord is not responsible.

Source: © Service Nova Scotia and Municipal Relations.

Performance Contract

LETTER OF AGREEMENT
Between Axis Theatre Society
(hereafter referred to as Axis Theatre Company) and
(*School name and address*)
(hereafter referred to as the Sponsor)
Contact: (*Teacher or Principal*)
Phone:
Fax:

1. Axis Theatre Company agrees to perform the production (*name of production*) on (*date and time*) 2005 in the facilities located at (*school address*).
2. In consideration of the above mentioned services, the Sponsor agrees to pay Axis Theatre Company the amount of (*$000.00*), plus (*$00.00*) GST. Total remuneration: (*$000.00*).
3. The Sponsor understands that the performance(s) must **start on time**. The Sponsor understands that Axis Theatre Company engages members of the Canadian Actors' Equity Association (CAEA), under the terms of the Canadian Theatre Agreement. Performance times have been carefully scheduled, so that Axis Theatre Company will **not** incur extra costs by violating the CAEA's rules for its members' lunch hours and for adequate travel time between schools/theatres.
4. One signed copy of the contract is to be sent back to Axis Theatre Company with a **non-refundable deposit** in the amount of (*$000.00*) plus (*$0.00*) GST. Deposit monies will be used to offset the sizable preproduction costs incurred in mounting this production.
5. The Sponsor agrees that a cheque representing the balance owing of (*$000.00*) plus (*$00.00*) GST will be made available at the completion of the final performance indicated on this contract. Please make cheques payable to **Axis Theatre Company**.
6. The Sponsor agrees to meet the technical requirements (if any) for Axis Theatre Company as listed on the attached addendum entitled "Technical Requirements." (Technical Requirements will be sent with the Study Guide.)
7. Axis Theatre Company will provide advance copy on the company (as requested) as well as Study Guides for educational presentations at no additional cost to the Sponsor. This **does not include house programs or posters**, unless otherwise stipulated in an attached addendum entitled "Publicity/Promotional Requirements."
8. The Sponsor agrees to prevent the photographing, broadcasting, filming or reproduction by any other devices of the Axis Theatre Company performance(s), unless given prior consent by authorized Axis Theatre Company personnel.
9. For special clauses and considerations, please see any attached addenda.
10. FORCE MAJEURE: If any performance or part thereof is prevented, rendered impossible or infeasible by any act or regulation by any public authority or bureau, civil tumult, civil strike, epidemic, interruption in or delay of transportation services, war conditions, or emergencies, fire or any cause beyond the control of the parties, it is understood and agreed that there shall be no claim for damage by either party to this Agreement and both their obligations herein shall be deemed waived.
11. Cancellation: Sponsors who cancel this contract less than 30 days in advance of the first performance (Force Majeure notwithstanding) will forfeit the deposit payable and may be asked to cover the costs incurred by Axis Theatre Company as a result of the cancellation.

Please sign both copies of this contract and return one copy to the Axis Theatre Company office within 14 business days.

Signed in duplicate this __ day of (*month*), **2005**

_____   _____
Per Sponsor (Signature)   Rosanna Ciulla for Axis Theatre Company

_____
Please print name here

Source: Courtesy of Canada Council for the Arts/Conseil des arts du Canada.

Renovation Contract

Renovation Contract

Between

Contractor (name of company) _____

Address _____

_____

Project manager _____

Telephone _____ Fax _____ E-mail _____

Business Number _____

Municipal Business License #, if applicable _____

and

Owner(s) _____

Address _____

Telephone _____ Fax _____ E-mail _____

Project address (if different from above) _____

1. Contract Documents

(a) This Contract form

(b) Drawings attached and/or referenced herein (if any)

_____

_____

(c) Specifications attached and/or referenced herein (if any)

_____

_____

(d) Additional documents signed by both parties during the course of this Contract. Extras and deletions to be documented on a Change Order Form and signed by both parties.

_____

_____

(e) Other

_____

_____

Omissions in the Contract Documents and any work requested in variance to the Contract Documents are considered extra to the Contract and are not included in the Contract Price. Any additional work, required due to site conditions known to the Owner and not disclosed to the Contractor, or which could not be reasonably anticipated by the Contractor, are not included in the Contract Price and shall be extra to the Contract Price.

2. Description of Work

Unless otherwise stated, the Contractor agrees to supply all materials, labour and supervision to perform the Work as (choose one):

_____ Described below

_____ Described in the attached Work Schedule

a. The Work entails the following _____

_____

_____

_____

b. The Work does NOT include the following

_____

_____

_____

_____

_____

_____

c. Permits

Work will be undertaken under the following permits which will be provided and paid for by the Owner or the Contractor as designated below.

		Owner	Contractor
(i)	Zoning variance	_____	_____
(ii)	Demolition permit	_____	_____
(iii)	Building permit	_____	_____
(iv)	Electrical permit	_____	_____
(v)	Plumbing permit	_____	_____
(vi)	Other	_____	_____

Any such permit obtained by the Contractor will be conveyed to the Owner within ___ days of receipt by the Contractor.

The following parties (specify Contractor or Owner) will contact the appropriate authorities for inspections:

_____

_____

d. Subtrades

The Contractor will use the following subtrades during the performance of the Work as listed below (company name and service provided):

_____

_____

_____

_____

If any subtrade listed above subsequently becomes unavailable for the Work, the Contractor will provide a suitable replacement, for Owner's approval prior to the subtrade commencing work.

Nothing contained in the Contract Documents is intended to, nor shall it, create any contractual relation between the Owner and any subtrade. The Contractor agrees that it is responsible for the enforcement of all material provisions of all subcontracts.

3. Timing

Work to commence on or before (date) _____

Substantial Completion on or before (date) _____

Full Completion on or before (date) _____

Substantial Completion means that the Work has been completed to such a percentage completion as is specified for substantial completion or substantial performance of such Work in the applicable legislation of the province where the Project is situated, that the Work has been completed to the point where it is ready for use for the intended purpose, and that an occupancy permit, where required, has been issued.

All time limits stated in this Contract are of the essence. Notwithstanding the foregoing, any delay in Substantial Completion or Full Completion of the Work (as the case may be) in accordance with the Contract Documents will be considered an excusable delay if arising from causes beyond the Contractor's control and not reasonably foreseeable by the Contractor with the use of the Contractor's best professional efforts. Excusable delays include but are not limited to such events as labour disputes, unavailability of materials, delays in obtaining a permit, fire, natural disaster, unfavourable weather conditions, delays (other than delays arising out of Contractor's breach of this Contract) by, or breach by any subtrades; or any delay by Owner of processing proposed changes, delays resulting from inaccuracies in information provided by the Owner, or delays resulting from the performance of tasks described in section 2b.

In the event of the occurrence of an excusable delay, Owner shall grant appropriate extensions to cover such periods of delays. Owner shall have no obligation to grant extensions if delays were not excusable delays, or otherwise resulted, directly or indirectly, from the Contractor's breach of this Contract. Where a delay occurs, the Contractor must inform the Owner at the earliest possible date of such occurrence, the reason for the delay and anticipated amended dates of completion.

The Contractor and Owner agree that should the Contractor not be able to commence the Work within ___ days from the commencement date specified in this Section, due to causes beyond the Contractor's control such as inability to obtain a building permit, then the Contractor or the Owner may cancel the Contract on written notice mailed to or delivered to the address of the other party shown in this Contract. The Contractor's liability to the Owner shall be limited to the refund of any monies paid by the Owner to the Contractor, less any cost incurred by the Contractor as previously agreed to by the Owner as specified below.

_____

_____

_____

_____

_____

_____

_____

_____

4. Terms of Payment

The Contract price is to be calculated as follows (select one):

(a) Stipulated fixed cost basis (all inclusive) $_____, plus GST/HST Payments shall be due and payable as outlined in the Payment Schedule.

(b) Cost plus _____% of cost, plus GST/HST Payments shall be due on a bi-weekly _____ or monthly _____ basis (check one).

(c) Cost plus fixed fee of $_____, plus GST/HST

Payment shall be due and payable as outlined in the Payment Schedule. A percentage of the fixed fee shall be paid on the presentation of each billing and shall be proportionate to the percentage of work completed for that billing period.

5. Payment Schedule

The Owner will make payments to the Contractor, minus a ___% holdback as required by provincial construction lien legislation, as follows:

	Gross	Payment	Holdback
Signing of Contract	$_____	$_____	$_____
Start-up of Work	_____	_____	_____
Upon completion of _____	_____	_____	_____
Upon completion of _____	_____	_____	_____
Upon completion of _____	_____	_____	_____
Substantial Completion	_____	_____	_____
Full Completion	_____	_____	_____
___% Holdback for ___ days after completion	_____	_____	_____
TOTAL	_____	_____	_____

Payment is due within ___ days of invoicing. Interest of ___% per annum, or the maximum rate allowable by law, whichever is less, will be charged on unpaid invoices after the due date.

All payments are subject to applicable legislation and shall be made in accordance with provisions of this Contract and the provisions of any applicable legislation. All payments must be made to the Contractor. Any payment to a subcontractor is not deemed a payment to the Contractor.

6. Changes in Work

The Owner may make changes by altering, adding to, or deducting from the Work, with the Contract and Contract Price being adjusted accordingly. Changes to the Work require a written Change Order Form, signed by both the Owner and the Contractor.

a) **Extras** will be calculated in the following manner (check one):

1) ____ Material cost plus hourly rate of $ ____

2) ____ Labour and material cost plus ____%

3) ____ A lump sum to be agreed on in advance by both parties.

Extras are payable upon (check one):

1) ____ Signing the Change Order

2) ____ Invoicing pursuant to the Change Order

3) ____ Completion of work specified in Change Order less ____% holdback in all cases.

b) **Deletions** will be calculated on a cost less ____% basis, to be deducted from the relevant or next scheduled payment.

7. Utilities and Washroom Facilities

The Contractor and the Owner agree that responsibility for the provision of utilities and facilities to meet work and worker requirements will be assumed in the following manner:

		Owner	Contractor
(a)	Water	____	____
(b)	Electricity	____	____
(c)	Washroom	____	____
(d)	Other		
_____		____	____

8. Standards of Work

The Contractor agrees to supply all labour, materials and supervision to complete the Work in accordance with the Contract Documents.

The Contractor agrees to undertake all Work diligently in a good and workmanlike manner, in accordance with good quality residential standards and practices, and in compliance with any applicable Building Code and all other authorities having jurisdiction.

The Owner accepts that there may be inconveniences from time to time, and the Contractor agrees to keep such inconveniences to a reasonable minimum. It is the responsibility of the Owner to take reasonable steps to provide a work area free of household obstructions, and to remove or protect household items in areas where it may be reasonably anticipated by the Owner that they may be subject to dust, damage or vibrations.

The Contractor agrees to keep the site orderly and reasonably free of debris. At the completion of the project, the Contractor shall clean the property and leave it fit for use. All equipment, materials, rubbish and similar material incidental to the project shall be removed by the Contractor.

9. Warranty

The Contractor shall correct, at its' own expense, any defects in the Work due to faulty materials and/or workmanship pursuant to this Contract for a period of ____ year(s) from the date of Full Completion.

The Owner shall give the Contractor written notice of such defects within a reasonable time, and in any event within the warranty period.

Special conditions limiting/affecting this warranty (if any)

_____

_____

_____

The Contractor will convey to Owner any warranties by manufacturers or suppliers on individual materials, products or systems supplied by Contractor under this Contract.

The Contractor does not warrant labour and/or materials supplied by the Owner or the Owner's subcontractors. The Contractor shall protect the Work, the Owner's property and the property of third parties from damage occasioned by the performance of its obligations under the Contract Documents.

10. Insurance

Prior to commencing the Work, the Contractor agrees to provide, maintain and pay for insurance during the time the Work is being performed, including commercial general liability in the minimum amount of $1,000,000 against claims for damages for personal injury or property damage by reason of anything done or not done by the Contractor, its employees or agents, in connection with the performance of this Contract. The Contractor will also provide proof of automobile liability insurance. The Contractor is responsible for all materials on site provided by the Contractor for the Work in this Contract until installed.

11. Compliance with Workers' Compensation and Other Laws

The Contractor agrees to provide evidence of compliance by the Contractor's own company and any of the Contractor's subcontractors with all requirements for registration and payments due under the province's workers' compensation statute.

The Contractor also agrees to comply with all laws, ordinances, rules, regulations, codes and orders in force during the performance of the Contract which relate to the preservation of public health or construction safety.

12. Other Contractors

Owner reserves the right to let separate contracts in connection with the Work or to do certain work by Owner's own forces as specified in Description of Work.

The Contractor shall include in his work co-ordination with Owner's separate contractors or forces, and Owner shall pay the Contractor $ _____ for coordination of same.

13. Dispute Resolution

The Owner and the Contractor agree that in the event of a dispute as to the interpretation of this Contract or the extent of the Work, the issues shall be submitted to arbitration as agreed to by both parties or under the province's arbitration statute.

14. Default by Owner

In the event that (a) the Owner does not perform its obligations under this Contract in accordance with the terms of this Contract and has not corrected the default within ___ days of written notice by the Contractor, or (b) the Owner becomes bankrupt or makes a general assignment for the benefit of its creditors, or if a receiver of the Owner is appointed, or (c) if the Work is stopped as a result of a court order, then the Contractor may cease work and treat the contract as repudiated forthwith on the occurrence of such default. In such event, an accounting shall be made between the Owner and the Contractor, and the Contractor shall be entitled to payment for such parts of the Work as are completed at the time of default.

15. Default by Contractor

In the event that (a) the Contractor does not perform the Work in accordance with the terms of this Contract and has not corrected the default within ___ days of written notice by the Owner, or (b) the Contractor becomes bankrupt or makes a general assignment for the benefit of its creditors, or if a receiver of the Contractor is appointed, then the Owner may finish the Work in accordance with the plans and specifications as the Owner may deem expedient, but without undue delay or expense.

In such event, the Contractor shall not be entitled to any further payment under this Contract, but upon completion of the Work, an accounting shall be made between the Owner and the Contractor. If the unpaid balance on the Contract Price shall exceed the expense of finishing the Work, the Owner shall pay the Contractor for such parts of the work as were payable or completed at the time of the default. However, if such expense shall exceed such unpaid balance, the Contractor shall pay the difference to the Owner.

16. Signs

The Owner agrees to permit the Contractor to display a sign on the project site until completion.

This Contract shall not be assigned, in whole or in part, without the prior written consent of the other party, which consent will not be unreasonably withheld or delayed.

This Contract shall be governed by and construed under the laws of the Province in which the project is situated, and supersedes all prior communications and agreements. There are no other terms outside of this Contract.

The Contractor assures that there is not now any claim, action, contract, rule or other circumstance which may interfere with the Contractor's ability to perform its obligations under this contract.

_____	_____	_____
Owner	Date	Witness
_____	_____	_____
Owner	Date	Witness
_____	_____	_____
Contractor	Date	Witness

Glossary

acceptance

when there has been acceptance of an offer made by one party in the bargaining process, the parties are assumed to have reached an agreement on contract terms, and a binding contract exists from that time

accord and satisfaction

a means of discharging a contract whereby the parties agree to accept some form of compromise or settlement instead of performance of the original terms of the contract

ad idem

see consensus ad idem

adequate notice

the requirement for a party who wants to rely on an exclusion clause in a contract to bring the clause to the other party's attention and explain its legal implications before the contract is signed

adhesion contract

a standardized contract for goods or services offered to consumers on a non-negotiable or "take it or leave it" basis, without offering consumers the opportunity to bargain over the terms of the contract

affidavit of execution

a sworn statement in writing, signed by the witness to a contract, stating that the witness was present and saw the person signing the contract actually sign it; the affidavit can be used to prove that a party to a contract actually signed it

anticipatory breach

an express repudiation that occurs before the time of performance of a contract

arm's-length transaction

a transaction negotiated by unrelated parties, each acting in his or her own independent self-interest; "unrelated" in this context usually means not related as family members by birth or marriage, and not related by business interests

assignee

a party to whom rights under a contract have been assigned by way of an assignment

assignment

a transfer by one party of his or her rights under a contract to a third party

assignor

a party who assigns his or her rights under a contract to a third party

asymmetric cryptosystem (public key encryption)

a form of electronic signature consisting of a private and public key; the sender controls both and sends them as the signature on a document; the recipient can access the public key to unlock the private key to decrypt the document and verify the signature, but the codes in the private key are not revealed to the recipient

beneficiary

a person who is entitled to the benefits of an agreement entered into between two or more other parties

breach of contract

failure, without legal excuse, to perform any promise that forms part of a contract

browse-wrap contract

an electronic transaction where the purchaser is able to click and see the terms of a contract on a website, but is not required to read or agree to them to complete the transaction

click-wrap contract

an electronic transaction where the purchaser sees the terms and must click on an icon that indicates the purchaser has agreed to the terms before the transaction is completed; also called a "click-through" agreement

common mistake

both parties to a contract are mistaken and make the same mistake

condition

an essential term of a contract, the breach of which denies the innocent party the benefit of the contract, or defeats the purpose of the contract

condition precedent

an event (or non-event) that must occur (or not occur) before a contract can be enforced

condition subsequent

an event that, if it occurs, will terminate an existing contract

consensus ad idem

when there has been acceptance by the offeree of an offer, the parties have reached an agreement on terms, and they have an intention to be bound by those terms; they are said to have reached a *consensus ad idem* (a "meeting of the minds"); sometimes a shorter form is used, and the parties are said to be *ad idem*

consequential damages

secondary damages that do not flow from the breach of contract but from the consequences of the breach, such as loss of future profits

consideration

the price, which must be something of value, paid in return for a promise

constructive trust

an implied trust, as distinguished from an express trust, where the person with legal title to property is unjustly enriched, the other party suffers a deprivation, and there is no legal reason for permitting one side to benefit disproportionately. A constructive trust does not depend on the intent of the parties.

contra proferentem rule

a rule used in the interpretation of contracts when dealing with ambiguous terms according to which a court will choose the interpretation that favours the party who did not draft the contract

contract/agreement

an agreement made between two or more persons that the law recognizes and will enforce; a binding contract

counteroffer

a response to an offer by an offeree that does not unconditionally accept the terms of the offer but proposes to add to or modify the terms

deed

a written contract, made under seal by the promisor(s); also called a formal contract

discharged

released, extinguished; a discharge of a contract occurs when the parties have complied with their obligations or other events have occurred that release one or both parties from performing their obligations

doctrine of frustration of contract

a legal doctrine that permits parties to a contract to be relieved of the contractual obligations because of the occurrence of some event beyond their control that makes it impossible for them to perform the contract

doctrine of laches

a common-law doctrine that states that the neglect or failure to institute an action or lawsuit within a reasonable time period, together with prejudice suffered by the other party as a result of the delay, will result in the barring of the action

due diligence

the attention and care that a reasonable person would exercise with respect to his or her concerns; the obligation to make every reasonable effort to meet one's obligations

duress

an unlawful threat or coercion used by one person to induce another to perform some act against his or her will

easement

an interest in land that permits certain uses without interruption or interference by the person who has legal title to the land

e-commerce

commercial transactions using the Internet; sometimes used interchangeably with e-contracts

e-contracts

contracts where the entire contracting process takes place on the Internet; sometimes used interchangeably with e-commerce

ejusdem generis

a rule of contract construction that requires that general words following specific words take their meaning from the specific words and are confined to the same category as the specific words

electronic agent

a computer program or other electronic means that can act (or respond to acts or documents) without review or oversight by an individual at the time the act or response occurs

equitable remedies

remedies developed by the court of equity that are based on fairness instead of the strict application of common law

estopped

stopped or prevented

exclusion/exemption clause

a clause in a contract that limits the liability of one of the parties

executory contract

a contract between a buyer and seller in which full payment is not made at the time of the contract; a contract to buy on credit

expectancy damages

damages that are based on a loss of expected profits

express repudiation/express breach

the failure or refusal to perform the obligations under a contract when they become due

express trust

a trust that arises as a result of an agreement, usually in writing, that is created in express terms

expressio unius est exclusio alterius

(Latin) "to express one thing and exclude another"; a rule of contract construction that requires that the use of one word implies the exclusion of another

fiduciary

a relationship where one person is in a position of trust to another and has a duty to safeguard the other's interests ahead of his or her own interests

force majeure

a major event that the parties to a contract did not foresee or anticipate that prevents performance of the contract and thus terminates the contract; such an event—for example, a natural disaster or war—is outside the control of the parties and cannot be avoided with due diligence

formal contract

a contract that is in writing and sealed by any party who is a promisor (which may be one or both parties); formal contracts are also called "deeds," and in English law are sometimes referred to as "covenants"

fraud

false or misleading allegations for the purpose of inducing another to part with something valuable or to give up some legal right

fraudulent misrepresentation

a false statement made to induce a party to enter into a contract that the maker knows is false

gratuitous promise

a promise made by someone who does not receive consideration for it

guarantee

a promise by a third party to pay the debt of another person if that person fails to pay the debt when it is due

guarantor

a third party who gives a guarantee to the creditor of another person

hyperlink

text or image on a web page that, when clicked on, takes the user to a linked page

implied repudiation

repudiation that is not express and must be implied or deduced from the circumstances

injunction

a court order that prohibits someone from doing some act or compels someone to do some act

innocent misrepresentation

a false statement made to induce a party to enter into a contract that the maker of the statement does not know is false

inquiry

questioning by the offeree as to whether the offeror will consider other terms or is willing to modify the terms of the offer; an inquiry does not constitute a counteroffer and is not a rejection of the original offer

intangible property
personal property where the interest in it or its value rests in rights it confers rather than in its physical properties

interlocutory/interim injunction
a temporary injunction granted by a court before the final determination of a lawsuit for the purpose of preventing irreparable injury

judicial interventionism
an approach to the interpretation of law that draws on social, economic, and political values in interpreting the meaning and application of legal rules and principles

lapse
the termination or failure of an offer through the neglect to accept it within some time limit or through failure of some contingency

legal tender
notes (bills) issued by the Bank of Canada and coins issued by the Royal Canadian Mint, subject to certain restrictions

licence
a grant of a right; in real property law, a grant of a right to some use of land that does not amount to a grant of an interest in the land

life estate
a transfer of interest in land for a term of years measured by the life of the transferee or by the life of another person; when the person dies, the life estate ends, and the property goes back to the transferor or other persons designated to receive the interest in land

liquidated damages
damages that are easily determined from a fixed or measurable standard, or can be assessed by calculating the amount owing from a mathematical formula or from circumstances where no subjective assessment has to be made

liquidated damages clause
a term in a contract that attempts to reasonably estimate the damages that will be suffered if the contract is breached

lost opportunity damages
damages that are based on a longer-term loss of business

mandatory injunction
an injunction that commands a person to do a certain thing

material alteration
a change in a contract that changes its legal meaning and effect; a change that goes to the heart or purpose of the contract

material representation
a statement of fact, not opinion, made by one party, of sufficient weight to induce the other party to enter into the contract

merger
the discharge of one contract by its replacement with, or absorption into, an identical contract

minor
at common law, an individual under the age of 21; minority status has also been defined by statute law, lowering the age of majority to 18 or 19 in most provinces

misrepresentation
a false statement that induces someone to enter into a contract

mitigate
to take steps to minimize or reduce the damages one will suffer as a result of another's breach of contract

mutual mistake
both parties to a contract are mistaken but each makes a different mistake

negative covenant
a promise in a contract to refrain from doing a certain thing

non est factum
(Latin) "I did not make this"; a defence used by one who appears to be a party to a contract but who did not intend to enter into this type of contract; in effect, the party is denying that he or she consented to this contract

novation
the creation of a new contract by the parties to an existing contract agreeing to substitute a new party in the existing contract, thus terminating the existing contract

null and void
of no force, validity, or effect

nullity
nothing; something that has no legal force or effect

offer

a promise to do something or give something of value to another person; if the other accepts the offer, a binding contract exists

offeree

a person to whom an offer is made during the bargaining process

offeror

a person who, during the bargaining process that precedes making a contract, agrees to do something for the other party; once the offer is accepted, the bargain is concluded and the parties have made an agreement

onus

the burden of responsibility or proof

option to terminate

a term in a contract that allows one or both parties to discharge or terminate the contract before performance has been fully completed

parol evidence rule

if a contract is in writing and is clear, no other written or oral evidence is admissible to contradict, vary, or interpret the agreement

past consideration

an act done or something given before a contract is made, which by itself is not consideration for the contract

penalty clause

a term in a contract that imposes a penalty for default or breach

persons under mental disability

a general term that includes persons who are delusional and insane so as to be a danger to themselves and others, and those who, while not insane and dangerous, lack the ability to manage their own affairs

PIN

a personal identification number used in a symmetric cryptosystem to identify one party electronically to another party

plain language drafting

the modern style of drafting legal documents that employs plain, ordinary language and emphasizes clarity, precision, and brevity

positivism

an approach to the interpretation of law that states that the meaning to be given to the words in legal rules should be the ordinary, dictionary meaning without resorting to social, economic, or political values to aid in interpretation

precedent

an essential doctrine of common law that requires judges to follow the rule in a previously decided case when that case deals with similar facts or issues to the case currently being decided

presumption of law

an inference in favour of a particular fact; a rule of law whereby a finding of a basic fact gives rise to the existence of a presumed fact or state of affairs unless the presumption can be rebutted, or proved false, by the party seeking to deny the presumed fact

privity

the relationship that exists between the parties to a contract

prohibitory injunction

an injunction that directs a person not to do a certain thing

promisee

the party to a contract who receives the benefit of a promise made by another party to the contract

promisor

the party to a contract who undertakes to do something

promissory estoppel

a rule whereby a person is prevented from denying the truth of a statement of fact made by him or her where another person has relied on that statement and acted accordingly

quantum meruit

an equitable doctrine that states that no one should unjustly benefit from the labour and materials of another; under those circumstances, the law implies a promise to pay a reasonable amount, even in the absence of a contractual term for price; loosely translated as "as much as is deserved"

recital

a part of a contract, at the beginning, that recites facts that establish the background of the parties and their purpose in entering into the contract

representation
a statement made to induce someone to enter into a contract

repudiate
to renounce or reject an obligation

rescission
the cancellation, nullification, or revocation of a contract; the "unmaking" of a contract

restitution
a remedy by which one seeks to rescind a contract; if granted, restitution restores the party, as far as possible, to the pre-contract position

restraint of trade
practices that are designed to artificially maintain prices, eliminate competition, create a monopoly, or otherwise obstruct the course of trade and commerce

restrictive covenant
a provision in a contract that prohibits certain activities or uses of property

resulting trust
an implied trust, as distinguished from an express trust, where the legal titleholder is presumed to be holding property for a beneficiary in circumstances where a common intent can be implied

revoke
to annul or make void by recalling or taking back; to cancel or rescind

setoff
in an action for debt, a defence where the debtor admits that he or she owes a debt to the creditor but also claims that the creditor owes a debt to him or her, and uses this to cancel or reduce the debt owed to the creditor

settlor
a person who creates a trust by transferring property to a trustee for the benefit of a third party

shrink-wrap contract
a transaction where there are additional terms or conditions inside the packaging or in documentation furnished after the purchase; the purchaser does not see these additional terms until after the transaction is completed

simple contract
a contract that can be oral or in writing and that is not a formal contract

specific goods
specific, identifiable chattels that have been singled out for contract purposes

specific performance
a remedy requiring the party who is in breach of a contract to perform his or her obligations under the contract

substantial performance
performance of contractual obligations that does not entirely meet the terms of the contract but nevertheless confers a benefit on a party

symmetric cryptosystem
a form of electronic signature that uses an alphanumeric code known to both sender and recipient that allows the recipient to verify who the sender is

tender of performance
offering to perform that which the contracted party is obligated to perform under a contract

term
a provision of a contract; terms are either conditions or warranties

terms of art
words, phrases, or technical terms that have a fairly precise, specific legal meaning, often as a result of being interpreted and defined in previous court decisions

tort
a civil wrong done by one party to another for which the law awards damages; the law of torts is much older than the law of contracts, and it is from tort law that modern contract law developed

trust
a legal entity created by a grantor for a beneficiary whereby the grantor transfers property to a trustee to manage for the benefit of the beneficiary

trustee
a person who holds property in trust for, or for the benefit of, another person

uberrimae fidei contracts

a class of contracts where full disclosure is required because one party must rely on the power and authority of another, who must behave with utmost good faith and not take advantage of the weaker party

under seal

bearing an impression made in wax or directly on paper, or affixed with a gummed paper wafer, to guarantee authenticity

undue influence

persuasion, pressure, or influence short of actual force that overpowers a weaker party's judgment and free will and imposes the will of the stronger party

unilateral mistake

one party to a contract is mistaken about a fundamental element of the contract

unjust enrichment doctrine

the principle that a person should not be permitted to inequitably gain a profit or benefit at the expense of another

unliquidated damages

damages that cannot be fixed by a mathematical or measured calculation but require information from a source outside the contract

vicarious performance

the performance of obligations under a contract by a third party in circumstances in which the original party remains responsible for proper performance

void ab initio

invalid from the beginning; no rights can arise under a contract that is void *ab initio*

void contract

a contract that does not exist at law because one or more essential elements of the contract are lacking; an unenforceable contract

voidable contract

a contract that may be avoided or declared void at the option of one party to the contract; once it is declared invalid no further rights can be obtained under it, but benefits obtained before the declaration are not forfeit

waiver

a voluntary agreement to relinquish a right, such as a right under a contract

warranty

a minor term of a contract, the breach of which does not defeat the purpose of the contract

Index

A

acceptance
> communication of, 17
> defined, 3
> performance as, 18
> reasonable time for, 21
> rules for determining, 19, 22
> silence as, 18, 19
accord and satisfaction, 166
ad idem, 3
adequate notice, 190
adhesion contract, 190
affidavit of execution, 45
anticipatory breach, 174
arm's-length transaction, 13
assignee, 121
assignment of contract
> by operation of law, 124
> defences, and, 122
> defined, 121
> equitable assignment, 121
> notice of, 123
> statutory assignment, 121-22
assignor, 121
asymmetric cryptosystem, 214

B

beneficiary, 115
breach of contract
> defined, 22, 174
> method of, 174-76
> nature of, 176-77
browse-wrap contract, 208, 209, 211

C

click-wrap contract, 207, 209, 210
common mistake, 105

condition, 131
condition precedent, 137, 167
condition subsequent, 167
consensus ad idem, 3
consequential damages, 178
consideration
> adequacy of, 26
> clause in contract, 249
> debtor–creditor relationships, 28
> defined, 23
> estoppel based on fact, 25
> existing legal obligation, 27-28
> future consideration, 27
> gratuitous promises, 24, 26
> past consideration, 26-27
> present consideration, 27
> promissory estoppel, 25
> *quantum meruit*, 29-30
constructive trust, 119-20
contra proferentem rule, 141
contract/agreement
> acceptance, rules of, 22
> administration
>> client questions, 257
>> electronic signatures, 255
>> errors, correction of, 257
>> execution, 254
>> form of party's name, 256
>> original protection of, 257
>> signing, 255, 256
>> under seal, 254-55
>> witnessing, 256
> assignment of, 121-24
> breach of contract, 22, 174-76
>> remedies, 181-93
> consideration, exchange of, 3, 23-30
> counteroffers and inquiries, 20

contract/agreement *(cont.)*
  defects
    duress, 83-85
    misrepresentation, 72-82
    mistake, 90-107
    unconscionability, 87-90
    undue influence, 85-87
  defined, 2
  discharge of, 160-68
  drafting of
    common language, 235-43
    construction rules, 243-44
    first draft, 234-35
    legalese, inappropriate use of, 244-47
  e-contracts, 200
  formality requirements, 5, 36-45
  formation, rules of, 23
  interpretation
    exclusion clauses, 139-45
    frustration, 148-55
    overview, 130
    parol evidence rule, 134-39
    penalty clauses, 145-47
    provisions, 131-34
  lapse of offer, 21
  legal capacity, 4
  legal enforceability, 2, 30-35
  legally binding relations, creation of, 3, 4, 12-14
  offer and acceptance, 3, 15-19
  preparation, 232-34
  privity of, 114-20
  revocation of offer, 21, 22
  structure of
    appendixes, 253
    consideration, 249
    format, 253-54
    layout, 253
    parties, identification of, 247-48
    recitals, 249
    schedules, 253
    terms, 249-52
    testimonium and attestation, 252-53
  weaker parties, protection of, 52-66
contract law
  case law, and, 6, 7
  development of, 5

positivism versus judicial interventionism, 7
  statute law, and, 6
counteroffer, 20

D
deed, 24
discharge of contract
  as of right, 167-68
  by agreement, 163-67
  by operation of law, 168
  by performance, 160-63
  overview, 160, 187
doctrine of frustration of contract, *see* frustration of contract, doctrine of
doctrine of laches, 168
drafting of contract
  common language, 235-43
  construction rules, 243-44
  first draft, 234-35
  interpretation, 243
  legalese, inappropriate use of, 244-47
  preparation, 232-34
  problems, , 235-43
drunkenness, 62-64
due diligence, 168
duress, 83-85

E
easement, 40
e-commerce
  browse-wrap contracts, and, 207, 209, 211
  click-wrap contracts, and, 207, 209, 210
  consent, effect on, 210-11
  defined, 200
  Electronic Commerce Act, 2000
    application, 202
    biometric information, 206
    documents not subject to, 206
    e-communications, 204-5
    electronic agents, 203-4, 216, 217
    electronic documents, 202
    electronic forms, 206
    electronic signatures, 202, 213-15
    freedom of information/privacy legislation, and, 206
    offer and acceptance, 203

overview, 201
public bodies conducting business, 203
regulations, 8
shipment of goods, 205
statutory override, 206
hyperlinks, 212-13
jurisdiction over, 216-19
shrink-wrap contracts, and, 207, 208
e-contracts, 200
ejusdem generis, 243
electronic agent, 203
equitable remedies, 181
essential collateral agreement, 136
essential implied term, 136
estopped, 23
exclusion/exemption clause
defined, 139
fundamental breach, 142-45
notice of, 140-41
public policy, and, 144
strict interpretation, 141
executory contract, 54
expectancy damages, 178
express repudiation/express breach, 174
express trust, 118
expressio unius est exclusio alterius, 243

F

fiduciary, 86
force majeure, 148
formal contract, 36
fraud, 26
fraudulent misrepresentation, 72, 78-79
frustration of contract
based on construction theory, 149-51
based on implied term theory, 149, 150
common-law remedies, 152-53
doctrine of, 148
factors affecting, 148
impossibility, distinguished from, 151-52
legislation governing, 153-55

G

gratuitous promise, 23
guarantee, 38
guarantor, 38

H

hyperlink, 212

I

implied repudiation, 175
injunction, 182
innocent misrepresentation, 72-77
inquiry, 20
intangible property, 77
interlocutory/interim injunction, 183

J

judicial interventionism, 7

L

lapse, 21
legal tender, 161
licence, 40
life estate, 40
liquidated damages, 178
liquidated damages clause, 145
lost opportunity damages, 178

M

mandatory injunction, 182
material alteration, 164-65
material representation, 72, 131, 132
mental disability, 64-66
merger, 167
minor
age of majority, and, 57
BC minors, 61
contract rights and obligations, 53
defined, 52
employment contracts, 55-56
necessaries, purchases of, 54-55
non-necessaries, contracts for, 57
ratification, failure to, 59
repudiation, consequences of, 58
void *ab initio* contracts, 59-60
void contracts, 59
misrepresentation
by omission, 80, 82
defined, 72
fraudulent misrepresentation, 78-79
innocent misrepresentation, 74-77

misrepresentation (cont.)
    overview, 72-74
    remedies for, 81-82
mistake
    common mistake, 105-7
    mutual mistake, 104-5, 107
    overview, 90-91
    principles, law of, 91-92
    treatment at common law, 92-102
    unilateral mistake, 102-4, 107
mitigate
    defined, 179
    duty to, 179-80
mutual mistake, 104

N

negative covenant, 182
non est factum, 100
novation, 116
null and void, 160
nullity, 21

O

offer
    acceptance, 3, 17
        communication of, 17-20
    communication of, 16, 17
    defined, 3
    invitation to treat, and, 16
    lapse of, 21
    mere puffery, 15
    nature of, 15
    revocation of, 21, 22
offeree, 2
offeror, 2
onus, 12
option to terminate, 167

P

parol evidence rule
    ambiguous language, and, 135
    condition precedent, and, 137
    defined, 134
    essential collateral agreement, and, 136
    essential implied term, and, 136
    exceptions to, 135
    rectification, and, 137-39

part performance doctrine, 41-43
parties to a contract, 247-49
past consideration, 27
penalty clause
    defined, 145
    overview, 145-47
    usurious interest rate, and, 147
persons under mental disability, 52
PIN, 214
plain language drafting, 245
positivism, 7
precedent, 6
presumption of law, 12
privity of contract
    defined, 114
    express trusts, 118
    implied trusts, 119-20
    lack of, 114
    novation, 116, 117
    statutory exceptions, 115
    vicarious performance, 116-18
prohibitory injunction, 182
promisee, 2
promisor, 2
promissory estoppel, 25
public key encryption, 214

Q

quantum meruit, 29, 188

R

"reasonable person" test, 13, 14
recital, 236, 249
rectification, 137-39
remedies, breach of contract
    choice of, 191-92
    damages, 178-80
    discharge, 187
    exclusion clauses, 190-91
    injunctions, 182-84
    overview, 193
    quantum meruit, 188-89
    rescission, 184-85
    restitution, 186
    specific performance, 181-82
    substantial performance, 189
representation, 131

repudiation
    defined, 174
    for intoxication, 63
rescission, 72, 184
restitution, 34, 75, 186
restraint of trade, 31-32
restrictive covenant, 33
resulting trust, 119
revoke, 21

S

setoff, 123
settlor, 118
shrink-wrap contract, 207
simple contract, 36
Slade's Case, 5, 6
specific goods, 154
specific performance, 181
Statute of Frauds, 37-45
substantial performance, 189
symmetric cryptosystem, 214

T

tender of payment, 161, 162
tender of performance, 160
terms in contract
    conditions precedent, 251
    definitions, 252
    obligation, 249
    overview, 131, 134
    representations, 250
    statements, 251
terms of art, 245
testimonium clauses, 152-53
tort, 36
trust, 118
trustee, 118

U

uberrimae fidei contracts, 81
unconscionability, 87-90
under seal, 24
undue influence, 85-87
unfair business practices, 89-90
unilateral mistake, 102
unjust enrichment doctrine, 186
unliquidated damages, 178

V

vicarious performance, 116-18
void *ab initio*, 53, 59-60
void contract
    consequences for, 60
    defined, 12, 184
voidable contract, 53, 184

W

waiver, 163-64
warranty, 131, 132